TOM PAINE
The Greatest Exile

David Powell

ST MARTIN'S PRESS
New York

First published in the United States of America in 1985

Library of Congress Cataloging in Publication Data
applied for:

CONTENTS

For Rachel

PREFACE

Two hundred and fifty years after his birth — and two centuries since he was central to the American and European Revolutions — Thomas Paine remains as much a contemporary as a controversial figure. Theodore Roosevelt, a former US President, once anathematised him as 'that filthy little atheist' (having never read *The Age of Reason* on which the charge was based); Michael Foot, a former leader of the British Labour Party, recently described him as 'the greatest exile ever to leave these shores'; while, in response to a BBC documentary of 1982, the *Daily Telegraph* of London felt compelled to carry a leader, for which the introduction set the tone:

> After MR KENNETH GRIFFITH's marathon television eulogy of TOM PAINE . . . it would be difficult for this newspaper to remain silent without disloyalty to its own traditions. For what was this man that we are invited to admire above all the national heroes who are actually known to us? He fought against his country in the American War of Independence and invited France to invade us during the French Revolution. Among decent Englishmen in his time his name was a synonym for treachery, blasphemy, and (whether justly or not) debauchery.

What the *Telegraph* failed to mention was that Paine was charged with treachery by what was possibly the most repressive British government of the past two centuries; that, as with Roosevelt, their leader writers had not read *The Age of Reason*, a diest's profession of a belief in God; and that, if the allegations relating to debauchery were based on Paine's drinking habits, then they had better look to the social practices of the eighteenth century when hard drinking was the rule — the premature death of their mentor, Pitt the Younger, possibly having been accelerated by his fondness for port!

Arguably, the innuendoes were unworthy of the traditions that the paper itself claims to represent, though it may be that such superficial charges disguised a deeper fear. Paine, they write, was 'the kind of philosopher whose natural forum was the pub'. Then, as now, the radical populist was deeply suspect, for he threatened the established order — and the only response of the Pitt government to the publication of the second part of *Rights of Man* (which sold 200,000 copies within the year in a country with a population of little more than ten million people) was to charge Paine with being a 'malicious, seditious, and ill-disposed person'.

And what was the basis of this bar-room philosophy of Paine's? The *Telegraph* supplied an answer: 'He made human liberty his supreme value; he talked glibly and abstractedly about the rights of man, evading all the dilemmas which are created by setting them in a social context.' Surely, even the *Daily Telegraph* could not deny the benevolence of such principles while, once again, they ignored the fact that Paine did, indeed, recognise the implications of his proposals — his carefully costed social programme anticipating Beveridge by almost two hundred years.

Not that the tenor of the *Telegraph* leader was unique; rather it was representative of the treatment that Paine has received since the late eighteenth century. In 1794, a handbill subsidised out of Pitt's Secret Fund was declaiming:

> as for them that do not like the PRESENT CONSTITUTION, let them have their deserts, that is the HALTER AND A GIBBET, and be burnt afterwards, not as PAINE hath been, but in body and person. To which every loyal heart will say Amen;

while in 1802, the New England Palladium was writing, on news of Paine's return to America: 'What! Invite to the United States that lying, drunken, brutal infidel who enjoyed in the opportunity of basking and wallowing in the confusion, devastation, bloodshed, rapine, and murder, in which his soul delights?'

In the years between, the United States has lived down its fears. Today Paine remains the towering figure of whom President Monroe wrote: 'The services which he rendered them (the American people) in their struggle for liberty have made an impression of gratitude that will never be erased, whilst they continue to merit the character of a just and generous people.' In Great Britain the bogy remains, if he is remembered at all. For all the occasional outbursts against 'A Radical Rascal' (the headline over the *Telegraph* leader), neglect more than abuse has ensured that Paine has remained little more than a disturbing footnote to English history.

The contrast is extraordinary, and reflects as much on America as on Great Britain. While the one was extrovert and open, willing to debate new ideas and concepts, the other was closed and reactionary — and, for half a century after Paine wrote, the answer to dissent was transportation or the hulks. While the one was exploring new constitutional forms, the other took precedent as its touchstone, to echo with Burke: 'The very idea of the fabrication of a new government, is enough to fill us with disgust and horror' — and suffrage was not to become universal until Paine had been dead for 120 years. In short, while the one was young and spirited, the other was old, paranoic and fearful of any change which threatened the established order, temporal or spiritual.

Paine tilted at both. *Rights of Man*, and the hopes it represented, was largely responsible for the coercive measures that Pitt was to take against the nascent radical movement that emerged in the last quarter of the eighteenth century; whilst *The Age of Reason*, a deist testament, shocked the nonconformist conscience and led to Paine's ostracism by a movement which was central to reform in the nineteenth. The irony is inescapable: that the political right and theological left combined to expunge Paine's memory in Britain, if not in the United States.

Yet Paine was as English as any free-born Englishman with a memory for the dissenting past, and the entire thrust of his work (whether related to the American or the European revolutions) was the product of the first 37 years of his life before he left England for the American colonies. For the biographer, so little is known of those early years that Hesketh Pearson (*Tom Paine, Friend of Mankind*) and Alfred Owen Aldridge (*Man of Reason*) each succeed in compacting them into 14 pages; while Conway's ageing, though still definitive, biography (*The Life of Thomas Paine*) condenses half of Paine's lifetime into three, brief chapters. The impression is that there was nothing to Paine's life before that day in late 1774 when he first landed in Philadelphia — to help nerve the Colonists claim their independence.

Clearly, the idea is absurd, the problem is to overcome it. Until comparatively recently what Hannah More once termed 'the nice arts' were largely the monopoly of the leisured class, a class with the education and the time to compose their diaries, their letters, their memoirs — which they did in abundance. If history was not written for them, then they wrote history for themselves — and Paine was not of their sort. The son of a staymaker, and a staymaker himself before entering the Excise, he had little time for those refinements recommended by Lord Chesterfield to his son, 'that easy good breeding, that engaging manner, and those graces, which seduce and prepossess people in your favour at first sight'.

They were the qualities of a world that Paine knew, but in which he had no part. Until his arrival in the Colonies, the everyday struggle for existence precluded the leisures of maintaining correspondence, of composing memoirs — thus the 'missing years' without which the later Paine is inexplicable. However, without some understanding of the isolation of his childhood, of his Quaker inheritance, of the world that he found in London, of his time with the Excise, the career of the man who coined the phrase the United States, and helped formulate the Declaration of Independence; of the man who first advocated that France should declare itself a Republic, then pleaded for the life of the King; of the man of whom Pitt once said 'Paine is right', to be party to his outlawry, is incomprehensible.

So again, what does the biographer do? How is it possible to reconstruct those early years on which all the rest depend? What was the genesis of Paine's achievements — the achievements of a man once described by Gouverneur Morris as being 'without fortune, without friends or connections' — in representing the aspirations of much of America and Europe during the Age of Revolution?

As I see it, the only answer is to adopt what might be termed an 'historical documentary' approach; to recreate something of the background in which Paine grew up and attempt to interpret his imagined response to all that he saw and heard. No doubt this will offend the historical purists. This work is not for them. Above all else, Paine was a populist. As such, he would be the first to reject the idea that his life was the preserve of that handful of academics who, inheriting the leisured practices of the eighteenth century, have the time to indulge in their specialisation, careless of wider audiences.

This said, however, the opening chapters are weighted towards the speculative in an effort to provide the background essential to understanding the development of Paine's later thinking and writing. In fact, without some appreciation of the social, economic and political conditions of Paine's early years, the later Paine is totally incomprehensible. Once established, however, and with an increasing amount of material available about Paine himself, I trust that the book gains a momentum of its own, for Paine's life was an extraordinary adventure. One writer went so far as to suggest that Baroness Orczy based *The Scarlet Pimpernel* on his time in France during the Revolution!

Far-fetched? Possibly, but then both the man and his times were extraordinary — not least, perhaps, for the resemblance they bear to our own day. Then, as now, the West was entering a period of radical transition. Then, as now, there was growing evidence of destabilisation — political, social, economic. Then, as now, governments attempted to readjust to new circumstances, and, while the United States claimed its independence, and France exploded into Revolution, Britain pioneered industrialisation and the Two Nations which Disraeli later described.

Two centuries later, at the onset of post-industrialism, the United States lives with the inherited problem of public affluence and private squalor, and the knowledge that with no new frontiers to explore it is no longer possible to relocate deprivation; France lives with growing evidence of political polarisation, with the renaissance of the far right and confrontation on the streets; while a British government adjusts to the problems of de-industrialisation by introducing measures in the name of 'law and order' of which Pitt the Younger would not have been ashamed.

The analogies may not be exact. They are disturbing, nevertheless; and, if history should repeat itself, then it is hoped that we have learnt something from our past mistakes, not least from a reflection of Thomas Paine writing at a time when: 'Freedom had been hunted around the globe; reason was considered as rebellion; and the slavery of fear had made men afraid to think.' Two centuries have passed since he voiced his concern. The fear remains.

Finally, I would like to thank all those who have indulged me for so long: Arthur Butler, Shirley Darlington, Diana Dixon, Liz Mandeville, Ian MacLaurin, Kay McLeod, Jacqui and Brian Morris, the staff of Lewes Library, Irene Brown (whose tolerance takes no account of the fact that there are any villains in history), Cora Kaplan (who provided me with an invaluable perspective of the times), Hilary Walford (who, whilst editing the text, taught me the correct usage of participles!), and, most especially, Rachel, to whom this book is dedicated.

Their encouragement, patience and advice has made this book possible. I can only hope that it does some credit both to them and 'The Greatest Exile'.

David Powell
Lewes

1 EARLY YEARS

The small town of Thetford bellied deep against the landscape, besieged by cold and darkness. The winter of 1737 was hard; the winds out of the east careened the Anglian flatlands, numbing all life and drowning out the birth cries of Thomas Paine, first son of Frances, née Cocke, and Joseph, staymaker of Bridge Street. It was no easy delivery. Childbirth was dangerous at the best of times. With Frances in her fortieth year the risks to both mother and child were increased, especially during the long march of winter when fresh food was scarce, when the cold and damp reached upwards and inwards through flagged floors and wattle walls, and the nights were 15 hours long.

The fear of darkness still lingers, a childhood bogy. In the mid-eighteenth century it was a palpable thing; the fear of winter nights darkened the mind, Blake's 'direful monster' that 'Withers all silence, and in his hand/Unclothes the earth, and freezes up frail night.' Only the great houses knew the comfort of candlelight, a luxury beyond the means of the masses. Once Joseph had stood and marvelled at the bright lit windows of the Duke of Grafton's country seat and wondered that the distance between them was so small, yet so great. The following morning all Thetford was *en fête*, for Elizabeth, Lady Fitzroy, had borne an heir to the Grafton line that held the town and its people in its feif.

But that was two years ago and now Joseph stood in the darkness of his small workroom, and looked out across the night-veiled town, and heard the child's first cries, and thanked his Quaker God. Now, perhaps, Frances would find the happiness that had been a stranger to their married lives. Sometimes, and to himself, he wondered why she had ever accepted his proposal; to dismiss as cynical the thought that at 36 she had been well beyond what was considered a marriageable age and that he, Joseph, had been a last resort.

Cynical, perhaps, but the doubt remained for, even before the banns were called at nearby Euston Church, her father had warned them both that the difference in their ages (she was eleven years his senior) would make for difficulties in the years to come but then, being a lawyer, he dissembled like all of his profession to cloak a different concern. In an age of rigid social demarcation, Joseph needed no one to tell him that Frances had married beneath her.

His own father had talked of the Paine line reaching back to one Sir

Joseph Paine, one-time Lord Mayor of Norwich, though the story remained unsubstantiated; as was the Cockes' claim to descent from Richard Cocke, author of *English Law, or a Summary Survey of the Household of God Upon Earth*. Whatever the past, however, the Cockes and the Paines were now of different social classes, for, while Joseph might be a well-found craftsman, Frances's family were professional people of 'the middling sort'. The prejudice, that anyone can get anywhere in trade so long as one gets out of it, had been a staple of the English social system; but in Hanoverian England it was not so much a prejudice, more an interdiction — and Joseph was well versed in the nuances of such differentiation.

As a Quaker, one of the handful in Thetford, he was one of that 'peculiar nation of people, quite different from ordinary English citizens by their language, manner of dressing, and religion'. During his visit to England only ten years before the young Paine's birth, Voltaire* may have found the Friends admirable (more especially, their belief in equality), but then he was French and, by definition, suspect. For Joseph Paine there was no disguising the fact that his religion set him apart from other people; not least, from his wife. Possibly they could have tolerated their age and social differences; but for Frances, an Anglican of Tory persuasion, Quakerism still smacked of the temporal and spiritual heresies of the early Friends who railed with Fox*: 'O ye great and rich men of earth, weep and howl for your misery is coming. All the loftiness of men must be laid low.'

Little more than two generations had passed since such levelling sentiments had threatened the whole political and social fabric of England. The fear remained; a memory prompted by the Quakers' continuing refusal to pay tithes to support the Anglican Church. Only last summer a number of Friends had been imprisoned for such defiance of the established order, which led the *Grub Street Journal* of March 1736 to call up Popish plots in a renewed attempt to discredit the sect:

Whether Quakers often turn Papists I cannot say, but I believe it is no difficult matter to produce instances of Papists turning Quaker, and the leader of the sect called Pennites has been seen in Jesuit garb in Rome . . . Upon the whole, should it be true that the Jesuits are at the bottom of the Quaker Tithe Bill, how little reason hath the State

---

* To avoid interrupting continuity, brief details about people, institutions and events of general interest in the eighteenth century are given in the Appendix, pp. 267–97. Entries are indicated by an asterisk when they first appear in the text.

to grant them more indulgence than any other set of people who are a cunning, fly, designing set of men.

The suspicion that the theological extremes of Catholic right and Quaker left shared a common interest in opposing the established church and its political masters was not lost on Joseph and the small congregation of Thetford Friends. They knew the practice well; the inheritance of their dissent reached back 90 years to that grey January day of 1649 when the English Commonwealth demonstrated that even kings have a bone in their neck (a fact that convinced George II that England was a nation of 'King killers and republicans'); since the radical Rainborough* had exclaimed:

I think that the poorest he in England hath a life to lead as the greatest he; and therefore, truly, sir, I think that it is clear that every man that is to live under government ought first, by his own consent, to put himself under government.

In 1737 such ideas were still dangerous to noise abroad, particularly for a Quaker, for those 'roundheaded rogues', the early Friends, had been in the van of the levelling movement; preach that there was a God in every man, and carrying their creed at sword point out of the north into Wales, the south, and the eastern counties where Old Nol had raised the cavalry troops that were later to form the nucleus of the New Model Army. The spirit of levelling might have been laid, and the Quakers abandoned their swords — but the legacy remained, to mock the pretensions of the new oligarchs and their Glorious Revolution of 1688.

The event was half a century distant now, distorted by time and journeying, though Joseph's father had remembered it well, and talked of it often: of James II's hurried flight; of Parliament's offer of the English crown to William of Orange on its own, carefully formulated terms. The Revolution Settlement was to exorcise, for once and for always, those dangerous times when the gentry had raised the people to further their own ambitions, and then became fearful, for 'Like unskilful conjurors they often raised those spirits they could not lay; and under cover of zeal for the cause, the poor levelled the rich of both parties.'

And they had succeeded well enough; the Graftons were evidence of that. The past two years had been hard, the agricultural wage accordingly low — £8 a year for a head ploughman, half that for his mate, and a shilling a day for casual labourers.[1] With the mass of the population dependent on the land for a livelihood, it was little wonder there was talk of unrest both in countryside and town. With the price of bread providing the most sensitive measure of well being, a fall in real wages and a rise in wheat prices was a sure recipe for trouble — though Thetford remained distanced from it.

The surrounding countryside was rich and prosperous, while the town itself, with no more than two thousand residents, still had two Members of Parliament, its own Mayor, Alderman, Mace- and Sword-bearers — all in the gift of the Grafton family. The Glorious Revolution has seen to that. The town might still boast of its character, but in practice it was little more than a Grafton monopoly and Joseph wondered that even now an Englishman was not free in his own country; that, even in a place such as Thetford, a man in search of work from another part of the country could be hounded out as if plagued.[2] So much for the Revolution and its Bill of Rights; and in the darkness he knew that his son's birthright was already flawed, then hushed himself for the thought.

Even the night was not safe for such ideas. If a man was to prosper it demanded quiescence and, according to his lights, Joseph had prospered well enough. Though a Quaker he had been elected a Freeman of the town only 18 months before; and his trade of staymaking, though no route to a fortune, provided a respectable income — as much as £30 in a good year. In contrast with the gentry, it was a pittance, yet it was more than most could expect — and all it required of Joseph Paine was that he should compromise his Quaker God, and, despising himself, he swore that this would not be the succession of his son.

Meanwhile, in the rushlight of the upstairs room, Frances held her son. Now there was no more bitterness; no frustration. The child, this Tom, redeemed the rest: the anger in her father's eyes when she had first talked of Joseph, the Thetford staymaker; the secret laughter of the women of the town, long married, when the betrothal was announced; and, most of all, the contempt in the eyes of the minister which reflected her secret fear that this marriage was a blasphemy, an unclean thing.

The Anglican Church, her Church, preached toleration, though within carefully circumscribed bounds; and, while Joseph was a good man, and well respected, his faith found no place in her catechism. Memories of the times when a Commonwealth trooper could swear an oath that 'This sword should never be laid down, nor many thousands more, whilst there was a priest left in England' were altogether too close for that, and sometimes she wondered to herself whether the Paines, too, had ever had the blood of the Church on their conscience.

Those had been savage times when a world was turned upside-down; nearer still, from her girlhood, she remembered the intrigues that had followed Anne's death and George I's succession; the fears aroused when the Earl of Mar had raised James Stuart's standard in the Highlands and gathered an army of three thousand men about him within the week. As that autumn of 1715 had deepened into winter, the news had grown more wild, more disturbing: of a rising in the west; of the Jacobites of Northumberland joining up with James's supporters; of their advance south through the Cumberland hills.

For an instant it had seemed as if savagery was to be unloosed again; though this time in the name of a different God for, as her father explained, the enforced restoration of the Stuarts with their Popish ways could only mean civil war. After all, it was less than 30 years since the Glorious Revolution had averted just such a blood letting; the Settlement of 1688 had provided England with a government sanctified by the established Church (for its authors well remembered Charles I's dictum that: 'Religion is the only firm foundation of power'), which was the envy of all the civilised world, even France.

After a season of rumour and fear, the Jacobite adventure had been still-born and, with his army dwindling about him, James Stuart had taken ship to France. Yet the fear remained. The stability of England and its Settlement was still a fragile thing, though, ironically, there was a steadily mounting clamour against George II's chief Minister, Walpole,* for his unremitting pursuit of peace:

> I have lived, Sir, long enough in the world to see the effects of war on this nation; I have seen how destructive the effects, even of a successful war, have been; and shall I, who have seen this, when I am admitted to the honour to share in his majesty's council, advise him to enter upon a war while peace may be had? No, Sir, I am proud to own it, that I always have been, and always shall be, an advocate for peace.

Yet now, even in Walpole's own county of Norfolk, men were drumming up the glories of war, and, remembering her husband and his torn conscience, Frances swore that there would be no compromise for her son. She, Frances, would make certain of that, for in three years of marriage she had learned what compromise meant.

As Frances wished, the child was baptised Thomas; and, as she feared, war soon came with Spain and, though Walpole resigned from office, he would still pass through Thetford on the way to his country seat at Houghton when Parliament rose for the long, summer recess. At one time it had been a whirlwind passage, a flying column of horses and coaches spurring north across the town bridge. Now it was a more leisurely parade, but none the less impressive, for Walpole had governed England for more than 20 years — the apotheosis of a class that had sent James and his Papist sympathies packing, to establish its own primacy in 1688.

For an impressionable child the passage must have made a powerful spectacle, for, though ageing now and heavy with good living, the stories that followed Walpole's name were legion: of how he had spent 16 years building Houghton, demolishing a whole village in the process; of how he had spent £12,000 on the drapes of his great velvet bed. The trimmings of power, perhaps, but enough to fill out a child's imagination with its majesty, for, as his mother never tired of explaining, this was the man that had brought stability to England, though his father called it a different thing — the rule of the oligarchs.

Together in the small workshop, Joseph would retell the story of the Commonwealth, and all that followed; of the Glorious Revolution and how, even then, the 'families of rank' had divided amongst themselves. While the infant Tory Party was torn in its allegiance between king, church, and Parliament, the Whigs had no such inhibitions and were relentless in pursuit of their new-won power — though it was to be quarter of a century, and more, before Walpole finally consolidated the authority of his class and its godhead, property.

For this was what these new men — the Walpoles and their kind — were about. Property was the ultimate measure of their standing. All else was subordinate to it — church, Parliament, the law itself. Concerned only with the 'dominion of property', and contemptuous of 'men of no property, and capable only of labour', the new masters of England pursued affluence with an even-handed rapacity — affluence based on landed interest, on capital speculation, on holding office under the crown; or a combination of all three.

And laying aside his tools, Joseph would describe the extravagance and list its antecedents. First, the historic wealth of the great landowning families such as the Devonshires and the Bedfords; second, an altogether more recent development, the mercantile affluence of men such as Lord Chandos who had lost more than £700,000 playing the markets in a handful of years, yet still maintained a full orchestra at his country seat; and finally, the new and burgeoning wealth of those who held government office that accounted for the rise of men such as Walpole, whose father had lived on a modest estate, whose son, when in office, put £150,000 through only one of his four bankers in as many years.

Hans Stanley, an opportunist if ever there was one, had summarised

the case neatly in a speech to the House almost too many years ago to
be recalled:

> If I had a son I would say to him 'Get into Parliament, make some
> tiresome speeches. Do not accept the first offer, but wait until you
> can make more provision for yourself and your family and then call
> yourself an independent country gentleman.'

It was advice which the Whigs pursued, assiduously. During Walpole's
days, corruption became a unifying force of government, administrations
depending as much on the length of their pockets as on promises of the
perquisites of 'place' to obtain, and hold, majorities — Horace Walpole
once listed the sinecures his father's family had reaped from his time
in office: one brother had been appointed Auditor of the Exchequer at
a salary of £8,000 a year; another to the Clerkship of the Pells; while
Horace himself was appointed Clerk to the Estreats before leaving Eton,
Usher of the Exchequer while still at Cambridge.

And, as they accumulated wealth, so they spent it, prodigiously: on
their wives and their mistresses, on their carriages and their cellars, and
always on their estates. Years later, on a visit to Lord Scarsdale's country
home, Dr Johnson remarked to his host: 'Why, sir, all this excludes but
one evil, poverty' — the one evil that the new elite feared most. To them,
it was a stigma they sought to banish with a display of conspicuous consumption made the more conspicuous by the condition of the four million
men, women and children lumped together as 'the poor' who lived out
their lives at subsistence level, or below.

And in growing numbers, they crossed the town bridge, too; a despairing army in search of work to contrast, vividly, with Walpole's passage.
These were the two nations of Paine's childhood. He needed no lessons
in their character, while even his grandfather, Henry Cocke, may have
remarked on the sight, though cautiously as became a lawyer who looked
for his fees from the landed classes who were rediscovering the benefits
of enclosure.

In the 1740s the movement was in its infancy, though growing apace:
400,000 acres of common land were enclosed in the first half of the century, a further three million by 1800. On this issue, at least, Tories and
Whigs shared a common interest, finding the system admirably suited
to serving two, complementary ends — on the one hand, improving the
levels of agricultural efficiency; on the other, increasing their own rent
rolls.

And the law, their law, concurred. Fourteen hundred enclosure acts were hurried through Parliament in the last 40 years of the century, denying smallholders and freeholders who made up the body of what, until then, had been largely an agrarian economy, either the time or the means to protest against measures on which their livelihoods depended. The wholesale eviction of villagers from the common lands of England may have provided the 'hands' necessary to work the new industries already emerging by the mid-century; their sequestered lands may have increased the food production for the new urban masses — but at the price of bitter hardship; and of Joseph's silence, save with his son.

But for Frances, it was different. She would watch the army of the dispossessed and pity them, yet knew that this was a cost that must be endured. The Reverend Vaughan at St Peter's and St Cuthbert's had explained it often enough. It was all very well for Joseph to wrestle with his God, and protest in the Quaker fashion: 'The earth is the Lord's and the fullness thereof. He hath given it to the sons of men in general, and not to a few lofty ones which lord it over their brethren.'[3] But where had such rantings led, and not so long ago?

No doubt the earth was the Lord's, but her church taught a different creed: that there was a set and established order of things in which each man and woman played out their pre-ordained role, and that without such a contract there could only be chaos. Yet Joseph persisted, and the lad was only seven when she came across him writing some lines to a dead crow:

Here lies the body of John Crow
Who once was high but now is low.
Ye brother crows, take warning all
For as you rise, so you must fall.

The boy had seen Walpole only recently and doubtless heard the talk that the old man was mortally sick, but there was no excusing such levelling thoughts, for, as the Reverend Vaughan said, it would be a little while before the meek could inherit the earth.

Ten years before Paine's birth, a Portuguese visitor had written of England:

The legislature here provides an abundance of excellent laws for the maintenance of the poor, and manufactures sufficient for all of them, and yet by indolent management few nations are so burdened with them, there not being many countries where the poor are in worse condition.

In the stews of England's towns and cities, ramshackle houses huddled together about unpaved and undrained streets, traps for infectious diseases like typhus and cholera. And in the countryside, conditions were little better. Most labourers' cottages continued to be built of mud, with earth floors; Defoe described one Derbyshire lead miner whose family of six shared a cave cut into the hillside — and suspected that many would envy them their 'clean and neat home'. As the poet Gray noted, 'chill penury' was generally the labourers' lot, whilst the despotism of 'little tyrants' spread a lengthening shadow across the land.

The labourer's wage rarely rose above subsistence level, and the story in Thetford was that his Grace's three footmen earned less between them in a year than their master spent on his chocolates. And if men fared badly, women fared worse. The use of sweated labour was not new, but employers of the eighteenth century refined the Protestant work ethic, true to the Duke of Albermarle's dictum that 'the mean people have no interest in the Commonwealth but the use of breath'.

With their conscience suborned by patronage, writers preferred to ignore the presence of 'the mean people'. Foreign commentators knew no such restraints. In 1740, a Swedish visitor described how he had seen women humping four baskets on their heads at a time at the lime kilns of Gravesend, all for sixpence a day, while Thetford was too small a place to keep the secrets of the girls who took the Norwich road to prostitution. In their cobweb of shawls the gossips of the town might chatter of scarlet women, and from his pulpit Mr Vaughan might thunder 'unclean' but they went none the less — a continuing mystery to the young Paine for, when he asked why they left, and where they had gone, and what they had done that was 'unclean', his mother became a scold and his father deaf.

Ultimately, however, children were the most utilitarian element within the labour force: cheap, malleable and totally expendable as far as the reserve army of child paupers was concerned. Apprenticed off at premiums of up to £10 as soon as it was possible for them to learn a trade, their contracts lasted until they were 24 years of age — if they survived that long. With government imposing no controls whatsoever either on their hours of work or their work conditions, many simply starved or were beaten to death.

The world of the poor — of a childhood which ended at five or six years of age; of a working life of twelve or fourteen hours daily; of the constant companionship of disease and death — was the world that Frances feared for her son. It was all very well to rail at the inequities of life, but the lad had to make his way in it, and with her tongue now sharpened by bitterness she would berate Joseph for his Quaker quiet-ism.

Little by little he was drawing away from her, haunted by the com-promise that he found within himself which he discussed alone with his son. The lad was already wary of the Friends' asceticism (what was it that he had said of them, that if their tastes had been consulted at the creation, neither a flower would have blossomed in its gaiety, nor a bird been permitted to sing?) but when it came to their humanity it was a dif-ferent matter.

He had learned their scriptures well, and was growing overfond of quoting them, not least the text that God 'made all men of one mould and one blood to dwell on the face of the earth'.

Even the thought was dangerous, yet there was no blinding him to the evidence. It was before him every day, among the workless who lived with the double damnation of being persecuted by a legal system for being unable to find work where it did not exist. John Locke* provided the Glorious Revolution with its philosophical legitimacy, though he was to be disappointed with the outcome; the Grandees exploiting his ideas for their own ends, and refining them with harsh judicial correctives.

To prevent pauper children absconding, they could be ringed by the neck or manacled. By an act of William III, men in receipt of poor relief could be made to wear a large roman 'P' on the right sleeves of their coats; while men and women caught in the act of begging could be strip-ped to the waist and 'openly whipped until his or her body be bloody'. But even the authorities flinched at the proposal that a propertyless per-son (a phrase that echoes down the eighteenth century) found guilty of counterfeiting the pass essential to travel from parish to parish in search of work 'shall loose his ears for forgery the first time . . . and the second time be transported to the plantations'.

As Joseph was never tired of repeating, it was little wonder that the times were troubled; that the workless carried talk (magnified by their hunger, a powerful aid to the imagination) of violence: of bread riots, wage riots, enclosure riots. Sporadic, lacking any form of leadership, isolated in small communities (only three or four towns in England had more than 20,000 inhabitants at the turn of the eighteenth century), and violated by their everyday struggle for existence, the poor lacked either the energy or the cohesion to represent the full grievousness of their distress.

Yet the fear of 'mobocracy', a word that only came into the language when Paine was a boy, continued to haunt the landed class, who were learning the age-old lesson that, the higher the value placed on property, the greater the need for its protection. With the bizarre contrast between private affluence and public squalor, the masters of the eighteenth century learned the lesson well. If the Act of Settlement had fixed their political and economic supremacy, and if Locke had legitimised their power, then the law provided them with the means to safeguard it, Oliver Goldsmith* writing that: 'Each wanton judge new penal statutes draws/Laws grind the poor, and rich men rule the law.'

Between 1688 and George III's death in 1815, the number of capital offences on the statute book rose by 190, two-thirds of the number being enacted before 1760, and the majority being concerned with crime against poverty: for forgery, for stealing (by 1740 the theft of a shilling handkerchief was enough to send a child to the gallows), for blacking the face (this a measure against smugglers), for uprooting fence posts around enclosed lands.

At their Sunday meetings the Friends of Thetford might deny the right of any man to take a life, but here, again, was their difference, for there was no escaping the peddled tales of public executions in London, Norwich or nearby Ely. The old city was only a morning's walk away, and the burning of Amy Hutchinson in 1750 must have made a rare spectacle. Seventeen years of age and condemned for the death of her husband: 'Her hands and face were smeared with tar, and having a garment daubed with pitch, after a short prayer, her executioner strangled her, and twenty minutes after the fire was kindled and burnt for nearly half an hour.'

In Thetford, the details were recounted with morbid fascination, but for the young Paine they must have been as confusing as fascinating. As long as he could remember his father had prayed to a merciful God, provoking Frances's tongue with his nonconforming creed, yet too often God remained merciless. Why, only recently at their Sunday meeting in Cage Lane, the spirit had moved a Friend to speak on the redemption of man by the death of the Son of God. The recollection lingered, disturbing. If one doubted God's charity, what else remained?

The answer could only be contradictions: of the Sunday peity of an established church which preached deference to a congregation that dare not be otherwise; of the measured tones of a constitution which called men free, to enslave them; of the majesty of a law that elevated itself, to mock justice.

To the adolescent Paine they may have been difficult concepts, but they found concrete form in Charles, Duke of Grafton, for 33 years Lord Chamberlain of England. When in Thetford, he prayed, occasionally, at the local church; attended the occasional town meeting; occasionally handed down law as a Justice of the Peace. It was a trinity of power that Joseph had long recognised of necessity rather than conviction and following necessity, and Frances's promptings, he enrolled Tom at the local Grammar School when the boy was 10 years of age. As she said, the boy needed an education if he was to make anything of himself.

The first days of school were an intimidating experience for Paine; the more so because his plain Quaker dress and manner of speech, and Joseph's insistence that he should learn no Latin, marked him out from the other new boys in the Reverend William Knowler's class. True, he had known most of them in the small gangs of childhood that roamed the town and nearby countryside; yet collectively they took on a different character that exposed and taunted his differences: a Friend without friendship.

It was a solitary experience, and there was little consolation to be gleaned from Joseph's explanation that he was fortunate to have any schooling — or that the family could not afford to send him away to school as the Grafton's had done with their heir. And here the otherwise taciturn man would smile a private smile, as if excusing his conscience for that at least.

The public schools of England were little better than a savage kindergarten to life for the gentry and those 'of the middling sort'. Run largely on the fagging system, the power of the older boys was virtually unlicensed and the young Grafton at Eton may well have seen Lord Holland's fingers, already grotesquely deformed from having to toast his fagmaster's bread before an open fire with bare hands. Such brutality was general rather than particular, and when discipline faltered the whole barbarous system often collapsed into anarchy — later in the century, the militia having to be called into Rugby School to quell a riot among the boys who had mined the headmaster's study.

And they were the fortunate ones. If the poor survived the trauma of birth, then work was their expectation; the sole purpose of education being to 'condition children to their primary purpose . . . as hewers of wood and drawers of water'. The advice dins down through the century, from the Bishop of London's warning in 1724 'that village schools should not encourage fine writing in boys, fine working in girls, or fine singing in either', to the pragmatism of that most Christian philanthropist, Hannah More,* writing 70 years later:

My plan of instruction is extremely limited and simple: they learn on weekdays such coarse works as may fit them for servants. I allow of no writing for the poor. The object is not to make them fanatics but to train up the lower classes in habits of industry and piety.

For all his isolation at Thetford School, for all his sense of difference, the young Tom Paine was fortunate — and there was even some compensation to be gleaned from being excused Latin. The subject was a staple of the eighteenth-century curriculum but, as his father explained to the Reverend Knowler on that first day, the Friends had a powerful objection to the books in which the language was taught. What the boy missed proved to be no loss for, freed of the classical affectations of the age, it did much to account for the vividness of his later prose style and, while Mr Knowler might question Joseph's reasoning, he sympathised with his problem and promised to keep an eye on the boy.

The old dominie was as good as his word. For the next three years, and recognising that as the constant butt of the schoolyard humour the young Paine was turning in on himself and finding an escape in work, he encouraged the boy to explore the world beyond the narrow boundaries of Thetford. Heaven knew, most of the pupils had little enough incentive to study as they lived with the expectation of inheriting a farm, or even a small estate. Paine, however, was different and not so much for his Quaker's ways but because of them, for he actively wanted to work.

The habit appealed, strongly, to Knowler and he took a personal pride in Paine's education, which the lad reciprocated. Together they studied the sciences (a subject for which the pupil was later to say that he had a 'particular bent'); poetry (a subject of which Frances and Joseph disapproved 'as leading too much into the field of imagination'); and a much used globe of the world, one of the master's few keepsakes of his time at sea. A one-time naval chaplain, Knowler sparked the boy's imagination with his adventures, recounting his voyages and the places he had known: India, the Indies, the African coast, but most of all America, America most of all.[4]

There was an old book in Mr Knowler's small library, *A Natural History of Virginia*, and from first reading it enthralled Paine: 'My inclination from that day for seeing the western side of the Atlantic never left me.' In their walks together, or in the small workroom, Joseph had talked often of the Colonies as if they offered an escape that he had never had the courage to take: of the Puritans of New England and the Friends of Pennsylvania who had fled English persecution in the belief that:

Wee shall be as a Citty upon a Hill, the eies of all people are uppon us; soe that if wee shall deale falsely with our god in this worke wee have undertaken and soe cause him to withdrawe his present help from us, wee shall be made a story and a by-word through the world.[5]

The globe, the book, the old chaplain's words brought Joseph's hearsay vision alive. Here was a purpose beyond the closed world of childhood. Suddenly, Thetford seemed a very small place indeed, too small when there was a world to be discovered, and at 13 Tom Paine quit school — for an adventure that took him no further than his father's workroom. For once, Frances and Joseph shared a common concern (that their son should not leave home) albeit for different reasons. A practical man, as his compromise with life testified, it was all very well for the lad to daydream, but that never earned an honest living. Better that he learn a trade. A lonely woman, and ageing (at 50 she was well above the average life expectancy of the mid-eighteenth century), Frances found little comfort in her husband and his brooding ways, and clung tenaciously to her son.

For the young Paine, that first day as an apprentice staymaker at his father's bench was the prelude to four, bitter years. Always a withdrawn man, 16 years of domestic feuding had driven Joseph further into himself, which only heightened Tom's sense of isolation — in a house where there was little laughter; in a congregation where there was little joy; in a town where he shared less and less in common with others of his age. It was as if he was being divided against himself by some infinite power beyond comprehension: he felt a growing confusion as to the name of God, yet rejected the alternative; he saw a temporal morality practised in God's name that denied his most fundamental precepts; above all else, he had the mounting certainty that it would only be beyond the close frontiers of Thetford that he would find himself, yet his parents insisted that he remain.

For four years he worked with Joseph waiting for a justification to escape and then, one morning, for no other reason than that he could wait no longer, he walked out of the house in Bridge Street, crossed the bridge over the Little Ouse and took the Lowestoft road. A spare built, but powerful 17-year-old, he made the 48-mile journey within the day and that evening signed as a hand aboard the *Terrible*, under its master Captain Death. His time aboard was short lived. Before the privateer sailed — to be sunk in an engagement with the French and the loss of nearly all hands — Joseph came aboard and persuaded her master to give Tom his discharge.

It was a weary journey back to Thetford, the silence between father and son punctuated only by Joseph's remonstrances: 'The good Lord knows, Thomas, your Mother and I looked upon you as lost. What got into you lad, what made you go?' There was a moment when he thought it worth trying to explain but it passed quickly enough, and for two more years he worked with his father, staymaking, while the small town suffocated him with its parochialism. It had a near tangible quality, and now his frustration was fused with the bitterness that only two alternatives remained, to resign himself to his craft, with all that that entailed — or to go. The outbreak of war decided it.

The troubles between England and France had been a long time brewing though, when safely distanced from Europe, they gave no cause for war. Since the 1750s the two powers had been in bitter dispute over sharing the spoils of India; but it was in North America that the clash of interests was sharpest, the French strengthening their Canadian defences, the English mobilising the Colonists for the conflict that had to come.

It all seemed remote from Thetford but then, in the mid-summer of 1745, came the report that a certain Colonel Washington* had overpowered a French detachment on the Virginian frontier — though had subsequently been forced to surrender to a larger force. The news was distorted by time (the clash had taken place in May), yet for the young Paine it vivified memories of the Reverend Knowler's old book on Virginia. For him, the distant Colony came alive.

In London, however, it was different. The government under Newcastle* was indecisive and for 18 months conditions in North America deteriorated, Newcastle himself confessing that the English holdings now amounted to a mere '*lisière* [a narrow strip] to the sea, to which the French could confine all our colonies and from whence they may drive us whenever they please'. What little news reached Thetford seemed almost wholly bad: of a French fleet slipping the English blockade to reinforce their Canadian garrisons, of the failure of the expeditions against Forts Niagara and Crown Point, of the ambush and decimation of a British force at Monongahela and of the death of General Braddock, the British C-in-C.

The phoney war finally ended in May 1756, to re-divide the Paine household, though this time on different lines. Now Tom had his excuse for quitting Thetford — and with Frances's blessing, too. The lath and plaster walls of Bridge Street were too thin to keep any secret and, through the nights following news of the formal declaration of war, he heard his parents' arguments before sleep: Joseph, the pacifist, in continual retreat before his wife's sense of patriotism.

The outcome was inevitable. In late summer Paine turned his back on Thetford for a second time, to ship aboard the *King of Prussia*, a merchantman pressed into service for the duration of the war. For the 19-year-old it was the final break with the pacifism of his youth, though if he was looking for adventure, he was soon to be disillusioned. Shipboard life in the eighteenth century mirrored the savagery and social discrimination of society at large.

With the notable exception of enlightened commanders such as Anson (and even he lost three-quarters of his complement in his circumnavigation of the globe in the 1740s), conditions at sea were brutal in the extreme. Discipline was maintained with the lash. Sickness was endemic (it is estimated that a hundred times more men died of disease than were killed in action during the Seven Years' War), and pay for the ordinary sailor amounted to less than £1 a month — while the glittering prospects of prize money were largely illusory. For the capture of Havana in 1762, Admiral Pocock obtained £122,697 10s 0d; the ordinary seaman £3 14s 0d.

To obtain a full complement in such conditions, impressment was the rule. In English ports, gangs scoured the docksides for hands, who were then distributed, indiscriminately, to any ship making ready for sea — pressed men making up 80 per cent of the fleet's strength throughout the century. Although certain officers recognised the weaknesses and the iniquities of the system — Admiral Vernon* writing: 'Our fleets, which are defrauded by injustice, are first manned by violence and then maintained by cruelty' — the Admiralty made little attempt to improve conditions, Admiral St Vincent* exclaiming in fury: 'The civil branch of the navy is rotten to the core.'

Thirty years before Paine shipped aboard the *King of Prussia*, the first performance of *Rule Britannia* had brought a London audience to its feet. Now he was to learn the reality behind the illusion, that life for the lower decks was little more than a caricature of hell, and recalling his schooldays' Milton — 'a universe of death, which God by curse/Created evil' — he wondered what had become of Reverend Knowler's romances?

The two worlds he found aboard the *King of Prussia* — of the hands being subjected to the absolute and arbitrary powers of the officers — reinforced his embryo suspicions about the absolute and arbitrary nature of power itself: social, economic, political. Within two years his disenchantment was complete; yet the impressions were still inchoate. They existed, none the less, the product of a lonely, and often loveless childhood which had compelled him to find his companionship within himself; of an upbringing which, in accentuating his 'difference', threw wider differences into sharp relief; and of his time aboard the *Prussia*, with its refinement of a system which his conscience abhorred.

Yet the pressures to conform remained, economic and social as much as personal, to divide him against himself. The miracle is not so much that Paine's sense of difference survived the experience of adolescence and early manhood, but that it provided the groundwork for the radical who was to be outlawed from England, more than 30 years after first sailing in the *Prussia*, for advocating that 'liberty, property, security, and resistance to aggression' were the rights of every men, not just of the privileged few.

2 LONDON: THE TWO CITIES

The *King of Prussia* swung at anchor in the long reaches below the Tower, one amongst a mêlée of ships, and Paine wondered at the sight — at the Thames with its double forest of masts; at the crowded wharves, the crush of small houses; and, to the west, at the great tumulus of St Paul's, now silhouetted against the evening sun. He was just 20 years of age, and from a village that called itself the town of Thetford (worldly wise, he smiled at the presumption), and the prospect was a fantasy, fantastic. This was a place where a man could be lost, to find himself; where he could disappear among the 660,000 inhabitants which, in 1757, made London the most populous city in the world. Here, if anywhere, he would find answers to the questions that he was only now learning how to ask.

Eighteen months at sea had refined the differences which he had learned, well enough, in childhood, but now — he looked about him, and the decision was made. Paine came to London. A clamour of life, the capital confused visitors with its mass, astounded them with its divisiveness. Archenholtz, the most placid of commentators, had recently wondered at the elegance of St James's and Whitehall, and recoiled at the squalor to the east of the Tower:

> The East End, especially the quarters along the banks of the Thames, consists of poorly built houses on narrow, crooked, and ill-paved streets. It forms an extraordinary contrast with the West End where one sees almost nothing but pretty houses, sumptuous squares, very straight and beautifully lighted streets and the best pavement in Europe.

In the coming 18 months the discovery of these two Londons was to confirm all that Paine had suspected in Thetford, all that he had learned at sea: of the affluence of the nobility in their 'pretty houses', safely distanced from the tenements of the poor, living ten to a room; of the majesty of the Lords and Commons assembled at Westminster, and their opposite, the disenfranchised mass 'out of doors'; of the panoply of the law, and its execution at Tyburn Tree.

And, over all, was a spectacle of a different sort, the Court of St James's. Ageing now, George II still loathed the country of which he had been king for 20 years. To Paine the irony was inescapable: of a man whose animosity to all things English was implacable (no Englishman could cook, no English player act, no English coachman drive, nor jockey ride; and there was no man nor woman in the kingdom whose conversation was fit to be borne), yet a man who remained the apotheosis of all the rest — of an established church, political distinction, partial law.

England repaid his contempt in full measure. Though George might be tiring of his *amours*, the wags never tired of reminding London of his past; posting notices at the gates of St James's: 'Lost or strayed out of this house, a man who left his wife and six children on the Parish', during the King's extended visits to his beloved Hanover; and composing doggerel to his notorious self-indulgence:

> The King this summer having spent
> Amoribus in teneris,
> Appoints his loving Parliament
> To meet him Die Veneris.

The lines provided Paine with an insight into both the mood and the mores of the times: of the court divorced from the reality of power playing the voyeur to its own, interminable affairs; of a government, which having drafted its own terms of reference, was still confident of its authority; and of the great mass of the labouring poor, haunted by fears of being thrown on the Parish.

Still largely confined to its Roman walls, the city turned in on itself; noisome, violent, flamboyant; and from his shared room above Mr Morris's staymaking shop in Long Acre (a couple of minutes' walk from Hogarth's Gin Lane), the young Paine must have wondered at the contrast and concluded, with Goldsmith, that 'the English make a splendid figure everywhere but at home'.

After all, hadn't he recently met up with Goldsmith's 'intrepid soldier'[1] as he tapped his way out of Drury Lane, past the bordellos of the Strand, into the raffish world of Mayfair with its 'sumptuous squares?' No doubt about it, the man was a rogue, but a compelling rogue for all that, with a hint of self-mockery for having lost a leg, then the laughing assurance that he had no grounds for complaint for 'there is some that have lost both legs and an eye'.

If the scoundrel was to be believed, his father, a labourer, had died when he was five years of age and he had been traded from parish to parish 'till I thought I belonged to no parish at all'. After five years in the workhouse he was bound to a farmer and later, for killing a hare on a magistrate's land, sentenced to transportation to the Colonies:

The passage was but indifferent, for we were all confined to the hold and died very fast for want of sweet air and provisions. I did not want meat because I had fever all the way. Providence was kind, when provisions grew short it took away my appetite for eating.

Sold to a planter, he served a seven-year term before returning to England and here, the melodrama always on cue, he would declaim: 'O Liberty, Liberty! that is the property of every Englishman,' at which, a chorus in counterpoint, the crowd would either jeer or applaud according to their mood.

Delighted, the old mountebank would conduct the bedlam with his crutch for a moment before crying them to order and continuing with his tale. Back in London he was soon impressed; served two campaigns in Flanders; volunteered for service with the John (East India) Company; was discharged, pressed again, then captured by the French — and there was uproar again.

'Now lads, let me finish for I almost forgot to tell you that in this last engagement I was wounded in two places, I lost four fingers on my left hand, and my leg was shot off. However, blessed be to God' (and the punctuation came, 'Amen, Amen') 'I enjoy good health and have no enemy in the world that I know of save the French and the Justice of the Peace.' (Wild hurrahs.)

The performance was a triumph, always, and Paine delighted at the broad satire for it crystallised much that he already knew: of the resignation that was characteristic of the poor, allied to a servility that disguised the deep-rooted hostilities that divided society; hostilities that occasionally flared into brief, but ferocious outbreaks of violence that were met with equal ferocity in return.

London celebrated ten holidays a year — Christmas, Easter, and the eight hanging days at Tyburn. *En fête*, the crowds would process the condemned from Newgate gaol and once, only once, Paine joined them to walk the last mile, to watch the 13, each lined below his noose; to hear their last words; to follow the executioner covering their faces, then lash the horses to drag the carts from beneath them; to see them hanging together, friends and relatives tugging at their still dancing feet; and that evening, walking alone, he took an oath never to make such a journey again.

It was all very well for him to swear that five minutes of life would not pass without acquiring some new knowledge, but Tyburn was too savage to be borne; yet it seemed that this ritual of death was inexorable, the end product of the system itself. God knew, he had been fortunate to learn a trade in Thetford, and so to find work with Mr Morris when he had first come up to town. Others were not so fortunate. They took the road to London (and now he laughed at the Whittington myth that the streets were paved with gold, and, looking down at his boots, saw they were covered with dung) to find only poverty — and hunger was not a postponable want.[2]

One day, or even a few hours, in such conditions was often the first step towards the gibbet. First came the little thefts and pilferings, but they soon led to greater things; in the ale houses they still told of Jack Sheppard, who rose from nothing to be a tearaway, and there would always be laughter at the description of him kicking out his life on Albion's tree. The evening, a fine one, closed about Paine and from a great house on Pall Mall he heard laughter of a different sort and wondered, again, at the contrast.

The week before the ugliest man in town, the young Mr Wilkes,* had been elected MP for Aylesbury at a cost, it was rumoured, of £7,000. The man, and his friends, were already a legend; not least, Sir Francis Dashwood and his Hellfire Club which included some of the most power- ful and wealthy in the land — among them my Lords Sandwich,* March and Orford. The whole affair was cloaked in secrecy, though there was talk of orgies and Satanic practices; one story, unverified, was that Wilkes had once dressed a monkey in a red cloak and strapped horns to its head and, when Orford began some diabolical prayer, Wilkes had released the creature and his Lordship had fainted away thinking that the Devil had, indeed, appeared.

And these were the men who ruled England. The whole thing was a caricature, no more; the intrepid veteran with his satire of patriotism; the crowds on their holy day of death; and always the grandees, puppet masters of all the rest. The differences multiplied, like the seventh ring of hell in some book he had once taken from the Reverend Knowler's shelves, and Paine turned for home trying to rationalise the irrational — and found the confusion worse than before.

Yet, as Dr Bevis had said, there must be an answer somewhere, if he only dared to know. Their first meeting had been a chance one; Paine had offered the old gentleman a hand across the Temple and, in return, had been invited up to the scholar's rooms, a sunlit place furnished with books. A member of the Royal Society and an astronomer, Bevis found Paine's curiosity compelling. The lad had a good mind, no doubt about it — why, he had even attended the lectures of those philosophical pedants, Martin and Ferguson. All that it required was an application of logic. The problem was, where to begin.

It was almost 150 years now since Bacon* had pioneered modern, inductive methods; almost a century since Newton* had explored 'the system of the world', and Locke had begun to formulate his theories of government. In the years between London had been at the eye of the storm that was blowing up over Europe — as much in science and economics as in theology and politics. This was the other London that the lad had to learn; the difficulty was to disentangle one discipline from another to create the whole.

The life of the eighteenth-century intellectual was a close-knit affair. Revered in France, but largely ignored elsewhere, the self-styled 'philosophes'* inhabited a small, yet eclectic universe whose influence was to prove quite disproportionate to its size.

The previous month, there had been a new translation of Monsieur Voltaire's *Elements de la physique de Newton*. The man had a quite extraordinary mind, though it was said that his morals left something to be desired, and, checking his abstractions, Dr Bevis recalled the young staymaker, Paine, Tom Paine. No good filling him out with metaphysics. He was confused enough as it was. But there again, where to begin? The answer, of course, was with reason but that in its turn, posed a problem, for where did reason itself begin?

Not with the mumbo-jumbo that God was some kind of cosmic clockmaker, that was for sure. True, the German upstart, Leibniz, had derided Newton's mechanistic philosophy, and the old man still felt anger at the words:

> Sir Isaac and his followers have an odd opinion of the work of God. According to their doctrine, God Almighty has to wind his watch from time to time, otherwise it would cease to move. He had not, it seems, sufficient foresight to make it perpetual motion.

The man had been a buffoon, and a German buffoon at that. Hadn't Voltaire himself attended Newton's funeral to write of his amazement that a true scientist could live 'honoured amongst his compatriots, to be buried like a king that had done well by his subject'. And that, Dr Bevis supposed, was as good a place as any for the young Paine to start: with the conviction that, given the right method, it was possible to explain the nature of both man and his universe.

After all, this was the theology of reason, the bequest of Bacon and Newton, and it was changing the world — even France, thanks very largely to Monsieur Voltaire. Why, in three short chapters of his *Letters on England* the man had finally, and irrefutably, exposed the 'occult qualities' of the metaphysical school and established a European reputation for the rigour of Newtonian methods, as much in science as in philosophy.

Yes, this must be the entrée, the *bien genèse* of this young philosophe's education, the *Letters* — though on handing over the volume he could see the lad's disappointment. It was only a slim work of no more than one hundred pages, which did not seem many to change the world. After one reading, however, Paine knew what the old man meant. For all its disguise as a guidebook to English customs, and for all its circumspect language, the whole thrust of Voltaire's essays was as revolutionary in tone as it was in content; no more and no less than a critique of the entire established order of things.

In the weeks that followed Paine read and reread the *Letters* to discover the nuances which had led the work to be outlawed in France. Not that Voltaire was building Utopias. He was altogether too practical for that. No, it was simply that, by contrasting the English experience with that of the French (albeit with considerable licence), he developed his case — against an established church: 'If there was one religion in England there would be a danger of despotism; if there were two, they would cut each others throats, but there are thirty and they live in peace and happiness.'

And against metaphysical speculation:

I am a body, and I think. I know no more than that and (to theologians) I would say 'Admit at any rate that you are as ignorant as I am; neither your imagination nor mine can conceive how a body has ideas, and do you understand any the more how a substance, whatever it be, has ideas? You don't comprehend either matter or spirit, how then can you dare to affirm anything whatever?' Then the superstitious come in their turn and say that those who suspect that one can think with the body alone should be burnt for the good of their souls.

And against absolutism in all its forms:

The English nation is the only one on earth which has succeeded in controlling the power of Kings by resisting them, which by effort after effort has at last established the wise system of government in which the prince, all powerful in doing good, has his hands tied from doing evil; in which the aristocrats are great without arrogance or vassals; and in which the people share in the government without confusion. The House of Commons and Lords are the arbiters of the nation, the King is the super-arbiter.

The man exaggerated shamelessly, and for an instant Paine wondered whether this was indeed the England that he knew (the England where kings remained arrogant, aristocrats absolute, and an established church blessed both); then he fathomed Monsieur Voltaire's purpose: that in taking England as his model, he was satirising all that he saw and making a fine stew of convention. Little wonder that the Parliament of Paris had ordered the public executioner to burn the work for being 'scandalous, contrary to religion, good morals, and the respect due to authority'.

The only problem with the *Letters*, so far as Paine could see, was that Monsieur Voltaire posed problems to which he had no adequate replies; that, like a petulant child, he had pulled the toy of creation to pieces — God, nature, man, thought — and was surprised when, on invoking reason, they did not fit neatly together again. It was all very well to select the pieces at random — Bacon's elevation of experimental science; Locke's rationale of government; Newton's exploration of the system of the universe — but the whole still remained in pieces.

At 21 years of age, Paine was as confused as before, and the good Dr Bevis merely compounded the problem, for, when taxed with Monsieur Voltaire, he would always reply: 'To find the right answers, you must first ask the right questions; that is where true reason begins.'

The reply was altogether too glib. For as long as he could remember (on the walks with his father, in the meetings at Cage Lane, in the class of the Reverend Knowler; and now in Dr Bevis's rooms) he had been asking what he thought were the right questions to find, with Archimedes, that: 'Had we a place to stand, we might raise the world.' Why, only this spring, Mr David Hume* had published his *Natural History of Religion* and the good Dr Bevis had read him an extract, as if savouring the words:

The whole is a riddle, an aenigma [*sic*], an inexplicable mystery. Doubt, uncertainty, suspense of judgement appear to be the only result of our most accurate scrutiny concerning this subject. But such is the faculty of human reason, and such the contagion of opinion, that even when this deliberate doubt could scarcely be upheld, did we not enlarge our view, and opposing one species to another, set them quarrelling, while we ourselves during their fury and contention, make our escape into the calm, though obscure regions of philosophy.

No doubt Mr Hume was right; the whole was indeed a mystery, and it was his good fortune that philosophy offered him an escape. But what of the less favoured: of the dispossessed who wandered England in search of work where there was none; of the huddled masses to the east of the

Tower; of the intrepid veteran of Drury Lane; of Amy Hutchinson 'her hands and face smeared with tar', and the 13 condemned beneath the Tyburn tree? It was all very fine for Mr Hume and his friends to toy with their theories, but that did nothing to fill the bellies of the poor.

Quite the reverse; in raising a Godhead to reason they dismissed reality to create . . . Paine searched for the word, and found it: chaos. In playing the iconclasts, they had discovered only chaos and, recoiling from the self-catechism, he remembered his mother and wondered whether she was right after all. There might be little to recommend the authoritarian ways that she adopted, but it was preferable to what he had found.

The problem was to escape. Eighteen months in the city had been enough. He had explored its mind and been frightened by what he found, an infinite multiplication of differences. Now he needed some place away from the crush and the noise where he had time to think; a place like the staymaking business which was looking for a new master at Sandwich. The journeyman who peddled the news had been full of its prospects, and Mr Morris was kind enough to say that he was more than capable of doing the job.

The opportunity was too good to lose and in the summer of 1758 Paine hung his sign, Master Staymaker, above the door of his new workroom in Kent. For a 21-year-old, well qualified in his trade, the future looked secure, and, confident of his prospects, he married Mary Lambert, a maid in the house of Richard Solly, woollen draper, in September of the same year. Both the marriage and the business were short lived — Mary dying the following year, and Paine abandoning his failing business within weeks of her death.

In years to come Pitt the Younger, fearful of Paine's reputation, was to fund dark rumours that Mary died of ill treatment at her husband's hands, a charge contradicted by all existing evidence that, far from being a wife beater, Paine was generous to a fault. As an old man in exile he once wrote some overnight lines in answer to the question: 'What is Love?'

> 'Tis that delightful transport we can feel
> Which painters cannot paint, nor words reveal,
> Nor any art we know of — can conceal.[3]

Though it could have been a memory of Mary that clouded the final lines:

> What are the iron chains that hands have wrought?
> The hardest chains to break are those of thought.

Think well on this, ye lovers, and be kind,
Nor play with torture — or a tortured mind.

The sentiment hardly tallies with the dark hints put abroad by Pitt,
while Paine's future conduct was to stand in sharp contrast with the general
mood of the period. The eighteenth century may have romanticised love,
but the lot of women was, at best, inferior; at worst, humiliating. Heiresses
were the prey to fortune hunters (the plot of half the novels of the time),
and those without any prospect were often the victims of violence, vice,
or both.

The great hiring fairs of the day were a regular market for prostitution, Hogarth's *A Harlot's Progress* showing a procuress recruiting a country girl into the ranks of the 50,000 prostitutes that worked in London
in the mid-century; while it was common practice for employers to take
on girls from the Parish authorities as much to pleasure themselves as
to provide a form of cheap labour. As an orphan, Mary Lambert had
been lucky; Richard Solly had been a good master, but now . . .

Paine followed the road west to London and thought bitterly of Mary's
death. The thing mocked God, for God knew they had loved enough,
and it seemed that for a woman that was a rare enough thing. Even in
England, where they might be thought to have a prospect of happiness,
they had few rights under the law, and were surrounded by tyrants in
breeches who tormented them first, then laughed at their tears.[4] Yet with
Mary there had been happiness, and now there was nothing; he wondered
what Dr Bevis might say, then cursed the imagined answer. For a very
short time he had known the right questions; and Mary's death was God's
reply.

At Deptford the road swung north to the river, but even before reaching
London Bridge Paine heard the bells tolling for the death of the King.
After 33 years on the throne George II had been a long time dying, as
if to spite his heir. The gesture was in character. If there was one thing
that the Georges disliked more than England and its constitution, it was
their successors to the throne.

Jealous of their sovereignty, successive Hanoverians publicly spurned their heirs, George II's wife once raged 'that canaille is the lowest
stinking coward in the world'[5] on being told that her son would represent his father at the State Opening of Parliament. Their children
reciprocated in kind, George's son, Frederick, having his wife driven
from Hampton Court to St James's during the agonies of childbirth to
prevent the delivery of their first-born under his parents' roof.

And now it was this first-born that was to inherit George II's throne. At 22 years of age, George III was as innocent of political arts as the arts of politics were corrupt — Pitt the Elder having recently described the Commons as 'a parcel of younger brothers', referring to the fact that in one session of Parliament alone 67 sons of peers sat in the Lower House, whilst a further 87 MPs were elected under the direct patronage of the Lords.

Gauche, stubborn and bitterly vindictive to all those who had anything to do with his grandfather, the young king determined to have nothing whatever to do with the jockeys of power, and his first proclamation declared his intention to encourage piety and virtue, and punish profaneness, immorality and vice. There was no mistaking his target, and the Whig grandees were not slow to interpret his first speech from the throne:

> Born and educated in this country, I glory in the name of Briton, and the peculiar happiness of my life will consist in promoting the welfare of a people whose loyalty and affection I consider the greatest and most permanent security of my throne.

The echo was of the patriot king, of the need to purge corruption and free the throne from the power of the Whigs, and the author was widely rumoured to be the Marquis of Bute.* A late developer who found writing and reading difficult even in his teens, George had formed a deep, adolescent attachment for the Scottish peer, deferring to his opinions on every issue and abasing himself when Bute was displeased.

The Whigs exploited the relationship shamelessly, resurrecting the Jacobite bogy (it was only 15 years since Prince Charles Stuart's army had reached south to Derby), allied to George's supposed ambition to restore absolute power. By the year's end, London was alive with rumours of cabal and intrigue, though the coffee house wits jested that it was simply a case of the new corruption replacing the old, and told of how Bubb Doddington had waited three days in the antechamber before kissing the young king's hand, 'changing his allegiance as deftly as his wigs'.

Contemptuous of politics, Paine laughed with the best of them. Power was no better than fashion on which even Goldsmith refused to comment for fear that 'the vogue should undergo some new revolution before it was finished'. In any event, he had troubles enough of his own without all the tittle-tattle of affairs behind the curtain at court — of one lord turning candleholder and another a groom of the stole, any office, in fact, to which a salary was attached that came out of the public purse.[6] It was not so much corrupt as distracting. How could a man be expected to find work when the whole town was embroiled in gossip? And work was what he needed most of all — any work, though preferably a solid occupation, for he had had enough of staymaking and being his own man; and enough of politics too.

In little more than three years it seemed that the whole world had shifted beneath him. Now he needed somewhere solid to stand, and the coffee house laughter echoed about him again as they talked of some new Lord of the Bedchamber or other; for, at 25 years of age, it seemed that the Duke of Grafton was the coming man.

One moment the talk was as remote as a Newtonian abstraction. The next it was as immediate as the child who had once ridden through Thetford on Walpole's knee; had once galloped his hounds through the town. In May 1757, Charles, Duke of Grafton, for 33 years the Lord Privy Seal of England, had died and his grandson, Augustus Henry (already an MP) had succeeded to the title. Within the year he was created Lord-Lieutenant of Suffolk, and appointed Lord of the Bedchamber to the young Prince of Wales, though there was already talk of a falling out with Bute. If true, Paine would have to move quickly.

It was all very fine to despise politics and all it entailed but, if men advanced by connection, then the Grafton connection was too influential to ignore. It was not that he was ambitious but surely, remembering Thetford, His Grace might find him a post where he could resolve his self-doubts; and, abandoning principle, the 22-year-old Paine approached Grafton and in the spring of 1761 received his first appointment with the Customs and Excise — as a cask gauger in Grantham, another of the Grafton seats.

For a man destined to become a prophet of radicalism, it was a paradoxical appointment, for the Excise was universally reviled as a dangerous extension of civil power. Introduced during the Civil War of the previous century, the service was responsible for raising taxes on imported goods through its bonded warehouses; for policing premises where bonded goods were stored; and, with the Customs, for the prevention of smuggling.

In the mid-seventeenth century the poet Marvell had caricatured the Excise as:

A monster worse than e'er before,
Frighted the midwife, and the Mother tore.
A thousand hands she hath, a thousand eyes;
Breaks into shops, and into cellars pries.

It was a far cry from Kipling's romanticism ('brandy for the parson/ Baccy for the clerk'), but Marvell's views were commonplace when all of England banded together to evade the Excise. During the 1720s (at a time when Walpole was using an Admiralty barge to run contraband ashore) over a million pounds of tobacco, and nearly 200,000 gallons of brandy were seized by the service; whilst in the 1740s some 300,000 pounds of tea were being imported illegally each year and a former smuggler, Abraham Walter, was telling a parliamentary committee that more than 20,000 men were employed, directly, in the smuggling trade.

But, if the public regarded evading the Excise as a legitimate pastime, it was the fear of a centrally organised standing force which made a bogy of the service itself. The free-born Englishman had had enough of standing armies and, when the author Henry Fielding* proposed the establishment of some form of permanent policing in the 1740s, the idea was rounded on bitterly as subversively un-English. Such was the service that Paine joined in 1761, to be embroiled within the year in the fury that exploded over Bute's proposal to tax cider.

Thirty years before, Walpole had tried to tax salt, and failed, to be smuggled from the Commons, ignominiously, to escape the anger of the mob. But Bute and his master would not compromise and, for all Pitt the Elder's horrifying sketch of England being overrun by excisemen, they bundled the Bill through Parliament, adding credence to the suspicion that George and his first Minister were intent on subverting the constitution and bringing in a more despotic regime.

When the news of the cider tax reached Grantham, a two-day ride north of London, it did not make Paine's job any easier, or his life any more pleasant. In the months since his arrival in the town, an off-comer, he had come to know the meaning of loneliness again; of a new difference that set him apart. As distinct from childhood, however, it was now his authority — the authority of Tom Paine. Exciseman — that made for the difference.

Where was the Quaker now ('O ye great and rich men of earth, weep and howl for your misery is coming'), or the child who had written on the death of a crow, or the apprentice philosophe who had read Voltaire to build anew a world of reason? How could he justify the differences he had long reviled, when he was now an agent of oppression himself? Isolated, he consoled himself by contrasting the tedium of staymaking with the security that he had found in the Excise — though Bute seemed bent on causing him mischief with this new tax of his.

Grantham was a safe Whig seat, the burgesses knew where their duty lay, and there was word that Grafton's break with Bute had become irreversible, and he had joined Pitt, Temple and 'that devil Wilkes' in opposition. The news delighted the town, for if Pitt was a national hero (and hadn't the man built England an empire from the Seven Years' War just ended?), then Wilkes was the champion of affairs closer to home; in his seat at the inn Paine recalled the misshapen figure, and the misshapen legends that had followed his name.

Now, it seemed, things were very different. Mr Wilkes was central to Whig affairs (and there was still laughter to be won from his epigram: 'Every person brought in by the Whigs has lost his post — except the King'), not least as editor of the *North Briton*. The thing was a virulent sheet, almost wholly devoted to satirising George and his Scots connections, past, present, and future: 'Some time since died Mr John Bull, a very worthy plain honest gentleman of Saxon descent. He was choaked by inadvertently swallowing a thistle which he had placed by way of ornament on top of his salad.'

By late 1763, Bute had had enough, the intensifying campaign culminating in claims of his supposed affair with the Dowager Princess of Wales; the implication that his high position had been obtained as a result of her favours; and cartoons showing a tartan Jack-Bute and his mistress riding roughshod over English liberty. On Bute's resignation, George III was to write:

> Though young I see but too much that there are very few honest men in the world; as my Dear Friend has quitted the Ministry I don't expect to see it there again. I shall therefore support those who will act for me and without regret change my tools whenever they are contrary to my service.

George's resolve was to have ominous consequences for, if the humiliation inflicted on his 'Dear Friend' incensed him, it also steeled his resolve. His short apprenticeship in kingship was over. For the next decade and more he was to try and set his personal stamp on British and American politics. In the meantime, however, there was Wilkes, always Wilkes.

Bute may have gone, but the *North Briton*'s campaign continued, unabated, treating the government and its supporters with equal contempt; its savage jibes reaching down even to Paine in Grantham. Dr Johnson,* despite the abuse of pensions in his dictionary ('In England it is generally understood to mean pay given to a state hireling for treason to his country'), had himself accepted a pension and become a government writer. This led Wilkes to suggest that he be given a place at the Board of Excise, which the good Doctor had described in the Dictionary as:

'a hateful tax levied upon commodities and adjudged not by the common judges of property but wretches hired by those to whom excise is paid.'

Paine understood the cut only too well, yet it was not only scoundrels that took pensions, and who would collect the Excise if it was not for wretches like him? He recognised the sophistry for what it was — a justification for the principles that he had sacrificed to obtain a steady post and £48 a year — and was relieved when the conversation turned to other things, to the state of the crops, to the promise of rain; though seemingly it always reverted to Mr Wilkes again.

Following the King's speech from the throne in 1763, Wilkes published *North Briton 45*. At last he had gone too far, describing George's ministers as 'the tools of despotism and corruption' and warning: 'They have sent the spirit of discord through the land and I prophesy it will never be extinguished but by the extinction of their power.'

Within the week a general warrant was issued for Wilkes's arrest, and he was held prisoner in the Tower, where Grafton was among his first visitors: 'to learn from himself his own story and his defence, and to show that no influence ought to stop the means of every man's justifying himself from an accusation, though it should be of the most heinous nature.'

In Grantham the story of the visit to the prisoner in the Tower was endlessly retailed and embellished. Wilkes had done no more than express a common fear, and, if detention was the King's reply, then what had become of English justice? In the silence that followed Paine recalled how the majesty of law could end: the slow procession down Tyburn way, the few spoken words, and then the noose. Pray God, that Wilkes's friends were too powerful for that; his wit too alert.

Taking the stand in his own defence, Wilkes argued that as an MP he was privileged and should be released, then carried the attack into the heart of the enemy's camp:

> The LIBERTY of all peers and gentlemen and, what troubles me more sensibly, that of all the middling and inferior sort of people, which stands in most need of protection, is in my case finally to be decided upon: a question of such importance as to determine at once, whether ENGLISH LIBERTY be reality or shadow.

The case was dismissed, and England acclaimed the new-found advocate of its rights. But George and his ministers were not to be denied. When *Number 45* was reissued in November 1763, the Commons declared it seditious libel, and in 1764 Wilkes was outlawed — though was already in self-imposed exile in France. The controversy flared again, not least in Grantham when the King dismissed the ageing General Conway (a Grafton nominee, and MP for Thetford) from his post in the royal Bedchamber for voting against the government.

Once again George had imposed his will on Parliament, and once again Grantham was alive with gossip. As an officer of the crown, Paine could not escape the meaning of all he heard: at his work, in his rooms, in the taverns of the town. Wilkes stood for LIBERTY and the liberty of free-born Englishmen was at risk. The man and his Whig friends, bitter at the loss of their long-standing power, may have employed the appeal expeditiously but, once the debate was opened, it could not be closed.

What was it that the Quaker James Nayler had written little more than a century before: 'God made all men of one mould and one blood to dwell on the face of the earth'? Paine knew the evidence mocked the words, and the knowledge only made it more difficult to bear, for where was the solution to the quandary to be found? Neither in God nor philosophy, whilst politics could be summarised in the one word: jockeyship.

The cynicism was deep-rooted. He had already seen too much, heard too much of the profession and was sceptical of Wilkes's new role as the people's friend. His conversion had been too facile for that. One day the man and his friends had ridden power; the next their nag had bolted and here they were whipping up the popular pack to hunt their prey — for their own profit. Whig or Tory it made no difference, power was their only concern; power and the pickings of office.

The curse was that there was so little alternative. It seemed that the choice was between absolutism (and that had been a stubborn enough burr to remove) or this — this farrago. Recalling Voltaire, Paine laughed wryly. The philosophes might dream up their ideal constitutions, but in practice little changed, and he shrugged off the thoughts — incestuous things living off one another to spawn dangerous notions of a liberty which Wilkes could never imagine. Such ideas were unbecoming to an officer of the crown, and personally he had few grounds for complaint.

The pay was not princely (£48 a year did not go far when one had to buy and keep one's own horse), but the job was easy enough (merely checking that the local brewers paid the necessary duties on their products) and, while still an off-comer, the townsfolk were coming to accept him in their cautious way. No, compared with what he knew, he had little to complain of; so long as he could keep his conscience down.

Paine served at Grantham for three years, then was posted to Alford, a six-mile ride on the Lincolnshire coast. A desolate spot flanked by sea and salt marshes, this was smugglers' country and he looked back to his time at Grantham with regret. If he had thought he had troubles then, he had hardly known what they meant compared with this wilderness forsaken by God and man — saving, that is, for the owlers.

The underworld of the eighteenth century was dominated by the professionals of smuggling, men who neither asked nor gave quarter in their long skirmish with the law. In Walpole's time, three customs men were overpowered by a gang of 50 smugglers after impounding a sloop laden with duty-free tobacco and brandy; in 1742, a Kent gang threatened to burn out a town for sheltering the militia; whilst only a couple of years previously Exciseman William Gilling and an informer had been taken by a smuggling band, tortured, killed, and their bodies dumped into a well.

The case sent a shock wave through England, but it was short lived, and by the time that Paine came to ride the Lincolnshire coast the gangs were as brazen as before. The posting lasted a year, then Paine was dismissed from the service for 'stamping' a victualler's goods without having examined them. The practice of 'stamping' goods unseen was common in the service and Paine frankly admitted his dereliction, pleading in extenuation that it was impossible to complete all his examinations thoroughly. The Board of Excise dismissed the plea and in August 1765 Paine was unemployed again, and again he turned to staymaking, though only for a handful of months for, by the spring of 1766 he was back in London, teaching at Mr Noble's school.

With certain notable exceptions, mainly in the Dissenting Academies, schoolteaching was a humble profession, and paid accordingly. The salary at Mr Noble's was £25 a year which, after paying essential expenses, allowed Paine little to spare to indulge his passion for improving himself — not least, after his Alford exile. It seemed that all of London was brewing around him, yet he could hardly afford the price of an ale; and, while it was all very well for the good Dr Bevis to moralise about poverty bringing its own rewards, he had never gone short of his dinner, or the bottle of port which followed.

It was always the way: those who had never gone hungry were the first to argue about the subjection of appetite, and those who had never been poor talked loudest of the power of principle — and since Paine's absence from London, Dr Bevis had indulged his appetite for both good living and high ideals. Aged now, and living the life of a semi-recluse in his rooms in the Temple, he fired off principles like a ship of the line, regular broadsides, more especially those of Jean-Jacques Rousseau.*

If Dr Bevis was to be believed, the man was a genius, though of a contrary sort; a philosophe certainly, yet challenging the most fundamental principles of the philosophes themselves. At which point the old gentleman had become quite disturbed, for it appeared that Rousseau had not only refuted Bacon and his followers' belief in the infallibility of reason, the inevitability of progress, but had gone so far as to suggest that the recent revival in the sciences and the arts had, indeed, corrupted morals; that progress was an illusion and mankind had been happier in a state of nature.

And that was by no means all. Why, only recently, this Monsieur Rousseau had published a *Social Contract* which concluded that men could be both ruled and free — if they ruled themselves. The notion, of course, was absurd; had not Mr Locke and Mr Hobbes* amongst others proved that a man had to choose between being governed and being free; that either he traded some personal liberty for the sake of security under government or settled for the alternative: anarchy? Surely, that was the essence of any social contract? All that remained was to define and limit the extent of sovereign power.

True, the issue had caused great problems; but, as Monsieur Voltaire had been kind enough to say, it seemed that England had resolved the difficulty with its balanced constitution, by establishing a harmony of power between the Commons, the Lords and the King. Yet here was Monsieur Rousseau maintaining that man was born free, but was everywhere in chains; that the only truly free man was the man who ruled himself.

In principle, the idea might be all very fine, but in practice even its author had to conjure up such vague and amorphous notions as 'the general will' of the people as the arbiter of power, as if such a thing could ever be balanced up in the constitutional scales. Clearly the man was an incurable romantic, harking back to the state of nature in all its barbarity, as if he could impose such primitive liberties on a civilised world. The whole thing was a tissue of contradictions, and yet . . .

Paine walked the night, and heard the uproar of a distant mob. The harvest had been bad and there were growing reports of food riots throughout the country, whilst in London the glass grinders and journeymen tailors had already taken to the streets, and in Middlesex five demonstrators had been cut down when marching for 'Wilkes and Liberty' by troops ordered out by the magistrates. Although outlawed from England since the *North Briton* affair of 1764, Wilkes's ghost fairly mesmerised the crowds; or was this an expression of Monsieur Rousseau's 'general will', the liberty to riot and loot — though, in truth, the people had grievances enough?

The past years had been hard, but the government took little note of the suffering, preferring to occupy itself in the continuing, internecine struggle for power. Since Bute's fall in 1763, Grenville, then Rockingham, and now Grafton held the seals of office as First Lord of the Treasury. No mistaking, George was changing his tools whenever they failed to suit his purpose; but for all that, matters went from bad to worse. There was controversy over the management of the East India Company's affairs; while it was widely rumoured that General Gage,* the Commander-in-Chief in North America, had warned London of serious unrest if there was not some easing of conditions in the 13 Colonies.

Relations between the government in London and the Colonists had been deteriorating since the end of the Seven Years' War. Superficially the dispute turned on whether the Colonies should pay for some share of the war (between 1756 and 1765 England had reimbursed the Colonists to the sum of £1.1 million for their military support); but this disguised the altogether more fundamental problem of a growing feeling of independence and self-sufficiency amongst the Colonists themselves, a feeling that they were increasingly capable of managing their own affairs.

Since the Pilgrim Fathers had pledged themselves as a 'City upon a Hill' more than 130 years before, the 13 Colonies had grown in territory, in population and in prosperity — yet they were still governed from London, a two-month passage away. Hard men, and independently minded, the Colonists too had read their Locke and Voltaire to place a revolutionary interpretation on their works — an echo of their own recent past when men had fled 'the depravations of Europe, to the American Strand'. Paine understood their mood well. As George and his ministers presumed in England, they presumed in America too.

Only two years before, Parliament had doubled the enumeration on Colonial goods. The practice, introduced at the Restoration, required that all Colonial products bound for northern Europe should be shipped through English ports, providing England with what amounted to a monopoly of the American trade: in tobacco, cotton, indigo, dyes, iron, copper, furs, skins, hides, pitch, tar, turpentine, masts, coffee, raw silk, potash. As a former officer of the Excise, Paine knew what such impositions meant, a continuing interference in the Colonists' affairs.

They could work their own iron mines, yet were forbidden to produce any secondary iron products. They could trap the native beaver, yet were prohibited from making beaver hats, save for their own use. They had new frontiers beyond the Alleghenies, yet were forbidden from settling there. The impositions were intolerable; little wonder that they now asked for a greater hand in the management of their own business.

Yet, stubborn as ever, the King regarded their ambitions as a personal affront, while Dr Johnson provided him with a voice, comparing the Colonies to 'the vestry of a large parish which may lay a tax on the inhabitants and enforce payments'. Much of England disagreed, but George and his ministers were unrelenting. In 1765, the Stamp Act was passed, to tax the Colonists on all legal and commercial documents, newspapers, pamphlets, cards and dice, to produce an estimated revenue of between £60,000 and £100,000 a year for the English Treasury.

Within the decade, it was to prove too high a cost to be borne. Though the Act was repealed in 1766, the seeds of revolution had been planted; the cry of 'No Taxation Without Representation' had been raised; while the ageing Pitt, now Earl of Chatham, had thundered to the Commons: 'I rejoice that America has resisted; three millions of people so dead to all feelings of liberty as voluntarily to submit to be slaves, would have been fit instruments to make slaves of all the rest.'

Liberty, it seemed, knew no licence, the call finding a more ominous voice on the streets nearer home, the Wilkes faction drumming up the mob to lead them God knew where. Philosophy and politics, politics and philosophy; the whole was a mess of pottage, though now that Grafton was the King's first Minister perhaps there was something to be salvaged from the stew and, recalling his hunger, Paine walked on. As early as July 1766, he had petitioned the Board of Commissioners to re-enter the Excise in what can only be described in servile terms:

> In humble obedience to Your Honour's letter of discharge . . . I delivered up my Commission and since that time have given you no trouble. I confess the justice of Your Honour's displeasure and humbly beg to add my thanks for the candour and lenity with which you, at that time, indulged me. And though the nature of the report and my confession cut off all expectation of Your Honour's favour then, yet I humbly hope that it has not finally excluded me therefrom, upon which I humbly presume and entreat Your Honour to restore me.

It is not the pedantry of the prose style that contrasts so vividly with the vitality of Paine's later writing, more the obseqiousness of tone when compared with the works of the radical who was to attack authority with an even-handed contempt — not least, His Majesty's Commissioners for Customs and Excise. But, at 29 years of age, Paine still lacked confidence in himself or his talents, still needed to find some purpose in life — and, as he already knew, employment with the crown appeared to offer both.

The only curse was that his conscience wouldn't be still. If only he could tame it; expunge the past; exorcise the memories of Joseph's torn mind, and the march of riches and poverty across the Thetford bridge; of the hanging figures on Tyburn tree, and the laughter in the great houses on the Mall; of Voltaire and reason, and Rousseau and his Noble Savage — though, for all their philosophies, neither explained Mary's death and that had hurt most of all. If only he could make a whole of the contradictions, then he might even know himself.

In the meantime it was better to settle for a taste of humility and an established place in the order of things for his past was a bleak enough reference — the more so in a city where the rewards for success, and the penalties of failure, stood in such stark and everyday contrast.

Late in 1766 the Board of Excise ordered that he 'be restored to a proper vacancy', and, after turning down a place at Grampound, in Cornwall, he was offered a post in Lewes which he accepted with gratitude. The posting put a temporary end to Paine's nomadic existence. For the next six years he was to make Sussex his home; they were six years of comparative stability in which he had time, and the stimulus, to interpret all that had gone before and develop a philosophy that was to play a seminal role in the Age of Revolutions that was to come.

3 'AN INGENIOUS, WORTHY YOUNG MAN'

In the nineteenth century a headstone still stood in a Lewes graveyard to the memory of Wm. Huntington, SS (Sinner Saved). A one-time coal heaver turned mendicant preacher, Huntington left a pen sketch of an Excise man remembered from his childhood in the early eighteenth century:

> At that time there was a person called Godfrey, a man of stern and hard-faced countenance, whom I took notice of for having a stick carved with figures, and an ink bottle hanging from a button hole in his coat.
>
> I imagined the man to be employed by God Almighty to take notice of, and keep account of children's sins and once I got into the market house, and watched him very narrowly, and found he was always in a hurry, and I thought he had need to hurry, as he must have a great deal to do to find out all the sins of children.

It could well have been Paine — a slender man of above average height at 5 feet 9 inches, with a ruddy face dominated by a hawk-like nose and soberly, even severely, dressed. It was a month past his thirty-first birthday and, determined to make a place for himself, Paine found the small Sussex town well to his liking, the keep of its Norman castle commanding a web of small streets and alleys on their freefall to the River Ouse.

Here was to be the quiet centre of his life and, as he first rode up School Hill, past the Pelhams' town house to his new lodgings in the shadow of the old West Gate, he must have wondered whether this would be the end of his wanderings; if this would be the place where the differences would be resolved, where he would find himself.

Paine was to spend the next six years secure in this retreat, distilling all that he had learned, while learning from Lewes itself. Steeped in traditions of dissent, the town was a sympathetic environment for the nascent radical. Five centuries before, following the Battle of Lewes in 1264, Simon de Montfort had dispatched the monks from the Greyfriars Priory to negotiate with Henry III and secure the 'Mise of Lewes', often regarded as 'the commencement of Parliamentary government'.

Three centuries on, during the Marian persecution, 17 Protestants were burned at the stake in the Market Square, while during the Civil War the town declared firmly for Parliament and three years after the Restoration of 1660 (a year in which Cromwell's son, Richard, took ship from Lewes to escape arrest) the town was still considered 'perverse' by the royalist faction. A century of comparative tranquillity, punctuated only by internecine theological disputes, had made Lewes a prosperous place by 1768; but its past was not forgotten, the great Bonfire Night fêtes of 5 November with their banners featuring 'Bloody Jesuits . . . and wanton friars' and 'Devils dancing attendance on the Pope' prompting memories of the town's nonconformist past.

By March 1768, however, Guy Fawkes night was four months gone, and there was more pressing business to hand: the election of two new members to represent Lewes in Parliament, though, as Paine's new landlord, Ollive, was to explain, the outcome was a foregone conclusion, the town being strong for the Newcastle connection. Always had been since God knew when — the Glorious Revolution certainly, and perhaps before that. A bluff man, Ollive was one of the town's two constables and as such would be acting as a teller for the election itself.

It interfered with the business, of course, but then a man had his responsibilities and never more so than now, what with George and his ministers continually meddling in affairs, though coming from London, Mr Paine would know all about that . . . Although only 60 miles south of the capital, news was still hard to come by, especially through the long winter months when the English roads became clogged with mud. Only recently John Wesley had come close to drowning when his horse stumbled on the Great North Road, while the ale house gossips of Lewes still retailed stories of the local dowager who had four oxen hitched to her coach each Sunday to draw her the half mile to church.

Paine knew the problem well, and remembered his lonely ride at Alford. When communications between town and town were so inadequate, it was small wonder that Mr Ollive was anxious for news, not least of Newcastle for it was rumoured that His Grace the Duke had suffered a stroke and now was mortally sick. If true, it had grave implications for the coming election. The man was a generous patron to the town, though he could afford it well enough, for word was that he collected £30,000 a year from his rent rolls alone.

A Whig grandee of the old guard, Thomas Pelham-Holles, first Duke of Newcastle, was born in 1698, served his political indentures under Walpole, was a minister at 33 years, and appointed First Lord of the Treasury in 1754. For the next six years his political power, buttressed by the votes his wealth and connections commanded, was virtually unassailable at Westminster. The accession of George III had undercut his power, but in Lewes his influence remained: an awesome figure whose Homeric banquets for his tenants and supporters were a legend within his own lifetime.

For Paine this was neither a political abstraction, nor an echo of Voltaire's 'happy blend' of government. The spring of 1768 was to provide him with a vivid insight into the workings of power itself — a skill at which Newcastle had long been an undisputed master. As polling day neared, however, the rumours hardened: His Grace was paralysed and dying. It was his agents who now managed his affairs, and badly at that. On the night before the election, they withdrew Newcastle's support from one of his Lewes candidates, and the following morning lost the vote of a member returned to the House to oppose Grafton's ministry.

The conjunction of power — of Grafton in Thetford and Grantham, Newcastle in Lewes — was no surprise to Paine. For all of George's early promise to purge political corruption (and the counter-charge that it was he who was corrupting the constitution), government remained the preserve of a handful of great families who gambled at politics with all the finesse that they brought to the gaming tables of Mayfair — though with fewer counters in play. In the mid-eighteenth century, less than a thirtieth of the population were entitled to vote; 84,000 electors returned 421 members to the House — of which Lewes, with 130 voters on the register, returned two.

The system was corrupt to the core. How was it possible to obtain an honest Parliament, when elections were made up of a mass of decaying constituencies; when in one seat the total electorate consisted of only two shepherds and, doubtless, their sheep? Parliament was a farce, and a corrupt farce at that. Little wonder that no man of honour or scruple would allow his name to go forward for such drudgery. To have any hope of success he would have to sacrifice all the qualities required of a good legislation and should he sacrifice them for the sake of election, was it likely that the representative would be any better than the man?

Such ideas were altogether too strong for Mr Ollive. A good man, but fixed in his ways and jealous, perhaps, of his office, he would maunder on about Lewes being an honest town; and what a great benefactor His Grace had been; and hadn't he, Samuel Ollive, once received a guinea from the hand of the Duke himself for his services as a teller; and what better way was there, anyway? Could Mr Paine answer him that? It was all very well playing the devil's advocate, but what was the alternative? For all his wit not even Mr Wilkes had been able to find one though he had tried hard enough and God bless him for it, for the man had served the Whig purposes well.

The whole was a mass of contradictions, though the old man had a point: what better way was there? Paine remembered the mobs on the London streets. Moreover, Mr Wilkes had now returned from France.

The man was either a rogue or a saint, there could be no in-between. Ten years ago there was no question of the one, his dissipation had been the talk of the town. His boon companion Lord Sandwich once remarked that he didn't know where Wilkes would end up, with the pox or on the gallows, to which the rogue had dared reply that it all depended on which he embraced first, his Lordship's principles or his mistresses.

To date he had escaped both, but there was no denying the courage of his convictions, whatever they might be. Though still outlawed, he had returned from France to fight the spring election and, on being defeated, had offered himself for a Middlesex seat. Returned at four elections in 13 months, Wilkes was expelled from the House on three occasions on the old charge of publishing seditious libel. The stalemate (of his election for Middlesex, and rejection by the Commons) was in danger of becoming permanent before George and his ministers devised a formula which satisfied even their constitutional scruples, declaring that, if Wilkes was not eligible as a member, then their own candidate (who had polled a fifth of his votes) should hold the seat.

The popular party, composed largely of disaffected Whigs, promptly denounced the decision as a fundamental violation of the rights of the electorate, and again the crowds took to the streets. Heaven knew, even if the man was no saint, the populace canonised him, for 'Wilkes and Liberty' was everywhere, finding its echo in Lewes and even further afield; not least in America where the Colonists had come to believe that his cause was their cause, that: 'The Fate of Wilkes and America stand or fall together.'

The conjunction was not coincidental. After eight years and more of meddling, the suspicion of George's constitutional intentions was taking on concrete form. The King's ambitions were clearly over-reaching themselves; at home, threatening the Revolutionary Settlement of 1688; in the Colonies, with the ill-conceived Stamp Act, then its substitute, the Declaratory Act ('to make laws and statutes of sufficient force to bind the Colonies and all the people of America, subjects to the Crown, in all cases whatsoever') allied to the imposition of new duties on Colonial goods to be managed by a strengthened Customs service under the Board of Commissioners in Boston.

When the news reached the town, it triggered off a wave of protests and the resolution: 'to restrain the expenses of funerals, to reduce dress to a degree of primitive simplicity and plainness, and in general, not to purchase any commodities from the Mother Country.' Within months similar resolutions had been adopted by the other Colonies. Then in June 1768, following the seizure of a sloop in Boston harbour, the Customs

House was attacked and the Board of Commissioners was forced to retreat aboard the man-o-war *Romney*.

George was incensed, Wilkes was lionised. Forty-five Friends of Liberty from the Whig Tavern, Boston, wrote:

> 'Tis from your endeavours that we hope for a Royal 'Pascite ut ante boves'; and from our attachment to peace and good order we wait for constitutional redress; being determined that the King of England shall have Subjects but not Slaves in these remote parts of his Dominions.

Paine was as confused as before. The contradictions piled one upon the other, but where was their reconciliation? As Paine rode the Downs above the small town he recalled Rousseau:

> The problem is to find a form of association which will defend and protect with the whole common force the person and goods of each associate, and in which each, while uniting himself with all, may still obey himself alone.

Surely such a thing was possible. The rub was to decide who was to defend and protect each associate; then he remembered his duties with the Excise, and hitching himself higher in his saddle, recalled what the alternative had offered.

The cursed thing was a web. The more he struggled, the more he became enmeshed. Better to have followed Frances and Joseph with their careful ways than always to be warring with himself — and with half the countryside, too. With its gently rolling hills and deep wooded valleys the place looked innocent enough but the appearance deceived for this was owlers' country, and those who weren't in the business of smuggling were involved in covering the smugglers' tracks. As a conspiracy, even old man Ollive had a hand in the game.

Nothing definite of course, no proof; but as the only tobacco merchant in Lewes the thing was as certain as day followed night. For sure there were smugglers down there somewhere, resting up, but come nightfall they would be up and about, and he spurred his horse into a trot. It was a long ride home.

With its short sea-crossing to France, England's south-east seaboard was the heartland of smuggling in the eighteenth century, the owlers running tobacco, tea, silks, and brandy up the Kent and Sussex beaches, or through the small harbours that punctuate the coastline. The local communities benefited, directly, from the cheapened luxuries that the trade in contraband produced; and from the high wages and employment (gangs of 50 and more were commonplace) that smuggling generated. Against them, the Customs and Excise service was largely manned by corruption and its officers were so thin on the ground that they could do little more than monitor the trade.

A score of years before Paine first rode into Lewes, the Duke of Richmond had broken the notorious Hawkhurst gang, executing 39 smugglers, while as late as 1833 it was being reported that:

> On Monday evening about 4 o'clock a boat laden with contraband goods came ashore near Number 28 Tower, Pevensey, which was perceived by one of the Coast Guards who discharged his musket for assistance, when a great number of smugglers rushed down to the boat and commenced upshipping her cargo . . . the boat being surrounded by armed smugglers who kept up a constant fire during the unloading of the boat.

And all this for £48 a year. If the odium of the profession was not enough, there were the dangers, too. For an instant Paine remembered the security and warmth of his father's old workroom, then crossing the ridge of the Downs looked down on Firle Place, the home of the Gage family, and recalled other, more pressing affairs. Twenty years had passed since the young Thomas Gage had ridden out of Firle on the first step of his journey to the Colonies. Now he had returned, C-in-C. of the British garrison in North America, though for a brief visit only. Conditions in the Colonies were too serious to allow a long stay, and he had business with the King in London before sailing for Boston again.

For the fifth time in ten years, George had found himself a new first Minister, a man well suited to the royal ways. Grotesquely ugly, yet with great personal charm, Lord North* had little personal ambition and seemed happy enough to play the puppet to his royal master; and, while complaining occasionally that it was a role to which he was ill suited, he was to serve George well for the next twelve years — twelve years of bitter political dispute in England, and unmitigated disaster in the American colonies.

Although distanced by three thousand miles, and a long sea-voyage, the two issues were inextricably linked: the Colonists' growing clamour against George's absolutism triggered off memories of England's own, radical past, whilst, in its turn, the movement for Wilkes and Liberty fuelled the Colonists' demands first for constitutional recognition, and then for complete independence. And through it all, the King appeared as autocratic, as intractable as ever, incapable of grasping where his own policies, as executed by Lord North, were leading.

A progression of disasters was to show him. He certainly had warnings enough, and no longer simply from the 'mass out of doors' on the streets of London, or the demonstrations of 'those damned rebels' in Boston Town. Those he might dismiss, with contempt — but not the growing coherence of the opposition which had found a new voice in Edmund Burke.*

The son of an Irish attorney, Burke obtained his BA at Trinity College, Dublin, before arriving in London to study law. After serving four years as secretary to the Rt Hon. William Hamilton, he entered Parliament in 1766 and immediately began to lay the foundations of a philosophy which for two centuries has been claimed as the covenant of both conservative and radical politicians: the one, to condemn change; the other, to denounce repression.

Such catholic usage tells as much about the man as his politics. An *arriviste*, haunted by a sense of social inferiority that was continually reinforced by the cavalier treatment he received from the Whig oligarchs he served so well (the Duke of Newcastle always maintained that he was a Jesuit priest in disguise), Burke's political life was spent balancing out his self-interest against his principles. Yet, for all this, his philosophy retains the inner consistency of a man who reviled injustice, whilst deprecating change.

Within months of taking his seat in Parliament, Burke set the tone for all that was to follow. Demanding a Committee of Inquiry into an order that troops be called out to disperse a crowd demonstrating for Wilkes (an order which had led to the death and injury of 20 demonstrators, and to George sending his 'gracious approbation' to the regiment concerned), Burke told the House:

> If ever the time should come when this House shall be found prompt to execute, and slow to inquire; ready to punish the excesses of the people, and slow to listen to their grievances; ready to grant supplies, and slow to examine the account; ready to invest magistrates with large powers, and slow to inquire into the exercise of them; ready to entertain notions of the military power as incorporated in the constitution — when you learn this in the air of St James's, then the business is done; then the House of Commons will change that character which it receives from the people only.

This, at least, was no metaphysical abstraction, no inexplicable mystery. While the philosophes might riddle with the universe, here was a man concerned with 'aenigmas' altogether closer home: the everyday practice of power.

Paine read Burke with the growing sense of conviction that his pursuit of philosophy had obscured an altogether more urgent concern, and for the next 20 years the two men were to point and counter-point each other's politics: first, sharing common ground in opposition to George III's North American policies; later, dividing, bitterly, in their attitudes to the French Revolution when Burke demanded Paine's arrest in response to the publication of *Rights of Man*.

But that was still far distant and, as Paine rode into Lewes, he remembered that this was an evening for a meeting of the Headstrong Club. He had much to say.

The White Hart still stands, its cool Georgian frontage facing across to the Law Courts with its 1717 sundial carrying Horace's admonition: 'Carpe Diem' — 'Time is Speeding, Live for Today.' The caution cannot have been lost on Paine as he stood with his back to the wood-panelled room at the first floor window of the inn. In his thirties he was already into what the eighteenth century considered middle age. Surely it was time to stop dabbling in the half world of Hume and Voltaire and their sort? There was no denying their importance (why, only recently Rousseau had had to flee France again), but now it was time that he, Tom Paine, was heard. And what better platform could a man have than this Headstrong Club?

True, Harry Verral and his crowd were as high Tory as one could find this side of St Peter, but they made a good audience, and disputatious, too. Give them a topic and they would wrangle over it till the mind begged for a truce, or there was no more ale left to cool the throat. And tonight would be no exception. Since the troops had cut down a Wilkite mob the summer before, Verral had taken to quoting variations of the King's thoughts on the subject of law and order ('I don't delight in blood letting but if it should be necessary to spill a little for the sake of law, then spill away I say'), while at the last meeting he had gone so far as to propose dispatching a Headstrong letter to Gage commending him on his sturdy treatment of the Colonists.

Clio Rickmann had put a stop to that soon enough and now this squib of his, 'To a Farmer's Dog',[1] put the law in its true perspective. No question, the story was bizarre enough even for Verral's tastes. Seems that a farmer on the other side of the County had voted against the wishes of the local grandees at election time — and they had proceeded to take

their revenge on his dog, Porter, by finding it guilty of the death of a
hare. Too long to read the whole poem; the last stanza should be enough,
then submit the rest for 'The Headstrong Book':

> So had the dog not chased the hare,
> She'd never had drown'd — that's clear.
> Thus logic, rhetoric, and wit,
> So nicely did the matter fit,
> That Porter — though unheard — was cast,
> And in a halter breathed his last.
> The justices then adjourned to dine,
> And whet their logic up with wine.

Rickmann, a close friend as well as a member of the Headstrong,
remembered Paine at the time:

> In politics he was a Whig and notorious for that quality which has
> been defined as perseverance in a good cause, obstinacy in a bad one.
> He was tenacious in his opinions which were bold, acute, and indepen-
> dent, and which he maintained with ardour, elegance, and argument.

And, as Paine matured in his six years at the Headstrong, he was to
become more independent in his views, more tenacious in his arguments,
inspired as much by the emergence of a new movement demanding
political reform in England, and the example of the American Colonists,
as by Burke's incisive criticism of George's meddling in constitutional
affairs. In 1769, while still fighting for the Middlesex seat, Wilkes and
his friends met at a city tavern to form the Society of the Supporters of
the Bill of Rights which was later to resolve 'to reduce the number of
placemen in the House . . . to endeavour to obtain a more fair and equal
Representation of the People' — a cause to which the Assembly of South
Carolina contributed £1,500.

A year later, William Dowdeswell, one of the old Newcastle connection, and a former Chancellor of the Exchequer, moved a Bill in the
House: 'for better securing the freedom of Election of Members to serve
in Parliament by disabling certain officers employed in the collection of
His Majesty's revenue from giving their votes at such elections.' Then
in 1771 Horne Tooke,* a one-time ally of Wilkes, broke with the Supporters of the Bill of Rights to found the Constitutional Society.

Talk of reform was the fashion, though George and his first Minister
would have none of it. They had troubles enough in their American

Colonies without being distracted by home affairs. Since the repeal of the ill-fated Stamp Act, George had shifted his policies as he had shifted his governments, though all the while hardening his attitudes — and hardening those of the Colonists in return.

The Townshend* duties of 1767, imposing an indirect tax on an range of goods imported into America from Britain, had again fused opposition in the 13 Colonies. Arguing that the duties were merely a disguised attempt to re-impose taxes without representation, and led by Massachusetts, seven Colonies introduced non-importation policies which, within two years, had halved the British trade to the Colonies. By 1770, when North abolished the Townshend duties, it was generally agreed that there was no feasible way of raising Exchequer taxes from the Colonies — but having once tested themselves against the ambitions of the King and his various ministries, the more radical elements amongst the Colonists had developed ambitions for themselves.

Mounting suspicions that 'the designs of the administration were totally to subvert the constitution' had led to an intensifying examination of the claims of English sovereignty itself; the moderate Andrew Elliot warned that, when tyranny was abroad, submission was a crime; a Boston Town Meeting of 1770 declared:

A series of occurrences affords great reason to believe that a deep laid and desperate plan of imperial despotism has been laid, and partly executed, for the extinction of civil liberty . . . The august and once revered fortress of English freedom — the admirable work of ages — the BRITISH CONSTITUTION seems fast tottering into total and irreversible ruin. The dreadful catastrophe threatens universal havoc, and presents an awful warning to hazard all if, peradventure, we in these distant confines of the earth may prevent being totally overwhelmed and buried under the ruins of our established rights.

Such fears were not exclusive to the Colonies. They were equally widespread in England, where they were finding vivid expression in Edmund Burke. While George might still protest that his sole interest lay in 'promoting the welfare of a people whose loyalty and affection I consider the greatest and most permanent security of my throne', Burke contended that: 'The power of the crown, almost dead and rotten as prerogative, has grown up anew with much more strength.'

Although conservative by inclination, Burke was in direct line of political descent from the Glorious Revolutiuon of 1688 — an inheritance which he treasured and which he saw threatened by George's policies and their mirror image, the mounting troubles on the streets:

> I am not one of those who think that the people are never in the wrong. They have been so, frequently and outrageously, both in other countries and in this. But I do say that in all disputes between them and their rulers, the presumption is at least on a par in favour of the people. Experience may in fact justify me in going further. Where popular discontents have been very prevalent, it may well be affirmed and supported, that there may be something sound amiss in the constitution, or in the conduct of government.
>
> The people have no interest in disorder. When they do wrong, it is their error, and not their crime. But with the governing part of the state it is far otherwise. They may certainly act ill by design, as by mistake . . . 'Pour la populace ça n'est jamais par envie d'attaquer qu'elle a soulevé mais par impatience de souffrir.' What he [Sully] says of revolution is equally true of all great disturbances. If the presumption in favour of the subjects against the trustees of power be not more probable, I am sure it is a more comfortable speculation.

Though Burke crystallised Paine's thinking, he did not go far enough. While he analysed the problems of contemporary power admirably, he failed, ultimately, to fix its locus; and while Voltaire might extol 'mixed government', and Rousseau conjure up 'the general will', Burke constantly reverted to the Settlement of 1688 as if a constitution could be fixed in place and time, immutable. Patently, the idea was nonsense. Why, if Mr Burke had been born a century earlier he might have found equal justification for the pre-Settlement constitution and what would have become of his Glorious Revolution then? Surely all government evolved according to circumstance, though that still left the problem: what was the ideal?

At the Headstrong Club the debates were long and vehement, providing Paine with the discipline and confidence necessary to assemble, and then to articulate, the motley ideas that had been gestating for so long and, in the process, driving him to the extreme to challenge the state as 'the great primaeval contract of all society'. Mr Burke and his friends had no monopoly of rights; what of the rights of man?

By the early 1770s Paine had established himself as the leading disputant in the Club, a man commanding attention as much for his powerful physical presence as for his mind. The long apprenticeship was ending, and as the most 'obstinate haranguer' in the Club he became the outright possessor of 'The Headstrong Book, or Book of Obstinacy':

Immortal Paine, while mighty reasons jar,
We crown thee General of the Headstrong War.
Thy logic vanquished error, and thy mind
No bounds but those of right and truth confined.
Thy soul of fire must sure ascend the sky,
Immortal PAINE, thy flame can never die.

The anonymous Headstrong poet proved to be more prescient than ever he can have imagined.

Samuel Ollive died in July 1769, and in March 1771 Paine married his only daughter, Elizabeth, at St Michael's Church, Lewes. For Paine, those were good years to be alive. Save for politics (and they were no more than a headstrong pastime), the doubts of the past seemed finally to have been laid. The Ollive's small tobacco business (in which he had taken a part share) prospered as well as the times allowed; he was an established, even a respected, figure in the town; the Board of Excise was well pleased with his service; and his fellow officers had recently invited him to compose a memorial to Parliament for an improvement in their conditions of pay.

The invitation was a compliment, though it needed some thinking about — while Elizabeth's mind was already made up. As soon as she heard the news, she had warned him of the dangers. The Commissioners were not men to toy with, as he had learned once before. Would he really risk the good reputation he had so carefully built up for the sake of a handful of words? If his fellow officers wanted an improvement in pay, then let someone else do the business for them. For their own part, weren't they comfortably off enough?

And she was right. Together with his income from the Excise, the business provided them with a fair living, while the members of the Board were not the most forgiving men; moreover, now that Grafton had gone, there was little prospect that he could work that connection again. Practically, there was no reason to accept the invitation, yet it was a compliment that could not be refused. Why, of all the officers in the service, should they have selected him, Tom Paine, an outrider on a comparatively isolated posting, to represent their views? Only one explanation was credible: that it was not only their Honours, the Commissioners of the Excise, who had a regard for him — though this was something Elizabeth refused to understand. However often he tried to explain, she would dismiss the idea as moonshine, and ask what had become of his common sense?

Common sense be damned, she should hear him at the Headstrong — though that was tricky ground, too. It was not that he neglected her, but he refused to abandon the Club. It took up two nights of the week, no more, yet within months of their marriage she had begun complaining that that was altogether too much; that he spent too much time with those ne'er-do-wells down at the White Hart and not enough time with her. What did she think marriage was, some sort of domestic yoke? Certainly he had sympathy and to spare for women, for most lived miserable lives, but there were times when a man had to take decisions on his own.

Paine received the invitation to write the Parliamentary memorial for the Officers of the Excise in 1772, and at first found the words hard to come by. This was like nothing he had attempted before, far different from the instant cut and thrust of the Headstrong. It demanded a consistency of logic, as much as of style, but slowly a technique evolved that was to become the hallmark of all his later writing: lucid, fresh and deploying the minutiae of the case to argue a larger cause:

> Poverty, in defiance of principle, begets a degree of meanness that will stoop to almost anything. A thousand refinements of argument may be brought to prove that the practice of honesty will be the same in the most trying and the most necessitous circumstances . . . But poverty, like grief, has an incurable deafness, which never hears; the oration loses all its edge; and 'To be, or not to be' becomes the only question.
>
> The rich in ease and affluence, may think I have drawn an unnatural portrait, but could they descend into the cold regions of want, the circle of polar poverty, they would find their opinions changing with the climate.

The echoes are of Walpole and the army of the dispossessed who still crossed Thetford bridge; of London with its foul stews and pretty squares; of the intrepid veteran, and the hanging men on Tyburn tree; and, further back, the inheritance of dissent, and the levelling voice of Richard Overton: 'I am confident that it must be the poor, the simple and the mean things of this earth that must confound the mighty and the strong.'

Paine wrote *The Case of the Officers of the Excise*, and elevated it into a powerful, humanitarian tract. Such advocacy, leading, as it did, to the contention that it was only equitable to pay the officers according to the trust that government itself placed in them to collect its revenues, did nothing to endear him to the Board of Excise, though there was little to be lost.

As all knew, the Excise was never the most popular of causes — the 'Monster . . . that on all Trades, like Caesar, feeds' — and the Commissioners could safely ignore the plea, knowing it would command little public sympathy. Better then to extend the case, and tax the conscience of the rich with the suffering of the poor. Elizabeth might think differently, and now she had taken to berating him openly for placing their livelihoods at risk, not least when his neglect of their business was damaging the trade. But still she did not understand; the more he wrote, the more he knew that this was a case that must be heard.

Four thousand copies of the work were printed, paid for by a three-shilling subscription from Excise men from throughout the kingdom, and Paine spent the winter of 1772 lobbying MPs and anyone else who cared to hear, among them the ageing Oliver Goldsmith:

> The enclosed case we have presented to most of the Members, and shall to all, before the petition appears in the House . . . Since the delivering of them I have received so many letters of thanks and approbation for the performance, that were I not rather singularly modest, I should insensibly become a little vain. The literary fame of Dr Goldsmith has induced me to present one to him, such as it is . . . I have some few questions to trouble Dr Goldsmith with, and should esteem his company for an hour or two, to partake of a bottle of wine, or anything else, and apologise for this trouble, as a singular favour conferred on
>
> His unknown,
> Humble servant and admirer
> THOMAS PAINE.

For all that Paine flattered himself on the progress of the case, the Board of Excise ignored the petition — though not his part in its submission. Elizabeth's fears were soon to be realised. The winter he spent in London was to cost him his job with the service, the tobacconist's business, and his marriage as well.

April 1774 was a bitter month for Paine. On the eighth the Board of Excise ordered his discharge for 'having quitted his Business, without obtaining the Board's leave for so doing', and six days later, to pay the debts accumulated during his winter stay in London, the tobacconist's business was auctioned:

> To be sold . . . all the household furniture, stock in trade and other effects of Thomas Pain [sic], grocer and tobacconist, near the West

Gate in Lewes; Also a horse tobacco and snuff mill, and with all the utensils for cutting tobacco and grinding of snuff.

It was just as Elizabeth had said. No question, she had warned him often enough, though he always knew what to do for the best. The members of the Board of Excise were hard men, with long memories — but he still knew what to do for the best. The business was difficult enough to manage without his long absences in London — but he still knew what to do for the best. The Headstrong might provide him with company, and she missed him during the nights — but he still knew what to do for the best. Paine, it seemed, loved the whole world, yet couldn't find time for his wife. Better, perhaps, if they part.

The broken marriage, following the earlier death of Mary Lambert, has become a part of the Paine legend: of a marriage that was never consummated, of the medical certificate obtained to establish Paine's virility; of a letter allegedly written by Frances to Elizabeth:

> I am heartily sorry that a woman whose character and amiableness deserve the greatest respect, love, and esteem, as I have always on enquiry been informed your's did, should be tied for life to the worst of husbands. I am, dear daughter, your affectionate mother, F. Paine.

Unearthed by one of Pitt the Younger's agents more than a decade after it was said to have been written, the letter is one of the patchwork of truths and half-truths surrounding a separation of which Paine himself would only say: 'It is nobody's business but my own; I had cause for it, but I will name it to no one.' Only one thing is certain, that they parted amicably enough, Paine settling all that remained of his Lewes property on Elizabeth, so that:

> He would not at any time hereafter claim or demand the said monies, which she should be entitled to at the sale of the said house in Lewes . . . or of any of the Monies Rings Plate Cloathes Linen Woollen Household Goods or Stock in Trade which the said Elizabeth should or might at any time thereafter buy or purchase.

At a time when married women were denied any property rights under law, the document's formality disguises its humanity, reflecting Paine's later sympathies that: 'Man with regard to woman, has been either an insensible husband or an oppressor.'

The separation ended his time in Lewes. Only six years before, he had ridden into the small Sussex town, 31 years of age, of liberal principles, middling prospects and as much a stranger to himself as to the town. Now nothing remained save, possibly, a resolution of the differences that had been a feature of the first half of his life: of the contradiction between a beneficient God, and the evidence of Christian practices; of a revered constitution, and its everyday corruption; of an Age of Reason, and its disciples who had never explored the 'cold regions of want'.

As he trudged for the last time past Pelham House, past the sundial with its admonition 'Carpe Diem', past the White Hart with its Headstrong memories, to turn north for London again, it could well be that Paine reviewed his past to conclude that there was little to be gained from compromising with a system which, governing according to its own inflexible rules, allowed of no compromise itself.

Superficially, London had changed little since Paine first arrived in the City 16 years before. Noble's Academy may have closed, Mr Morris moved his staymaking business, and Dr Bevis died; but otherwise the familiar landmarks remained, St Paul's towering above the City and all its contrasting ways. The difference in mood, however, was an almost palpable thing. Wilkes had taken his politics on to the streets and, after six years of bitter, and sometimes bloody controversy had finally been allowed to take his seat in the House.

Once the constitutional debate had been opened, however, it could not be closed. The days when politics were the exclusive preserve of a handful of grandees were ending, and during the early 1770s a series of reform proposals were tabled in Parliament, while in 1776 the Earl of Chatham was warning that, by the turn of the century 'either the Parliament will reform itself from within or be reformed with a vengeance from without'.

George and Lord North were unmoved. For all that the dispossessed Whigs might rail at 'corruption and Treasury influence, as well as aristocratical tyranny', the King's friends commanded an overwhelming majority in the House — besides which, there was more pressing business to hand. The repeal of the Townshend duties, with the exception of that on tea, had done little to placate Colonial unrest, or that nest of vipers in Boston.

Since before the passage of the Stamp Act, Massachusetts and Boston had been the focus of Colonial dissent. Rugged individualists of Puritan stock, the Colonists had developed a deep distrust of the constitutional ambitions of the government in London, and, while Mr Johnson of Connecticut might think that 'a little discreet conduct on both sides would perfectly re-establish that warm affection and respect towards Great Britain for which this country was once so remarkable', Boston radicals such as John Hancock* and Samuel Adams* thought otherwise. Whether they wanted independence or not still had to be decided, though attitudes were hardening rapidly.

In March 1770, 13 days before George signed the bill rescinding the Stamp Act, British troops in Boston fired on a crowd of demonstrators. Five died, and six were injured. The radicals had their martyrs and, though there was to be a truce for the next three years, it was always an uneasy one — George smarting at what he regarded as the humiliations inflicted on his sovereignty, the Colonists waiting, tensely, for any new move by London.

The end came suddenly. In 1773 North endorsed a scheme aimed at persuading the Colonists to buy Townshend-taxed tea in increased quantities in an attempt to assist the hard-pressed finances of the East India Company. No taxation without representation was again the issue, and on the night of 16 December a party of Colonials masquerading as Indians boarded three English ships in Boston Harbour and dumped 340 cases of tea valued at £15,000 into the sea.

Five weeks later the packet *Hayley* dropped anchor at Dover with the news. This was treason. On home leave, Gage told the King: 'While we're lambs, they'll be lions.' George concurred: 'If we take the resolute part, they will undoubtedly be very meek.' His resolve was reflected in his actions. Within weeks four new Acts were hustled through the House: to close Boston Harbour; to suspend the charter of Massachusetts province; to empower the Governor to remove any case he chose for trial in Britain or another colony; and to extend the Canadian frontier and transform it into a Loyalist stronghold where George could raise an army to turn the flank of the New Englanders if they dared to resist.

The Colonists would learn that two could play at games; but in the meantime there was an example to be made closer to home. For 17 years Benjamin Franklin,* agent for Pennsylvania and Massachusetts, had been the Colonists' unofficial ambassador in London. Author, scientist, inventor and philanthropist, the homespun diplomat was widely respected, though his position had become increasingly isolated as relations between England and the Colonies deteriorated — the more so since the publication of the Hutchinson letters.

Six years before, Governor Hutchinson and Lieutenant-Governor Oliver of Massachusetts had written a series of 13 letters to Thomas Whateley in London suggesting, among other things, that: 'There must be an abridgement of what are called English liberties' in the Colony.

The letters came into Franklin's hands and, as agent for Massachusetts, he returned them to the Colony with instructions that they be held in confidence. In June 1773, however, the Massachusetts House of Representatives published the letters — and petitioned the King to replace both Hutchinson and Oliver.

On 29 January 1774, the Lords of the Plantation Committee of the Privy Council met at the Cockpit in Whitehall to consider the application, with Franklin, the agent for Massachusetts, in attendance. Six months later the hearing was still the scandal of the Whig taverns and coffee houses and Paine listened, astonished, to the humiliation of Mr Franklin. He was known as a mild enough man, and a good friend of England besides, as Lord Chatham and Mr Burke testified. The curse was that North and his flunkeys couldn't read the longitude of friendships from a bribe, as that lickspittle Wedderburn had proved.

Not to be wondered though; the man was a Scot, after all. He had come south to line the Wedderburn reputation, and what better way than through George and his friends! He had won a seat in the House through the Bute connection, was Solicitor-General before he was 40 and, how he had preened himself at the Cockpit when Franklin was called. Didn't give a damn for the Massachusetts petition, went straight for Franklin himself:

I hope, my Lords, you will mark and brand this man for he has forfeited the respect of societies . . . Into what companies will he hereafter go with an unembarrassed face? Men will watch him with a jealous eye, they will hide their papers from him and lock up their escritoires. He will henceforth esteem it a libel to be called 'a man of letters'.

This and much more, all dressed out in the choicest flowers of Billingsgate, while North's flunkeys had laughed and applauded: 'Hear him. Hear him.' No wonder Mr Wedderburn had been drummed off the Scottish bench for failing to control his tongue. If George gave him enough of it, he'd hang himself for sure — though that would be small consolation to Franklin. He had not said a word in his own defence; just stood there silent till Wedderburn had done, then returned to his place in Craven Street, and told his servants he was home to no one; not to Burke, not to Goldsmith, nor the Lord Mayor himself.

The talk was interminable, but Paine was lost to himself. Only last year Mr Goldsmith had shared an hour or two with him over a bottle of wine, and here was another connection, though not of the Grafton sort. This was a connection of quite another kind, and he remembered Joseph's quiet talk of the men who were 'as a Citty upon a Hill', and the Reverend Knowler's old book on Virginia and, late that summer of 1774, with an introduction from Mr Goldsmith, Paine called on Benjamin Franklin.

It was the beginning of a friendship that was to last until Franklin's death, and how they had talked: of Mr Franklin's extraordinary lighting rods and how a certain Dr Price of Massachusetts had preached against their impiety for attempting to defy the Will of God; of Newton and Locke, and Voltaire and Rousseau and a social contract that would make men equal; of Wilkes and Burke and what liberty meant, or whether it was all an illusion; but mostly of the Colonies, of the American cause. That embraced all the rest, the hopes of men who once had promised to turn the world upside-down.

But what of their hopes now? Only recently Admiral Montagu had been heard to boast that Boston had had its Indian capers, and the reckoning was to come. And it had. In midsummer the new Governor of Massachusetts, General Gage, had sealed off Boston Harbour and 'raised a flame from one end of the Colonies to another and united all the old Colonies in one common cause'.

At such a time, London was no place to be. The Colonies needed men of courage and principle, and had not Mr Burke recently intimated that the New World knew more of freedom than England herself? But the rights of man were no abstraction; they had to be won and, at his desk, Franklin wrote Paine's letter of introduction to America:

> The bearer, Mr Thomas Paine, is very well recommended to me as an ingenious, worthy young man. He goes to Pennsylvania with a view to settling there. I request that you give him your best advice and countenance as he is quite a stranger there.

The letter was short, but it would suffice. In September 1774, Thomas Paine — former staymaker, exciseman, tobacconist, seaman and schoolmaster — took ship for Philadelphia, a man no longer a stranger to himself. Within twelve months he was to write:

> Society is produced by our wants, and government by our wickedness, the former promises happiness *positively* by winning our affections, the latter *negatively* by restraining our vices. The one encourages intercourse, the other creates distinctions. The first is a patron, the last a punisher.

It was a difference he learned in Lewes, at the quiet centre of his life, which he took to America to help change the course of history.

4 COMMON SENSE

The *London Packet* made the passage to Philadelphia in nine weeks, a better than average time considering the season. Autumn was a bad time for the crossing, the westerlies making a mill race of the Atlantic, and it was no idle formality when Franklin wished Paine a safe passage. Having made the crossing eight times before, he knew what the undertaking meant.

It took hardy, or desperate, stock to make the 3,500-mile voyage westward in the eighteenth century. Depending on weather conditions the average sailing time was between ten and thirteen weeks, if, that is, the vessel was not blown off course to land its passengers as far afield as Portugal, Spain or the West Indies — though, as Paine well knew, this was one of the lesser hazards.

The real fear was of starvation or disease. Only last year a brig out of the Clyde with 300 passengers had docked in New York after a three months' passage; and only 200 passengers had been put ashore. The remainder had starved to death, to be buried at sea. The tragedy was commonplace; masters crowded their vessels yet took in too few provisions, so that by the mid-passage food was so scarce that a rat could be sold for eighteen pence, a mouse for sixpence, and water fetch sixpence a quart.

The passengers became weakened by hunger, and were crowded into damp and fetid quarters between decks where disease was prevalent. A Palatine, Gottlieb Mittelberger, described a crossing in the 1750s:

> During the voyage there is on board . . . terrible misery, stench, fumes, horror, vomiting, many kinds of sea sickness, fever, dysentry, headache, heat, constipation, boils, scurvy, cancer, mouthrot and the like, all of which come from old and salted food and meat, also from very bad and foul water, so that many die miserably.
>
> Add to this want of provisions, thirst, frost, heat, dampness, anxiety, want, afflictions and lamentations, together with other troubles, as c.v. the lice abound so frightfully, especially on sick people, they have to be scraped off the body. The misery reaches a climax when a gale rages for two or three nights, so that everyone believes that the ship will go to the bottom with all human beings on board.
>
> Children from one to seven rarely survive the voyage, and many a time parents are compelled to see their children miserably suffer

and die from hunger, thirst and sickness, and then to see them cast into the water. I witnessed such misery in no less than 32 children in our ship, all of whom were thrown into the sea.

Five weeks out, the first case of typhus appeared abroad the *London Packet*. Paine knew the symptoms well; first the headache and pains in the back and limbs; then on the third day the sudden rise in temperature so that the body was wracked with heat, the eyes and face congested, burning; followed on the fifth or sixth day by the mulberry rash that spread from the belly to cover the back and chest and the intensifying delirium so the days and nights fused into one, for the mind itself was torched. On 30 November 1774 he was carried ashore at Philadelphia, too weak to know that he had made his American landfall.

A month passed before Paine was strong enough to explore the city, though as his condition improved his physician, John Kearsley, supplied him with news of the two missing months of his life: of the universal demonstrations against Parliament's latest legislation, more especially the Boston Port Act; of the Assembly of Virginia setting aside a day for humiliation, fasting and prayer for the passage of the Act; of the muffled bells tolling throughout the countryside, and colours flying at half-mast on the river in New York; of the old warhorse Israel Putman driving seven score sheep on to Boston Common to feed the beleaguered townsfolk, and on being told that twenty English regiments were expected in the town, gravely replying: 'If they come, I am prepared to fight'; but most of all, of the meeting of the first Continental Congress* in Philadelphia itself.

Ironically, it was the Tory Loyalists who first proposed the Congress as a counter to suggestions that the Colonies sign a solemn league and covenant implying a fight to the death with England. The sessions had continued through September and deep into October — and closed with the radicals having won an unqualified triumph. Until Parliament agreed to the repeal of all legislation enacted since 1763, a ban was to be imposed on all imports and exports to England; no American taxes were to be raised for the Treasury, and plans were to be drawn up to defend the Colonies in the event of an English attack.

The Colonies, Kearsley explained, were a powder keg. All that was required was to torch the mood of the people and there would be rebellion. Paine walked the streets of Philadelphia in the late December days of 1774, a gaunt figure, face shrunken to a mask of yellowed skin taut across the bone, and wondered at the contrast between the incessant talk of war and the pleasant prospect of the city around him. Penn* and the early Friends had done well by the place, and it thrived, with its quays and

its docks, and its fine public buildings, and everywhere places of worship — though he had heard talk of bad blood between Quakers and
Presbyterians who both struggled for civic power.

It was always the same. Wherever men raised a church to the denominations of God, there was always a falling out; and, recalling Voltaire, Paine
knew he was wrong. If England had 30 religions, then why not more?
Why couldn't each man find his own God, for who was to limit such
Holy Experiments if, as Mr Hume had contended, the whole was indeed
an 'aenigma'? That at least might resolve one riddle, though the temporal
one still remained. Monarchy, aristocracy, democracy: where should the
power lie? Maybe he would find the answer here, in Philadelphia. In the
meantime there was the more pressing business of finding an occupation
and he delivered Franklin's letter at the house of his son-in-law, Richard
Bache.*

Six months previously Paine had discussed with Franklin the idea of
establishing an Academy in Philadelphia on the lines of those to be found
in London, but Bache soon explained that such ambitions were altogether
too high-flown for a newcomer to the city, and for the next weeks Paine
earned his living giving private coaching to the children of Philadelphia's
leading families — all the while becoming more restless.

Conditions between England and the Colonies continued to deteriorate,
and a second Continental Congress was to be held in Philadelphia in May.
It seemed as if the whole world was changing around him, while he was
confined to teaching the three R's. He had not risked the Atlantic passage
for that. Surely there was more to make of the talents which Goldsmith
and Franklin had admired — not least, with the pen? In January 1775,
the printer Robert Aitken founded the *Pennsylvania Magazine, or
American Monthly Museum*, and invited Paine to contribute an introduc-
tory essay on 'The Utility of Magazines Evinced'.

It was rich ground for speculation, for the press was among the most
powerful tools of both Loyalists and Patriots in the years immediately
before the Revolution. Thirty-eight newspapers were published in the 13
Colonies, together with a proliferation of periodicals, while between 1750
and 1776 more than four hundred pamphlets discussing the Anglo-Colonial
dispute appeared. Paine remembered Wilkes, the publicist, and wrote:
'There is nothing which obtains so general an influence over the manners and morals of the people, as the press; from that, as from a fountain, the streams of vice and virtue are poured forth over a country.'

The words sounded well, and with a glass of rum and water to hand
the ideas came easily, especially when contrasting the Old World with
the New:

Degeneracy here is almost a useless word. They who are conversant with Europe would be tempted to believe, that even the air of the Atlantic disagrees with foreign vices; if they survive the voyage, they either expire on their arrival, or linger away in an incurable consumption. There is a happy something in the climate of America which disarms them of all their power.

It was 150 years since the Pilgrims had agreed the Mayflower compact:

solemnly and mutually in the Presence of God and one another, to convenant and combine ourselves together in a civil Body Politick . . .; and by virtue hereof enact, constitute and frame, such just and equal Laws, Ordinances, Acts, Constitutions and Offices, from time to time, as shall be thought most meet and convenient to the general Good of the Colony; unto which we promise all due Submission and Obedience.

This was the 'happy something' that provided the basis for all the rest: the theological conviction that the colonisation of North America had been ordained by God combined with memories of the radical, social and political ideologies of the English Civil War and Commonwealth. For the Patriots of 1775 these were no abstractions. Reinforced and refined by the writings of Locke (who once had written 'In the beginning all the world was America'), Voltaire and Rousseau, they provided an ethos of which John Adams wrote at the passage of the Stamp Act:

The liberties of mankind and the glory of nature is in their keeping, America was designed by Providence for the theatre on which man was to make his true figure, on which science, virtue, liberty, happiness and glory were to exist in peace.

This was the faith for which men would die — and that was to provide Paine with his purpose. Individually, George's legislation was offensive. Collectively, it threatened the providential belief in the Colonist's mission and the covenant under which the Pilgrims had bound themselves together to form a community presupposing equality between man and man. Once they had been little more than words to Paine. In Philadelphia they began to take on concrete form, not simply of a rebellion against kingship but of a revolution of society itself.

In February 1775, Paine was offered the editorship of the *Pennsylvania Magazine* at a salary of £50 a year, and his career as a professional writer began. Although the journal under Paine gave extended coverage to the sciences and the arts, it was soon to develop a sharp cutting edge. In May, he was writing on titles:

> The Honourable plunderer of his country, or the Right Honourable murderer of mankind, create such a contrast of ideas as exhibit a monster rather than a man . . . the title of My Lord overawe the superstitious vulgar, and forbid them to enquire into the character of the possessor;

in June, the anniversary of his separation from Elizabeth, on broken marriages:

> As ecstasy abates coolness succeeds, which often makes way for indifference, and that for neglect. Sure of each other by the nuptial bond, they no longer take any pains to be mutually agreeable;

in August, 'An Occasional Letter on the Female Sex':

> Man with regard to them, in all climates and in all ages, has been either an insensible husband or an oppressor; but they have sometimes experienced the cold and deliberate oppression of pride, and sometimes the violent and terrible tyranny of jealousy . . . Over three-quarters of the globe Nature had placed them between contempt and misery.

Paine reread the piece, remembered Mary and Elizabeth, and caught the echo of Rousseau ('Man is born free . . .'). The man had drawn his boundaries too close. He had never seen a black cargo coming ashore. Philosophe be damned; the practice mocked such abstractions — and the ambitions of the Colonists besides. How was it possible to reconcile slaving with the 'Patriots' concern for liberty? Here, at least, there could be no dissembling: either humankind was free, or in bondage. True, the Quakers of Pennyslvania and others had long stood out against the practice, but as the Colonial debate intensified, there was fresh need to expose the contradiction in the case, and under the signature 'Justice and Humanity' Paine wrote:

> Christians are taught to account all men their neighbours, and love their neighbours as themselves; and do to all men as they would be done by; to do good to all men; and man stealing is ranked with enormous crimes.

Thirty-five days after the article appeared on 9 March, the first American Antislavery Society was formed in Philadelphia, an event soon to be overshadowed by an altogether more ominous development. On 19 April, as final plans for the second Continental Congress were being drawn, General Gage in Boston dispatched a force to seize a cache of Colonial arms stored at James Barrett's farm in Concord — and the shot was fired that 'was to be heard around the world'.

Since the passage of the Coercive Acts, the C-in-C.'s civil administration had virtually collapsed, and everyday he received fresh intelligence of the Colonists' preparation for war: of minutemen drilling on the village greens of Massachusetts, Connecticut and Rhode Island; of Colonel Israel Putnam riding towards Boston at the head of a force of 15,000 men; of a force assaulting the royal fortress at Portsmouth, and carrying off its cannon and supplies; of the Congress voting to raise an army of 18,000 men.

By early spring 1775, Gage's position was virtually untenable, while the only consistency to be found in London was from the King. Now he demanded total submission, nothing less: 'The New England governments are in a state of rebellion, blows must decide whether they are to be subject to this country or independent.' George's government, however, still failed to grasp the magnitude of Gage's problems, or of his needs. He had asked for a force of 20,000 men, to be promised half that number — when weather conditions allowed. The decision was not unexpected.

A year before, Burke, no friend of the government, had asked: 'Have you considered whether you have the troops and ships sufficient to enforce a universal proscription to the trade of the whole continent of America?' North had not troubled to reply, and done little to reinforce Gage's command. The mood in London was sanguine, the 'Liberty Boys' had no taste for a fight, and as late as January 1775 Lord Sandwich (now a Secretary of State in the Cabinet) was dismissive of the Colonists' military potential, telling the Lords: 'They are raw, undisciplined, cowardly men. Believe me, my Lords, the very sound of a cannon would carry them off as fast as their feet could carry them.'

Gage knew better. He had campaigned with the Colonists during the Seven Years' War, and knew their fighting calibre. Whatever his personal reservations, however, they were subordinate to his orders from London; and London had ordered that he take a 'more active and determined part' against the insurgents.

At 8.45 a.m. on 19 April 1775, 1,200 men under the command of Earl Hugh Percy marched out of Boston with colours flying and drum and fife band playing. Their orders were clear: to seize the Colonists' supply dump at Concord, 16 miles away. The foray was to end in war. Alerted by Paul Revere, Percy found Colonial minutemen waiting on Lexington Common. The first shots were fired, eight Americans fell, and for the next twelve hours the British force fought a bitter rearguard action against continuous American skirmishing — to cross the neck into Boston carrying 273 dead and wounded with them.

The American Revolution had begun, in fact if not formally, for Britain and the Colonists were still unwilling to accept the progress of events. Three hundred miles north of Boston, the delegates assembled for the second Continental Congress and, while agreeing that they must now assume responsibility for the defence not only of Massachusetts but of all America, they drafted the Olive Branch petition for immediate dispatch to the King:

> Knowing to what violent resentments and incurable animosities civil discords are apt to exasperate and inflame the contending parties, we think ourselves required by indispensable obligations to Almighty God, to your Majesty, to our fellow subjects, and ourselves, immediately to use all means in our power, not incompatible with our safety, for stopping the further effusion of blood, and for averting the impending calamities that threaten the British Empire. Thus called upon to address your Majesty on affairs of such moment to America, and probably to all your dominions, we are earnestly desirous of performing this office with the utmost deference to your Majesty . . .

The same ambivalent mood prevailed in London. Satisfied with the success of the Concord expedition, George reflected: 'The object of sending the detachment was to spike cannon and destroy military stores; this has been effected . . . I therefore hope that you will not see in this a stronger light than it deserves', while North still sought a formula for reconciliation.

While the talk was of moderation, however, both sides prepared for war, and in Philadelphia the summer of 1775 passed in a welter of speculation and rumour. A major engagement had been fought at Bunker Hill.* The Congress was suing for peace. Gage was preparing to march. The King had acceded to the Colonists' demands. In Mr Smith's elegant City Tavern and Mr Bradford's London Coffee House the patrons played pitch-and-toss with truth and Paine listened to the talk and was tortured by it, as if all his previous conflicts had crystallised at a moment in time: the conscience of a Quaker set against the Friend's pacifism.

True, he had fought once, but that was half a lifetime ago when he had been a boy and knew little better; and whilst that had been a war of sovereign powers, this would be for principles. A century and more had passed since the Friends rode with Cromwell in the belief that: 'Freedom is the man that will turn the world upside down, therefore no wonder he hath enemies.' Surely that had been a just war, yet now the enemy rode down freedom again and this would be a just war, too. The talk eddied about him, sweet or bitter according to the mood, and Paine called for a final drink. He had work to do and a little rum always sharpened the mind, for, while he might justify his actions to himself, there were others to be considered.

Five months had passed since he had first become editor of the *Pennsylvania Magazine* and in that time its sales had trebled. Now, in the city of Quakers, he had to write of a Friend's duties in the event of war:

I am thus far a Quaker, that I would gladly agree with all the world to lay aside the use of arms, and settle matters by negotiation; but unless the whole world wills, the matter ends, and I take up my musket, and thank heaven he has put it in my power . . . We live not in a world of angels. The reign of Satan is not ended, neither can we expect to be defended by miracles.

There was no more to be said. Now it turned on each man's conscience, though, for all their talk of reconciliation, George and his ministers seemed bent on alienating even their friends. It was reported that, on its receipt in London in late August, the King had refused to receive the Olive Branch petition and two days later had issued a proclamation accusing the Colonists of 'traitorously preparing, ordering and levying war against Great Britain' and ordering full military preparations 'to suppress such rebellion and bring the traitors to justice'.

Inexorably, the two sides closed for action; yet it seemed that only the most radical amongst the Colonists could contemplate a complete break with the crown. What was it that Washington had shouted to Jonathan Boucher as he crossed the Potomac River on his way to the second Congress: 'Independence, sir? If you ever hear of my joining in any such measures you have my leave to set me down for everything wicked?' The man, the self-same George Washington who had drubbed the French on the Virginian frontier 15 years before, now commanded the Continental Army about Boston — yet still he had his doubts.

As Dr Rush* had said only recently when they met at Mr Aitken's shop, the whole Colony was not in two minds, but in three: the Tory

Loyalists seeking to remain within the empire; the moderates searching for an eleventh-hour compromise; the Patriots pressing for independence though with due deference to the King. If only George stepped gently, he could still divide and rule damned nearly as absolutely as he had done before.

What was needed was more of Paine's latest essay, a felicitous piece: 'I hesitate not for a moment to believe that the Almighty will finally separate America from Britain. Call it Independency or what you will, if it is the cause of humanity it will go.' It seemed that Rush himself had been considering a pamphlet on the subject, and not least on George's arcane role in the whole affair, but he had neither the time nor the aptitude with words. Perhaps Mr Paine would consider undertaking such a squib?

Paine wrote *Common Sense* in the early winter of 1775. After six months as successful editor of the *Pennsylvania Magazine* his confidence was burgeoning — it appeared that half the Philadelphia establishment waited to read what he wrote, though this was to be different from anything that he had attempted before. The pamphlet was a staple of eighteenth-century Colonial literature. Cheap, easy to print, and flexible, tracts averaged between 5,000 and 25,000 words; long enough to develop a reasoned argument, and yet not too long to be tedious.

Not that Paine had any doubts about the latter. His subject was incendiary enough to compel attention — nothing less than demolishing the Colonist's seemingly superstitious reverence not only for George III but for the institution of kingship and all it entailed. Burke might plead for reconciliation — 'The Americans will have no interest contrary to the grandeur and glory of England, when they are not oppressed by the weight of it'[1] — but now it was too late.

Fifteen years had passed since George had succeeded to the throne with a pledge to root out the old corruption — and America still remained oppressed by the weight of his grandeur and glory. If only the Colonists would weigh his words rather than his majesty, they would soon understand that he gave them short measure. Yet even now there were those who still believed that the King's ministers were the architects of all their troubles, and George the innocent victim of affairs.

The idea was an indulgence, an echo of a romanticised past, though it had received powerful reinforcement from Voltaire. The principle of power-sharing under mixed government was all very well as long as power, indeed, was shared. Otherwise it was no more than a new cloak for the old despotism, and Paine wrote:

I know it is difficult to get over local or long standing prejudices, yet if we shall suffer ourselves to examine the component parts of the English constitution, we shall find them to be the base remains of two ancient tyrannies, compounded with some new Republican materials.

First — The remains of Monarchical tyranny in the person of the King.

Second — The remains of the Aristocratical tyranny in the persons of the Peers.

Third — The new Republican materials, in the persons of the Commons, on whose virtue depends the freedom of England.

To say that the constitution of England is a union of three powers, reciprocally checking each other, is farcical; either the words have no meaning or they are contradictions.

And the Colonists knew enough of that. For a decade and more they had lived with the contradiction: of George making a godhead of the constitution, and mobilising the troops to enforce it; of Wilkes drumming up liberty, and ending in the Tower for his pains; of an Olive Branch that was cut down with the sword. The whole was a contradiction, and its author was the King for the crown remained the overbearing part of the constitution; the fate of Charles I only served to make monarchs more subtle, not more just.

George was as absolute as before, and took a pride in the inheritance of his absolutism; he was a man who looked upon himself as born to reign, and had grown insolent in the practice, for wasn't it true that:

England since the Conquest hath known some few good monarchs, but groaned beneath a much larger number of bad ones; yet no man in his senses can say that their claim under William the Conqueror is a very honourable one. A French bastard landing with an armed Banditti and establishing himself as King of England against the consent of the natives, is in plain terms a very paltry rascally original. It certainly hath no divinity in it.

And that was the key: that there was so little divinity in either kings or their inheritance. The Colonials would understand that; they had been reared on the scriptures and dissent was as much their inheritance as absolutism was that of kings. The Lord knew, they had raised enough denominations to him — Lutheran, Calvinist, Presbyterian, Quaker, Baptist — yet they still shared one thing in common, the belief that no man should be exalted above the rest for: 'Monarchy is ranked in scriptures as one of the sins of the Jews, for which a curse in reserve is denounced against them.'

Yet, curse or no, they still craved for kingship; only recently one New York Loyalist had gone so far as to trace the Colonies' dependence upon the English crown, as much in the future as in the past: 'England purchased for some of her subjects, who found themselves uneasy at home, a great estate in a distant country.' Like so much else, the words masked the truth:

> I have heard it asserted by some, that as America has flourished under her former connection with Great Britain, the same connection is necessary for her future happiness, and will always have the same effect. Nothing can be more fallacious than this kind of argument. We may as well assert that as a child has thrived upon milk, that it is never to have meat, or that the first twenty years of our lives is to become the precedent for the next twenty.
>
> But even this is admitting more than is true; for I answer roundly that America would have flourished as much, and probably much more, had no European power taken any notice of her. The commerce by which she hath enriched herself are the necessities of life, and will always have a market while eating is the custom in Europe.

So much for the notion that the 13 Colonies were the result of royal benevolence, and for the merchants' concern for the future of their trade. But there was more to it than this. It was 18 months now since Louis XV of France had died, and his successor had inherited all the arrogance of the Bourbon line. At 21 years of age, Louis XVI was slow, dull-witted, and had only one, abiding passion in life — the chase. As for the rest, he left matters to his first Minister, Turgot,* who had troubles enough at home (only recently there had been a march of starving sansculottes to Versailles) without concerning himself with foreign affairs — though it was said that the Treaty of Paris which had ended the Seven Years' War still rankled with the young King.

There was little credence to be placed in the gossip coming out of Versailles, though one thing was sure, that French agents in the Colonies had long been reporting to Paris on the likelihood of an American revolt, maintaining that:

> it was the business of France and Spain to bring about such circumstances. All that would be required to secure independence of the

colonies was arms, a leader, and a feeling of self-reliance in the minds of the inhabitants.[2]

There could be little doubt about the Colonists' self-reliance while if there was to be a final falling out between England and America, France's power would weigh heavily in the scales. The notion of calling up one king to redress the grievances of another amused Paine, though he recognised the sophistry for what it was, expedience, and justified it to himself in the name of independence. If it came to an all-out war with England, then the Colonies would need what friends they could find.

But to what end, that was the rub? It was all very fine to play the iconoclast and drum up liberty, but what if the Royal Brute was removed and independence was achieved? What then? In his critique of Rousseau, old Dr Bevis had always maintained that nature abhorred a vacuum; yet that is how this new country would be, a vacuum of power, unless there was a new constitution to hand — though heaven preserve America from the whimsy of the general will and the metaphysics of the social contract.

Something altogether more practical, more substantial than that was required: a working constitution based upon reason to secure the freedom, security and happiness of the governed. The thing was easily said, more difficult to achieve. At best government was a necessary evil; at worst, an intolerable one, for:

> When we suffer, or are exposed to the same miseries *by a Government* which we might expect in a country *without Government*, our calamity is heightened by reflecting that we furnish the means by which we suffer. Government, like dress, is the badge of lost innocence; the palaces of kings are built upon the ruins of the bowers of paradise.

Monsieur Rousseau might extol the simple democracy of city states (after all, he came from Geneva and had spent his early life in the rustic culture of a Swiss canton), but how was it possible to extend his principles to embrace a nation of three million souls scattered through 13 Colonies? In comparison to this, all the rest (the corruption of kings, the wealth of nations, independence itself) was simple, for:

> if there is any true cause of fear respecting independence, it is because no plan is yet laid down. Men do not see their way out.
>
> Wherefore, as an opening into that business I offer the following hints; at the same time modestly affirming, that I have no other opinion of them myself, than that they may be the means of giving rise

to something better. Could the straggling thoughts of individuals be collected, they would frequently form material for wise and able men to improve into useful matter.

Paine poured another rum and water. The unmaking of power was easy enough, its reconstruction an altogether more difficult task, and his thoughts came fragmented, a patchwork of ideas:

> Let the assemblies be annual with a president only . . . Let each Colony be divided into six, eight, or ten convenient districts, each district to send a proper number of delegates to Congress . . . let the Congress choose (by ballot) a president out of the Delegates . . . in order that nothing may pass into law but what is satisfactorily just, not less than three fifths of the Congress to be called a majority . . .
>
> But as there is a peculiar delicacy from whom, or in what manner, this business must first arise, and as it seems most agreeable and consistent that it should come from some intermediate body between the governed and the governors, that is, between the Congress and the People, let a Continental Conference be held . . . The conferring members being met, let their business be to frame a Continental Charter, or Charter of the United Colonies (answering what is called the Magna Carta of England), fixing the number and manner of choosing the Members of Congress . . . with their date of sitting; and drawing the line of business and jurisdiction between them.
>
> Immediately after which, the said conference to dissolve and the bodies which shall be chosen conformable to the said charter, to be the Legislators and Governors of this Continent for the time: Whose peace and happiness, may God preserve. Amen.

The plan needed the disclaimer, for the thoughts straggled enough. Little wonder that Mr Locke and Monsieur Rousseau had either trimmed the old forms or resorted to primitive fantasies when it came to constitution-building. Best leave such business to them. He had other, more pressing affairs to hand, for, if the latest reports from London were correct, time was moving against the Colonists. A decision had to be taken, soon:

> These proceedings may at first seem strange and difficult, but like all other steps we have already passed over, will in a little time become familiar and agreeable; and until an independence is declared, the Continent will feel itself like a man who continues putting off some

unpleasant business from day to day, yet knows it must be done, hates to set about it, wishes it over, and is continually haunted with thoughts of its necessity.

Satisfied, Paine signed the pamphlet simply 'Author' and wondered what Dr Rush would make of the work?

Common Sense was published on 10 January 1776, price two shillings. Nine days before, and imitating the example of Admiral Graves at Falmouth (now Portland), Maine, the previous autumn, Lord Dunmore had launched a sea-borne attack against Norfolk, Virginia. After a heavy cannonade, the Governor of the Colony — in exile aboard the British flagship *William* for the past six months — ordered marines ashore to fire the town. By the morning of 3 January, Norfolk was a smouldering ruin and Dunmore well pleased. His slight by the Colonists had been avenged; his dignity restored.

The reckoning, however, had still to come. By the month's end, and having read Paine's pamphlet, General Washington was writing from his headquarters with the Continental Army entrenched around Boston:

A few more of such flaming arguments as were exhibited at Falmouth and Norfolk, added to the sound doctrine and unanswerable reasoning contained in the pamphlet *Common Sense* will not leave numbers at a loss to decide upon the propriety of separation.

He was not alone in his views. The work literally exploded in the American consciousness. A second edition (by rival publishers) appeared in late January, and sales totalled an unprecedented 120,000 within three months, leading Dr Rush to exclaim that it had 'burst from the press with an effect that has rarely been produced by types and paper in any age or country'.

Which was all very gratifying for Paine's vanity, save for the anonymity of the piece. Doubtless it was admirable to have withheld his name because 'the object of attention is the Doctrine, not the Man', but the gesture had provoked almost as much controversy as the contents of the work itself; some said it was by the ageing Franklin, others by the young Virginian, Jefferson, and still others by Dr Rush. If they warred as hard for independence as they did over the 'Author' of *Common Sense*, then there would be no cause for alarm.

Yet every day they speculated, fresh intelligence arrived from England. In early January, the King had appointed Richard, Lord Howe (brother of William who had replaced Gage as C-in-C. British land forces in North America following the débâcle at Bunker Hill) as commander of all naval forces operating in American waters; whilst, altogether more ominously, George was recruiting troops in Germany to reinforce his American command. Since late the previous year the King's Minister Plenipotentiary had been negotiating first with Brunswick, then with Hesse-Cassel, and, at a cost of £522,628 to the English Treasury (or levy money of 30 crowns for every foot soldier), had raised a force of 16,000 men.

The auguries were threatening, but still the debate as to the identity of the 'Author' continued though now, as Washington's camp adopted the toast 'May the Independent Principles of Common Sense be confirmed throughout the United Colonies', a new controversy was emerging. The Scot Robert Bell was Paine's first publisher. The agreement between them was straightforward: that, if *Common Sense* incurred any losses, Paine would meet the costs and, conversely, that any profits would be evenly divided between Bell and a fund to provide mittens for Continental troops posted north to the Canada border — an agreement which, considering the work's future sales, was to cost Paine a fortune.

But, if the loss did not trouble him (and as a writer, Paine must be unique in never accepting any income from any of his published works), then Bell's constant money-grubbing did. By the end of January — and having already placed an advertisement for the second edition with the *Pennsylvania Evening Post* which revealed that *Common Sense* was 'Written by an Englishman' thus eliminating Franklin, Jefferson and Dr Rush from the guessing game — Bell was claiming £29 12s 1d from Paine for original publishing costs.

The demand was absurd. Paine had made less than nothing from the work, and what credit there was to be won from its authorship was disguised by anonymity; yet here was Bell denying that he had profited from the venture, refusing to make any payment to the aid fund, and dunning him for a share of the print costs besides. The man was a rogue, and a tight rogue at that. None the less, Paine paid the bill, at the same time offering the rights of the second edition to William and Thomas Bradford — and late in January the second edition of *Common Sense** appeared under a double imprint.

Bell was incensed. In an advertisement for his own reprint of *Common Sense* he derided his competitor's publication of its 'smallness of print and scantiness of paper', adding that the Bradford edition bore as much resemblance to his own 'in figure and utility as much as a British shilling in size and value resembleth a British half crown'.

Not to be outdone, the Bradfords released the story of Bell's

short-changing the fund for the Continental Army in the same edition
of the *Pennsylvania Evening Post* as their rival's advertisement appeared
— while offering their own edition at half Bell's price. By early February,
the controversy was the talk of Philadelphia, and Bell had switched his
attack from the Bradfords to Paine himself:

> Your head being whirligigged by imaginary importance, you got your
> eye upon public money, and you were immediately the self constituted
> treasurer. It was certainly very shallow and impolitic to give the public
> money so early away, without convincing them you had some merit
> than mere noise as a claim upon it.

Tired of the whole pettifogging dispute, Paine withdrew all claims to
the copyright of *Common Sense* and offered it for publication to anyone
who cared to print the work. By the spring, publishers throughout the
13 Colonies were peddling *Common Sense* and, as its sales mounted, so
its critics emerged; notably the President of Dr Rush's own College, the
Reverend William Smith, writing under the pseudonym 'Cato'. An
Anglican and Tory Loyalist, Dr Smith was quick to exploit the fact that
Common Sense was the work of an Englishman, writing of 'the foul pages
of interested writers, and strangers intermeddling in our affairs' to which
Paine (under the pseudonym Forrester) retorted: 'A freeman, Cato, is
a stranger nowhere — a slave, everywhere.'

The controversy — crystallising the Patriot and Loyalist positions —
raged in the correspondence columns of the Colonial press late into the
spring of 1776, but, as the debate became more bitter (by April the
Mechanic's Committee of New York were burning pamphlets opposed
to *Common Sense*), Paine divorced himself, increasingly, from the furore
that his work had caused. The pamphlet had more than achieved its purpose; it was said that Philadelphia alone had close on two hundred taverns,
and the issue was debated in every one and as he walked towards State
House he wondered at the differences that a year had made — as much
to his own fortunes as those of the Colonies.

Little more than twelve months previously he had been carried ashore,
as near to death as made no difference, a stranger to the city with no
more than an introduction from Mr Franklin in his pocket; while only
recently the self-same Franklin had been complimenting him on *Common Sense* and the London press reporting that: 'it is read to all ranks,
and as many as read so many become converted; tho' perhaps the hour
before were most violent against the least idea of independence.'

Fortune had been good to him though, with all due modesty, he had given it a little help. Why, hadn't he tripled the sales of the *Pennyslvania Magazine* with his writings; and wasn't he admitted to the best circles in the town and listened to with respect? Harry Verrall at the Headstrong should see him now, and his mother, too. Then, perhaps, they would know Tom Paine's worth; and, shrugging off the thought, he turned into the State House. It would not do to keep the young Mr Jefferson* waiting. He was a coming man of power.

Only 33 years of age, Jefferson had already won a powerful reputation for himself, though when first they met at Mr Bradford's London Coffee House the man had hardly spoken, thinking, possibly, that he had said enough in the *Summary View of the Rights of America* which had placed him at the forefront of the revolutionary movement and given him a Congressional seat for Virginia. Whatever the reasons, it had been Paine who talked: of the plans by Congress to send Franklin on a mission to France; of Turgot's dismissal from office and Louis's new interest in American affairs; of the Duke of Grafton's latest proposal for reconciliation.

His Grace, it seemed, had matured with time. Six years had passed since he quit his post as the King's first Minister, and now he was one of that permanent, though vociferous, minority of Whigs who sapped at the foundations of North's colonial policy. The effort was unavailing, the King's parliamentary 'friends' made sure of that; but, even as a new army was embarking for the Colonies, Grafton was tabling a motion in the Lords for one last, meaningful attempt at reconciliation:

> I once more conjure your Lordships to reflect that the honour of Parliament, the prosperity and dearest interests of both countries, the lives of thousands of British subjects, are at stake; that the present is probably the only moment you will ever have to snatch them from the ruin that will otherwise inevitably await them; and that the consequences of neglecting this opportunity will be the source of endless mourning and lamentation to ages yet unborn.

The vote (90 to 31 against the motion) reflected George's command of the House. However, while there could be no conciliating the rebels, Admiral Lord Howe still sailed for America with new terms from George to the Colonists. Jefferson dismissed the whole idea — more like revenge in the guise of conciliation — and Paine agreed. The King was a man who lived off his pride, and he would have been mortally wounded when he heard news of the events that had occurred at Boston only three days after Grafton spoke.

On Sunday, 17 March, after pulling the last British garrison back from Bunker Hill, General Howe had evacuated the town; a British convoy of almost 100 ships sailed north for Halifax with more than 10,000 people aboard — including 1,100 Loyalists. The long seige was over, and when Washington's troops entered the town they raised their new flag of 13 red and white stripes with the ensign's crosses of St George and St Andrew in the upper left canton above Fanueil Hall.

But that was close on two months ago, and, as Paine entered the State House, he knew that the young Mr Jefferson had other matters to discuss. In January, New Hampshire had been the first of the Colonies to adopt its own constitution, to be followed in March by South Carolina, and in early May Congress had instructed all Colonies to begin forming their own governments and finally suppress what authority was still vested in the crown. Wryly Paine remembered the Declaratory Act of how many years ago was it now — eight maybe nine? The whole procedure was illegal, and yet . . .

Jefferson was waiting, and with news. The Virginia Convention at Williamsburg had voted, unanimously, to instruct their delegates to the Continental Congress to propose that independence be declared, and had agreed that the Convention itself should draft a Declaration of Rights and a new form of government. Their instructions were unequivocal, Paine could read them for himself:

> Propose to that respectable body to declare the United Colonies free and independent states, absolved from all allegiance to, and dependence upon, the crown or Parliament of Great Britain . . . and give assent of this colony to such declaration and whatever measures may be thought proper and necessary by the Congress for forming foreign alliances, and to a confederation of colonies, at such times and in such manner as to them shall seem best.

Lord Dunmore, one-time Royal Governor of Virginia, had fired more than Norfolk that January day of five months ago. Paine read, and the two men talked of a Declaration of Rights and independence as synonymous, the one postulating the other. If they were, indeed, to be as a 'Citty upon a Hill' then Virginia must understand that all men are by nature equally free and independent, and have certain inherent rights, notably the enjoyment of life and liberty; and that all government should be for the common benefit, protection, and security of the people.

The echoes might be of Locke and the English Bill of Rights, but this was to be a new Declaration and the two men contrasted past with present to build the world anew: of corrupt government ('that all men having sufficient evidence of common interest . . . have the right of suffrage'); of partial law ('a man hath a right to demand the cause and nature of his accusation and . . . to a speedy trial by an impartial jury without whose common consent he cannot be found guilty'); and of an established church ('all men are equally entitled to the free exercise of religion, according to the dictates of conscience').

The Virginian Declaration of Rights, intended as the 'basis and foundation of government', was approved by the Convention in Williamsburg on 12 June 1776 — 20 days before the American Declaration of Independence. The two documents share much in common — not least, their omission of any reference to slavery. During their meetings, Jefferson and Paine agonised over the question, agreeing that it was 'the most horrid of all traffics', yet recognising that an emancipation clause would meet powerful opposition from the southern states and northern merchants with an interest in the trade.

The old contradiction remained: that their demand for liberty was particular, not general — but now the problem was compounded by expedience. At Williamsburg a toast had been drunk to the United States, and unity was essential if there was to be a war with England. The new nation could afford no dissenters, yet neither could 'the most horrid of all traffics' be ignored. In the second week of June, Jefferson was appointed to the five-man committee to draft the Declaration of Independence.* The only paragraph struck out of the document read:

> He has waged cruel war against human nature itself, violating its most sacred rights of life and liberty in the persons of a distant people who never offended him, captivating and carrying them into slavery in another hemisphere, or to incur miserable death in their transportation thither. This piratical warfare, the opprobium of INFIDEL powers, is the warfare of the CHRISTIAN King of England . . .

On Thursday, 4 July 1776, the Declaration was read, and agreed to, by Congress:

> We hold these truths to be self-evident; that all men are created equal; that they are endowed by their Creator with certain inalienable rights; that among these are life, liberty and the pursuit of happiness. — That to secure these rights, governments are instituted among men, deriving their power from the consent of the governed . . .

The words are Jefferson's, the sentiments those of men who had dared to turn the world upside-down: of Rainborough and Winstanley, of Locke, Voltaire, Rousseau and Thomas Paine. Forty years on, William Cobbett asserted that, whoever wrote the Declaration, its author was the Thetford Quaker — though, on that Thursday morning of 1776, he was two days' journey from Philadelphia, serving with Washington's army on the approaches to New York.

5 'THE TIMES THAT TRY MEN'S SOULS'

Four days before the publication of the Declaration of Independence, Colonel Harry Knox breakfasted early at his headquarters on Lower Broadway in New York. It was a custom he enjoyed, for this was the best time of the day. Behind him, the city still slept whilst, to the south, across the harbour, he watched the morning mist lifting above the New Jersey shoreline and was curious at what he saw: the topmasts and rigging of what appeared to be a veritable armada lying off Sandy Hook like 'a swarm of locusts escaped from a bottomless pit'. The British had arrived.

It was now four months since General Howe had pulled his force out of Boston; four months of intense speculation as to where he would make a new landing reinforced by a new army being shipped out of Europe. With a 1,100-mile coastline, well supplied with good harbours, the 13 Colonies provided Howe with an abundance of choice — but Washington had read his mind well. Within a week of taking Boston, the advanced units of the Continental Army were *en route* for New York and by mid-summer he had established his headquarters in the city.

Strategically, New York and New Jersey held the key to Howe's North American campaign. They were midway between the northern and southern Colonies, and a bridgehead in the area would not only provide him with a natural jumping off point for seaborne expeditions, but also with command of the land routes between New England and the south; a position that would be reinforced if he could win control of the Hudson River reaching north-west from New York towards the Canadian border. As one of his staff wrote: 'As long as a British army held the passes of that noble river and her cruisers swept her coasts, the colonists would have found it almost impossible to have joined or fed their respective troops.'

For two weeks the 138 vessels of the British fleet swung at anchor off Staten Island, while General Howe put his troops ashore. They met with no resistance and, when, on the evening of 12 July, his brother, Admiral Lord Howe, led a fleet of 150 ships through the Narrows between Staten and Long Island, he studied the long lines of round tents that made up the British encampment and was pleased with what he saw. Together with his own force, the army totalled 30,000 men — the largest expeditionary force ever mounted by Great Britain. And even this was not all: a further 10,000 troops were assembling in Canada under General Carleton in readiness for a push southwards to link with the main force on the up-per reaches of the Hudson, while in the south Admiral Peter Parker with a force of 2,000 men was attempting to gain a foothold in the Carolinas.

As evidence of the King's intent, the display was unprecedented. The Colonials would soon learn the nature of sovereignty, though first there was to be one last attempt at reconciliation — even if they had declared for independence. For, backed by force, the Howes were under instruc-tions to act as peacemakers. Eight days after Howe's fleet had dropped anchor, Washington inspected the guard before Colonel Knox's head-quarters before meeting the emissary from the British commanders, Lieutenant-Colonel Paterson.

The formalities over, Paterson explained that Lord Howe and his brother were empowered by the King to settle the differences between Great Britain and her American Colonies, to which Washington replied that for his part, he had no powers to negotiate peace terms — and of-fered the Colonel a drink. Paterson declined and, turning to leave, ask-ed: 'Has Your Excellency no particular commands with which you would please to honour me to Lord and General Howe?'

'Nothing', replied Washington, 'but my particular compliments to both.' The peace initiative had failed; only force remained.

Paine joined General Roberdeau's Flying Camp at Amboy, 20 miles behind the front, in midsummer. Since the publication of *Common Sense* six months before, his reputation had burgeoned, though John Adams* was already suggesting that his opinions were too 'democratical'. The view was significant for what it revealed of the ambitions of the Colonists — ambitions that were later to polarise between Adams's belief that govern-ment should be the prerogative of the high-born and the affluent, and Paine's contention that: 'The Nation is essentially the source of all sovereignty; nor can ANY INDIVIDUAL, or ANY BODY OF MEN be entitled to any authority which is not expressly derived from it.'

With the Declaration just signed, however, there were more pressing matters to hand than polemics. While it was all very well to state the principles of independence, it was a different matter to fight for them. For six months and more the Friends of Pennsylvania had been playing the doubting Thomas, while the Tories had found a new confidence in their cause since the return of the British. And with reason. They had seen the Continental Army for themselves.

At most, Washington had 20,000 troops under his command; amateur soldiers, the majority of whom were ill equipped, ill trained and expected to buy their own uniforms from their pay of seven dollars a month. Since the formal establishment of the Continental Army by Congress the previous year, there had been an improvement in both organisation and discipline, though one, overriding factor still conditioned all the rest — Washington's entire force was composed of men on a one-year enlistment and, with the autumn, the service of many of them would come to an end.

Congress might be pleased to call it a Grand Army. Washington knew better. Yet this was all he had to pit against Howe's professionally commanded, iron-disciplined, plentifully supplied, and numerically superior force. Little wonder that Loyalists crowded the beaches of Staten Island when the British fleet dropped anchor, or that the Tories of New Jersey were already counting off the days to their liberation.

They had good reason for optimism for the Patriots' euphoria was not enough to win this contest — and already it was wearing thin as the tension mounted before Howe's first assault. For five weeks he bided his time on Staten Island and then, on the afternoon of 22 August, Paine heard the distant crackle of gunfire. The British thrust had begun. The cannonade, little more than a frieze of sound, continued late into the evening, and by the morning of the twenty-third the first riders spurred through Amboy on their way south to Philadelphia with the news: the British had landed in force on Long Island; Washington was retiring northwards.

In the days that followed, the reports arriving at Roberdeau's headquarters were generally fragmentary, always bad: Howe advances . . . Hessians encamped before Flatbush . . . Washington withdraws. In the Flying Camp, the tension mounted. Clinton's Dragoons overrun Flushing . . . Howe advances. Roberdeau and his command grew fretful for action. More than a 1000 Continental troops killed or wounded in major engagement at Flatbush Pass . . . Washington retires. Order to Flying Column: disband. Howe advances . . . Brooklands falls. For a week the British fought their way northwards and by the end of August Long Island was theirs.

The Colonial press could call the operation what they liked (a tactical withdrawal; a redeployment on prepared lines), but there was no disguising the fact that the Continental Army had been bettered in its first brush of the war with the British professionals. Small wonder that the Tories' confidence blossomed by the day, or that there was a growing flood of desertions from Washington's command.

Like one of Dr Bevis's equations, it had a certain symmetry: the predominance of the Continental force was reduced in direct proportion to the weight placed in the Loyalist scales, while the Howes had timed their latest peace initiative with rare precision — driving a wedge of doubt further into the Colonists' resolve. The story had come together piecemeal, but from the British standpoint the approach made good sense.

Apparently a certain General Sullivan had been taken by the British when Long Island fell. Within 72 hours the man had convinced the British commanders that, having learned the lesson of the débâcle, Congress might well be in the mood to negotiate and that he, John Sullivan, would be happy to serve as an agent between the parties. The idea had recommended itself to Lord Howe and his brother and, on 30 August, Sullivan was passed through the British and American lines on his way south to Philadelphia.

Three days later, the go-between appeared before a session of Congress, maintaining that the Howes were fully empowered to negotiate a settlement, and would be happy to meet members of Congress 'as private citizens' to discuss peace terms. The news of the new British initiative spread fast, and faced Congress with a nice dilemma — to reject the offer of exploratory talks and be accused of wishing to prolong the war; or to accept the offer while doubting both the intentions and the credentials of the British commanders.

The decision wracked Congress (by inference, the Howes' offer to talk with them as 'private citizens' denied their independent status), but by the week's end it was agreed that Benjamin Franklin, John Adams and Edward Rutledge* should meet with the British commander:

to know whether he has any authority to treat with persons authorised by Congress for that purpose on behalf of America, and what that authority is, and to hear such propositions as he shall think fit to make respecting the same.

Only a skeleton force remained in Amboy on 11 September as Franklin, Adams and Rutledge rode down to the quay on their way to Howe's headquarters. Paine had hoped for a few words with Franklin, but there was no time for conversation. The Admiral's barge was waiting to ferry them to Staten Island, and peace was not a matter to be kept waiting — however illusory the prospect might be. The British had made capital enough out of their supposed good intentions. Now they would be put to the test. If, Howe explained, they acted solely as 'private gentlemen of character', then the negotiations could begin. 'Your Lordship may consider me in what light you please,' retorted Adams, 'except as a British subject.' The charade continued for a little longer; effectively, however, the negotiations were at an end. Four days later the British took New York.

As Paine rode north along the Jersey heights to his new posting at Fort Lee, he looked out across the Hudson and saw the British fleet. Admiral

Lord Howe now had some 400 ships under his command, while his brother, only recently knighted, had more than 30,000 troops stationed about New York alone. Once he might have taken a pride in the situation, but that was another lifetime ago — a lifetime of contradictions and frustration and, too often, despair. Now he was Mr Thomas Paine, and even the children had taken to calling him 'Old Common Sense' — and he smiled at the thought, though not for long, for where was the common sense in this farrago, and he could only thank God that the weather still held.

The Continental Army was in poor condition to fight a winter campaign, not least when weakened by men reaching the end of their twelve-month term of service, and, with the day well advanced, he spurred his horse on. Loyalist country, this was no place for a Patriot to be after nightfall, besides which, there was an appointment that had to be kept with General Greene.

The man was already a legend. A one-time Quaker blacksmith, he had been rejected as an officer by the Rhode Island Kentish Guards (one of the crack units in New England) in 1774 because of a limp caused by a stiff right knee — and immediately volunteered as a ranker. Within the year, however, the Rhode Island Assembly voted to raise a 1,500-man force to 'Preserve the Liberties of America' — and gave Greene the command, leading Colonel Knox to write: 'He came to us the rawest, most untutored being I ever met, but in less than twelve months, he was equal in military knowledge to any General Officer in the army, and very superior to most.'

On 19 September 1776, Paine was appointed Greene's aide-de-camp with the rank of Brigadier. At 39 years of age, and recently described by General Lee as 'a man who has genius in his eyes', it was late to go a-soldiering but he shared Greene's fierce contempt as much for the fireside independents as for the Quakers who were making a growing clamour of their conscience, especially in the light of what their misgiving was doing to the morale of the front line troops. It was bad enough having to hold a command together knowing that the Continental Army was both outnumbered and outgunned without having to face continuous sniping from the rear as well, though Greene's troops seemed in good enough spirits. Only days after joining his staff there had been a night alarm, and in the hurry and confusion of rising Paine had been unable to find either his wig or his boots — to learn the following morning that both the alarm and the loss of his gear had been part of an elaborate jape staged for his benefit by the young Major Blodget.

The incident was merely an interlude in the altogether more serious business of war. Greene's command held the bluffs above the Hudson River little more than 20 miles to the north of New York — and already there was intelligence of Howe preparing for a new advance, while Carleton moved down from Canada. It was here that the fate of independency would be decided, but Greene was confident, too confident perhaps. A square-cut figure, he would stand on the heights overlooking the Hudson and boast that, given a couple of weeks, his two strongpoints — Fort Washington on the east bank, and Fort Lee on the west — would be capable of withstanding anything that the British sent against them and then, by God, he'd bloody Howe's nose.

The mood was infectious, and did wonders for the men's morale, while with his staff in the evening Greene would shrug off all anxieties and turn the talk to other things — of London and England and science and government. Recusant Quakers, Paine and Greene shared much in common and over brandy and rum talked long into the nights about why it was that men could make a science of reason, yet still failed to apply reason to government.

Surely, if men entered into a contract of any sort — whether to shoe a mare or make a constitution — it must be on equitable terms; for who would take up arms and spend their fortunes *not* to maintain their rights; rather to maintain that they had no rights? The idea was nonsensical, but this was how it was the world over: the Hessians were sold like beasts (it was said that Frederick of Prussia was levying a cattle tax on every armed man that crossed his land) to side in a quarrel which was no concern of theirs; the Irish regiments were manned by men who hated the British at home, yet carried their colours overseas; and even now, with their Declaration only recently signed, Congress had begun debating the small print of liberty while dispatching a mission to France to negotiate aid for independence from the autocrat of Versailles.

Only the ends of independence could justify such means though it might be that France itself would learn something of liberty in the process, and Paine quoted Rousseau whilst Greene wondered at what he had heard of Mr Silas Deane. The man, it seemed, had a dark character, yet already he was entrusted with the delicate task of trading with the French. A one-time blacksmith like himself, it was reported that Mr Deane had talent and ambitions in equal proportions, in which case he would be well employed stoking the French hatred of Britain.

Twelve months before the Declaration of Independence, the French Foreign Minister, Charles Gravier, Comte de Vergennes, had dispatched Caron de Beaumarchais* to London to test out the British mood to the Colonists' ambitions. His conclusion was succinct: 'All sensible people in England are convinced that the English colonies are lost to the mother country, and that is my opinion too.' It was exactly what Vergennes wished to hear, and by the spring of 1776 he had established an undercover company, headed by Beaumarchais, to supply the Colonists with arms and munitions — Hortalez et Cie. The morality of the project troubled Paine, that liberty should be compromised by such an arrangement, but then the business of war always made for strange bedfellows and hopefully Mr Deane could make something of the scheme, for the Continental Army needed all the help that it could recruit.

For more than a month Howe checked his forces whilst Greene strengthened his positions (the third defence line to the south of Fort Washington was already nearing completion) and wondered that the British commander did not exploit the continuing fine weather to extend his bridgehead. The New Jersey winters were notorious, and if Howe did not move soon he would be pinned down on Long Island until the spring. The delay was inexplicable and it was not until 12 October, with autumn already closing in, that Howe made his move for the north, bypassing Fort Washington to drive at the main body of the Continental Army on White Plain.

British progress was slow, almost stately, and it was three weeks before the army was drawn up before Washington's line and the order given to advance on the American positions — to find that the Colonials had withdrawn yet again. Since the opening of the campaign two months before, Washington's tactics had become clear. Recognising that his heavily outnumbered, ill equipped and partially trained command was no match for the British in a set piece battle, he took full advantage of his one asset, space, to play cat and mouse with Howe — and again he had pulled the main body of his force northwards, leaving Greene on the British flanks.

Innately cautious, Howe would not contemplate any further advance without securing his lines of communication and on 5 November he turned his army southwards towards Fort Washington — heartened by intelligence from a deserter who had brought with him full plans of Greene's fortifications. In theory, the fort might appear impregnable. In practice, however, the concentration of Greene's defences were south-facing — whilst the main body of the British army was now advancing from the north.

The situation alarmed Washington and from his headquarters at Hackensack, five miles west of the Hudson, he wrote to Greene: 'It will not be prudent to hazard the men and stores at Mount Washington, but as you are on the spot, leave it to you to give such orders as to evacuating Mount Washington as you judge best.' The implication was clear, but Greene ignored it and two days later Colonel Paterson, the same officer who had parleyed with Washington in New York, rode slowly towards the Fort under a flag of truce with the ultimatum: surrender or recognise the alternative that, under the rules of war, the entire garrison will be put to the sword.

Colonel Robert Magaw, the American commander, was defiant: 'Give me leave to assure His Excellency that, actuated by the most glorious cause that mankind ever fought for, I am determined to defend this post to the very last extremity.' As night fell on the evening of 15 November, Paterson and his small party returned to the British lines, and Greene's aide-de-camp dictated an urgent dispatch to General Washington: the battle for Fort Washington was on. In the early hours of the following morning the American commander and Greene met in midstream on the Hudson River — while in the darkness close by British flat boats loaded with infantry moved silently into the assault.

The conversation was hushed, anxious, but Greene remained confident; the men were in good spirits and would put up a stout defence; knowing that there was no more that could be done, they returned to Fort Lee. As the sun rose Paine stood with Washington's staff on the New Jersey heights and traced the progress of the British assault: the frigate *Pearl* pounding the outworks from the Hudson; General Percy storming the main defensive lines from the south; and, to the hammer of drums, Lieutenant-General Baron von Knyphausen leading the main assault at the head of 3,000 Hessians from the north.

This was war as Howe knew it, a precise ritual as conducted between gentlemen — even to the courtly gesture of a second offer of surrender. Magaw asked for four hours to consider the terms. Knyphausen granted him 30 minutes. At four in the afternoon of 16 November, Colonel Robert Magaw offered up his sword, and his force of 2,900 officers and men marched out of the Fort under the guard of Howe's troops. From their vantage point a mile to the west, Washington, Greene and Paine followed the disaster, helpless, and their despair was almost palpable.

In half a day, Washington had lost almost a fifth of his entire force and within the next 24 hours the Massachusetts units would complete their term of service — while every regiment raised by Congress the previous year was scheduled to disband by the end of December. So much for the brave hopes of 4 July, and Paine wondered, for a moment, where independence itself would finally be surrendered and cursed the gentlemen of Philadelphia. Surely they could grasp the need to arm their principles, and he watched the last of Colonel Magaw's command being marched away into captivity and remembered a dispatch captured from the British on the condition of Continental troops:

It is a fact that many of the rebels who were killed in the late affairs were without shoes or stockings . . . They are also in great want of blankets. The weather during the former part of the campaign has been so favourable that they did not feel the want of these things, but in less than a month they must suffer extremely if not supplied with them. Under all the disadvantages of want of confidence, clothing and good winter quarters it will be astonishing if they keep together till Christmas.

The report was no more than the truth; and now the stores at Fort Washington were lost, and Fort Lee threatened — while General Washington had fewer than 2,500 men under his direct command to the west of the Hudson. True, Charles Lee* had 7,000 men in a force lying to the north of White Plain (though there were already reports that, with their service up, the Massachusetts units were marching for home); and William Heath* had a further 4,000 men guarding the passes to Canada, but New Jersey remained the lynch pin of the British campaign. With 30,000 men at his command, and the lower reaches of the Hudson now commanded by the British fleet, a river crossing posed no problems to Howe, and, if Fort Lee was to fall, a wedge would be driven between the northern and southern colonies and the route to Philadelphia would be open to him.

Not that Washington was to repeat the mistake of 16 November and commit his small force to fighting on fixed lines in defence of Fort Lee. To retain flexibility of movement was now of paramount importance and, within 24 hours of the fall of Fort Washington, he ordered Greene to evacuate the stores from his west-bank strongpoint with all possible haste. For two days, lines of heavy waggons left Fort Lee loaded with powder and supplies and then, early on the morning of 20 November, Howe made a lighting strike across the river. By sun up Fort Lee was in British hands, with hardly a shot having been fired; the garrison having evacuated in such haste that Howe's forward units found breakfast kettles still simmering on the fires.

By evening, the remnants of Green's command were regrouping five miles to the west of Hackensack — and rain had begun to fall. The Indian summer had ended; the bitter winter campaign had begun. And as a fighting force the Continental Army had virtually ceased to exist. Two abreast, wrapped in their blankets, and some without shoes on their feet, what remained of Greene's brigade straggled through the town in search of warm food and some place to rest — and Paine watched them go. Was it only four days ago that Greene had insisted to Washington that these men would check the British and now . . . now it seemed that he was witnessing the death throes of the Revolution itself.

And still the column shuffled past, exhausted men with defeat in their eyes, while safe in Philadelphia the fireside generals marched and counter-marched their tankards across the tavern tables between ordering up fresh drinks in which to toast 'Liberty' — so long as it was at no cost to themselves. For a moment Paine's anger flared that the fine words of July — 'We hold these truths to be self-evident; that all men are created equal . . . ' — should have come to this, and he wondered whether there was a drink to be found in Hackensack for this was an anniversary of sorts. Twelve months before he had begun to write *Common Sense*. Now, perhaps, he should write again . . .

The rain was incessant, the road to the south already a mire. For three days Washington's small force had been falling back on Newark, shadowed by the 16th Dragoons of Cornwallis's* command and waiting for Howe to strike. The British might call it a rout, but still they failed to press their advantage home; their van still held off; still Howe failed to launch his flanking force across the lower Hudson to cut Washington's line of retreat. The delay was incomprehensible. A single clean thrust and all would be ended, but for 72 hours the British commander hesitated, and at Newark Washington temporarily checked his withdrawal to await Lee's army and regroup his broken command.

The decision was as much a matter of compassion as expediency. Hackensack might be only a twelve-mile march to the north — but for his men it had been a march into hell. A broken column, many slogging through the mud barefoot, their blankets and threadbare uniforms sodden by the downpour, they were no longer in any condition to fight. Cold as death and exhausted, they trudged their way south through the rain-lashed Jersey landscape, too tired even to answer the taunts of the Tories who mocked their passage.

Scavenging confidence from the disaster (only recently Howe had issued a broadsheet offering a $5 bounty and the promise of 50 acres of land to every American who would serve under his command), the Loyalists watched the small army pass and, as he crossed the Passaic Bridge north of Newark, Paine remembered another time and another place — the dispossessed army that had straggled through Thetford many years ago — and cursed his God. It seemed that humanity itself was in retreat; and that night he talked with Greene.

His confidence broken like the summer, the bluff Rhode Islander was close to despair, and small wonder. Washington himself contemplated that the affair was almost done, unless a miracle occurred — and they put little faith in such things. Once, maybe, the words of the creed had been enough ('WHEN, in the course of human events, it becomes necessary for one people to dissolve the political bonds which have connected them with another . . .'), but the practice was very different, and Greene drowned his anger in another drink. The latest intelligence reports had it that Howe intended reinforcing Cornwallis with fresh regiments out of New York, and, while there was still no news of Lee's brigade, Washington was left with barely 5,000 men and the empty promise of aid from Congress. With Philadelphia less than eighty miles to the south, it surely was not too much to hope that they would have roused themselves to the dangers; yet in the past weeks their promises had proved chimerical, and together the two men drank to a miracle in which neither had faith before Greene went into the night to inspect his pickets, leaving Paine to the half-empty bottle and his angry thoughts:

These are the times that try men's souls. The summer soldier and the sunshine patriot will, in this crisis, shrink from the service of his country, but he that stands it NOW, deserves the love and thanks of man and woman. Tyranny, like hell, is not easily conquered, yet we have this consolation with us, that the harder the conflict, the more glorious the triumph. What we obtain too cheap, we esteem too lightly; 'tis dearness only that gives everything its value. Heaven knows how to put a proper price upon its goods, and it would be strange indeed if so celestial an article as FREEDOM should not be highly rated.

His thoughts became words and he liked them, and Paine poured himself a drink. The principles for which they fought needed reiteration, and who better to express them than 'Old Common Sense'? This time there would be no pseudonyms; he had had too much of that, too much of playing at political games. This time it would be Thomas Paine who stamped his name on this crisis to make room on earth for honest men to live, and tomorrow he would write more.

For a fortnight Paine marched by day and wrote by night. At first the form was fragmentary; a scatter of ideas lacking in logic:

Let it be told to the future world that in the depth of winter, when nothing but hope and virtue could survive, the city and the country alarmed at one common danger, came forth to meet and repulse it . . . Panics in some cases, have their uses, they produce as much good as hurt. Their duration is always short, the mind soon grows through

them, and acquires a firmer habit than before . . . The heart that feels
not now is dead; the blood of his children will curse his cowardice,
who shrinks back at a time when a little might have saved the whole,
and made *them* happy . . . I dwell upon the powers of the imagination; I bring reason to your ears; and in language as plain as A. B.
C. hold up truth to your eyes.

And that was it: that the language and the logic should be as plain
as ABC. With Greene beside him, and the ragged column about him,
Paine rode south through the bitter weather across the Jersey flatlands:
'with a handful of men, we sustained an orderly retreat for near an hundred miles, brought off our ammunition, all of our field pieces, the greatest
part of our stores, and had four rivers to pass.' South across the Passaic,
the Rahway, the Raritan and the Delaware, already icing over in the first
frosts of December, where Washington turned to face the British, and
where Paine completed his first 'Crisis' paper.

The words were unsparing, the reasoning taut:

Britain with an army to enforce her tyranny, has declared that she has
a right *not only to TAX but 'TO BIND us in ALL CASES WHATSOEVER'*
and if *being bound in that manner* is not slavery then there is no such
thing as slavery upon earth. Even the expression is impious for so
unlimited power can belong only to God.

This was the key on which all the rest turned: the King's presumption
('I cannot see on what grounds the King of Britain can look up to heaven
for help against us; a common murderer, a highwayman, or a house
breaker has as good a pretence as he'); the British tactics ('Howe's first
object is partly by threats and partly by promises, to terrify or seduce
the people . . . Is this the madness of folly, to expect mercy from those
who have refused to do justice?'); the Tory dealings ('And what is a Tory?
Good God! what is he? Every Tory is a coward, for servile, self-interested
fear is the foundation of Toryism, and a man under such influence, though
he may be cruel never can be brave'); and independence itself:

A noted Tory, who kept a tavern in Amboy, was standing at his door,
with as pretty a child in his hand, about eight or nine years old, as
I ever saw, and after speaking his mind as freely as he thought prudent, finished with this unfatherly expression : '*Well, give me peace
in my day.*'
    Not a man lives on the continent but fully believes that separation
must some time or other finally take place, and a generous parent

should have said: *'If there must be trouble, let it be in my day, that my child may have peace,'* and this single reflection, well applied, is sufficient to awaken every man to duty. Not a place on earth might be so happy as America. Her situation is remote from all the wrangling world and she has nothing to do but trade with them. A man can distinguish himself between temper and principle, and I am as confident as I am that God governs the world that America will never be happy till she gets clear of foreign dominion.

Wars, without ceasing, will break out till that period arrives, and the Continent must in the end be conqueror; for though the flame of liberty may sometimes cease to shine, the coal can never expire . . . 'Tis the business of little minds to shrink, but he whose heart is firm, and whose conscience approves his conduct, will pursue his principles unto death.

The work, little more than 3,000 words in all, was finished and by the third week of December was with a printer in Philadelphia, appearing first in the *Pennsylvania Journal* on 19 December and then in pamphlet form. By the twenty-third copies were at Washington's headquarters. Since fixing his line on the Delaware, there had been little improvement in his position. The weather continued to deteriorate, Lee's force had still failed to arrive, whilst his own command of 5,000 men were 'most so thinly clad as to be unfit for service'. On the seventeenth, Washington was writing to a relative in Virginia:

Your imagination can scarce extend to a situation more distressing than mine. Our only dependence now is upon the speedy enlistment of a new army. (The one-year enlistment for what remained of the Continental Army was due to expire on 1 January.) If this fails, I think that the game will be pretty well up, as from disaffection and want of spirit and fortitude, the inhabitants, instead of resistance, are offering submission and taking protection from General Howe.

All that remained was one last throw, to go out and surprise the British who had grown complacent with their long run of success. And what better time for such a venture than 25 December? As darkness fell on Christmas night, Washington's ragged force paraded at McKonkey's Ferry and by the light of their lanterns, the picket guards read Paine's words: 'These are the times that try men's souls. The summer soldier and sunshine patriot will, in this crisis, shrink from the service of his country . . .'

Twelve hours later, having crossed the ice-bound Delaware and marched eight miles through a violent snowstorm, the remnant of the Continental Army under Washington's command drove the British out of Trenton, taking 23 officers and 886 men. Seemingly, there were still some miracles left, and not even Paine's most vehement critic, Cheetham, could gainsay the impact of his words:

> The number was read in the camp to every corporal's guard, and in the army and out, it had more than the intended effect. The convention of New York, reduced by dispersion, occasioned by alarm, to nine members was rallied and reanimated. Militiamen who, already tired of war, were straggling from the army, returned. Hope succeeded to despair, cheerfulness to gloom, and firmness to resolution. To the confidence which it inspired may be attributed much of the brilliant little affair which in the same month followed at Trenton.

6 'CRISIS' PAPERS

On the evening of 21 December 1776, Benjamin Franklin reached Paris to take up his post as the first US Ambassador to France — to the alarm of the British envoy, Lord Stormont, and the delight of the salons. To the formalised world of Parisian society, the 71-year-old diplomat (simply dressed and carrying a rugged staff rather than a sword) seemed as much a prophet of natural philosophy as an ideal citizen of the free world; the Comte de Ségur wrote:

> Nothing was more astonishing than the contrast between the luxury of Paris, the elegance of our fashions, the splendour of Versailles, all those living survivals of the Autocratic pride of Louis XIV, the polite but arrogant loftiness of our great nobles — with the almost peasant clothes, the simple but proud deportment, the outspoken but honest language, the uncurled and unpowdered hair, in a word with that air of a distant age, which seemed suddenly to transport to Paris in the middle of the decadent and servile civilisation of the eighteenth century a philosopher of the time of Plato or a republican of the age of Fabius or Cato.

The appearance was deceptive. No one knew better than Franklin the role he had to play — committing the French to the American cause — and his arrival in Paris was to prove even more momentous to the future than the 'brilliant little affair' at Trenton. Since the Declaration of Independence, Silas Deane had been negotiating for supplies through the bogus company, Hortalez et Cie, while Lord Stormont had been urging on the Comte de Vergennes, the French Foreign Minister, the importance of France's continuing neutrality in what George III still regarded as a domestic concern. Vergennes, however, had remained non-committal, though he was privately reported to have remarked: 'If the Colonies are determined to reject the sovereignty of His Britannic Majesty, it would not be in the interest of France to see them reduced by force.'

The remark captured the full ambiguity of the French position: on the one hand, the pleasurable anticipation of Britain's discomfiture; on the other, the innate caution of being too closely drawn into a venture which the French exchequer could ill afford. For five months Vergennes and Stormont had played out their diplomatic charade, as courteous as it was inconclusive. Franklin's arrival, however, further limited Vergennes's room for manoeuvre. The man was fêted by court and salon, playing on the long-standing enmity between Britain and France and discreetly hinting at the benefits to be gained from an alliance with the young nation.

By the end of January 1777, Stormont was taxing Vergennes with reports that five ships were being loaded with military supplies intended for the Americans, 'contrary to the friendship this Court has expressed to us'; and again Vergennes evaded a direct reply. Under the combined influence of Franklin's 'sensible gracefulness', and the occasional reports of American successes, however, France was inexorably being drawn into war with England.

The Year of the Hangman, as 1777 was already being called by the more superstitious Patriots who saw, in the last three digits, the gibbets that would await them if their cause should fail, began well for Paine. If any proof was needed, which he doubted, the first of the 'Crisis' papers had established his place as the foremost propagandist in North America, and this in less than a year since *Common Sense* had nerved the Colonists to declare for independence. It was all very well for men such as John Adams to whisper that his radicalism was too heavy to be borne; there could be no denying that Thomas Paine, one-time staymaker and ex-ciseman, was now a figure of standing in American affairs — and, from his lodgings on Second Street, Philadelphia, he followed the comings and goings of the Friends at their Meeting House across the way.

Once he had been one of them, but that was before many things: before a Sabbath at the Thetford meeting when the Friends had talked of God as if he were 'a passionate man that killed his Son'; before the bitterness of the campaign just passed; before Brother Pemberton had published his testimony counselling all Quakers to respect 'that happy Constitution under which they and others long enjoyed tranquillity and peace'. With friends like that at his back, it was little wonder that Washington was demanding that all American citizens should take an oath of allegiance to the young Republic; and, watching their scurryings, Paine began writing the second of the 'Crisis' papers:

> From concern that a good cause should be dishonoured by the least disunion among us, I said in my former paper, No. 1, that 'should the enemy now be expelled, I wish with all the sincerity of a Christian that the names of Whig and Tory might never more be named;' but there is a knot of men among us, of such a venomous cast, that they will not admit even one's good wishes to act in their favour.
>
> Instead of rejoicing that heaven had . . . providentially preserved this city from plunder and destruction, by delivering so great a part

of the enemy into our hands, with so little effusion of blood, they stubbornly affected to disbelieve it, until an hour, nay half an hour of the prisoners arriving; and the Quakers put forth a testimony, signed John Pemberton, declaring their attachment to the British Government. These men are continually harping on the great sin of our bearing arms; but the King of England may lay waste the world in blood and famine and they, poor fallen souls, have nothing to say.

In some future paper, I intend to distinguish between the different kinds of persons who I have decided to denominate Tories.

Paine checked himself; in the meantime, there was other work to hand. The Council of Safety in Philadelphia had already approached him with an invitation to act as secretary to the Commissioners being dispatched by Congress to negotiate with the Indians at Easton, Pennsylvania. The salary was generous, £300, for the role was crucial — both the British and the Patriots vying for the loyalty of the tribes.

On Columbus's landing three centuries before, the population of North America was estimated to have totalled 1,250,000, a population subsequently decimated by smallpox, tuberculosis, drink, VD — and the ruthless ambition of frontiersmen to open up the rich, western lands of Ohio, Kentucky and western New York. Indeed, the British government's determination to check their advance had been a subsidiary cause of the Revolution itself. Ten years before, Grenville's ministry had attempted to fix the western frontiers of the 13 Colonies, legislation which provoked a powerful backlash, yet did nothing to check the savage depredations of the frontiersmen.

None the less, the tribes on the frontier remained an important consideration in the strategy of Howe and Washington and as early as 1775 Congress had created three departments to handle Indian affairs, voting a sum of $17,000 to purchase gifts and rum. The mission to Easton was part of this strategy and on 21 January Paine left Philadelphia at the start of his trek to the western frontier. Six days later, after drinking a toast to the outcome of their talks, and to the accompaniment of the organ, the Commission held their first meeting with King Last Night at the First (German) Reformed Church.

The negotiations lasted for two months and news of the war was difficult to come by, though what little arrived was almost exclusively bad: of Howe receiving further reinforcements; of a new army assembling in Canada and awaiting the arrival of Major-General 'Gentleman Johnny' Burgoyne* before moving south; of Tories in the Jerseys flocking to sign the oath of allegiance to the King, and the faint-hearted in Pennsylvania only waiting for the opportunity to follow suit. Though his English was makeshift, King Last Night made for better company. At least he had the measure of George.

While his judgement turned on a single impression formed long ago, it still remained sound. Once, it seemed, he had seen some English ships of the line off the Canadian coast, and, though impressed by 'the great war canoes', he concluded that: 'The King of England is like a fish. When he is in the water, he can wag his tail; when he comes on land, he lays down on his side.' The Commission had laughed at the metaphor, but it was apt none the less and Paine stored it away for later use. The Royal Brute as a fish stranded on the American shore: the image was a powerful one, of Howe and Cornwallis and Gentleman Johnny cast up high and dry and suing to be sent back from whence they came — the prospect seemed as incredible as any angler's tale.

The talks lasted until late into March, and by April Paine was back in Philadelphia and writing where he had left off when the mission began — the third of the 'Crisis' papers. Three months had passed since he had promised to expose the hidden Tories, and he was as good as his word. The words fairly crackled on the paper. If George claimed the 'RIGHT TO BIND THE COLONIES IN ALL CASES WHATSOEVER', then by the same token he bound their citizens as slaves and made a play of the Tories' talk of freedom. This was the die by which to test the issue, the touchstone to try men by:

> He that is not a supporter of the Independent States of America, in the same degree that his religious and political principles would suffer him to support the Government of any other country, of which he called himself a subject, is in the American sense of the word, A TORY; and the instant that he endeavours to bring his Toryism into practice, he becomes A TRAITOR.

The definition served well enough, though the Quakers still remained. Had they minded their religion, they might have lived at ease through troubled times, but certain of them preferred to shield behind their principles, whilst promoting dissension:

> The common phrase with these people is 'Our principles are peace'. To which may be replied, and your practices are the reverse; for never did the conduct of men oppose their own doctrine more notoriously than the present race of Quakers. They have artfully changed themselves into a different sort of people to what they used to be, and

yet have the address to persuade each other they are not altered; like antiquated virgins, they see not the havoc that deformity hath made upon them, but pleasantly mistaking wrinkles for dimples, conceit themselves yet lovely, and wonder at the stupid world for not admiring them.

Did no injury arise to the public by this apostasy of the Quakers from themselves, the public would have nothing to do with it; but as both the design and the consequence are pointed against a cause in which the whole community is interested, it is no longer a subject confined to the cognisance of the Meeting only, but comes as a matter of criminality before either the authority of the particular state in which it is acted, or of the Continent against which it operates.

Across Second Street, the Friends made their way to Meeting and, wondering where his childhood God had gone, Paine despised them. A convert to a new faith, he was jealous of independence, the more so for knowing the consequences of failure. The Year of the Gibbet was no old wives' tale. They would hang for their principles if they failed. The general order book taken from the British at Trenton made that clear: 'His excellency the Commander in Chief orders, that all inhabitants who shall be found with arms, not having an officer with them, shall immediately be taken and hung up.' Such thoughts were too dark to be borne and, pouring a rum and water, Paine recalled King Last Night and wrote:

The enemy have long lain idle, and amused themselves with carrying on the war by proclamations only. While they continue to delay, our strength increases . . . Like a wounded, disabled whale, they want only time and room to die in; and though in the agony of their exit, it may be unsafe to live within the flapping of their tail, yet every hour shortens their date, and lessens their power of mischief.

That would have to do; there was more urgent business to attend to. Two days before the publication of the third 'Crisis' on 19 April (the second anniversary of the Battle of Lexington), Paine was appointed Secretary of the Committee of Foreign Affairs of Congress on the nomination of John Adams — though not before coming under ferocious, personal attack from the New Jersey delegate, John Witherspoon.

A Scot and a Presbyterian, the man was as narrow as his creed, though he had served independence well enough. There was talk of his descent from John Knox and, while it remained only talk, he was a conservative as much by inheritance as by inclination and there lay the contradiction

— that he adopted a cause whose conclusion was a radicalism that he found intolerable. Yet that was no ground for his charge 'that he [Thomas Paine] was very intemperate . . . a bad character, and not fit to be placed in such a situation' — and even less for the claim that he was a turncoat who had written 'against the American cause' on his arrival in the Colonies.

The charge was a lie. None the less, there were those who gave it credence; not least, certain of the larger merchants and landed proprietors who were strong for the cause, as long as the outcome served their own ends; who drew independence as tight as their own self-interest. It was the same the world over. Little more than a century had passed since the gentry had raised the people against the crown to become 'frighted by what they unleashed'; and what of a Glorious Revolution that had found its gospel in Locke and the reign of property?

Paine shook off the thoughts, for who was this Dr Witherspoon? Once the title might have impressed. No longer; modesty forbade men to assume honours, though if the Reverend gentlemen cared to play the game then he, Thomas Paine, was well prepared.

In ten days' time he would be 40 years of age, of which the first 38 had been a prelude to the two just passed, and he tolled off his credentials — author of *Common Sense* and three 'Crisis' papers; an aide to General Greene; a member of the Committee of Correspondence of the Whig Society of Philadelphia, and Secretary of the Foreign Affairs Committee of the Congress of the United States — before recognising that he had sprung his own trap. Vanity was an insidious thing, yet he even impressed himself. To the devil with Dr Witherspoon and his temperance; there was work to be done, and he drank a toast to his fortieth year.

Paine's burgeoning self-esteem, allied to his excoriation of both Tories and Quakers and his growing contempt for the conservative wing of Congress, were to have far-reaching consequences. In the Year of the Gibbet, however, they were disguised by more pressing events. 'Common Sense', it seemed, had become indispensable to the cause, managing the affairs of his Committee; corresponding with American agents overseas; publicising the case for independence ('by the wish of the Generals, wielding his pen'); and serving as agent with Washington's command.

After his service at the front the army trusted him, which only tempered the jealousy of Paine's critics in Philadelphia. Their whispering campaign as to his loyalty may have failed, but eventually he would make a slip. In the meantime, they could wait while Paine wrote to Franklin in Paris: 'There has been a wonderful and visible chain of matters without the disorder of a single link, in bringing this important affair to an issue that a man must be an infidel not to think heaven had some hand in it.'

The critics bridled that Paine called up heaven when he disavowed his own Church, yet there was no denying his endeavour, and it was never needed more. The affair at Trenton may have lifted the Patriots' morale and Howe wasted the spring in paper manoeuvres, but by June there were clear indications of the British intent. In the Jerseys, Howe's command only waited for the order to strike at Philadelphia, while Burgoyne had already launched his army south out of Canada, with the aim of establishing a foothold on the upper reaches of the Hudson, then linking up with the main British force.

Paine to Wm. Bingham, Agent of Congress to Martinique, 16 July 1777:

We are under some apprehension for Ticonderoga for we have found the enemy unexpectedly come into that Quarter. The Congress have several times had it in contemplation to remove the Garrison from that place — and by Experience we find that Men shut up in Forts are not of so much use as in the field, especially in the highlands where every hill is a natural fortification.

The apprehension was well founded. Ticonderoga, one of the world's most powerful defensive positions and gateway to the Hudson, had fallen to the British ten days before he wrote. On hearing the news, George III burst into the Queen's bedroom elated: 'I've beat them, I've beat all the Americans', by which time Burgoyne's column was a hundred miles further south and Howe was positioning himself for the final thrust against Philadelphia. On 11 September, Washington came close to defeat at Brandywine Creek, but managed to pull back his army under the cover of darkness.

The following day, Paine wrote 'Crisis Four':

The event of yesterday is one of those kinds of alarms which is just sufficient to rouse us to duty, without being of consequence enough to depress our fortitude [though defeatist rumours were already widespread in the city]. It is not a field of a few acres of ground, but a cause we are defending; and whether we defeat the enemy in one battle or by degrees, the consequence will be the same . . .

Shall a band of ten or twelve thousand robbers, who are this day fifteen hundred or two thousand men less in strength than they were yesterday, conquer America, or subdue even a single state? The thing

cannot be, unless we sit down and suffer them to do it . . . Gentlemen
of the city and country, it is in your power by a spirited improvement
of the present circumstances to turn it to real advantage. Howe is now
weaker than before, and every shot will contribute to reduce him. You
are more immediately interested than any other part of the Continent,
your all is at stake.

All that remained was a footnote to Howe:

We fight not to enslave, but to set a country free, and to make room
upon the earth for honest men to live in. In such a case we are sure
we are right; and we leave to you the despairing reflection of being
the tool of a miserable tyrant.

Seven days later, British forward units were on the west bank of the
Schuylkill River on the approaches to Philadelphia. The early morning
was fine and moonlit, the streets crowded with women and children but
there were few signs of military preparations. The place might as well
have been *en fête* as being readied for defence and twelve hours had already
been wasted since Colonel Bayard, Speaker of the Pennsylvania Assembly,
had agreed that, however slight, some evidence of preparations might
have checked the British advance — while given three thousand armed
citizens, the city would give a good account of itself.

The problem, it seemed, was one of command. By noon on the nine-
teenth, Bayard and Colonel Bradford had accepted Paine's plans for
defence but refused to issue any orders while the senior serving officer,
General Mifflin,* remained in the city. Pleading illness, however,
Mifflin declined to take command. The City of Brotherly Love be damned.
It was altogether too generous with its favours. They could ring their
Liberty Bell as well for enslavement as independence — and on Sunday,
21 September, Paine quit Philadelphia *en route* for the Continental Army.

Five days later the city fell without a shot being fired and by 2
October Paine was at Greene's headquarters. Careless of the past, the
old Quaker was spoiling to fight, for Washington planned a night march
on Howe's position at Germantown, with Greene's three divisions (totalling
two-thirds of the entire, 8,000-strong force) leading an enveloping movement against the British flank. Almost twelve months had passed since
the débâcle at Fort Washington and this time there would be no mistakes,
though Paine was to have no part in the venture. Those were his, Nat
Greene's, orders. In the past ten days, the Secretary of the Foreign
Affairs Committee of Congress had travelled far enough. He could wait

until sunrise to enjoy the victory.

And at first it seemed that Greene was right. By five the following morning Paine was riding south through thick fog for Germantown. The countryside was quiet, deserted; a good omen. If Washington's surprise had failed, then there would already be signs of flight. That was always the way of it. The line cracked or an assault failed, and the faint-hearted turned and ran. Instead of which the first news he received came from a solitary horseman riding back to speed up supplies of ammunition. The enemy had broken; the road to Philadelphia was open.

Maybe this was the turning-point. Maybe the times that tried men's souls had finally been redeemed and what then of the sunshine patriots? God knew, a victory was almost too much to hope for and he pressed south towards the sound of sporadic gunfire and imagined Howe's retreat and met up with Colonel Biddle who:

> – called after me that if I went further on that road I should be taken, for the firing I heard was the Enemy's. I never could, and cannot now learn, and believe no man can inform truly the cause of that day's miscarriage.
>
> The retreat was extraordinary. Nobody hurried themselves. Everyone marched at their own pace. The Enemy kept a civil distance behind, sending every now and again a Shot after us, and receiving the same from us . . . The Army had marched the preceding night 14 miles and having full 20 to march back were exceedingly fatigued. They appear to me to be only sensible of a disappointment, not a defeat.

Germantown was an inconclusive engagement. Again Howe failed to press his advantage and again Washington was allowed to regroup with the Continental Army in high spirits. The battle had been a close run thing. They had taken the British head on, and damned near won, while within the week there was news that it could, indeed, be done: that the British were beatable. Since the fall of Ticonderoga in July, Burgoyne's column of 6,000 men had been pushing southwards and by mid-September was only a handful of miles north of Albany. Gentleman Johnny, however, had troubles. He had lost the majority of his Indian scouts, his supply lines were tenuous, and desertions were mounting whilst the American position improved by the day.

Under their new commander, Horatio Gates,* the son of the Duke of Leeds' housekeeper, the Northern Army, with 7,000 men, was well entrenched at Saratoga. On 19 September, Burgoyne launched a reconnaissance in force against the position and, while claiming victory, his losses were double those of the Americans. Three weeks later, on 7 October, he launched his second assault which resulted in total defeat. Ten days later, after his officers had unanimously agreed that they should treat for surrender, Burgoyne drew his sword and handed it to Gates. The northern campaign had ended.

The news of Saratoga reached Europe seven weeks later, and, whilst in London, Burke castigated the government: 'We employed the savages to butcher them, their wives, their aged parents and children and yet, generous to the last degree, they gave our men leave to depart on parole' (an undertaking soon to be broken with the imprisonment of Burgoyne's men); Vergennes in Paris was informing Franklin that France would recognise American independence and Lord Stormont was writing: 'This unhappy event has greatly elated all our secret enemies here and they break out in the most intemperate joy.'

In the autumn of 1777, however, Paine had little time for celebration. On 10 October, the Pennsylvania Assembly had formally invited him to be their agent to Washington's command, writing: 'It is a duty of importance that there are few, however well disposed, who are capable of doing in a manner that will answer all the intentions of it.' Within the week he was out with a patrol in force hunting a British unit on the Schuylkill: 'But the enemy either on the approach of McDougal or on information of it, called in their party and the expedition was frustrated.'

The tactic was becoming commonplace. Like children, Howe and Washington played tip and run across half of Pennsylvania: Germantown; the Schuykill; then Forts Mercer and Mifflin, though the latter were altogether different. It was all very well for Congress to rage that Howe had lost his taste for a fight since discovering the pleasures of Philadelphia when they were safe at York, 70 miles and more from the front. They should have been with Varnum's brigade on the Delaware when the Hessians launched their assault on Fort Mercer, or when the British fleet razed Fort Mifflin before it was overrun. Paine knew, he was there in an open boat before the Fort when the fleet opened fire. For a moment it seemed that the earth itself had exploded and then he watched, helpless, as gun and mortar batteries made a charnel house of the place.

The incident redoubled Paine's standing among the Patriots and temporarily silenced the critics who whispered about the quality of his courage. Momentarily, he was as much hero as propagandist, and in the months that followed there was as much need for the latter as the former. In December, the Continental Army had gone into winter quarters at Valley Forge — a site that had been chosen by speculators, traitors or a 'council of ignoramuses' according to General Kalb.*

Only 18 miles from Philadelphia, the spot was bleak, isolated and inhospitable, and by the year's end Washington was writing bitterly: 'Unless some great and capital change suddenly takes place . . . this army must inevitably be reduced by one or other of these three things. Starve, dissolve, or disperse, in order to obtain subsistence in the best manner they can.' The auguries of the Year of the Hangman had proved ill founded — though a quarter of Washington's force of 10,000 men were to die at Valley Forge before they broke camp in the spring of 1778.

And this was not all. As a young French officer serving with the Continental Army was later to write of Valley Forge: 'The greatest difficulty was that in order to hide this evil from the enemy, it had to be hidden from the people.' Two years had passed since the Marquis de Lafayette,* scion of the French aristocracy, had first been fired by the Americans' cause, but it was not until April 1777 that he sailed from France to join Washington's command — prompting Franklin to write to the Committee of Foreign Affairs asking that he should not be placed in too much danger for the sake of his 'beautiful young wife'.

Paine saw the letter, but Lafayette rejected its advice. Within weeks of landing in the States, and having been commissioned a Major-General by Congress, the 19-year-old was in action against the British. At Germantown, he helped check the British advance and was slightly wounded; and in November routed a superior force of Hessians while on reconnaissance for Greene's division.

A legend was in the making, though a legend with substance. Lafayette symbolised the mood of France, as Lord Stormont knew. At the close of a meeting with Vergennes on Christmas Eve 1777, the French Foreign Minister wondered whether he had anything new to report. 'Nothing from England, Sir,' came the reply, 'but if one half the news of Paris is true, it seems to me very doubtful that I will have the opportunity of wishing Your Excellency a Happy New Year.'

In the twelve months since his arrival in Paris, Franklin had done his job well. The French were making their dispositions for war. All that remained was to choose the time. On 8 January 1778, Vergennes informed Franklin that France was willing to enter into an alliance with the United States. On 13 March the French Ambassador to the Court of St James's delivered a note to the British government stating that Louis had signed a treaty of amity and commerce with the young Republic, and on 4 May Congress ratified both treaties. In principle, if not in practice, England and France were again at war.

The early months of 1778 were hard and Paine spent much of his time on the roads between Valley Forge, the temporary seat of Congress at York, and the home of William Henry at nearby Lancaster. The old house was a good place to rest after two years of campaigning and writing, writing and campaigning. At times the one blurred into the other, so there was no distinguishing between them — between *Common Sense* and the furore which followed its publication; the retreat through the Jerseys and the first of the 'Crisis' papers; the correspondence for Congress and the fall of Philadelphia.

But now there was to be a short-lived pause, though the fifth of the 'Crisis' papers demanded completion. Addressed to Sir William Howe it had begun well: 'To argue with a man who has renounced the use and authority of reason . . . is like administering medicines to the dead, or attempting to convert an atheist by scripture. Enjoy, Sir, your insensibility . . .' — but surely it would wait a little while? In the meantime there was this new scheme to build a ship powered by steam. How long now was it since he told Clio Rickmann back in Lewes that he would as soon build artefacts as revolutions, and here in Lancaster Wm. Henry shared his interests. The Treasurer of the town, Henry was as enthusiastic for independence as science and, between discussing the rumours that surrounded Washington's future as Commander in Chief, the two men argued through the feasibility of applying James Watts's* newly developed steam engine to ships.

The prospect was visionary, of transforming the nature of seafaring, though the discussions always ended with the reality that independence had first to be won — a cause not helped by the secret clamour for Washington's removal. Since the autumn campaign of 1776, the American commander had faced a series of challenges to his authority. First there were the ambitions of Charles Lee who, as his direct subordinate, had divided the Continental Army on its retreat to the Delaware in the hope of discrediting Washington and assuming command from a man who '*entre nous* . . . is damnably deficient'. Then, following Saratoga, a small cabal had begun to tout the qualifications of General Horatio Gates for the post of Commander-in-Chief.

Led by Sam Adams, Thomas Mifflin and Benjamin Rush, the group played on public doubts about Washington's qualities as a commander to screen their private ambitions to regain the leadership of the Revolution. By late 1777, they had circulated an anonymous tract maintaining that: 'The people of America have been guilty of idolatry in making a man their God', while Gates and the most junior Brigadier in the Continental Army, Thomas Conway, were actively conspiring with the politicians to have Washington removed.

By early in the New Year, the cabal was broken — but the memories remained. It was damaging enough that certain Congressmen appeared doubtful in their loyalty to Washington; it was worse that they had publicly attempted to undermine confidence in his command. Washington might not be infallible, but nothing but mischief would come of continually dividing not only the people but the army itself against their commander. The plans for steamships could wait. 'Crisis Five' could not.

The trick was to feature Washington's achievements by exposing Howe's failures. Paine drank and wrote:

> If the principle events of the three campaigns be attended to, the balance will appear strongly against you [Howe] at the close of each . . . At the close of the campaign in seventy-five, you were compelled to retreat out of Boston . . . Through the whole of the campaign of seventy six you had nearly double the forces which General Washington immediately commanded.

And there was the rub, the sheer weight of professional numbers that Howe had put into the field in 1776, when set against the small, and ill-trained army at Washington's command:

> You were formidable. Your military knowledge was supposed to be complete. Your fleets and forces arrived without an accident. You had neither experience or reinforcements to wait for. You had nothing to do but to begin . . .
>
> When I look back on the gloomy days of last winter, and see America suspended by a thread, I feel a triumph of joy at the recollection of her delivery, and a reverence for the characters who snatched her from destruction. To doubt *now*, would be a species of infidelity, and to forget the instruments that saved us *then*, would be ingratitude.

Even a dullard should take the meaning. Washington had saved the Revolution in 1776, and had done the same in 1777:

> You have now, Sir, tried the fate of three campaigns, and can fully declare to England, that nothing is to be got on your part, but blows and broken bones; and nothing on hers but waste of trade and credit, and an increase of poverty and taxes . . . The full amount of your losses since the beginning of the war exceeds twenty thousand men, for which you have nothing in exchange. Our expenses, though great, are circulated within ourselves . . . *Here*, in *this* spot is our business to be accomplished; our felicity secured.

The more so with the new French alliance, though better save that for another time. The business needed careful study, not least as far as England's future strategy was concerned. Paine's fifth 'Crisis' was published on 1 March 1778, 17 days before George III had been formally informed of the alliance. On 18 March his Cabinet met at the home of the Secretary of State for the Southern Department, Lord Weymouth, to discuss the crisis. The French had made it clear that, if the commercial treaty was interrupted in any way, she would 'support the dignity of the flag' and had two fleets in preparation to enforce her promises; meanwhile there were disquieting rumours that Spain was arming herself for war.

With the bulk of her forces pinned down in North America, England faced the prospect of war on two fronts — and Ireland was growing restless again. The war had undermined the fragile Irish economy and, while the Protestant landowners were raising a volunteer movement to garrison the country, it could as well be used to challenge Westminster's authority. Lord North, always a reluctant first Minister, pressed the King to allow him to stand down in favour of Lord Chatham, but George would have nothing of it: 'I would rather lose the crown I now wear than bear the ignominy of possessing it under their [the Whigs'] shackles.'

North stayed, and the Cabinet made its dispositions. Even before final news of the French alliance, a new Peace Commission under the young Earl of Carlisle had been dispatched to treat with Congress, with powers to offer everything the rebels demanded — save independence, and even this was hinted at in a secret clause. Since 17 March, the mission had taken on a new urgency, if only to create time in which the government could implement its revised strategy of retrenching in North America: of reinforcing the garrisons in the West Indies; and, cardinally, of maintaining its maritime supremacy.

By late April, the Cabinet's foresight was well rewarded. On the twenty-seventh, intelligence reached London that a French fleet under Comte d'Estaing had sailed from Toulon for an unknown destination. A month passed before a frigate docked in Portsmouth with reports that d'Estaing had passed through the Strait of Gibraltar on a south-westerly heading. Vice-Admiral Byron was ordered to sail for New York with all speed.

Within two months, the whole course of the war had changed, and by 5 June Paine was writing to Washington of likely British campaign plans:

> As a general opinion prevails that the Enemy will quit Philadelphia, I take the Liberty of transmitting to you my reasons why it is probable they will not.

I put the immediate cause of their evacuation, to be a declaration of War in Europe made by them or against them; in which case their Army would be wanted for other services, and likewise because their present situation would be too unsafe, being subject to being blocked up by France, and attacked by you and her jointly.

Britain will avoid a war with France if she can; which according to my arrangement of Politics she may easily do — She must see the necessity of acknowledging, sometime or other, the Independence of America; if she is wise enough to make the acknowledgment *now*, she of consequence admits the Rights of France to the quiet enjoyment of her Treaty, and therefore no War can take place upon the Ground of having concluded a Treaty with revolted British Subjects.

This being admitted, their apprehension of being doubly attacked, or of being wanted elsewhere, cease of consequence; and they will then endeavour to hold all they can, that they may have something to restore, in lieu of something else which they will demand; as I know of no Instance where conquered Plans were surrendered up prior to, but only in consequence of a Treaty of Peace.

Paine's appraisal was right, though it was soon overtaken by events. Britain was anxious to avert war with France and talk peace with America but on 17 June Admiral Kepple, leading a squadron of 20 sail out of Portsmouth, fired on two French frigates. The two countries were at war again. It was what London feared, yet had anticipated, and on 18 June General Sir Henry Clinton,* who had assumed command of the British land forces from Howe, ordered the withdrawal from Philadelphia on instructions just received from London. In preparation for an extension of hostilities, he was to concentrate his forces in New York — and the long retreat north through the Jerseys began.

If the heavens ever dealt in martial justice, then it was now, and from his old room in Second Street Paine thought back 18 months to echoes of a picket guard reading: 'These are the times that try men's souls.' But now it was the British who retreated north across the Delaware close by Trenton, north across the Rahway, close by Newark, with its ghosts of a broken army and a guttering fire: 'The summer soldier and sunshine patriot will, in this crisis, shrink from the service of his country.'

It was Clinton and the British who were tried now, and it seemed that even the elements were against them. For ten days after the withdrawal from Philadelphia the Continental Army shadowed the flanks of the retreating army. Then at Monmouth on 28 June they struck. The day was hell-fired (Greene later claimed that the temperature had reached 100°

in the sum), and by evening Clinton had lost 1,200 men — more than 60 of sunstroke. If the Royal Brute still pretended to any divinity, he would be hard pressed to explain this, or the value of his German connection for that matter. Within a week of the engagement, close on 500 Hessian deserters had come into Philadelphia and more were still wandering the countryside.

Paine drank to the victory: little wonder that George and his agents were now active for an American peace. A week before Clinton's evacuation of Philadelphia, Lord Carlisle had arrived in the city — bag and baggage, for on best authority it was reported that the party included his wife, and 'the best dancer and skater in London'. The idea appealed. After Monmouth, Carlisle would need to dance a pretty jig, and on thin ice too, and Paine laughed at the mixed metaphor.

Not that the Commission should be lightly dismissed. It could prove damned divisive and already there were rumours that one of Carlisle's party, Mr Johnstone, had attempted to bribe certain Congressmen — one for as much as £10,000. The plot had failed, and Mr Johnstone been exposed, but the thing deserved its epitaph:

> Must he exhibit to a laughing mob,
> A turn-coat patriot conquer'd by a jobb;
> And prove from under his adult'rous pen
> How few are just of all the sons of men?

The doggerel served well, but Carlisle remained dangerous none the less — the more so when he abandoned attempts to negotiate with Congress and appealed to the public above its head. The proclamation, from Clinton's new quarters in New York and dated 3 October, offered a general pardon to all Americans, and a full pardon to all officers serving in the Continental forces who asked for it within 40 days. Paine was incensed, as much by the patronage of the sheet as the realities of the British position. The mischief demanded a reply:

> In the course of your proclamation you say, 'The policy, as well as the BENEVOLENCE OF GREAT BRITAIN, has thus far checked the extremes of war' . . . What you mean by 'the BENEVOLENCE OF GREAT BRITAIN' is to me inconceivable. You have already equalled, and in many places excelled, the savages of either Indies; and if you have yet a cruelty in store, you must have imported it unmixed . . . from the original warehouse of hell.

So much for the benevolence which the British were in no position to offer. Their charity was a chimera, no more. Twelve months before, when Howe took Philadelphia, they might have been in a position to patronise but now:

> Remember at this time you do not command a foot of land on the Continent of America. Staten Island, York Island, a small part of Long Island, and Rhode Island, circumscribe your power, and even these you hold at the expense of the West Indies. To avoid defeat, and prevent a desertion of your troops, you have taken up your quarters in holes and corners of inaccessible security; and in order to conceal what everyone can conceive, you must now endeavour to impose your weakness on us for an act of mercy.

Mercy? They tarred the word, then hoped to dress it with American feathers. Paine drank, there was still much to write: of Clinton's dubious blandishments of serving a rightful sovereign, for: 'You go a-begging with your King as with a brat, or with some unsaleable commodity you were tired of; and though every body tells no, no, still you keep hawking him about'; of the hollow threat of British vengeance, for: 'be assured of this, the instant you put a threat in execution, a counter-blow will follow it'; and of the French treaty, that most of all.

Clinton had styled France as Britain's 'natural enemy' and now, by some strange association, she was to be America's enemy too — as if the Creator himself arranged such things. The charge needed answering, for the alliance was crucial to the Revolution:

> I deny that she [France] ever was the natural enemy of either, and there does not exist in nature such a principle . . . We have a perfect idea of a natural enemy when we think of the Devil, because the enmity is perpetual, unalterable, and unbeatable. It admits of neither peace, truce, or treaty; consequently warfare is eternal, and therefore is natural. But man with man cannot arrange in the same opposition.

Distantly, the watch called the hour, and the words blurred before Paine's eyes. The world was full of them — in the beginning was the word and they multiplied in contention! For tonight, however, he had had enough of them and signing the paper 'Common Sense' Paine went to rest. The sixth 'Crisis' was published in Philadelphia on 20 October 1778, and within weeks Paine was embroiled in a new crisis of his own.

7 'THE WORLD TURNED UPSIDE-DOWN'

Two months before the publication of 'Crisis Six', Silas Deane, until recently an American Commissioner to France, had appeared twice before Congress to explain the internecine affairs of Hortalez et Cie, the Paris-based company established to channel French aid to the Revolution. The hearings had been highly unsatisfactory and, if Deane's friends were to be believed, the matter was by no means closed. Too many reputations were at stake for that, for the whole business smacked of graft and, though Paine held the papers for the Paris mission as Secretary to the Committee for Foreign Affairs, it was the devil's own problem to get at the truth of a matter which had been cloaked in secrecy from the outset.

Only one thing was sure. In the early spring of 1776, at least three months before the Declaration of Independence, the French Foreign Minister, Vergennes, and the adventurer Pierre de Beaumarchais (a darling of Paris society since his authorship of *The Marriage of Figaro* the previous year) had established Hortalez et Cie as a front to supply the Colonists with money and arms, the French government itself having no wish to be seen aiding George III's 'damned rebels'.

Who conceived the idea — Beaumarchais with an eye to personal gain, or Vergennes for the advantage of France — still remained to be determined. Some said one thing, some another, though it was whispered that it was Vergennes who had persuaded Beaumarchais to put his signature to a series of letters to Louis urging his support for the venture by extolling the prospects of defeating England as an ally of America, for: 'to sacrifice a million to put England at the expense of one hundred million is exactly the same as if you advance a hundred to gain ninety nine.'

At first, Louis hesitated. The finances of France were in chaos, the Treasury would be hard pressed to raise such a sum; but Vergennes and Beaumarchais were not so naïve as to suggest that the money should be an outright gift. At least half the sum would be spent on buying arms and munitions from French magazines — then sold at inflated prices to Congress. The idea was appealing, and provided commercial justification for Marie Antoinette's and the court's romanticised intercessions on behalf of the Colonists.

What was more, Vergennes was in correspondence with Arthur Lee,* the American agent in London, who also pleaded the cause on practical grounds for:

We offer to France, in return for her secret assistance, a secret treaty of commerce, by which she will obtain for a certain number of years after peace is declared all the advantages with which we have enriched England for the past century.

Such blandishments, allied to memories of the humiliations imposed on France at the close of the Seven Years' War, were too tempting to resist. In May, Louis agreed to the plan for funding Hortalez and, four weeks before the publication of the Declaration of Independence, Vergennes gave orders to the French Treasury to pay Beaumarchais a million livres in gold — a contribution soon to be doubled by the Spanish government, and trebled by French financiers.

One crucial point, however, remained unresolved. Were France's million livres a gift or a loan? The French government insisted on the former and, when Deane arrived in Paris in mid-July 1776, were quick to assure him that the money was a royal gift. Beaumarchais thought otherwise. Now comfortably installed at the Hôtel des Ambassadeurs de Hollande, he regarded the million as a purely commercial transaction, though emphasising to Lee the generous nature of the scheme.

On 18 July, Beaumarchais met Deane for the first time, and denied that he had already received £200,000 from the French government for the use of Congress. Deane believed him. The British Ambassador, Lord Stormont, did not. On his arrival in Paris, Deane had employed a fellow American, William Bancroft, as his secretary. The arrangement suited Deane admirably, for Bancroft had once been a student of his and now had powerful connections in London — not least with the British government for whom he had agreed to act as an agent for the income of £400 a year.

Within hours of the Beaumarchais–Deane meeting, Bancroft left his first message for the British Ambassador in a hollow tree in the Terrace des Tuileries. It appeared that the immediate plan was to supply the Colonists with enough cannon, muskets, powder, blankets, clothes and shoes for 25,000 men. Incensed, Stormont complained to the French government who, whilst denying all knowledge of the arrangement and protesting that 'You cannot conceive what engines are at work, what wheels within wheels', agreed to issue ordinances against smuggling supplies of war.

It was a gesture, nothing more. By late 1776, Beaumarchais had three frigates laden at Le Havre and, while waiting for favourable weather, he attended a performance of *The Barber of Seville* at the town's small theatre. A British agent in the audience recognised Beaumarchais, reported to Stormont, who again complained to Vergennes and only one of the small fleet, *L'Amphitrite*, managed to slip the French authorities and sail for Portsmouth, New Hampshire. The setback was only temporary, however, and by 1777 Beaumarchais had twelve ships operating out of various French ports.

To Washington, the supplies were a Godsend but for Congress the question still remained — were they a gift or a loan? The Commissioners to France said one thing, assuring Congress in October 1777 'that no repayment will ever be required from us for what has already been given either in money or military supplies'; Beaumarchais said another, sending an agent to Philadelphia for settlement of his bill. Only one man could sift the truths from the half-truths, and, in the spring of 1778, Congress issued an instruction for the recall of Silas Deane.

Deane and the new French Minister, Alexandre Gérard, made the Atlantic passage with Comte d'Estaing's fleet in July 1778, and on 9 August he made his first appearance before a closed session of Congress. Six days later he was given a second hearing which split Congress into pro-Deane and anti-Deane factions leading the President, Henry Laurens,* to regret 'that my fellow labourers had as absolutely taken sides as it can be supposed Gentlemen are capable of in a pure unbiased Assembly'.

The Hortalez affair had all the makings of a first-class scandal which Congress could ill afford. The newly struck French alliance was a sensitive thing, easily disturbed, yet Deane's friends seemed determined to take the issue out of doors which could only serve the British interest, as much by revealing the diplomatic underbelly of the negotiations as by exposing the differences within Congress itself.

As Secretary to the Committee for Foreign Affairs, Paine was at the centre of the dispute. The correspondence with the French mission had always been fragmentary, and it was only in March that he had received five packets dispatched the previous October — three on commercial matters, one to Richard Lee, brother of Arthur Lee, and the other to the Committee for Foreign Affairs: 'these two last Packets had nothing in them but blank white French paper.'

The condition was not unusual. Stormont's agents, more especially Bancroft, had ample opportunity to tamper with official American dispatches, though the blank dispatch which was alleged to have confirmed that the million livres were a royal gift would have been useful to set against Deane's private correspondence to Congress which enforced Beaumarchais's claims for payment. Someone lied, and Paine suspected Deane, a 'vain, desultory, and subtile' man according to British Secret Service reports.

How convenient that he had left all his papers in France on his return to America. How convenient that he had taken a loan from Beaumarchais to pay for the expense of his passage. And how convenient that among his 'friends' in Congress were a number of hidden Tories who, like Deane himself, still dreamt of kingship and connived to embarrass the cause of independence.

As Laurens rightly said, Deane 'would not say nay to any Frenchman who called himself Count or Chevalier' and it was widely reported that while in France he had been actively engaged in trying to recruit a young German princeling to replace Washington as commander of the Continental Army — with, no doubt, the offer of the crown of America if he should succeed.

Little wonder that the man's credentials demanded scrutiny, yet he and his friends still pressed for a wider debate. Without knowing better, the campaign might as well have been orchestrated from Whitehall: Carlisle and his mission suing for peace on honourable terms; Deane and his faction dividing Congress and, with it, the public mind. It seemed that, for the moderates and Tories, independence had gone far enough. They would profit from what George had to give.

The notion was contemptible, the exchange of three years of sacrifice to pleasure the Royal Brute. Paine wrote his seventh 'Crisis' paper to 'The People of England' in November 1778, and dismissed the idea contemptuously:

> The breaking out of hostilities opened a new suspicion in the politics of America, which though at that time very rare, has since been proved to be very right. What I allude to is 'A secret and fixed determination in the British cabinet to annex America to the Crown of England as a conquered country' . . . Reconciliation never appears to have been the wish or the object of the Administration, they looked on conquest as certain and infallible, and under that persuasion, sought to drive the Americans into what they might style a general rebellion, and then crushing them with arms in their hands, reap the rich harvest of general confiscation, and silence them for ever.

The same remained true, though disguised by Carlisle's blandishments, to those who fought for independence with one eye on the enemy, the other on their pocket books, and who now grouped themselves around Silas Deane. Patrician by birth, conservative by inclination, men such as the lawyer John Jay* and the financier Robert Morris* had opposed independence until the movement gained momentum, whilst even then

Morris regarded it largely as a commercial transaction.

No one could deny John Adams's assertion that he had 'an open Temper and an honest Heart' or his skill at managing the finances of the young Republic, but his involvement with Deane in the Hortalez affair was equally indisputable. The thing was indefensible: of commercial interests happy to trade independence for a turn in the market set against the political integrity of men such as Laurens who set a higher price on the Declaration than self-interest; of private greed and public confusion.

What was it that he and Jefferson had discussed in the State House little more than three years, yet so many lives, ago: that all men are created equal and endowed by their Creator with certain inalienable rights; and that among these were life, liberty and the pursuit of happiness? But even then there had been compromise to ease the sensibilities of the moderates. The clause on slaving had been dropped to mock the words themselves.

The trick was always the same, and Paine remembered his father in the workroom at Thetford talking of a time when the gentry had raised England to topple a crown but always with 'an eye to property . . . for if man shall vote equally, men shall soon pass to taking hold of the property of other men'. It was all very well for Monsieur Rousseau and his kind to talk of *égalité*. The notion was an abstraction, no more. In practice it was very different, and here were the oppportunists again in the person of Silas Deane, the men who had doubted Paine's loyalty; had questioned Paine's courage; and had gulled the people with the belief that they, too, deserved a share of life and liberty and the pursuit of happiness — so long as they held the measuring scales.

Four years had passed since he had been carried ashore in Philadelphia; hard years, often savage, but until now never bitter. Then on 5 December Paine read Deane's open letter in the *Pennsylvania Packet* 'to the free and virtuous Citizens of America' denouncing Congress for its ignorance and neglect of foreign affairs.

Four days later, Henry Laurens resigned the Presidency to fight the issue on the floor of the house, to be succeeded by John Jay; and by the month's end a further article under the signature 'Plain Truth' was claiming that, though a stranger to France, it was Deane who had first arranged the American supplies through Hortalez et Cie.

The lie was shameless, and with it came the bitterness. Laurens had gone. The true Patriots were reviled, and the Tories were in the saddle — men who had connived at Washington's removal, who had toyed with Carlisle's peace proposals, who would as soon have a king as liberty. The affair offended all that Paine had campaigned for since the publication of *Common Sense* three years before, since he had first written:

I am inclined to believe that all those who espouse the cause of reconciliation, may be included within the following descriptions. Interested
men, who are not to be trusted; weak men who cannot see; preju-
diced men who will not see; and a certain set of moderate men who
think better of the European world than it deserves, and this last class,
by an ill-judged deliberation will be the cause of more calamities to
this Continent than all the other three.

And he was right; but, while they had dismissed him as a stranger
then, even the children now touched a forelock to Mr Common Sense
in the streets and this time he would Common Sense them for sure. Paine's
latent arrogance, allied to his sense of rectitude (features of his character
which were to have a profound effect on the remainder of his life), sparked
his contempt for the 'certain set of moderate men' whose enmity he had
aroused in the past three years — the slavers: 'man stealing is ranked
with enormous crimes'; the Quakers: that 'knot of men . . . of venomous
cast'; the Tories: 'As disaffection to independence is the badge of a Tory,
so affection to it is the mark of a Whig.'
They were powerful haters, but despising them Paine wrote to expose
Deane's lie:

If Mr Deane or any other gentleman will procure an order from Congress to inspect an account in my office, or any of Mr Deane's friends
in Congress will take the trouble of coming themselves, I will give
him or them my attendance and shew them in handwriting with which
Mr Deane is well acquainted that the supplies he so pompously plumes
himself upon were promised and engaged, and that as a present, before
he ever arrived in France . . .

The rebuttal of Deane's claim appeared on 2 January 1779, and four
days later Paine was called before Congress to explain his charge — on
the insistence of the French Minister, Alexandre Gérard. To maintain the
charade of France's neutrality until the signing of the 1778 alliances and
the subsequent declaration of war, it was essential to refute Paine's allegations. The thing was a farce, all available evidence substantiating his
charge, but the pro-Deane faction under John Jay was in command in
Congress and they were determined to make an example of Paine to press
home their new-found advantage over the radical wing.
On the morning of the sixth, Paine wrote a memorial to Congress:

Understanding that exceptions have been taken to my conduct, which exceptions I am unacquainted with I cannot reply to: I therefore humbly beg leave to submit every part of my conduct public, and private, so far as relate to public measures, to the judgement of the Honble. House to be by them approved or censured as they shall judge proper.

It was exactly what the pro-Deane faction wished to avoid. To open the books of Hortalez et Cie to public inspection, or submit Deane himself to a close examination of the affair, would expose the dubiety of their own case. Yet the problem remained: to silence Paine. The solution was as simple as it was crude. If the man requested a hearing, he should have one; but only one question would be asked. Was he, indeed, the author of the recent offending article signed 'Common Sense'?

Jay put the question, Paine answered 'Yes' and was immediately ordered to withdraw. Twenty-four hours later, Paine submitted a second memorial, and again pressed for a full hearing of the case:

I cannot in duty to my character as a freeman submit to be censured unheard. I have evidence which I presume will justify me. And I entreat this House to consider how great their reproach should be should it be told that they passed a sentence upon me without hearing me, and that a copy of the charge against me was refused to me . . .

I make my application to the heart of every gentleman in this House, that, before he decides on a point that may affect my reputation, he will duly consider his own. Did I court popular praise, I should not send this letter. My wish is that by thus stating my situation to the House, they may not commit an act they cannot justify.

I have obtained fame, honour, and credit in this country. I am proud of these honours. And they cannot be taken from me by any unjust censure grounded on a concealed charge, therefore it will become my duty afterwards to do justice to myself.

The threat was clear, that Paine would take his case out of doors; but a combination of the French interest and the pro-Deane faction within Congress again ensured that he went unheard — the former using the Alliance to shield Beaumarchais's part in the affair; the latter smearing Paine's character for, as Gouverneur Morris* argued, he was 'a mere adventurer from England, without fortune, without family or connections, ignorant even of grammar'.

The charge exactly reflected the mood of the patrician faction. Two years previously they would have hesitated to whisper such sentiments but now they had found a new confidence, and, on 8 January 1779, Paine resigned his post of Secretary to the Committee for Foreign Affairs of Congress and addressed a final letter to its members:

> My wish and my intentions in all my late publications were to preserve the public from error and imposition, to support as far as laid in my power the just authority of the Representatives of the People, and to cordialise and cement the Union that has so happily taken place between this country and France.
>
> I have betrayed no Trust because I have constantly employed that Trust to the public good. I have revealed no secrets because I have told nothing that was, or I conceive ought to be secret. I have convicted Mr Deane of error, and in so doing I hope I have done my duty.
>
> I beg likewise to have it understood that my appeal to this Honourable House for a hearing yesterday was as a matter of Right in the character of a Freeman, which Right I ought to yield up to no power whatever. I return my utmost thanks to the Honourable Members of this House who endeavoured to support me in that Right, so sacred to them and their constituents; and I have the pleasure of saying and reflecting that as I came into office an honest man, I go out with the same character.

After four days of debate behind closed doors, Congress disavowed Paine's exposure of Deane, concluding that Louis 'did not preface the alliance with any supplies whatever sent to America'.

The mendacity of Jay and his clique had saved French honour and Silas Deane, and it was little consolation to Paine that John Adams should write: 'There are certain infallible proofs of vanity, presumption, ambition, avarice, and folly in Mr Deane as to render him unworthy of confidence.' No doubt all that, and more was true, yet what was the value of truth? Deane had lied. Gérard had lied. Jay had lied. And behind closed doors Congress had elevated their lies into a truth, whilst as for himself — and Paine counted the cost of integrity.

It was not so much the loss of the post of Secretary of the Foreign Affairs Committee, or even the $70 a month salary that went with it, more the death of an ideal. How long since he had written: 'The Sun never shined over a greater cause . . . Now is the seedtime of Continental union, faith and honour?' Two years or three, it made little difference. He should have known better, should have heeded Dr Bevis's caution that 'scrupulous people are not suited to great office' and developed a cynicism that was the hallmark of office-holders who believed, with Lord Chesterfield, that politicians neither loved nor hated, simply pursued self-interest.

The thought flavoured the bitterness not so much of his own betrayal, but of his vision — and Paine drank a toast to lost innocence. Confound innocence, Congress had hardly closed their books on the affair before Monsieur Gérard, having been party to his dismissal, came tapping at his door to ask whether he would write for the French cause? Once the man's gall would have astounded him. No longer. The past month had changed all that, and he identified the sudden generosity for what it was: a bribe to keep his silence.

And Paine was correct. In a letter to Vergennes of 17 January 1779, Gérard was writing cynically:

> I foresaw the loss of his office, and feared that, separated from the support which restrained him, he would seek only to avenge himself with his characteristic impetuosity and impudence.
>
> All the means of restraining him would be impossible, considering the enthusiasm here for the license of the press, and in the absence of any laws to repress audacity even against foreign powers. The only remedy, my Lord, I could imagine to prevent these inconveniences, and even to profit by the circumstances, was to have Payne [*sic*] offered a salary in the King's name, in place of that he had lost.

The salary was to be $1,000 a year and: 'You know too well the prodigious effects produced by the writings of this famous personage among the people of the States to cause me any fear of your disapproval of my resolution.' Gérard was right to value Paine's writings and to fear his 'impudence'. In mid-January, Paine made one, brief reference to the Hortalez affair in print, maintaining that he had 'never laboured to prove that the supplies were or are a present', but by early spring had returned to his pursuit of Congressional corruption — to Gérard's dismay and alarm.

In late May, the Minister was writing to Paris:

> In it [an article in the *Gazette*] M. Payne declares that he is the only honest man thus far employed in American affairs and demands that the nation shall give him the title and authority of Censor-general, especially to reform and purify Congress. This bit of folly shows what he is capable of.

Little more than three months after resigning his Congressional office, Paine's high opinion of his own rectitude had reasserted itself. If no other man could call himself honest, then he would appoint himself to the role. In truth, he had asked little enough recompense for his part in events since the first publication of *Common Sense* three years and more ago. That pamphlet alone would have made a tolerable fortune if he had taken an author's normal profits; and since then there had been six 'Crisis' papers, not to mention M. Gérard's bait, from which he had earned nothing at all.

To Paine, the case was indisputable. To his critics it smacked of cant; of a man who reached above himself to pull his betters down. As Gouverneur Morris said, he had neither family nor connections yet, since his first arrival in Philadelphia, he had presumed to dictate to the conscience of the Republic — and its masters. Half a year since, he and Laurens and the radical faction had been party to the charge that Robert Morris was guilty of fraud in his transactions with the French and, though cleared by Congress, Paine still pursued the vendetta, unremittingly.

The winter of 1779 had been hard, the British blockade close and, as imports grew scarce, prices rose. It was a rich field for the speculator and Paine suspected that Morris and Holker, the French Consul-General, were playing the markets for personal gain. In May the suspicions were redoubled with the berthing of the *Victorious* in Philadelphia with the whole cargo down in Morris's name. On 25 May a citizens' meeting appointed a committee to investigate charges of profiteering (specifically by Deane and Morris), and elected Paine to its membership.

Once the issue was opened for debate, the charges against Morris multiplied: that he and Matthew Slough were profiteering from sales of flour; that he and Holker were exploiting the French connection; that purchases for the French fleet were being diverted to private trade. Morris made no attempt to deny his commercial interests (indeed, Congress welcomed his mercantile skills), but during a war it was easy to confuse them with exploitation and, through the summer of 1779, the Citizens' Committee unavailingly searched Morris's accounts and records for concrete evidence of profiteering, while Paine sapped at his reputation in the Philadelphia press.

The city was dividing against itself, the patrician and mercantile interest on the one hand, the radicals on the other, and on 26 July a town meeting came close to violence, though not before declaring that Paine be considered 'a friend of the American cause'. The compliment was appreciated, though it did little to pay his debts, among them the cost of repairing his suit. Walking home late one evening, he had been set on by Slough and his companions, one shouting 'There comes Common Sense', Slough replying 'Damn him, I'll Common Sense him', before tripping him into the gutter.

It made a good story for the coffee houses and taverns, but to Paine the humiliation was deeper than a torn coat, for he was hard pressed to pay the cost of its repair. Since resigning his post with Congress he had worked as a clerk in the office of Owen Biddle, and earned what little extra he could from his writing. It was subsistence living, poor return for a man of whom Ralph Izard, the aristocratic Congressman from South Carolina, was writing:

> America has been fortunate in having her cause supported by so able an advocate as Mr Paine, but it is much to be lamented that she should stand in need of protection from an adopted son, against the assaults of so many of her own unnatural offspring.

Paine's poverty, however, did nothing to dampen his passion for his adopted cause. Through the spring and summer of 1779, he published a stream of articles, arguing one day for the French alliance, on another denouncing 'the mighty bugg of peace'. Meanwhile in private correspondence with Nathaniel Greene he volunteered to visit England as an undercover agent to explain the American case. It was an extravagant notion:

> could a certain person possessed of a knowledge of America, and capable of fixing it in the minds of the people of England, go suddenly from this country to that, and keep himself concealed, he might, were he to manage his knowledge rightly, produce a more general disposition for peace than by any method I can suppose,

and Greene persuaded him to reconsider the venture in view of the hazards involved.

In the meantime, his debts mounted so that by mid-September he was confiding to Henry Laurens:

> I find myself so curiously circumstanced that I have both too many friends and too few, the generality of them thinking that from the public part I have so long acted I cannot have less than a mine to drawn from — What they have had from me they have got for nothing, and they consequently suppose I must be able to afford it.
>
> I know but of one kind of life I am fit for, and that is a thinking one, and, of course, a writing one — but I have confined myself so much of late, taken so little exercise, and lived so very sparingly, that unless I alter my way of life it will alter me.

The moderates and secret Tories in Congress might delight at his misfortune, but in Pennsylvania the mood was different. The summer-long campaign against the speculators had strengthened the position of the popular party; a situation reflected in the political tone of the Assembly which in the three years since the drafting of the State Constitution (in itself the most progressive to be adopted before the French Constitution of 1793) had become increasingly radical. In late September, Paine wrote to the Executive Council requesting a pension for his past services, and six weeks later he was appointed Clerk to the Assembly.

Twenty-four hours later, the Assembly appointed a committee to draft a bill for the abolition of slavery — an echo of one of Paine's earliest campaigns on his arrival in the Colonies, and part reparation for the clause deleted from the Declaration of Independence. In 1775, he had written: 'Under gospel light all distinctions of nations, and privileges of one above another are ceased. Christians are taught to account all men their neighbours, and love their neighbours as they do themselves' — a sentiment recaptured, exactly, in the preamble to the bill:

> It is not for us to enquire why, in the creation of mankind, the inhabitants of several parts of the earth were distinguished by a difference in feature or complexion. It is sufficient to show that all are the work of the Almighty Hand . . . We esteem it a peculiar blessing granted to us, that we are enabled this day to add one more step to universal civilisation, by removing, as much as possible, the sorrows of those who have lived in undeserved bondage.

The words were a trigger to memory: of the dispossessed labourers of East Anglia; of the young lads that came up to London to make their fortune but 'by many small causes' ended on Tyburn's tree; of a veteran who tapped his way down Drury Lane mocking, always, English liberty: 'O, Liberty, Liberty, Liberty; that is the property of every Englishman'; but most of all, of himself.

The bondage was there, always, as if he was snared by the contradictions of his own making: of the rights of man denied by the rights of contract; of the benevolence of God dealt out amongst the creeds so that each held a card to be played in the winning of souls. Once the answers had appeared straightforward, there had been no confusion between the right and the wrong, and yet now, when it seemed that he knew even less than when he began, there was this invitation to him, Thomas Paine, to accept an Honorary Degree from the University of Pennsylvania.

The gesture was laughable — had he not derided honours enough?

— the more so since the Trustees who had unanimously extended the invitation included an Anglican Bishop, a Presbyterian minister, a Lutheran pastor and a Roman Catholic priest. If ever God dealt a powerful hand it was now, and, while he accepted the degree of Master of Arts, the conflict remained to be reconciled.

In the meantime, more urgent business was to hand. The campaign of 1779 had been desultory; in the north, Clinton had done little more than mount a series of skirmishes out of New York; while in the south, d'Estaing had taken the islands of St Vincent and Grenada but had been forced to break off his seige of Savannah, Georgia, in early October. By the year's end, however, the British were planning to take the offensive again — and Washington was ill-prepared.

It was not so much that the reorganisation of the Continental Army in the spring of 1779 had reduced his force by seven regiments, more that provisions were again in desperately short supply. At New Year 1780, Washington was writing:

> The troops, both officers and men, have borne their Distress with a patience scarcely to be conceived. Many of the latter have been four or five days without meat entirely and short of Bread, and very scanty supplies — Some for their preservation have been compelled to maraud and rob from the Inhabitants, and I have it not in my power to punish or reprove the practice. If our condition should not undergo a very speedy and considerable change for the better, it will be difficult to point out all the consequences that will ensue.

There was a punishing familiarity about the appeal. For three years the commander of the Continental Army had been pleading with Congress for improved supplies, and for three years his pleas had gone largely unheeded. The French alliance had improved the situation marginally, though by the early months of 1780 Washington could only field a force of 25,000 enlisted men and late in May (a fortnight after Charleston, South Carolina, had fallen to Clinton with the loss of 5,000 men) Paine was reading Washington's latest dispatch to the Pennsylvania Assembly:

> I assure you, every idea you can form of our distresses will fall short of reality. There is such a combination of circumstances to exhaust the patience of the soldiery that it begins at length to be worn out, and we see in every line of the army the most serious features of mutiny and sedition.

When Paine finished reading there was a 'despairing silence' before a member rose and quietly contemplated that: 'If the account in that letter is true . . . it appears to me vain to contend the matter any longer. We may as well give up first as last.' After five years of war, it seemed that the cost of independence was too high. Washington's command was close to breakdown, many of his men had not been paid for months; inflation was rampant throughout the 13 States, the American dollar was worth one cent; and Jefferson had recently exchanged his annual salary as Governor of Virginia to obtain a new riding saddle.

Bankruptcy rather than defeat in the field threatened to break the Republic — and Paine's response was immediate. Within hours of reading Washington's letter he had drawn his full salary from the Assembly, and enclosed a third of it with a letter to a Philadelphia merchant, Blair M'Clenaghan, proposing the establishment of an army relief fund. That evening, M'Clenaghan read Paine's letter to a meeting held in a city coffee house and by mid-June £300,000 had been raised to establish a bank (later to become the Bank of North America) that was to supply Washington's army throughout the remainder of the war.

For all the success of the fund, however, Paine knew the impossibility of fighting a war on charity. Though it might serve as a temporary expedient, in the long term the Republic's finances had to be placed on a sounder footing. While drumming up American confidence with a short 'Crisis' (the Ninth), published on 9 June 1780 — 'It is the remark of the enemy that everything in America has been done by the force of government, but when she sees individuals throwing in voluntary aids . . . it will convince her that the cause of America stands not on the will of a few, but on the broad foundation of property and popularity' — Paine was working on a series of altogether more radical fiscal proposals.

Until now, he had shown little interest in financial affairs, a subject as alien to his taste as to his temperament. The summer of 1780 was to change that. For four months he steeped himself in the intricacies of finance, reading, amongst other things, a long dissertation on the state of English taxation by Dr Richard Price (a name that was to re-occur later in an even more tempestuous context) before publishing his 'Crisis Extraordinary' on 6 October.

While there was still much to be learned, one thing was already clear, that the whole war resulted solely from English avarice and 'how truly wretched and deplorable would the condition of this country be, were she, by her own remissness, to suffer an enemy of such a disposition, and so circumstanced, to reduce her to subjection'? That much was easily said. The problem was to explain the balance sheet of the Republic in terms that not only those with counting-house minds would undersand. He had found it difficult enough to grasp the complexities himself but now: 'Suppose Britain was to conquer America and, as conquerors, was to lay her under no other condition than to pay the same proportions to her annual revenue which the people of Britain pay, our share in that case would be six million yearly' — and this without mention of the five shillings per gallon tax on rum; the twopence per gallon tax on beer; the six shilling per pound tax on coffee; or the eighteen pence annual window tax.

The English fashion of taxation was punitive, that much, at least, was beyond dispute. But what of the alternative? What of the cost of safeguarding the independence of the Republic?

> I have already stated the number of souls in America to be three millions, and by a calculation I have made . . . the whole expense of the war and the support of the several Governments may be defrayed for two million pounds sterling annually; which, on an average, is thirteen shillings and fourpence per head, men, women, and children, and the peace establishment at the end of the war, will be but three quarters of a million, or five shillings per head.

The arithmetic of the difference was simple enough; it was in raising the money that the difficulty lay:

> that the people do not understand the insufficiency of the taxes to carry on the war, is evident, not only from common observation, but from the construction of several petitions, which were presented to the Assembly of this State, against the recommendation of Congress of the 18th March last, for taking up and funding the present currency at forty for one, and issuing new money in its stead.

As ever, the popinjays of independence wanted their liberty at a discount price. The hope contradicted itself, yet, if he had balanced the costs of defeat, the price of success still had to be paid: 'half of which I propose should be raised by duties on imported goods and prize goods, and the other half by a tax on landed property and houses.' The detail of the scheme was complex (of Congress determining the level of duties to be 'ingrafted . . . in the law of each State'; of individual States determining how to raise their own tax quotas). But ultimately one thing was clear, for whilst: 'The subject . . . was entangled with perplexities, and enveloped in obscurity; yet such are the resources of America, that she wants nothing but a system to insure succcess.'

What of the interim before such a system was agreed, however? The army could not fight a war on charity indefinitely, and, even if his financial package was accepted, it would take time to introduce — if the Republic hadn't gone into liquidation in the meantime. The need was for short-term funding and there was only one place where it could be raised — France.

In the autumn of 1780, as he was completing 'Crisis Extraordinary', Paine wrote to Vergennes asking that the French Treasury should provide Congress with a subsidy or loan of a million pounds per annum. Eighteen months had passed since the alliance had been ratified and, save for d'Estaing's excursions (which had been dilatory enough), France had proved a lackadaisical ally, concerned more with European than trans-Atlantic affairs. Now they could pay the price of their friendship. In Paris, the proposal was received coolly (the war was running the French Treasury ever deeper into debt), but in Philadelphia it received Congressional support.

Colonel John Laurens, son of Henry Laurens, and an aide to Washington, was invited to head an envoy to Paris — and agreed on the understanding that Paine was allowed to accompany him. In a farewell note to Nathaniel Greene, Paine wrote:

> I leave America with the perfect satisfaction of having been to her an honest, faithful, and affectionate friend, and I go with the hope of returning to spend better and more agreeable days with her than those which are passed.

It was a hope that was to be stillborn.

On 11 February 1781, Laurens and Paine sailed from Boston in the *Alliance*. During the two months' passage, the frigate was briefly trapped in an ice pack, and later freed a Venetian merchantman which had been taken prize by a Scottish cutter. Early in March, however, the *Alliance* docked in L'Orient for a reception that was far different from Paine's departure from Europe almost seven years before.

Then he was unknown. Now his reputation preceeded him and among the first men aboard was the Port Commandant, anxious to compliment him on the success of his writings. It was the same throughout the journey to Paris — though in Nantes, where the Mayor and a deputation of leading citizens called on him to pay their respects, one commentator reported: 'He was coarse and uncouth in his manners, loathsome in his appearance, and a disgusting egoist, rejoicing mostly in talking of himself, and reading the effusions of his own mind.'

Careless of the memory of his humiliation by Congress, the old arrogance had reasserted itself. If he had taught the New World the meaning of liberty, then he could teach the Old World its meaning, too, though his audiences in the Paris salons were altogether more sophisticated than those of the Philadelphia coffee houses and taverns. Only three years had passed since Voltaire had been interred in the Pantheon, since Rousseau had died at his cottage in Ermenonville, though a new generation of philosophes carried on their radical traditions.

It was a society that needed few lessons in the theories of the social contract, so long as they remained theoretical. If London was a world of contrasts, then it was far outdone by Paris where the young rakes flaunted like peacocks; where the women of fashion flitted from an opera to a review of the troops before dancing at some ministerial reception then gambling the night away; while at Versailles, the court set the tone for the rest, as if vying in the extravagance of its fashions with the extravagance of the more extreme philosophes.

Arriving in Paris, the talk was still of the birth of a son to the Queen and the great events that surrounded it — the 'Grand Processions to the Cradle', the 'Feasts of Morals' with their prize givings and speeches — though it was fast being displaced by a new sensation. Word had it that the King's brother, Monsieur d'Artois, had new breeches of a fabulous kind such that four, strapping lackeys had to haul him into the air to ensure that he fell into the garment without causing a wrinkle to the fabric — and this for a man who flattered himself on his advanced opinions.

The contradictions were everywhere, yet here were he and Laurens having to bend a knee for French charity. The fight for liberty made for strange companions. The negotiations lasted for three months, and, if Laurens's inexperience in protocol was to draw a reprimand from Vergennes, Lamartine* was later to write that 'the King loaded Paine with favours'. In years to come, Paine was to remember Louis's kindness. In the meantime, there was news of a more immediate sort.

Silas Deane was in Paris counselling anyone who cared to listen (including the agent, Bancroft, who was quick to publish the story in the British press) on the advisability of France breaking her alliance with America. The man was finally exposed for what he was, and on hearing the news even Gouverneur Morris 'hopped around on one leg, swore that they had all been duped, himself among the rest'.

In late May, the mission left Paris — with Paine still toying with his old fancy of visiting England to publicise the American cause. Six years had passed since Burke had written:

Nothing less than a convulsion that will shake the globe to its centre can ever restore the European nations to the liberty by which they were once distinguished. The Western world was a seat of freedom until another, more Western, was discovered; and that will probably be its asylum when it is hunted down in every other part.

Since then much had changed. The American spirit, it seemed, was infectious. In 1778, there had been troubles in Ireland; in 1779, revolutionary disorders in London and only last year 25 English counties had supported a petition from the County of York which, after charging George with 'great and unconstitutional influence which may soon prove fatal to the liberties of this country', requested a root and branch reform of the Exchequer, and those who managed it. The demand was modest enough compared with those of the radical John Jebb (secret ballots, universal male suffrage, annual Parliaments, and equal constituencies), but it was a beginning; whilst if they were to hear from 'Common Sense' . . .

Laurens, whose father was in the Tower of London having been captured *en route* to Holland from Philadelphia, eventually dissuaded Paine from taking such a foolhardy risk, and on 1 June 1780 they sailed from Brest in a convoy of three ships laden with supplies and carrying two and a half million livres in silver. On arriving in Boston in July, 16 oxen teams were needed to haul the money to Philadelphia — whilst Paine found himself penniless.

Seven months before, he had resigned his clerkship of the Pennsylvania Assembly to accompany Laurens, paying for all the expenses of his passage to France out of his own pocket. And now, again, he faced poverty. The irony of his situation was as inescapable as it was bitter.

More than two years before he had lost his post as Secretary to the Foreign Affairs Committee for challenging Deane's lies whilst now, having bailed out the Revolution, he had not even the cost of the repair of Colonel Laurens's boots:

I went for your boots the next day after you left town, but they were not done, and I directed the man to bring them to me as soon as finished, but have since seen nothing of him, neither do I wish him to bring them just now, as I must be obliged to borrow some money to pay for them.

The receptions in Boston and Philadelphia were all very gratifying, but they did nothing to pay the rent. Not that he asked for much and, remembering the luxuries of Paris, Paine wondered that he managed on such a small account. Surely the occasional rum and water and pinch of snuff were small extravagances for a man the Republic lionised for trading in millions with a king? Yet even this seemed too much, and close to starvation Paine wrote to Washington. Five years had passed since they had campaigned through the Jerseys, since the picket guards had read 'Crisis One' on the Delaware, but now the whole tide of the war was turning.

The French mission had eased the supply problems of the Continental Army, the arrears of pay were being made up, and, on 18 October 1781, Yorktown fell to Washington. Since the spring, a British army under Cornwallis had been extending its southern bridgehead in North Carolina and Virginia but in August, and under orders from Clinton, he regrouped his entire command at the mouth of the Chesapeake Bay. It was a trap that would soon be sprung, a French squadron of 29 sail under Admiral de Grasse shutting off the seaward escape route, and a combined American and French force commanding the landward side.

For six weeks Washington tightened the seige about Yorktown and then, on 9 October, the first bombardment of the British positions began. Five days later, two major British strongpoints fell and on 17 October (the fourth anniversary of Burgoyne's surrender at Saratoga) a 100 French and American pieces went into action against the British positions — drowning the call for a parley tapped out by a redcoat drummer on the parapet before the British lines.

Forty-eight hours later, Cornwallis surrendered his force of 8,081 men, as a regimental band played the old British marching song, 'The World Turned Upside-down':

> If buttercups buzzed after the bee,
> If boats were on land, churches on sea,
> If ponies rode men and if grass ate the cows.
> And cats should be chased to holes by the mouse,
> If summer were spring and the other way round
> Then all the world would be upside-down.

The news stunned London and, in the first week of March 1782, the Commons passed a motion that: 'The House would consider as enemies to His Majesty . . . all those who should advise, or by any means attempt, the further prosecution of the war on the continent of North America.'

It was the end of North's twelve-year ministry and, while George threatened to abdicate if there was any change in his North American policy ('His Majesty therefore with much sorrow finds He can be of no further Utility to His Native Country which drives Him to the painful step of quitting it for ever'), his bluster failed. There was no longer any escaping the inexorability of events. Effectively, the War of Independence ended at Yorktown — and, momentarily, the one-time fears of Washington's deification were realised.

Throughout the 13 United States the commander's name was toasted, while in France the King decreed that: 'All inhabitants of Paris will illuminate on November 27 the fronts of their houses to celebrate with due respect the great victory gained in America . . . over the English, by the armies of the King commanded by General Washington.' The man had risen high, but surely not so high as to have forgotten 'Common Sense'?

From his old lodgings in Second Street, Philadelphia, Paine wrote to Washington on 30 November. The words were hard to come by. He had begged for America, but never for himself, and, though penniless, he still had his pride. Some said too much, and damned if he'd ask for charity now. Better to speak frankly:

> I never thought (if I thought at all on the matter), but that as I dealt generously and honourably with America, she would deal the same by me. But I have experienced the contrary — and it gives me much concern, not only on account of the inconvenience it has occasioned to me, but because it unpleasantly lessens my opinion of the character of a country which once appeared so fair, and it hurts my mind to see her so cold and inattentive to matters which affect her reputation.

As his own case did. While American fortunes waxed, so his waned. Once the Republic had been hard pressed to pay the price of his talents. Now it was different. Now the financial crisis was resolved and the war almost won.

> While it was everybody's fate to suffer I cheerfully suffered with them, and tho' the object of the country is now nearly established and her circumstances rising into prosperity, I feel myself left in a very unpleasant situation. Yet I am totally at a loss what to attribute it to; for wherever I go I find respect, and everybody I meet treats me with friendship; all join in censuring the neglect and throwing blame on each other, so that their civility disarms me as much as their conduct distresses me.

The room was cold, it promised to be another hard winter, and there was little point in being further chilled:

> In this situation I cannot go on, and as I have no inclination to differ from the country or tell the story of her neglect, it is my design to get to Europe, either France or Holland . . . after all there is something peculiarly hard that the country which ought to have been to me a home has scarcely afforded me an asylum.

Paine's sense of exile was strong. In Thetford, the exile from his family and his father's faith; in London, the exile from his workmates in Mr Morris's staymaking establishment with their long days and bawdy nights; in Lewes, after the deception of belonging, the exile from his home and friends; and now, again, the exile from America. Where did he belong, or was he cursed to be like the wandering Jew always looking for a place to rest?

Surely that wasn't the way of it. He was no vagrant wanting the world to remain as it was, as long as he could shirk its responsibilities. The reverse. How long was it since he had written in his note on the Excise that: 'The rich in ease and affluence, may think I have drawn an unnatural portrait, but could they descend into the cold regions of want, the circle of polar poverty, they would find their opinions changing with the climate?' Eight years, maybe nine? Yet the same remained true; that he was an exile from the system, because he wanted the system changed. Then he would find a home.

Christmas and the New Year passed before Paine heard any news of his letter to Washington, then, on 26 January 1782, he was asked to a meeting with Robert Morris, now Superintendent of Finances. Eighteen months had passed since Morris had been close to disgrace, in part as a result of Paine's campaign against speculators. Now the situation was reversed, but the 'Financier of the Revolution' bore Paine no grudge and by February the two men were meeting with Gouverneur Morris to discuss the prospect of Paine again becoming a propagandist for the American cause — for a salary of $800 a year, and with no restrictions being placed on what he wrote. On 10 February, Paine received a formal invitation to accept the post, signed by Washington, Robert Morris and Robert Livingston (Secretary of the Committee for Foreign Affairs):

> The subscribers, taking into consideration the important situation of affairs at the present moment, and the propriety and even necessity of informing the people and rousing them to action; considering also

the abilities of Mr Thomas Paine as a writer, and that he has been of considerable utility to the common cause by several of his publications: They are agreed that it will be much in the interest of the United States that Mr Paine be engaged in their service for the purpose above mentioned.

Within the month, Paine had completed 'Crisis Ten' — 'On the King of England's Speech'. After all that had happened, after Saratoga and Yorktown, after the call from Parliament to 'end the prosecution of war', George still had the gall to claim that 'no endeavours have been wanting on my part . . . to restore to the deluded subjects of America, that happy and prosperous condition which they formerly derived from a due obedience to the laws' — and to call up 'the protection of Divine Providence' to bolster his claims.

By what right Divine? By contract, or arms — Locke's contract; Cumberland's* arms? For a moment he was back in Thetford, an eight-year-old listening to Joseph telling of the Young Pretender's long retreat to Culloden, of Cumberland's victory, and the butchery which followed so that 'in a few days there was neither house, cottage, man nor beast to be seen within the compass of fifty miles; all was ruin, silence, and desolation'.

For America, it was a cautionary tale, as much because Cumberland was George's uncle, as because of England's own fears that the constitution was again imperilled by royal ambitions. Like a whirligig of power, it turned endlessly on itself: and men had once fought believing that 'God, the mighty Leveller' would make all men equal, yet the Commonwealth had come close to despotism; and the Glorious Revolution was 'An Act for declaring the rights and liberties of the subject', yet had soon become a tool of oligarchs; and now, here again, was George calling up Providence in the name of Hanoverian ambition.

The process appeared irrevocable and he looked out across the spires and steeples of Philadelphia and counted their Gods and wondered, an instant, whether this is where independence would lead — to Liberty subordinate to power? But that was to speculate. For the present it was enough that America wanted nothing of George's 'happy and prosperous condition', rather: 'Let Britain leave America to herself and she asks no more. She has risen into greatness without the knowledge and against the will of England, and has the right to the unmolested enjoyment of her own created wealth.'

Once the ambition may have seemed far-fetched. No longer. Clinton was shut up, tight, in New York; there was mounting talk of a British peace initiative; and Washington felt confident enough to leave his staff and spend an increasing amount of time in Philadelphia. The battle front was now political and, on 17 March, Paine wrote to Morris and Washington:

> You will do me a great deal of pleasure if you make it convenient to yourself to spend part of an evening at my apartments, and eat a few oysters or a crust of bread and cheese; for besides the favour you will do me, I want much to consult with you on a matter of public business, tho' of a secret nature.

Two topics rather than one dominated the conversation: the state of American taxation, and reports that Britain was attempting to buy France out of her alliance with America. As to the former, while 'We began with paper, and end with silver and gold', there was still a need to raise finance to meet interest on foreign loans. As to the latter, twelve months had passed since Vergennes had shown Paine the first overtures towards an Anglo-French *rapprochement*, and the pressures for a settlement mounted daily. Both demanded urgent attention, but the second was the more pressing and, on 22 May, Paine published 'Crisis Eleven' to expose 'an insidious era in British politics'.

The material was all there, a mare's nest of intrigue: of British emissaries in Paris trading with both Franklin and Vergennes in an attempt to persuade one to abandon the other; of Whitehall's secret approach to the Spanish Court to act as an intermediary 'for the purpose of negotiating a peace with France, leaving America out of the question'; of the proposition to convene a congress to discuss peace proposals — without any American representation.

Until the French alliance, George's ministers had bent all their efforts on dividing America against herself and, having failed in this: 'A peace with France and Spain she anxiously solicited; but America, as before, should be left to her mercy.' Mercy? George's actions had made the word meaningless in the lexicon of humanity, and it was to the credit of France ('with an open, noble, and manly determination') that she would hear no proposition for a separate peace.

And now, with the prospect of military humiliation on both sides of the Atlantic, there was talk that Britain would

> try on America the same insidious arts they tried on France . . . We sometimes experience sensations to which language is not equal. The conception is too bulky to be born alive, and in the torture of thinking we stand dumb. Such must be the sensations of America, whenever

Britain, teeming with corruption, shall propose to her to sacrifice her faith.

As little as a decade ago, conciliation might have served. That time was long passed. Then a little humility from George and his ministers might have saved an empire. Now it was too late. In Paris, the first tentative steps for a negotiated peace had begun and in early August, General Guy Carleton, replacing Clinton in command of British forces following the débâcle at Yorktown, was writing to Washington:

> A mail has now arrived, sir, by authority, that negotiations for a general peace are now commenced at Paris. And we are further, sir, made acquainted that his Majesty, in order to remove any obstacle to that peace which he so ardently wishes to restore, has commanded his ministers . . . that the independence of the Thirteen United Colonies, should be proposed to him in the first instance, instead of making it a condition of a general treaty.

While George might rail at his new ministers one moment, and indulge in the melancholy of his own ill humour the next, the thing was virtually over, done. To all intents, American independence was secure, and already the wiseacres had begun to pick over the bones of the affair. Only recently, a translation of Abbé Raynal's *Revolution of America* had come to hand which asserted that there was no moral justification for the American rising; that the King and his ministers did, indeed, have the power 'to bind America in all cases whatsoever'.

Surely the cleric could understand that the Declaratory Act knew no limits, that there was no despotism to which the law did not extend. 'It stopped no where. It went to everything. It took in with it the whole life of man . . . It is the nature of law to demand obedience, but this demanded servitude.'

And if this was the British case, what of the American? While one passed a Declaratory Act, the other published a Declaration of Independence. Was not that distinction enough; that, whilst George demanded servitude, America demanded liberty — not for the benefit of a few, but in the interests of the whole? It was this that made the Revolution like no other — 'that America had no particular family to set up or pull down, that nothing of personality was involved in the cause'. Here the value of liberty, the nature of government and the dignity of man were known and understood, and it was an attachment to these principles that produced the Revolution as a natural and unavoidable consequence.

This was the heart of the matter, and, while the cleric might toy with subsidiary causes, it was this that posterity should understand or the memory of the men who had fought, and died, would be traduced. Paine completed his 'Letter of Abbé Raynal' in early September and mailed 50 copies to Washington with an ironic covering note on the English concept of time:

> The British have accustomed themselves to think of seven years in a matter different from other portions of time . . . They serve seven years' apprenticeship — they elect their Parliament for seven years — they punish by seven years' transportation, or the duplicate or the triplicate of that term — they let their leases in the same manner, and they read that Jacob served seven years for one wife, and after that seven years for another . . .
>
> They have now had seven years of war, and are no further on the Continent than when they began . . . The superstitious and populous part will therefore conclude that *it is not to be*, and the rational part of them will think they have tried an unsuccessful and expensive venture long enough . . . unless, consistent with their former sagacity, they should get over the matter by an act of parliament *'to bind TIME in all cases whatsoever',* or declare him a rebel.

The notion appealed — of George reviewing time and, finding it tiresome, holding a Tyburn Fair — though there was talk that public executions were soon to be abolished. It seemed that, since North's departure and the arrival of Shelburne's* ministry, things were changing, if not always to the King's liking. The new men, following nationwide support for Mr Burke's proposals for economical reform, had introduced legislation to curb the power of the crown by prohibiting government contractors from taking seats as MPs; by curbing government expenditure; and by disenfranchising the officers of the Customs and Excise.

In his room in Philadelphia, Paine remembered the Lewes elections, and his own role in them. It had been all very well to serve in the Excise, but the price it had demanded was the surety of a man's vote. He had had difficulty enough in squaring his conscience to the practice then; now, having come to know independence, he reviled it. If Shelburne and his ministers truly sought reform, they should introduce secret ballots and extend the franchise, rather than trimming it so that no more than one man in fifteen could go to the polls; the one would ensure that every man's vote was his own affair; the other would diffuse corruption so thinly that it would no longer be a cause for concern. As it was, the Whigs simply decked their concern to curb George's power with the name of reform, then declared with Burke: 'I cannot, indeed, take upon me to say that I have the honour to follow the sense of the people. The truth is, I met it on the way, while I was pursuing their interest according to my own ideas.'

The sentiment was admirable, so far as it went, but it did not go far enough. There was little of the people's interest in the bill, and less of their representation. Yet there was no diminishing its significance. The Whigs had tightened the strings around George's purse, which was always a painful experience as Paine knew only too well. While there might be a million or two difference between his own and George's prospects, it was damnably hard to adjust to economies as much in private as in state affairs.

Six months had passed since he had written on the state of American taxation, three since his meeting with Washington and Morris, but there was still no resolution to the pressing problem of raising finance to pay the interest and capital on America's overseas debts. Although Congress had recommended a 5 per cent duty on all imported goods, the proposal demanded the unanimous consent of the 13 States under the Articles of Confederation — and Rhode Island steadfastly refused to accede to the scheme.

With Morris's approval, Paine visited the State capital, Providence, and, in an attempt to contain the controversy, limited his appeal to the Rhode Island press. Under the pseudonym 'A Friend of Rhode Island and the Union' he argued that, if America had raised capital to gain its independence, it must make arrangements for repayment — and that a 5 per cent duty was a small enough sacrifice to pay for liberty. The appeal made little impression and, when his identity was revealed, Paine was accused of being a tool of Congress, at the expense of local autonomy — an augury of the bitter controversy that was soon to wrack the Republic.

As it was, the recalcitrance of the Rhode Islanders was temporarily dwarfed by other events. In September 1782, Shelburne had authorised his agents to treat with the American mission in Paris; in November, the terms agreeing American sovereignty were agreed by both parties; in January, Britain signed preliminary peace articles with France and Spain; and on 11 April 1783, Congress officially proclaimed that hostilities were at an end.

Eight days later, Paine published 'The Last Crisis': 'The times that tried men's souls are over — and the greatest and completest revolution that the world ever knew, gloriously and happily accomplished.' The achievement defied comprehension, yet peace demanded as much as war.

Eight years had passed since America set out, and everything about her wore the mark of honour: 'Her cause was good. Her principles just and liberal. Her temper serene and fine.'

It was a rich inheritance. None ever began with higher character than America, and none was under a greater obligation to preserve it:

> It would be a circumstance ever to be lamented and never to be forgotten, were a single blot, from any cause whatsoever, suffered to fall on a revolution, which to the end of time must be an honour to the age that accomplished it; and which has contributed more to enlighten the world, and diffuse a spirit of freedom and liberality among mankind, than any human event (if this may be called one) that ever preceded it.

Cynics might say he exaggerated, but it was no more than the truth. Hadn't Irish Protestants and Catholics only recently united to demand improved representation in Westminster? Only last year, hadn't the burghers of Geneva allied with their workers to seize power in the old republic in an attempt to introduce a more liberal constitution (an appropriate enough gesture for Monsieur Rousseau's 'City state'). And even now, there were reports of an insurrection being raised under the banner of liberty in the United Provinces. It seemed that the spirit of independence was infectious.

Yet already, there were those who would divide the sovereignty of the new Republic piecemeal, and, remembering Rhode Island, Paine poured himself another rum and wrote:

> But that which must forcibly strike a thoughtful penetrating mind, and which includes and renders easy all the rest, is the UNION OF THE STATES. On this, our great national character depends. It is this which gives us importance abroad and security at home . . . Sovereignty must have power to protect all the parts that compose and constitute it; and as UNITED STATES we are equal to the importance of the title, but otherwise we are not . . . Our citizenship in the United States is our national character. Our citizenship in any particular State is only our local distinction. By the latter we are known at home. By the former to the world. Our great title is, AMERICANS.

It was done. What had been begun so long before was complete. Alone, Paine toasted the memories: to Dr Rush and that first meeting in Aitken's bookshop; to Jefferson and the long summer days when they had talked of a Declaration of Independence; to a shattered army that marched south through the Jerseys to Trenton; to Gates at Saratoga, and Washington at Yorktown, and Louis at Versailles; and to the nameless thousands who had died without having known independence — and signed the work 'Common Sense'.

Only one thing marred Paine's pleasure: money. With peace, the contract arranged by Washington and Morris came to an end, and what little capital he had had been spent on buying a home at Bordentown. Set in quarter of an acre of ground, the house was small, but it was close to the home of his old friend, Colonel Joseph Kirkbride. The two Quakers had known each other since they had helped frame the Pennsylvania constitution seven years before, and they shared much in common; not least, an interest in science.

But while peace provided Paine with the opportunity of renewing his old interests (eight years had passed since the early days of the *Pennsylvania Magazine* when he had written on subjects as diverse as the utility of a new electrical machine and the instructional value of a cabinet of fossils), it was continually overshadowed by the fear of poverty. As early as June 1783, Robert Morris was advising him to approach Congress for a financial settlement for past services, and having received no reply he wrote again four months later pointing out that: 'the State I have lived in scarcely knows me as a citizen or anything but the Tax-book.'

Congress agreed, and appointed a committee to investigate Paine's case which, in its turn, concluded that he should be appointed official historian of the Revolution — but took no action on the proposal. For the third time in as many years Paine was close to destitution. Although specious, Congress did have grounds for his discharge during the Deane affair. Although inconsiderate, Pennsylvania needed to appoint a new clerk during his absence in Paris. But now . . .

Paine considered the cost of his services to the Republic, and wondered that he had sold himself so cheap. When they had needed 'Common Sense', they had been easy enough with their compliments; yet, once their ends were served, they were quick to foreclose on their debt. America had her independence; as for Thomas Paine, he was expected to live on a reputation he could no longer afford. In the streets, folk still pointed him out as the 'author of our liberties' — yet he could hardly meet the price of fresh ink. In the taverns, well-wishers still stood him drinks — though he was hard pressed to repay the hospitality. To the devil with common sense; it showed few returns save, perhaps, for the friends that he had made when there was only independence to play for.

They, at least, still remembered and in late September he was writing to accept an invitation from Washington to visit his headquarters at Rocky Hill:

> I am hurt by the neglect of the collective ostensible body of America, in a way which it is probable that they do not perceive my feelings . . . Their silence to me is something like condemnation, and their neglect must be justified by my loss of reputation, or my reputation supported at their injury; either of which is alike painful to me.

The mood at Rocky Hill was carefree, the lifestyle elegant. Only two years before these men — George Morgan and Ben Lincoln and the rest — had wintered at Valley Forge. Now they dined in style, and drank French wine from silver cups. No one could begrudge them their pleasures, but their circumstances contrasted strongly with his own condition and, on Guy Fawkes night 1783, Washington and Paine rode together in a scow down the creek below the camp and, while one set the water alight, the other remembered Lewes many years ago.

Then they burned other Gods, not these; and as Washington ordered the troops to stir the river bed to release more of the ignitable gases, Paine saw in the flames the ghosts of the Liberty Boys who had roared down the long hill of the small Sussex town to torch their effigies before hurling them into the Ouse, crying: 'No Pope; No Popery here.'

Scientific experiment was all very well, but this was to forget that there were altogether more dangerous forces in play. Only recently, Lord Gordon* had raised a mob which had burned out half London in the name of their Protestant God. Now it seemed that they were bent on deifying Washington, too. In the past days, all the talk was of the new Egyptian statue that Congress had ordered to be raised to his name, while one visitor to headquarters had been heard to remark that: 'No honours short of those which the deity vindicates to himself can be too great for Genl. Washington.'

Temporal or spiritual, spiritual or temporal, there seemed little sense in affairs. Yet Washington himself was little changed. Wrapped in a cloak against the night, he pursued his experiment as single-mindedly as he had discussed Paine's problems only that afternoon. He would do what he could to help, though it must be remembered that he was not necessarily the most fortuitous of allies, that there were still some who suspected the designs that others foisted upon him. How long was it since Sam Adams, and Rush and the rest had accused America of idolatry 'in making a man their God', or Colonel Nicola had suggested that he accept the crown of America?

What was it that he had written then: 'Let me beseech you, if you have any regard for your country, concern for yourself or posterity, or regard for me, banish these thoughts from your mind.' Yet they still persisted, whilst others continued to suspect him of ambitions which he had never entertained. It defied comprehension, but they would not grasp that he had had enough of power, and what's more, the climate was not suited to Egyptian draperies!

In the darkness the two friends laughed together, and, within the week, Paine had returned to Bordentown. A month later, on 4 December 1783, Washington bade farewell to his troops, returned his commission to Congress, declared he was 'taking leave of all employments of public life' and, after more than eight years of soldiering, retired to his home at Mount Vernon.

But Washington did not forget his pledge to Paine. In the spring of 1784, New York was the first American state to recognise his services by making him the gift of a farm and 267 acres (formerly the property of a Tory loyalist) at New Rochelle which eased his immediate financial pressures — though Congress still failed to recognise his claims, or implement their own proposal to commission a history of the Revolution. Four days before Paine took possession of New Rochelle on 16 June, Washington was writing to James Madison*:

Can nothing be done in our [Virginia] Assembly for poor Paine? Must the merits and services of Common Sense continue to glide down the streams of time, unrewarded by this country? His writings have certainly had a powerful effect upon the public mind — ought they not then to meet an adequate return? He is poor! He is chagreened! and almost if not altogether in despair of relief.

Twice within the following month, the Virginian legislature voted out bills to make land grants to Paine, and by early July Madison was writing to Washington:

Should it finally appear that the merits of the man, whose writings have so much contributed to enforce and foster the spirit of independence in the people of America, are unable to inspire them with a just beneficence, the world, it is to be feared, will give us little credit for our policy as for gratitude in this particular.

But, while Virginia spurned Paine, and Congress still quibbled over his settlement, Washington continued to lobby on his behalf. By November he was in touch with John Dickinson, President of the Pennsylvania Assembly, and in March 1785, the legislature voted him £500, referring the matter of additional payments to Congress. Together with the farm at New Rochelle and the house at Bordentown, Paine was temporarily secure and, when Congress moved to New York in the summer, he could afford to follow them.

The euphoria of victory remained (it was only six months before that the last British squadron had sailed from the harbour), the city was *en fête*, and for the first time in his life Paine could afford the price of self-indulgence. At 48 years of age, a well-cut figure and newly elected to the prestigious American Philosophical Society, he was lionised by the New York establishment. Twelve months before, he had been hard pressed to pay his bills. Now he spent his days between Congress and the home of Commodore Nicholson, headquarters of the leading republicans in the city.

The contrast was extraordinary, and again Paine's confidence burgeoned. There was little point in dwelling on the past. Here men recognised him for what he was; not for any title or honour but as plain 'Common Sense', the man who had taught America the alphabet of independence. That was enough to satisfy any man's vanity, though perhaps the letter to Franklin was a little strong, smacking more of arrogance than humility to his former patron:

> Should Fate prolong my life to the extent of yours, it would give me the greatest felicity to have the evening some resemblance of what you now enjoy . . . so far as I have hitherto gone, I am not conscious of any circumstance in my conduct that should give you one repentant thought for being . . . my introducer to America . . . It would give me great pleasure to make a journey on purpose to see you, but an interesting affair I have with Congress makes my absence at this time improper.

The note would have to suffice; there was other business to hand, for only recently Congress had agreed that he was entitled to 'a liberal gratification from the United States' and now the matter was finally to be decided. Paine's own view was that he was entitled to a reimbursement of $6,000 but, on 6 October, Congress halved the sum and resolved to pay him $3,000. It was a niggardly gesture, the more so in the light of the intense controversy that was already brewing over the funds of the

Bank of North America.

In the winter of 1780, when Washington's command at Valley Forge had been decimated by lack of supplies, Paine had given $500 of his salary as Clerk to the Pennsylvania Assembly to establish a subscription fund for the Continental Army. The gift was the first deposit in the Bank of North America whose charter the Assembly of Pennsylvania was now threatening to remove. Paine was incensed. The proposal was 'an ill digested, precipitate, impolitic, faithless piece of business, in which party and prejudice is put for patriotism'.

Paine's vehement outburst disguised a paradox that he could not disguise from himself. The Assembly was only reflecting the public's sentiment against what they regarded as the vested interests of the Bank. As a radical populist, there was no question as to where his loyalty should lie, yet reason demanded otherwise. In itself, the affair of the Bank was of small concern though, through the winter of 1785, it came to symbolise all the rest — the faith in man and reason on which Paine had built his creed.

And there, again, was the paradox. Once, and not so distantly, he had been the voice of the people, but now all he heard was the mob. It wasn't the first time he had known the sound but then they had echoed his own sentiments — and while all London had cried for 'Wilkes and Liberty', all America had chorused 'No Taxation Without Representation'. And subscribing to their reasons he, Tom Paine, had agreed. But now it was different. Now Tom Paine and reason stood apart from the rest. No question that the paradox had to be reconciled or nothing remained, and Paine began to write:

> In republics, such as those established in America, the sovereign power, or the power over which there is no control and which controls all others, remains where nature placed it — in the people; for the people of America are the fountain of power . . . This sovereignty is exercised in electing and deputing a certain number of persons to represent and act for the whole and who, if they do not act right, may be replaced by the same power that placed them there.
>
> In a republic, the people retaining the sovereignty themselves, naturally and necessarily retain freedom with it: for wherever the sovereignty is, there must the freedom be; the one cannot be in one place and the other in another.

Dr Bevis had been dead these many years but he would have approved the sentiment, for surely it was no more than what Monsieur Rousseau had called the General Will? The curse was that it did little for his case. Without qualification, the notion was no more than a licence for anarchy. Even Rousseau himself had recognised the point for hadn't he written that, if the General Will was the ruler of all, then it might be necessary to compel a man to be free?

The idea was absurd. That way lay slavery to the sovereignty of the mob for: 'Despotism may be more effectually acted by many over a few, than by one over all.' But what of the alternative? How could the sovereignty of the people be safeguarded as much in the people's interests as against the innate despotism of the General Will? Since time immemorial it seemed that men had argued the question and that only one answer was reasonable, possible. Paine drank, and wrote:

> When a people agree to form themselves into a republic . . . they mutually resolve and pledge themselves to each other, rich and poor alike, to support and maintain this rule of equal justice among them. They therefore renounce not only the despotic form, but the despotic principle, as well of governing as being governed by mere will and power, and substitute in its place a government of justice.
>
> By this mutual compact the citizens of a republic put it out of their power, that is, they renounce, as detestable, the power of exercising at any future time, any species of despotism over each other, or doing a thing, not right in itself, because a majority of them have strength of numbers to accomplish it.

Surely, that was the essence of the Declaration of Rights that prefixed the constitution of Pennsylvania itself, itself an echo of its leveller antecedents: that under law, all men were born equally free and independent, and had certain natural and unalienable rights including the freedom to enjoy and defend life and liberty? Nine years had passed since he and Kirkbride had helped draft the contract, but then, as now, all turned on the defintion of law:

> All laws are acts, but all acts are not laws. Many of the acts of the assembly are acts of agency and negotiation . . . An act of this kind, after it has passed the house, is of the nature of a deed or contract, signed, sealed, and delivered; and subject to the same general laws and principles of justice as all other deeds and contracts are; for in a transaction of this kind, the State stands as an individual and can be known as no other character in a court of justice.

Critics might say that this was special pleading but the thing was as much a defence of the social contract ('the people in their original compact of equal justice or first principles of a republic, denounced as despotic, detestable and unjust, the assuming a right of breaking and violating their engagements, contracts and compacts . . . with each other') as of the Bank's charter (a 'contract entered into, and confirmed, between the State on the one part and certain persons included therein on the other').

The reasoning was close, compact. The irrational had been made rational, but a suspicion remained — that he, Tom Paine, had betrayed himself. The notion disturbed him. He was 'Common Sense' and no casuist, and the argument read common sensically. Yet somewhere within the reasoning a contradiction remained.

At the Headstrong in Lewes it had been straightforward enough. In practice it was different. What with the General Will and the Social Contract and the Sovereignty of the People, the thing was a regular cat's cradle of logic which would take time to unravel. Meanwhile, the paper would have to stand.

In February 1786, Paine published his *Dissertations on Government and Affairs of the Bank*, an extended attempt to reconcile his conflicting attitudes towards government and a precursor to his later controversy with Burke. The work contributed to an explosive debate (the critics largely ignoring Paine's rationale to accuse him of being 'an unprincipled author whose pen is let out for hire'), but eventually the dispute was settled in the Bank's favour — Paine's hostile biographer, Cheetham, accepting that the *Dissertations* effectively prevented the Pennsylvania Assembly's 'act of despotism'.

The spring of 1786 was a good time for Paine. At last he had the peace to absorb himself in the sciences for, like 'many thousands who had borne a part in that memorable Revolution, I returned with them to the enjoyment of a quiet life'. More than eleven years had passed since he had first come ashore in Philadelphia, more than ten since the publication of *Common Sense*, and the years between had been such a pell-mell that it seemed that time itself had become foreshortened in his mind. How long was it since he had ridden the shores of the Hudson and seen Howe's fleet riding at anchor below? When was it that he and Henry Laurens had first explored the intricacies of Mr Deane's affairs? Not that it mattered. Now, at last, he was his own man with time to call on Colonel Kirkbride and discuss his latest idea.

While in Paris, four years before, he had heard talk of Monsieur de Montpetit's scheme to build a single span, iron bridge and wondered whether the idea could be applied to the Schuylkill River which was a torrent of ice floes through the winter? The arch would have to reach 300 feet, but if only the practices of nature were applied it might well be possible to reduce the weights involved to increase the strength of structure: 'as is evidenced in the bones of Animals, Tails of Birds, Reeds, Canes etc, which were they solid with the same quantity of Matter, would have the same weight with a much less degree of Strength.'

By June, Paine had completed two models of his bridge (one wooden, the other cast iron) and sent them by stage boat to Franklin together with a covering letter:

> The European method of bridge architecture, by piers and arches, is not adapted to many of the rivers of America on account of the ice in winter. The construction of those I have the honour of presenting to you is designed to obviate the difficulty by leaving the whole passage of the river clear of the encumbrance of piers.

For the next five months, Paine worked at refining his designs but then, in November, the Pennsylvania Agricultural Society petitioned the Assembly for exclusive rights to build a traditional, piered bridge across the Schuylkill. Paine was sceptical ('they may sink money, but they will never sink piers that will stand') and he accelerated his own efforts to obtain the contract. In December, he had completed a second, cast iron model and, after a demonstration to Franklin, exhibited it at the State House.

The members were impressed, but concerned at the costings. Peace or war, it was always the same; they applauded the principle, but shied at the price. For himself, he had had enough of their tight-fisted ways.

In a handful of days he would be 50, and the thought exploded in his mind. Fifty: did life really pass away so quickly? It was as if he was being robbed of time, yet so much remained to be done. A year and more had already passed since he promised himself a visit to Thetford, and there was still the bridge to be built. Perhaps he had had enough of America. Perhaps it was time to return home.

8 'LA BASTILLE EST PRISE'

When Paine sailed for France in late April 1787, the delegates were already gathering for the Constitutional Convention. Since the New Year, individual States had been appointing 'Commissioners to meet at Philadelphia on the Second Monday of May next to . . . devise such provisions as shall appear to them necessary to render the constitution of the Federal Government adequate to the exigencies of the Union' — though no one saw fit to invite Paine.

It was not so much his qualities that were in question, more his politics, for with the war's end America had entered a period of conservative retrenchment. Their goals achieved, the majority of the 54 delegates who attended the Convention remembered Paine's works on titles, on slavery, on the rights of men and women and suspected his radicalism. The end of government might be liberty, though on carefully circumscribed terms. The aristocrat Alexander Hamilton* could idealise: 'civil liberty . . . as the greatest of terrestial blessings', but others were more realistic in recognising that the constitution-makers of 1787 had little ambition to extend the principles of 'life, liberty and the pursuit of happiness' as promulgated in the Declaration of Independence.

Ten years before the words had served well enough, but now there was no further need to drum up high-sounding principles. On the contrary, there was general agreement amongst delegates that what America needed was firm government by practical men of affairs. In such circumstances Paine was as much an embarrassment as a liability; his arrogance and rectitude served as an uncomfortable reminder of the young Republic's more egalitarian past.

While the French packet made a fast crossing, Paine still had time to consider the irony that men only invoked ideals to serve their own ends; that, having won independence, the Revolution was only partly complete when Patriots like John Adams could write that America should be governed 'by the rich, the wellborn and the able'. Wryly Paine recalled a remark of Colonel Rainborough at the close of the English civil war 140 years before: 'I would fain know what the soldier hath fought for all this while? He hath fought to enslave himself, to give power to men of riches, men of estates, to make himself a perpetual slave.'

Then the Puritans had told the poor that they were damned of God because they were not Elect. And now this new Elect, direct descendants

143

of those same Puritans who had raised England in their own self-interests, would deny a share in government to the poor because of their poverty. So much for the self-evident truth that all men were created equal; he had better things to do and on 26 May Paine disembarked at Le Havre to supervise the unloading of the model of his bridge.

In the following week, Paine journeyed through northern France, admiring the richness of the Normandy countryside but astounded by the poverty of the peasantry. The contradiction was everywhere — the fertility of the land, the hunger in the faces of the poor — and he remembered how Rousseau had told of country folk hiding their bread and wine to avoid the tax gatherers. That was forty years and more ago; yet it seemed that conditions were now worse than ever before.

Since the accession of Louis XVI, the price of France's two staple farm products (corn and wine) had been severely depressed due to overproduction; but in years of famine the peasantry still paid two-thirds and more of their income for bread — or starved. The countryside might be prosperous, but those who worked it were paupers, the more so since the demands of the Exchequer became increasingly voracious to pay for the pleasures of Versailles and the cost of the American war.

Although exact figures were hard to come by, it was said that the war had cost France 2,000 million livres, that by 1787 the Treasury's annual deficit was running at 112 million livres, and that the annual cost of handling the public debt totalled a further 300 million livres — all of which had to be raised by taxes, the bulk of which fell on the peasantry. The nobles and clergy were exempt from direct taxes levied by the *taille* (a 'cut' of all production) and *capitation* (a tax on income reckoned in terms of production); whilst indirect taxes on necessities such as salt (the *gabelle*) and shoe leather (*marque de cuir*) also discriminated heavily against the poor.

At least in America no one starved to pay for a court and its profligacy, and in Rouen they still retailed the story of the 'Queen's necklace', and laughed at its black humour. Some years before, the young Cardinal de Rohan — grandson of the Chevalier who had ordered Voltaire's beating 60 years previously — had been appointed Ambassador to Vienna and had offended the court by his ostentation (it was said that the mules that hauled his baggage from Paris had been shod with silver) and frivolity. The fiasco culminated when he wrote a dispatch in which he described Marie Thérèse drying her tears with one hand, while carving up Poland with the other.

Hearing the story in Paris, Marie Antoinette conceived a bitter loathing for the man who had dared to mock her mother. Recalled from Vienna,

Rohan determined to regain the favour of the Court; more especially of the Queen. At first it may have been little more than a conceit. It was soon to become an obsession which he shared with anyone who cared to listen — among them, Jeanne de la Motte, daughter of an army officer and a Paris street walker.

Alleging descent from the Valois line, de la Motte had ingratiated her way into the fringe of Versailles society and begun to boast that the Queen herself recognised her as a cousin of the blood. Rohan was intrigued, the more so when de la Motte showed him forged letters from the Queen and hinted that Marie Antoinette would be happy to meet him secretly.

A prostitute was rehearsed for the late evening assignation in the Bosquet de Venus at Versailles. Rohan advanced and kissed the hem of what he took to be the royal gown; the bogus Queen whispered a few, carefully chosen words ('You can hope that the past will be forgotten'), and the Cardinal withdrew — entranced. How could he show his devotion to such Majesty? Madame de la Motte had the answer. The jeweller Bohmer had created what was said to be the finest diamond necklace in the world, and valued it at 1.6 million livres; a gift worthy of a queen. Rohan, armed with a forged letter from Marie Antoinette indicating her interest in the necklace, visited Bohmer, drew up a memorandum of purchase, collected the necklace — and handed it to de la Motte. Within hours, the necklace had been broken up and its stones were being sold in Paris, and later in London.

The case was heard in June 1786; de Rohan was acquitted and retired to a monastery, while de la Motte was sentenced to life imprisonment still protesting her Valois lineage. Although on the grand scale, the affair of the 'Queen's necklace' exactly reflected the mood and extravagance of the Court, the cost of which ultimately had to be borne by the taxpayer — though since the trial Marie Antoinette had not dared visit Paris where the public were convinced of her complicity and she was known as 'Madam Deficit'.

As Paine rode for Paris, he recalled the quick generosity of Louis XVI, and now understood how it was afforded. The evidence was inescapable, and entering the city he passed through the customs barriers where the country folk queued to pay their tolls on their products. Everywhere it was the same, the peasantry bearing the burden of the state debt; yet France was again close to bankruptcy which accounted for the Assembly of Notables that had been convened in February to examine tax reforms, and dismissed by the King only the week before.

Twelve months had passed since the Controller-General of Finances, Calonne, had recommended the Assembly to Louis in the hope of introducing revolutionary changes in the tax system, in particular the annulment of the tax privileges of the *ancien régime*. At first, Louis procrastinated but Calonne was determined and, in November 1786, the King agreed that the Notables should be called — 14 churchmen, 53 princes of the blood and great nobles, 37 high magistrates meeting to abolish their own privileges.

The idea was absurd and by April the Assembly had broken Calonne who was replaced as Controller-General by Loménie de Brienne, a favourite of Marie Antoinette and the scarcely less than agnostic Archbishop of Toulouse. Within the month, de Brienne had pirated Calonne's proposals and, when they were again rejected, Louis dismissed the Assembly — though not before Lafayette had demanded the convocation of a National Assembly.

'You demand Estates General?' asked the Comte d'Artois. 'Yes, Monseigneur, and even better than that,' replied Lafayette. The call had echoes of the American experience, that there should be no further taxation without representation, and by June it dominated talk in the salons. The Estates General had not met for 175 years and now all of Paris waited for the King's response, while Paine wondered what part he could play in events and what was to become of his bridge.

As to the latter, he could only await the arrival of his model from Le Havre. As to the former, the political developments of the past months affected Britain almost as much as France. A more democratical government in Paris could only enhance the relations between the two nations, the more so since the recent signing of a trading treaty to consolidate 'the good harmony which actually subsists between them'. Sceptics had laughed at the phrase (if France was no longer the enemy, who was there left to fight?) and Mr Pitt (still only 28 years of age, though already Prime Minister for four years) had met some hostility from the chauvins on the floor of the Commons. He could have expected little else. The need for a better understanding between the two countries remained, none the less.

France and England had been at each other's throats for so long that cynics maintained that the Channel ran blood, and within days of Paine arriving in Paris no less a person than Mercy de Soufflet, private secretary to de Brienne himself, raised the matter with him. The impolicy of the two countries, and the madness of continual wars, had resulted in taxation that had bled both nations dry. Now was the time for a lasting peace, and who better to serve as an emissary between the two nations than an Englishman who shared the French government's aspirations? Paine welcomed the approach, formulated the proposal, and submitted it to de

Brienne. Through June and July, however, the Controller-General had more pressing concerns to occupy his mind and Paine could only wait for his reply and turn, once again, to his bridge project.

Before sailing for France, Franklin had given him letters of introduction to the Duke de la Rouchefoucauld and the Comte d'Estaing, while he was already well acquainted with Thomas Jefferson, the American Minister at the Court of Versailles, and though they pressed his case it was always against the background of rising political expectations. In late June, the model of the bridge arrived from Le Havre and on 21 July he presented it to the French Academy of Sciences who appointed a committee to examine its feasibility. The prospects were promising (Paine had already established contacts with one member of the committee, Jean-Baptiste le Roy), but it was overshadowed by the charge of political developments.

On 16 July, the Parlement de Paris had added its weight to Lafayette's demands, and when Paine dined with Jefferson later in the week the bridge was very much an afterthought of discussion. Both men knew Lafayette well from his time in America, though neither had ever suspected that he would apply his cavalry tactics to tilt at the throne of France. Then he had been the hothead of Washington's command, and they recalled stories of his éclat at Germantown and Monmouth.

Now he was committed on an altogether different scale. Jefferson called him 'the head and Atlas' of the Patriots, and only recently he had persuaded a mutual acquaintance, the Marquis de Condorcet*, to abandon his faith that: 'If the people had bread and justice, freely given, one could put up with everything else and patiently wait the decline of superstition.'

It was a notable conversion. Still in his early forties, Condorcet was among the last of the school of D'Alembert and Diderot and Voltaire, whom he had numbered amongst his friends, working for the great *Encyclopédie* and winning a seat in the Academy of Sciences when he was only 22. Once he had been a disciple of gradualism, but the American war had sown the first doubts; what was it that he had told Paine only last week: that men who read philosophic books had become enthusiastic over the liberty of America and 'seized with joy the opportunity to avow publicly sentiments which prudence had prevented them from expressing'?

The recollection might not be word perfect, but the sentiment was exact and Paine wondered, again, that he, a former staymaker and exciseman, should now share the confidences of statesmen and aristocrats. If life was a bagatelle, then he had drawn a fine hand to dine with Jefferson and call the Marquis de Condorcet a friend, though there was no cause to diminish himself. He had played his own part in the making of events and there could be no disguising that they respected him for what he was — an author of America's freedom who now had a bridge to build. The curse was that all other business was secondary to the affairs of state, and there was already talk that Louis intended to call a 'lit de justice'.

The royal session to register the new taxes which the Parlement of Paris had already repudiated on the grounds that only the Estates General could approve new taxation was held at Versailles on 4 August, with Louis presiding. The following day, the Parlement again declared the King's plans 'null and void' and the streets of Paris were thronged with crowds cheering: 'Long live the fathers of the people. No taxes.' Louis reacted sharply. The recalcitrant Parlement was exiled to Troyes, which immediately united the provincial Parlements in its support, whilst, when the Comte d'Artois rode into the capital on 17 August to register the new taxes, he was mobbed by a crowd of ten thousand rioters.

Civil order was close to breakdown, the lawyer Malesherbes confiding that the contest between King and Parlement could be 'the first spark of what, if not quenched, may become a great conflagration'. The words had a familiar ring; Paine had heard them before. It was on an August day very similar to this that Charles had raised his standard against the English Parliament 145 years before, while he recalled his father's more recent memories of the flight of James II and the Glorious Revolution. And now here it was in France, and men called on America as the talisman of their freedom, though only twelve years had passed since Paine had written:

> Men who look upon themselves as born to reign, and others to obey, soon grow insolent. Selected from the rest of mankind, their minds are early poisoned by importance; and the world they act in differs so materially from the world at large, but they have so little opportunity of knowing its true interests, and when they succeed in the government are frequently the most ignorant and unfit of any throughout the dominions.

Twelve years! So much had changed and yet so little, and now Louis played the simulacrum to George. Was life to be a permanent revolution, with himself at the eye of the storm? Surely, he had already played his part and, while the temptation to dabble in politics remained (de Brienne had given tacit support for his mission to England), it was the bridge that commanded his attention.

On 29 August the Academy of Sciences reported on his model that it was

ingeniously imagined; that the construction of it is simple, solid and proper to give it the necessary strength for resisting the effects resulting from its burden, and that it is deserving of a trial. In short, it may furnish a new application of a metal which has not hitherto been used in any works on an extensive scale.

To the devil with politics. Here was something altogether more tangible. Now, with the prospect of some future purpose, he could cross to England and visit Thetford again. The following day, Paine left Paris, carrying a note to Edmund Burke and considering whether, merely to pass the time, it might be useful to compose a short pamphlet on the state of current affairs?

The journey to London took five days, crossing at Dover and then south past Sandwich with its memories of Mary Lambert and his early love 'that delightful transport we can feel/Which painters cannot paint, nor words reveal'; south past Gravesend where women still humped their baskets to the lime kilns for sixpence a day; south past the anchorages to the east of the Tower with their double forest of masts; and then north across London Bridge. The city had not changed a great deal in 13 years, it was still the mêlée he remembered. The change was in himself.

Paine delivered his letter, approved by de Brienne, at Burke's town house, though Burke was in the country, resting. Little wonder. For ten years he had held the reforming wing of the Whig party together virtually single-handed, while in the months just passed he and Charles James Fox* and the playwright Sheridan* had been pressing their case against Warren Hastings* — 'that great object which engaged in a peculiar manner the House of Commons'.

Since his return from India in 1785, Burke had relentlessly pursued the charge that, as the late Governor-General of Bengal, Hastings had been guilty of 'high crimes and misdemeanours', of oppression, injustice and corruption. Individually, the indictments were damning enough. Together they made an indictment not so much of Hastings as of the John (East India) Company's government of India as a whole. Two years and more after Burke had levelled his first charges, there were still those who recalled his opening speech:

There is a secret veil to be drawn over the history of all governments. Ours, in India, had an origin like those which time has sanctified by obscurity. Time, in the origin of most governments, has thrown this mysterious veil over them. But, whatever necessity might hide or excuse or palliate in the acquisition of power, a wise nation, when it has once made a revolution upon its own principles, rests there. The first step to empire is revolution, by which power is conferred; the next step is good laws, good order, good institutions to give that power stability . . .

By conquest, which is a more immediate designation of the hand of God, the conqueror succeeds to all the painful duties and subordination to the hand of God which belonged to the sovereign whom he has displaced, just as if he had come into it by the positive law of some descent or some election. To this at least he is strictly bound — he ought to govern them as he governs his own subjects. But every wise conqueror has gone much further than he was bound to go. It has been his ambition and his policy to reconcile the vanquished to his fortune, to show that they had gained by the change, to convert their momentary suffering into a long benefit, and to draw from the humiliation of his enemies an accession to his own glory.

This was the substantive charge against Hastings and the East India Company, that they had abused the trust of power and failed to convert the momentary suffering of India into a long benefit. Paine knew. Among the first articles he had written for the *Pennsylvania Magazine* 13 years ago before had been one 'On Lord Clive'* in which he had drawn heavily on the report of a Select Committee of the Commons into the state of East India affairs. In introducing the findings the Chairman, General Burgoyne, the self-same 'Gentleman Johnny' who had surrendered at Saratoga, had said 'that the reports contained accounts shocking to human nature, that the most infamous designs had been carried into execution by perfidy and murder'.

And the same remained true. As with Clive, so with Hastings. They were party to, rather than scapegoats for, the Company's plunder of a continent: 'Oh India! thou loud proclaimer of Christian cruelties, thou bloody monument of unnecessary deaths, be tender in the day of enquiry, and show a Christian world that thou canst suffer and forgive.' Always it was the same, whether in the Indies or the Americas, this begging forgiveness in the name of God for crimes committed in God's name.

In his room in York Street, off fashionable St James's Square, Paine again wondered at the contradiction, then turned to correcting his latest paper. There were troubles enough in Europe, let alone those further afield, for now George and the young Mr Pitt were meddling in Dutch affairs. Seven years had passed since the *Stadtholder*, William V (one of the Orange family that had held the title for a century and more) had begun to consider changing his title to that of King, and strengthening his powers — and this at a time when all Holland clamoured for liberty and was at war with England for America's independence. The issue had divided the Provinces, and at the war's end the Patriots demanded extensive reforms of the man who would make himself king, among them, the establishment of a more democratic regime and the removal of the Duke of Brunswick* as Commander-in-Chief.

Between times, Holland had verged on civil war and in May, William had appealed to his brother-in-law, the King of Prussia, and his father-in-law, George III, to put down the Patriots by force. The Prussians were pleased to oblige, and were busily restoring William to power — while a British fleet cruised off the Dutch coast. Such provocation was madness, and extravagant madness at that. The recent enmity between England and Holland was nothing new. They had been rivals for trade for two centuries and more:

> The English navigation act was levelled against the interest of the Dutch as a whole nation and it is not to be supposed that the catching of the accidental circumstances of one man, as in the case of the present Stadtholder, can combine the interest of that country with this.

Yet now there was talk of a new tax to fund the *Stadtholder*'s cause.

> If half the money which nations lavish on speculative alliances were reserved for their own immediate purposes, it would be more productively and advantageously employed. Monarchs and Ministers . . . often contemplate to themselves schemes of future greatness, and set out with what appears to them the fairest prospect; in the meanwhile, the great wheel of time and fate revolves, and something never dreamed of turns up and blasts the whole. A few fancied or unprofitable laurels supply the absence of success, and the exhausted nation is HUZZAED INTO NEW TAXES.

But if the affairs of Holland were little more than a bubble of the day, they would be none the less disastrous if they embroiled England and France on different sides and, recalling de Brienne, Paine wrote:

> What has at this moment the appearance of disorder in France, is no more than one of the great links in that chain of circumstances by which nations acquire the summit of their greatness . . . The French were once the freest people in Europe; and as nations appear to have their periodical revolutions, it is very probable that they will be so again. The people of France are beginning to think for themselves, and the people of England are resigning up the prerogative of thinking.

He read the words again, and questioned them. It was not so much the people who were unthinking, more the newspapers who pretended to reflect their views. Day in, day out, they touted the most barefaced lies, the most abandoned principles. Day in, day out, they peddled a total disregard of national faith and obligations. Yet public opinion still rejected the view of Pitt and his hacks that Holland was worth a new tax. All that now had to be answered was whether George and his Minister were parading under the banners of Prussia simply to exploit the present troubles in France?

If so, if this is all that the recent treaty between the two nations was worth, then Mr Pitt and his master were again inviting troubles for England.

A disposition for peace was growing up in every part of France, and there appeared at the same time a mutual one in England. A silent wish on both sides, was universally expanding itself, that wars, so fatal to the true interest and burdensome by taxes to the subjects of both countries, might exist no more.

Instead of which it seemed that Mr Pitt ('a young and ambitious Minister . . . fond of himself; and deficient in experience') was making counters of his principles, and dicing away the new-found friendship between England and France:

By this means the sparks of ill will are afresh akindled between the nations, the fair prospect of a lasting peace is vanished, and a train of future evils fills up the scene, and that at a time when the internal affairs of France, however confused they at present appear, are naturally approaching to a great and harmonious increase in its power.

All that remained was to find a title. Before, and even during, the American war there had been much talk in Parliament of Caesar's passage of the Rubicon. Today, England was still on the peaceable side of the river, but it would be well if they considered the 'Prospects on the Rubicon', and he wrote the title, signed the paper, and put away his writing desk. How often had he sworn to give himself a rest from politics? Too many times for sure, but tomorrow he would leave for Thetford where he could occupy himself with other things.

Paine's father, Joseph, had died five months before his son returned home, but Frances still lived in the same small house on Bridge Street, though she was no longer the woman whose bitterness had shadowed his childhood, who had sympathised so keenly with her son's second wife, to write on their separation: 'I am heartily sorry that a woman whose character and amiableness deserves the greatest respect, love, and esteem . . . should be tied for life to the worst of husbands.' In her early nineties, Frances had mellowed towards her only son, possibly because he had been making small, but regular payments to his parents since his early days in America.

Whatever the cause, Tom Paine was home and she was proud. A spare man, he cut a fine figure in his drab breeches, snuff-coloured coat and olive green vest, though she was still uncertain of the reasons for his success. It was all very well when he talked of his time in London stay-making; of his service with the Excise in Grantham and Lewes. That she understood; but America was a world away and when they rode by the Duke of Grafton's country seat in the carriage he had hired there was no comprehending his talk of friends who he said made a Lilliputian figure of His Grace. How could the President of the United States, so lately a rebel, compare with a family who traced their line back to the Conquest? Of what significance was this Mr Franklin when set against a nobleman who had been Lord in Waiting to King George himself? Whilst, as for the Marquis de Lafayette, he was a Frenchman and that was enough.

The world of Thetford was as small and as insular as ever and on Sundays they attended service together at the Friends' Meeting House on Cage Lane, for Frances was a convert to Quakerism, and in the silence of the meeting Paine wondered how it was that she could change her God — then see no other? Almost half a century had passed since he had heard his parents dispute religion. Then there had been no compromise. To his mother, the Anglican Church had been the only faith — but if with time's passage she had come to accept a second God, then why not more?

Why not a multiple of two to an infinite power until there was something of God in everyman? What was it that Monsieur Rousseau had written: 'I feel my own heart and know men. I am differently made from any of those I have seen. I dare to believe that I am different from any man who exists?' It was true: all were different, Gods as much as men. Once he told Frances of how Voltaire had maintained that, as a free people, the English went to heaven by whatever route they chose — but she had never heard of Voltaire and dismissed the idea as infamous.

In Thetford or London it was always the same. Only this spring the Commons had debated a motion for a repeal of the Corporation and Test Acts,* in which the proposer had to defend dissenters from charges of being republicans, while the opposition had raised spectres of a Godless revolution. The motion had been defeated, heavily; and all sects but the Anglicans remained disenfranchised, in the name of God.

Such intolerance mocked Mr Pitt's talk, yet Frances had been born within seven years of the Glorious Revolution which pretended to make men free, while shackling conscience almost as close as the constitution. But there was little point pressing the issue. She was too old, too fixed in her ways for that; a letter to Jefferson would have to suffice:

> After I got home, being alone and wanting amusement, I sat down to explain to myself (for there is such a thing) my ideas of national and civil rights, and the distinction between them. I send them to you to see how nearly you agree.
>
> Suppose twenty persons, strangers to each other, meet in a country not before inhabited. Each would be a Sovereign in his own natural right. His will would be his law, but his power, in many cases, inadequate to his right; and the consequence would be that each might be exposed, not only to each other, but to the other nineteen. It would then occur to them that their condition would be much improved, if a way could be devised to exchange that quantity of danger into so much protection; so that each individual should possess the strength of the whole number.
>
> As all their rights in the first place are natural rights, and the exercise of those rights supported only by their own natural power, they would begin by distinguishing between those rights they could individually exercise, fully and perfectly, and those they could not. Of the first kind are the right of thinking, speaking, forming and giving opinions . . . or the rights of personal competency. Of the second kind are those of personal protection, of acquiring and possessing property, in the exercise of which the individual natural power is less than the natural right.
>
> Having drawn this line they agree to retain individually the first class of Rights . . . ; and to detach from their personal possession the second class, or those of defective power, and to accept in lieu thereof a right to the whole power produced by a condensation of all the parts. These I conceive to be civil rights, or rights of compact, and are distinguishable from natural rights because in the one we act wholly in our own persons, in the other we agree not to do so, but act under the guarantee of society.
>
> It therefore follows that the more of those imperfect, natural rights, or rights of imperfect power we give up, and thus exchange, the more security we possess . . . But it does not follow that the more natural

rights of *every kind* we assign, the more security we possess, because if we resign those of the first class we may suffer much by the exchange; for where the right and the power are equal with each other in the individual, naturally, they ought to rest there.

The letter and its thoughts made him restless, the days in Thetford passed at a leisurely pace. By late autumn, Paine was planning his return to Paris. He had neglected his bridge for too long whilst, if what little he heard of the outside world was true, events were moving apace. In November he took his leave of Frances (after providing her with a nine shilling a week settlement for life) and left Thetford for the last time.

By early December, Paine was in Paris where there was only one topic for discussion: the crisis in French affairs. Condorcet, Jefferson, Lafayette could talk of little else. When Louis dismissed the Assembly in May, the bourgeoisie of the cities and towns had been whole-hearted in their support of the nobility. Since then, however, events had progressed, more especially since the recent Royal Session. Throughout the autumn, de Brienne had been working on plans to raise new revenues, and on 19 November the King had brought two edicts before the Seat of Justice: one for Protestant Emancipation, a liberal measure to mollify the philosophes; the other for a state loan. For eight hours the debate had continued and when, towards the close, the radical Duc d'Orléans* had charged Louis with acting illegally, the King had retorted: 'No, it is legal because I will it.'

The Session broke up in disarray and, while it was reported that the King had promised to call the Estates General 'before 1792', Orléans was immediately exiled to his estates, and two of the King's most outspoken critics jailed. The whole fabric of government was being sapped for, whereas the bourgeoisie had sided with the nobility during the summer, they had now begun to talk of 'enlightenment' and liberties which the nobility may have considered, but never conceded. Although the most dynamic, single element of the French eighteenth-century economy, the emergent middle class was debarred from a range of offices in government and the army (where all Commissions were subject to proof of pure, noble blood), which united it in rejecting the time-honoured system of privilege based upon birth.

Professional men, financiers, businessmen, they had patronised, and learned from the philosophes, remembering the lesson of the *arriviste* Voltaire who had once been horsewhipped, then imprisoned for daring to cross swords with a de Rohan. But that was a lifetime ago. In the meantime much had changed and now the bourgeoisie were quick to exploit the division between Louis and the nobles, for, as the Abbé Sieyes* wrote, the aristocracy was like 'some horrible disease eating the living flesh on the body of some unfortunate man'.

The disease was privilege; the body, France. Though having little time for artisans or peasants, the bourgeoisie drew their definition closer. Having established their financial credentials, they now demanded social equality — but in a limited sense. It was a risky game that had been played before, and while Paine recalled Rainborough and a world turned upside-down, Jefferson prompted the radicals to: 'Be moderate; take what you can get without violence; encourage the King to travel quietly along the road which leads to tolerable and workable government.'

The advice was sound, but the realisation questionable. Unlike America and England, the entire edifice of French taxes, laws and institutions was based on the concept of inequality. To remove the keystone was to remove the whole. Paine and Jefferson, close friends of radicals such as Condorcet and Lafayette, urged caution, but they were already being outpaced by the public mood. If Sieyes and the rest spurred on the bourgeoisie in the name of circumscribed liberty, there were already deeper forces at work.

Since the previous summer, French journals and handbills had been pursuing revolutionary politics with growing intensity: Parisian graffiti had become increasingly virulent ('So long as he was but a fool,/"Forgive the fool" we said,/But now he wants despotic rule/Let's knock him on the head'); and, while the author Chamfort was contemplating that: 'To overawe the weak we have that resolute class that sees nothing to lose in change and believes that it has everything to gain', a young Arras lawyer, Maximilien Marie Robespierre,* was considering that: 'Most of those living in our towns and countryside are weighed down with poverty, in that extreme state of degradation where man . . . is unable to reflect on the causes of his afflictions and to acknowledge the rights nature has bestowed on him.'

Jefferson was right that under a mass of misrule 'the people might justly press for reformation', but as a diplomat his room for manoeuvre was limited; whilst Paine . . . what of Paine? If anyone had a taste for the mix that was brewing, he was surely the man, yet he remained uncharacteristically ambivalent about his future plans. Almost two years had passed since he had begun work on his bridge; six months since he had submitted his model to the French Academy of Sciences; four since their favourable report — yet still he waited for progress. No doubt it was flattering for the French to call on 'Common Sense' for advice on the meaning of liberty and the remaking of constitutions, but were those two years to be wasted. Was the bridge to be abandoned in favour of yet more political jockeying?

Early in 1787, while still in Bordentown, he had written to the President of the Royal Society, Sir Joseph Banks, about the dynamic mood of American science which had inspired his bridge project ('Even the war with all its evils had some advantages. It energised invention and lessened the Catalogue of Impossibilities'), and had received a warm reply:

> I expect many improvements from your countrymen, who think with vigour and are in a great measure free from the shackles which are imposed on the minds of our people before they are capable of exerting their mental faculties to advantage.

To the devil with France, she was too embroiled in her own affairs, while Jefferson had promised to mind his interests if he returned to England again. Early in 1788, Paine was back in London, to be adopted by the Grand Whiggery; to be dined by the Duke of Portland (Leader of the Party), wined by the Marquis of Lansdowne (who had gone so far as to say that Pitt's continental policies 'cut the throat of confidence' between England and France), and to spend a week with Burke at his country house near Beaconsfield. The reception was extraordinary, not so much that he was the son of a staymaker who had been dismissed from the Excise twice; more because it was his influence that had helped nerve the Colonists to declare their independence by breaking the spell of the Royal Brute.

Yet that was exactly the reason for the new-found friendships: as pragmatists they trusted that he, Tom Paine (who they had taken to calling 'the unofficial American ambassador'), could help repair the damage inflicted by the recent conflict between England and her former Colony. The whole thrust of Burke's case against the crown's North American policies had turned as much on the harm it would do to English trade ('Let us get an American revenue, as we have got an American empire'), as on constitutional matters. And now here they were, the oligarchs Paine had so long despised, courting his favours for a turn in the market, and he despised them again — save, that is, for Burke. With Burke it was different.

Since the days in Lewes when he had first read *Thoughts on the Causes of the Present Discontents* ('The people have no interest in disorder. When they do wrong, it is their error, and not their crime'), Paine had admired the man, and he admired him still. A stooped figure, bespectacled, the wits had taken to calling him 'Dinner Bell Burke' for the length of his speeches in the Commons. And small wonder. He talked seemingly interminably: on Indian government and Hastings's impeachment ('Of one thing I am certain, that the man is guilty of general evil intention'); on America ('In the character of Americans, a love of freedom is the predominating feature which makes and distinguishes the whole'); on toleration for dissenters ('Do not promote diversity; when you have it, bear it; have as many sorts of religion as you find in your country. There is a reasonable working in all of them'), but always, underlying all the rest, on the constitution of civil society.

At times it was as if he was obsessed by that vision, condemned by a personal demon to reconcile the public interest with the private good, yet knowing the impossibility of the task. What was it he called it: the Bedlam of the system — the wretchedness and contempt in which society had placed its *enfants perdus* whose sole purpose was to administer to the idleness and follies of the rich? Indeed, if the poor were blind to their slavery, then the rich had an interest in their blindness for it ensured their continuing servitude.

At some point, the system had to be broken — thus India and Hastings; America and independence; England and reform — though with caution, always with caution. It was easy enough to undo a constitution, hard to mend once undone. Only five years had passed since Parliament had approved Burke's own programme for economical reform, yet already men such as Fox (and Burke had few closer friends) were demanding more. And this was the centenary year of the Glorious Revolution. Unless carefully managed, it would raise unwelcome memories.

Throughout the spring and summer of 1788, Revolution Societies were planning their anniversary dinners and celebrations to entertain the friends of liberty, and defend against 'any oppression or invasion they might suffer from the undue exertions of misplaced power or the venal influence of the enemies of freedom'.

The words could well have been Burke's, but he had grown sharp when taxed with them. It was not that he did not honour the Revolution. The reverse: he regarded it as the capstone of the constitution, and invoked it often enough. No, it was not the past that he feared; rather its power to bewitch the present, for even now there were those who would boil the constitution in some magician's kettle, to brew it into youth and vigour. The notion was madness, not to be talked of again.

Burke's vehemence astounded Paine. It seemed that the man was haunted by a contradiction he could not resolve: on the one hand, by his compassion for the *enfants perdus*; on the other, by his fear, amounting to a phobia, lest they should have any share in the improvement of their own affairs. Small wonder that he had had such short shrift for Rousseau when the ageing *philosophe* had visited England 20 years before. It was not so much Rousseau's vanity that had troubled Burke (though he had written that it was a characteristic that Rousseau possessed 'to a degree little short of madness'), more his metaphysics and talk of a General Will. If Burke despised the one, he feared the other.

And the conflict remained. Only recently, Burke had been writing of what France had learned from America of those 'glorious scenes of equality, security, and prosperity' — yet already he seemed fearful of the recent events in Paris. His ambivalence was extraordinary and Paine wondered at the irony that it was Burke who had once helped to resolve his own contradictions, whilst now it was Burke who was riven by them himself.

As far as France was concerned, however, he had little cause for alarm now that the Estates General had been called — though not before Louis's intransigence had provoked further disorders. Early in May 1788, after the Paris Parlement had again denied the King's authority to levy taxes, Louis had stripped both the Parisian and the provincial Parlements of their powers to oppose his will. The country erupted into violence. In Paris, crowds burned de Brienne in effigy. In Rennes, the military governor had to shelter in the governor's palace. In Grenoble, rioters turned on the troops, while in Pau the Patriots imprisoned the King's intendant, and reinstated the Parlement.

The country was close to civil war, when, on 5 July, de Brienne announced that the Estates General would be summoned to Versailles the following May. Lafayette's demand had finally been met and, as Jefferson had written, it seemed that France would now follow 'the good model of England' and go step by step to a good constitution. What had Burke to fear from that? He must be sure to ask him the next time they met. Meanwhile the affair of the bridge was progressing well.

Early in 1788, Paine had submitted his model to the Royal Society, and applied for a patent on his design:

> No 1667, Specification of Thomas Paine. Constructing Arches, Vaulted Roofs, and Ceilings . . . on principles new and different from anything hitherto practised. The idea and construction of this arch is taken from the figure of a spider's circular web, of which it resembles a section, and from a conviction that when nature empowered this insect to make

a web she also instructed her in the strongest mechanical method of constructing it.

The patent was registered in the first week of September, and within days Paine had reached an agreement with Saml. Walker & Co. of Rotherham to cast an experimental arch in either wrought or cast iron. A month later Paine travelled north to Yorkshire and, even if the speed of the journey did not impress him (in the previous quarter century the journey time between London and Norwich or Manchester had been halved, and the London–Edinburgh run cut from six days to 60 hours), his first sight of the Walkers' works did.

There had been a small foundry in Lewes that cast cannon for the fleet but it bore no resemblance to this prodigy. Small wonder that Parliament had denied the Americans the right to work their own iron to protect their investment in such a colossus with its furnaces and forges and rolling mills, and when they tapped off the molten iron even the daylight seemed to pale. Here, if anywhere, they could build his bridge and, if the original notion of a 200-foot span was not feasible, then a 90-foot arch could easily be worked, and in less than half the time.

Paine remained in Rotherham until late November and, between overseeing work on the bridge, went on a week's tour of northern industries with Burke. He had long heard of how Arkwright's spinning frame, Crompton's spinning mule, and Hargreaves's spinning jenny were revolutionising the cotton industry, while when last in London he had inspected the latest model of Bolton and Watts' great Albion steam mill.

Now he saw the impact of nascent industrialisation for himself: the mills, and mines, and manufactories. They inspired awe, and something besides. No doubt about their ingenuity — this was the very apotheosis of reason — but what of the people; what of their place in this new order of things? Samuel Walker may have been so devout a Methodist that he raised a chapel to glorify the new works of God, yet there was a darker side to such beneficence.

Almost half a century had passed since he had watched the ragged army of dispossessed cross the small bridge at Thetford; almost 30 years since he had wondered about the fate of London's orphan poor. Their poverty may not have been a postponable want, but was it any worse than this? In the past two decades, nearly two million acres of common land had been enclosed. Now the only property that was left to the poor was their labour; and as for children, manufacturers had been buying them up in growing numbers from the workhouses of London and Westminster and bringing them up north.

Only recently Dr Thomas Percival (the youngest ever Fellow of the Royal Society) had reported on an outbreak of infectious fever in the mills around Manchester, and was in no doubt that it was 'supported, diffused, and aggravated by the ready communication of contagion to numbers crowded together; by the accession to its virulence to putrid effluvia, and by the injury done to young persons [especially those under fourteen years of age] through confinement and too long continued labour'.

He did not exaggerate. Paine saw for himself children of seven and eight who worked the mills for 15 and 16 hours a day, and heard the story of how, only recently in Cragg Dale, a boy had been beaten awake, having worked for 17 hours at his loom. Carried home by his father, but unable to eat any supper, he woke at 4 a.m. the following morning, asked his brothers if they could see any lights in the mill as he was afraid of being late, then died.

The incident might not be commonplace, but it was by no means unique. It seemed that all of England was being ravaged in the name of progress — and Paine recognised the contradiction instantly. For ten years and more he had been an apostle of reason, of progress; yet was this where it led, to this new hell? What point in calling up the rights of man, if they were to be destroyed by machines; by this new system in which humankind itself was converted into a mere machine, ignorant, brutalised, damned?

It was all very well promoting such abstractions as 'life, liberty, and the pursuit of happiness' when life was so cheap, liberty so confined, and happiness non-existent. It was all very well excoriating slavery ('Our traders in MEN, an unnatural commodity!, must know the wickedness of that SLAVE-TRADE, if they attend to reasoning, or the dictates of their own hearts') when here was a new slavery, as bad as before. Either progress was beneficent, and the new machines served the ends of humankind, or there was nothing — except, it seemed, in the eyes of God.

In his journey through the north, he had seen almost as many new chapels as mills and manufactories: Presbyterian, Baptist, independent, but most of all Methodist, Methodist most of all. They spawned across the land — Tent Methodists, Primitive Methodists, Independent Methodists — all glorying Mr Wesley's* God. Twenty years before, on his Lewes ride, Paine had happened across an open-air meeting of one of their ministers, Whitefield, at Brighthelmsea, and, while the sect had multiplied wonderfully, its ministry remained the same — the same groaning and weeping, swooning and ranting: 'Glory, glory, glory to God.'

Half a century had passed since Wesley, an Anglican clergyman, had felt himself 'strangely warmed. I felt I did trust in Christ, Christ alone, for salvation; and an assurance was given me that he had taken away my sins, even mine.' In the years between, Wesley had covered a quarter of a million miles on horseback preaching the blessedness of poverty and salvation through temporal submission, holding with Luther that: 'Even if those in authority are evil or without faith; nevertheless, the authority and its power is good and from God.'

The tenets of Methodism were well suited to industrialisation's need to break the spirit of the working people (work being 'a pure act of virtue . . . inspired by the love of a transcendent being') in order to establish the relentless code of factory discipline; well suited to the manufacturer's requirement 'to organise his moral machinery on equally sound principles with his mechanical' — for the fate of backsliders was always that dreadful hell: 'where sinners must with devils dwell,/In darkness, fire, and chaos.'

Paine wondered which hell was to be preferred, the sacred or the profane, but hesitated to raise the question with Burke. The man had little enough to fear from dissent if it took the Methodist form. Mr Wesley's salvation had gelded the word. And as he rode with Burke for Lord Fitzwilliam's northern seat at Wentworth House, Paine remembered that Rousseau had somewhere written that 'it is manifestly against the laws of Nature . . . that a handful should gorge superfluities while the multitude starve from lack of necessities' — but hesitated to mention that either.

The news at Wentworth was astonishing. On 24 October George III had held a levée at St James's Palace and then returned to Windsor. The following day, driving through the Great Park, he had called to his coachman to pull up and proceeded to address an oak tree as the King of Prussia. There had been hints of insanity as far back as 1765 when a Regency Council had been established, but now there could be no further doubt. George was mad, quite mad, and the question was not so much whether the condition was temporary or permanent, rather how the Whigs could best exploit the situation?

Like all Hanoverians, no love was lost between George and his heir, the Prince of Wales; yet Pitt depended on the King's patronage to retain himself in power. If the King was to be declared incurably insane, and a Regency established, it would break Pitt and the Tories, and it was already reliably reported that certain Government supporters were contemplating a shift in their allegiance. At such a time, Yorkshire was no place to be and Burke hurried south to London, to be followed by Paine after he had entrusted the completion of his bridge to the Walkers.

For the next two months, London was a political tumult as the rumours multiplied to contradict one another. George was temporarily mad; incurably insane; dying. The Prince of Wales was making his dispositions for a new government, between gaming at Brooks's where the wits with a topical interest now referred to a court card as 'The Lunatic'. Fox, who had made the journey from Bologna to London in nine days to lead the Opposition, was confident: 'I think it certain that in about a fortnight we shall come in'; meanwhile Pitt, after declining an offer of £100,000 from the City of London to provide for him out of office, fought a long rearguard action for his political life.

Paine to Thomas Jefferson, 16 December 1788:

> That the King is insane is now old news. He yet continues in the same state, and the Parliament are on the business of appointing a Regent . . . An embarrassing question, whether the Prince of Wales has a right in himself by succession during the incapacity of his Father, or whether the right must derive to him through Parliament, has been agitated in both Houses. This day is fixt for bringing the matter on in the House of Commons. A change of ministry is expected, and I believe determined on. The Duke of Portland and his friends will in all probability come in.

Paine to Thomas Jefferson, 15 January 1789:

> I am in some intimacy with Mr Burke, and after the new Ministry are formed he has proposed to introduce me to them. The Duke of Portland, at whose seat in the country I was a few days last summer, will be at the head of the Treasury, and Mr Fox Secretary for Foreign Affairs. The King continues, I believe, as mad as ever.

The Whigs' hopes of power were to be disappointed. Although George's state of health was sporadic (on one occasion an equerry heard the King praying piteously 'that God would be pleased either to restore him to his senses, or permit that he might die directly'), George had recovered sufficiently by late February for his doctors to announce that he was now convalescent. London celebrated and Paine wrote to Jefferson that 'he [George III] has fixed April 23rd for a public thanksgiving and he is to go in great Parade to offer up his Devotions at St Pauls on that day'.

Tory or Whig, they would all be there, making a nonsense as much of man as his Gods and, in his rooms at the White Bear, Paine considered the infamy of power: of a mad king, now apparently recovered; of a profligate heir, now temporarily put down; of a Government of royal patronage, and an opposition as careless of virtue as it was quick to vice. For all of Burke's fine talk of economical reform, it had made little difference. The political jockeys still rode the state; the corruption was as deep as before.

What was it he had written in the Rubicon paper little more than twelve months before: that, while the people of England were resigning up the prerogative of thinking, the people of France were beginning to think for themselves? Jefferson's latest news confirmed the opinion. Affairs in France were progressing well. Since Louis had agreed to convene the Estates General, the country's main business had turned on drawing up the *cahiers de doléances* (lists of grievances) for the first meeting of the Estates.

Throughout France, the Three Estates (Nobles, Clergy and Commons) compiled their complaints, each being discussed in detail before being accepted. Individually, there were variations between the Estates, as there were between the districts and regions. One demand, however, was common to all — that France should be a constitutional monarchy with a liberal, decentralised constitution that would guarantee the rights of individuals, the Third Estate of Paris adding that:

> Every year on the anniversary of its receiving Royal assent the Constitution will be read out in all churches, courts of justice, and schools, to all members of the armed services and on board ship; and this day will be observed as an official holiday in every country ruled by France.

The drafting of the *cahiers* not only focused the mind of France on its historic grievances, thus raising the level of political consciousness; it also held out the promise of their redress, thus lifting the level of public expectations. It was a volatile combination, especially when related to a fundamental grievance about the Estates General itself: that, because of its historic composition, the Third Estate (though representing the great majority of the population) could always be out-voted by the Nobles and the Clergy.

In answer to the title of his own pamphlet, *What is the Third Estate?*, the Abbé Sieyes wrote: 'Everything. What has it been up until now? Nothing. What does it desire to be? Something.' The only way the demand could be realised was by granting the Commons the right to have as many representatives as the other two Estates combined, and to have the votes of the Estates General counted by head, rather than by order. The tinder for revolution had been laid. It only remained to be lit. In the spring of 1789, however, the growth of public expectations and the composition of the Estates General appeared to pose small problems, and, from London, Paine was writing to Jefferson:

> I am much rejoiced at the account you give me of the state of affairs in France. I feel exceedingly interested in the happiness of that nation. They are now got or getting into the right way, and the present reign in France will be more Immortalised . . . than any that have ever preceded it.

As for England, George III was again firm on his throne. Burke and Fox and Sheridan continued their case against Hastings (it had been running for more than a year already, yet Burke himself said this was only a beginning); Pitt again opposed a motion to lift the Corporation and Test Acts, whilst easing restrictions on hawkers and beggars which encouraged the wits to wonder whether dissent would now register itself indigent; and Paine returned, once more, to the matter of the bridge. The business had gone so far, it deserved completion.

By early in April 1789, Paine was looking for a London site where the bridge could be demonstrated, and later the same month visited the Walkers in Rotherham to see its trial erection — the three-ton iron arch bearing a deadweight of six tons. Already the Royal Society had expressed 'great satisfaction' with the design, whilst in Dublin, London and Paris there was agreement on the need for new bridges across the Liffey, the Thames and the Seine. All that was required was a public demonstration of his prototype, and Paine was convinced there would be contracts for his design.

Yet all the while there was the distraction of the business in France. The Estates General met at Versailles on 5 May, in seeming fulfilment of Robespierre's words written only weeks before:

> You, generous nation, which alone among the peoples of the world, without a fatal revolution, without any bloody catastrophe, by your own magnanimity, and the virtuous character of your King, have resumed the exercise of the sacred and imprescriptible rights that have been violated in every age . . . Here is the basis of that social contract of which people talk so much, which is far from being an agreement produced by human volition; its fundamental conditions, written in heaven, were determined for all time by that supreme legislator who is the only source of all order, of all happiness and of all justice.

The young lawyer's words anticipated events. On 7 May the Nobles and Clergy verified their credentials, but the Third Estate refused. The King had still done nothing to amend the voting procedures which meant that it would remain in a permanent minority. For a month the stalemate continued and then, on 10 June, and at the instigation of the Abbé Sieyes, the Third Estate invited the other two orders to join it in the joint verification of 'all the representatives of the nation'.

For two days nothing occurred, then, on the morning of the thirteenth, three priests from Poitou joined the Commons. They were soon followed by others and, by the fifteenth, Sieyes had coined the title National Assembly for the new legislature. Effectively, the Revolution in France had begun. The Third Estate (which immediately voted itself powers to legislate on all taxation) had established an authority independent of the King, and by 19 June the majority of the clergy, and 80 nobles had opted to join the new assembly.

The following day, Versailles was placarded with notices announcing a *séance royale* for the twenty-second, and the hall of the Third Estate was closed on the pretext of preparing for the session. The deputies were undeterred. They moved to the royal tennis court and, with only one dissenting vote, took a solemn oath that the Assembly would 'go on meeting wherever circumstances may dictate, until the constitution of the realm is set up and consolidated on firm foundations'.

The King had two alternatives: either to make significant concessions as recommended by his liberal first Minister, Necker;* or to side with the reactionary party in court, headed by the Queen and the Comte d'Artois. He compromised, fatally. At a royal session on 22 June, Louis produced his own reform programme (parliamentary control of taxation, reform of the law, freedom of the press, internal free trade), but closed the proceedings with a veiled threat that he might well dissolve the Estates General altogether, and the explicit ruling that the three orders of the Estates should examine his proposals separately.

At the King's withdrawal, his Master of Ceremonies gave the deputies their instructions: 'Gentlemen, you know what the King's orders are . . .' The Comte de Mirabeau* replied instantly: 'Go and tell those who sent you that we will not move from our places here except at the point of the bayonet'; the President of the Assembly, Bailly, more diplomatically: 'The nation in assembly cannot receive orders.' The impasse was absolute. Either the Assembly or the King stood down. After five days of bitter internal wrangling at the Palace of Versailles (with the Queen now calling for the use of arms), and disturbing news of mounting unrest in Paris, Louis accepted the inevitable. On 27 June, he invited 'his loyal clergy and nobility' to reassemble with the Third Estate. That night Paris was illuminated — and Louis issued marching orders to six regiments to concentrate around the capital.

Reaction was on the move. On 1 July, ten further regiments received orders to deploy around Paris (a manoeuvre denounced by Mirabeau as counter-revolutionary), and on 11 July the King exiled Necker and his other liberal Ministers, while Jefferson was writing to Paine in London:

> The next day [26 June] the King wrote a letter with his own hand to the Chamber of Nobles and the minority of the Clergy, desiring them to join immediately the Common Chamber. They did so, and thus the victory of the Tiers became complete. Several days were then employed about examining returns & it was discovered at length that great bodies of troops and principally of the ancien corps were approaching Paris from different quarters. They arrived in the numbers of 25,000 to 30,000 men.
>
> Great inquietudes took place and two days ago the Assembly voted an address to the king for an explanation of this phenomenon & removal of the troops. His answer has not yet been given formally, but he verbally authorised their president to declare that these troops had nothing in view but the quiet of the Capital; and that once being established they should be removed. The fact is that the king never saw anything else in this measure; but those who advised him to it assuredly meant by the presence of the troops to give him confidence and to take advantage of some favourable moment to surprise some act of authority for him . . .
>
> But it is now out that these troops shew strong symptoms of being entirely with the people, so nothing is apprehended from them. The National Assembly then (for that is the name they take) having shewn through every stage of these transactions a coolness, wisdom, and resolution to set fire to the four corners of the kingdom and to perish with it themselves rather than to relinquish an iota from their plan of a total change of government, are now in complete and undisputed possession of the sovereignty. The executive and the aristocracy are at their feet; the mass of the nation, the mass of the clergy, and the army are with them and they have prostrated the old government, and are now beginning to build one from the foundation . . .

RECAPITULATION

Declaration of the rights of man. Principles of the monarchy. Rights

the nation. Rights of the king. Rights of the citizen. Organisation &
[functions?] right of the national assembly. Forms necessary for the
enaction of laws. Organisation and functions of the provincial and
municipal assemblies. Duties & limits of the judiciary power. Functions and duties of the military power.

You see that these are the materials of a superb edifice; and the
hands which have prepared them, are perfectly capable of putting them
together, & of filling up the work of which these are only the outlines.
While there are some men among them of very superior abilities, the
mass possess such a degree of good sense as enables them to decide
well. I have always been afraid their numbers might lead to confusion, 1,200 men in one room are too many. Another apprehension
is that a majority cannot be induced to adopt the trial by jury; and
I consider that the only anchor, ever yet imagined by man, by which
government can be held to the principles of its constitution . . . I am,
with great esteem Dear Sir your friend and servant

Th. Jefferson

In London five days later Burke and Paine considered the news, though
from rapidly diverging viewpoints. For some months Paine's relationship with the Whig establishment had been cooling ('I believe I am not
so much in the good graces of the Marquis of Lansdowne as I used to
be — I do not answer his purposes. He was always talking of a sort of
reconnection of England and America, and my coldness and reserve on
this subject checked communication'), but he was still hopeful that Burke
would be sympathetic towards the latest developments in France. For all
the political furore, Louis had still conceded less than England had known
for a hundred years, and here was Jefferson confident that France was
moving towards a balanced constitution.

Burke thought otherwise; indeed he became quite agitated on reading
Jefferson's news, the more so when Paine suggested that England itself
could do with some reforms:

Do you really imagine, Mr Paine, that the constitution of this kingdom
requires such innovations, or could exist with them, or that any reflecting man would seriously engage in them? You are aware that I have,
all my life, opposed such schemes of reform, because I know them
not to be Reform.

For all his principles (or possibly because of them), it seemed that

Burke was still bedevilled by contradictions. He had extolled the liberty of America; prosecuted the injustice of Hastings; pleaded the rights of dissent; accepted that 'where popular discontents have been very prevalent, it may well be affirmed and supported, that there has been generally something sound amiss in the constitution . . .'; and once had gone so far as to pity France her grievances. Yet now? Now he fled his own principles, for what was reform if not the redefinition of the rights of man, as much as the rights of kings?

Burke's economic palliatives might serve the Whigs' interests (they required no redistribution of either power or property), but what of more general measures for the welfare of the constitution? The answer was unrelenting. Burke railed: 'Do you mean to propose that I, who have all my life fought for the constitution, should devote the wretched remains of my days to conspire to its destruction?' And again: 'Do you not know that I have always opposed the things called reform.'

Such protests made nonsense of reason, grounded as they were on his irrational fear of what he called the venality and profligacy of the common people. Yet even here Burke was cursed by the irony that the mass was only venal, only profligate in proportion to the venality, the profligacy of its masters — and he had castigated them often enough. Not that there was any point in pursuing the issue further. He had become too intractable for that. The best that could be hoped was that he would learn from the progress of events in France — and on 14 July 1789, the day Jefferson's letter reached London, the Bastille fell.

At noon on Sunday, 12 July, Paris heard of Necker's dismissal. For more than two weeks, as royal troops were deployed around the capital, there had been growing suspicion of a court conspiracy against the National Assembly and the hopes it represented. The latest move reinforced such fears. By late afternoon the young lawyer Camille Desmoulins* was calling a crowd of six thousand to arms, while Jefferson crossed the Place Louis XV between a line of German cavalry and Parisians armed only with stones.

The moment he had passed, the crowd attacked the cavalry; the Germans charged, but a hail of stones drove them back.

This was the signal for universal insurrection; and this body of cavalry, to avoid being massacred, retired towards Versailles. The people now armed themselves with such weapons as they could find in armourers' shops and private houses, and with bludgeons; and were roaming all night through all parts of the city without any decided object.

The commander of the royal troops regrouped his forces in the Champs de Mars, while elected representatives from the city's 60 districts formed a standing committee to co-ordinate their response. By the morning of the fourteenth, on a rumour that an attack on Paris was imminent, barricades began to appear on the approaches to the city, and a search for weapons began. None was found at a Carthusian monastery where they were alleged to have been stored; whilst the arms and munitions that had been stocked at the Arsenal had already been transferred to the Bastille, a sombre fortress whose eight huge gates faced on to the Faubourg Saint-Antoine.

At 10 o'clock, the Bastille's governor, the Marquis de Launay, met a Paris deputation, offered them breakfast, ordered the cannon on the battlements to be withdrawn, and gave an undertaking that his command (a hundred men in all) would not open fire unless attacked. Two hours later, as a crowd of sightseers jostled in the outer court, de Launay conducted a second deputation around the battlements. The cannons had been withdrawn, though he refused to surrender up his command to the mob.

As the deputation was reporting back to the *Hôtel de Ville*, there was a burst of gunfire from the direction of the Faubourg Saint-Antoine. De Launay had fired on the crowd; a hundred were dead; the assault on the fortress had begun. By late afternoon, the Bastille had fallen, and its seven prisoners released from their cells. De Launay, who had been guaranteed safe conduct at the surrender, was beheaded by a furious mob processing through the city carrying at their head a tricolour, the keys to the fortress, and a banner inscribed: 'La Bastille est prise et les portes sont ouvertes!'

Paris that night was tense. The fall of the Bastille might be regarded as near miraculous, but how would the King react? At Versailles, Louis went to bed after hearing all that had happened, but could think of nothing more to write in his diary than: 'Rien.' The crisis had again robbed him of his day's sport. He had killed neither a stag nor a boar. At his *levée* the following morning, Louis was inclined to dismiss the previous day's troubles: 'Is this a rebellion?' he asked the Duc de la Rochefoucauld-Liancourt, the Grand Master of the Wardrobe. 'No, sire,' replied the Duke, 'this is a revolution'; and, while the Comte d'Artois advised him to flee to the protection of the troops that remained loyal, Marie Antoinette began burning her papers, packing her jewels.

The King remained, to compromise with the National Assembly. On the fifteenth he ordered the withdrawal of all troops from Paris and Versailles (a 'surrender of discretion' as Jefferson was to write), and the following day he rode into Paris to announce the recall of Necker. At the *Hôtel de Ville*, Louis, with a tricolour cockade pinned to his hat, mounted the staircase to the great hall to the roar of 'Vive le Roi' from the crowd, and the whisper from the Comte d'Estaing, 'Sire, with that cockade and the Third Estate you will conquer Europe.'

In his dispatch to London the following day, the British Ambassador, the Duke of Dorset, was reporting:

> Thus, my Lord, the greatest revolution that we know anything of has been effected with the loss of very few lives: from this moment we may consider France as a free country, the King as a very limited Monarch, and the Nobility as reduced to a level with the rest of the Nation.

Having curbed Louis and his nobles, the bourgeoisie now turned to consolidating their legislative powers. A fortnight after the fall of the Bastille, the National Assembly opened a discussion on the Declaration of Rights, and through the night of 4 August debated a motion for the abolition of feudalism.

Armed with the promises of the *cahiers*, and aggravated by grave food shortages (symbolically, the price of bread in Paris on 14 July was the highest recorded in the eighteenth century), there had been growing disturbances throughout France; estate owners were attacked, chateaux burnt and legal documents (the source of almost superstitious fears) destroyed. If Louis and the Assembly disappointed the peasantry's hopes, then they would act for themselves. By the morning of 5 August, however, it seemed as if their expectations had indeed been fulfilled. In a night-long session, the National Assembly has repudiated virtually all that the *ancien régime* represented. Serfdom, tax privileges, judicial and civil distinctions; one by one the nobility voluntarily surrendered up their seigneurial rights, the priests their tithes and annates, the towns their administrative and fiscal privileges.

For the bourgeoisie, few of whom were major landholders, it cost them little to abolish feudalism, and nothing to sacrifice serfdom. They had made their revolution at the expense of the *ancien régime*. There were others still to come, inspired as much by the rapid politicising of the working classes as by the Declaration of Rights approved by the National Assembly on 26 August:

1. Men are born and always continue free and equal in respect of their rights. Civil distinctions, therefore, can only be founded on public utility.

2. The end of all political associations is the preservation of the natural and imprescriptible rights of man, and these rights are liberty, property, security, and resistance to oppression.
3. The nation is essentially the source of all sovereignty; nor can any individual, or any body of men, be entitled to any authority which is not expressly derived from it.

In all there were 17 clauses which were to provide the text of the Revolution. Only one problem remained: to implement the Declaration's intentions. Ultimately it was a problem that would break the Revolution itself, though, in September 1789, it appeared a trifling difficulty, and in London Paine was writing to the Walkers with the latest news he had received from France:

Mr Jefferson concludes his letter by saying 'a tranquillity is well established in Paris and tolerably well throughout the kingdom, and I think that there is now no possibility of anything hindering their final establishment of a good constitution which will in its principles and merits be about a middle term between that of England and America'.

Inevitably, Burke disagreed. For all of Jefferson's assurances, for all the Duke of Dorset's dispatches, he had become increasingly suspicious of the progress of affairs in France since the first meeting of the Estates General in May. Whilst recognising the Revolution, he wondered if it meant reformation. Whilst applauding the new liberty, he doubted its moderation. Whilst congratulating France on tearing off the mask of despotism, he feared the ideologues and the common people who came behind them. It was always the same, there was no reconciling the conflicts, and the distance between Paine and Burke widened daily.

As Paine's relations with the main body of the Whig party deteriorated, his contacts with an emergent group of radicals — with the wayward aristocrat, Charles James Fox; the playwright and politician, Richard Brinsley Sheridan; the teacher and commentator, William Godwin* — increased, and, the morning being fine, on 19 September he walked to Hackney to visit Dr Richard Price.* The bridge was not mentioned. All the talk turned on the happenings in France, and their meaning to England. For the first time since the civil war, a national political movement involving the working classes was in the making, and even Pitt had been heard to say that when he first came to power there was no public, only politicians, whilst now men were looking beyond party jugglery towards the government of their affairs.

Within months a crop of new constitutional and reform societies had emerged, and Dr Price himself was planning to move a resolution at the Revolution Society of London hailing the events in France as the forerunner of more general European liberties. The details had yet to be finalised, but their thrust was clear: that France had provided an example to all mankind to assert its inalienable rights and, thereby, introduce a general reformation in government to make the world free and happy. Burke might dismiss such a declaration as metaphysical. For Paine, its appeal was irresistible, a synthesis of all his beliefs. In Paris they were building the world anew, while he frittered away his days in London. Surely once the details of the bridge were settled, he could afford a little time in France.

In a final letter to Jefferson before his return to America on the completion of his term as Minister to France, Paine wrote: 'I am looking out for a place to erect my Bridge, within some of the Squares would be very convenient . . . I expect it will be ready for erecting in London by the latter end of October.' His optimism was stillborn. The dispatch of the bridge from Rotherham was delayed until early in 1790, and by early November Paine was in Paris.

The city was alive with politics, a synthesis of all the rest — the aspirations of the philosophes who dared to know; the logic of the economists who recognised the 'imperious necessity' of the law of self-preservation; the rationale of the constitution-makers who understood that to prevent the abuse of power, it was necessary to have power to check power — all fused by Rousseau's 'pure act of understanding which reasons in the silence of the passions'.

Here was the Age of Reason in tangible form, and, on 25 November, the Duc de la Rochefoucauld presented Dr Price's address to the National Assembly and was instructed by the President to express

> the lively and deep sensibility with which the National Assembly of France receive the Address of the Revolution Society in England which breathes those sentiments of universal benevolence that ought to unite together in all the countries of the World the true friends of Liberty and of the happiness of Mankind.

At such time it was small wonder that the Marquis de Lafayette, now commanding the National Guard, decorated his study with a great cartoon in two columns; the one inscribed with the American Declaration of Independence; the other blank, awaiting the Declaration of France.

Eleven years had passed since Lafayette and Paine had first met at Washington's winter quarters at Valley Forge. Now they had shared two revolutions together. It was a proud enough boast for any man, and Lafayette presented Paine with a key of the Bastille for forwarding to President Washington.

Paine to Washington:

Sir — Our very good friend the Marquis de La Fayette has entrusted to my care the Key of the Bastille . . . as a present to your Excellency, of which his letter will more particularly inform. I feel myself happy in being the person thro' whom the Marquis has conveyed this early trophy of the spoils of despotism, and the first ripe fruits of American principles transplanted into Europe, to his great master and patron.

When he mentioned to me the present he intended you, my heart leaped with joy. It is something so truly in character that no remarks can illustrate it, and is more happily expressive of his remembrance of his American friends than any letters can convey. That the principles of America opened the Bastille is not to be doubted, and therefore the Key comes to its right place.

And later:

In the partition in the Box, which contains the Key of the Bastille, I have put up half a dozen Razors, manufactured from the Cast-steel made at the Works where the Bridge was constructed, which I request you accept as a little token from a very grateful heart.

There was no ceremony between the two men. They knew each other too well for that. Lafayette handed over the key. Paine promised to carry the American flag in the triumph through Paris when the constitution was proclaimed. With a single toast — 'Liberty' — they shared memories, oblivious of the fact that, in London, Burke was considering what more could be done with a brief letter he had recently dispatched to a young correspondent, Monsieur Dupont, who had asked for his reflections on the Revolution in France; whilst, in Paris, Gouverneur Morris was smarting at Lafayette's presentation to Paine, regarding it as an insult to his new office as Minister to France. Both events were to have profound consequences for Paine's future career.

9 RIGHTS OF MAN

The winter of 1790 was mild, and Paris was quiet again. Each morning, Louis and Marie Antoinette walked in the garden of the Tuileries flanked by grenadiers and an officer of the National Guard. Each evening, *The Barber of Seville* played to full houses of theatre-goers, whilst throughout the day the talk in the cafés of the Palais Royale and Place Vendôme was of politics, and yesterday's business at the National Assembly.

Since moving into the capital from Versailles in October, the Assembly had been meeting in a riding school built for the young Louis XV; an uncomfortable place, ill lit and heated by a single stove modelled on the Bastille set in the middle of the floor. The proceedings were always noisy, with several speakers often on their feet at the same time; sometimes wild, the public gallery pelting the deputies below with oranges and apples. For all this, the Assembly and its 31 Standing Committees were slowly hammering out a body of legislation that would make a reality of the Declaration of the Rights of Man.

Superficially, at least, it seemed that the transfer of power was progressing smoothly enough, though the deputies of the Assembly were fully aware not only of the fickleness of the public mood, but also of the danger of counter-revolution. In public, Louis might appear amenable to the new order and be pleased to call himself 'King of the French'. Too often, however, he forgot the caveat: 'by the grace of God and the constitutional law of the state.' Prompted by Marie Antoinette, the man still hankered after his lost absolutism, and only recently had been heard to remark: 'I would rather be King of Metz, than continue to be King of the French.'

There was no mistaking his meaning. Under the Marquis de Bouille, a royalist army lay just across the frontier. Once there, he could call up the support of both Spain and Austria. As was so often the case, however, Louis equivocated, whilst royalists made a mare's nest of plots — of a march of eight hundred from Versailles to free the King; of English funds promoting unrest in Britanny; of the plan of the Marquis de Favras to assassinate Lafayette. On 14 January 1790, that indefatigable traveller, Arthur Young, was writing in his diary:

> Plots! Plots! Plots! The Marquis La Fayette, last night took two hundred prisoners on the Champs Elysée; out of eleven hundred that were collected. They had powder and ball but no muskets. Who they are

175

and what they are is in question; but an answer is not so easily to be had. Brigands, according to some accounts, that have collected in Paris for no good purpose; people from Versailles by others; Germans by a third; but everyone would make you believe, they are an appendix to a plot laid for counter-revolution.

The rumours were so various that they cancelled each other out, and Paine shrugged them off. They were phantoms, no more, even less substantial than the recent divide between the Monarchists and the Patriots in the Assembly. Immediately, the matter was of little consequence and it could be that, as the vote of the old guard in the Assembly diminished, so they encouraged the rumours out of doors; but if such rifts were to become commonplace it could cause problems in the future. As it was, the business of government progressed satisfactorily and, now, perhaps, was the time to chronicle the history of recent events.

By January 1790, Lafayette was reporting that Paine was already at work on such a project, noting in a letter to Washington: 'Common Sense is writing for you a brochure in which you will see a portion of my adventures. The result, I hope, will be happy for my country and for humanity.' The Marquis anticipated Paine. With France apparently on course towards stable government, there was time enough for such a venture. The bridge, however, would not wait. The Walkers had completed their work, and by the spring it was *en route* to London.

Paine had written to Burke from Paris in the winter of 1790, commending the course of events in France and inviting his assistance in 'propagating French opinions throughout Europe . . . to advance the cause of Freedom'. Burke did not reply, having opened his case against the Revolution in a letter to Monsieur Dupont.

The name, a pseudonym, disguised an acquaintance of Burke's who had written requesting his views on French affairs as the man whose 'feint and glimmering taper' had lit 'the splendid flame of liberty'. Suspecting censorship, and careful for his correspondent ('In the ill-connected and inconclusive logic of the passions, whatever may appear blameable is easily transferred from the guilty writer to the innocent receiver'), Burke couched his reply cautiously.

No one could doubt that he welcomed any cause that promoted liberty ('It is not the reward of our merit, or the acquisition of our industry. It is our inheritance,') or that despotic government should be changed ('If necessary, by violence') if it could not be reformed — but 'You may have made a revolution, but not a reformation. You may have subverted monarchy, but not recovered freedom.'

Burke teased out the doubt, to question the new legislature, the new judiciary, the new rights of man. 'You have theories enough . . . it may not be amiss to add a small degree of attention to their nature and disposition. It is with man in the concrete; it is with common human life and human action you are to be concerned.'

The indictment was masterly, by implication. Within weeks Burke was to take a stronger line. On 4 November 1789, Richard Price had delivered his 'Discourse on the love of our Country' to the Revolution Society from the pulpit of the dissenters' Meeting House in Old Jewry; and on the twenty-fifth, the National Assembly had welcomed Price's declaration applauding recent developments in France as the precursor of more general, European liberties.

The combination triggered Burke's worst fears — of dissent wracking England in imitation of the metaphysical principles of the French. Although his family was of 'the middling sort', Burke had been adopted as the philosopher of the Whig oligarchs; although baptised and educated in the Church of England, Burke came of Irish Catholic stock, with its bitter memories of Protestant supremacy — yet here, again, was dissent applauding French practices with its equalising tendencies, and exposing the 'superstition and error' of the Romish kind.

The notion threatened the entire fabric of beliefs that Burke had so carefully constructed for himself but which, at centre, was still flawed by the contradiction that he represented an aristocratic critique of the bourgeoisie — whilst remaining bourgeois himself. The conflict haunted Burke, driving him to extremes in defence of his adopted position, for after more than three decades he still remained that 'Irish upstart from the Catholic underworld across the Bristol channel'.

A quarter of a century before, he had offered to resign his post with Rockingham when charges were laid as to his Catholic antecedents; then, when the Whigs finally came to power, he was offered a post inferior to that which either his talent or his service to the party deserved. It was always the same; their need of him levened by their patronage. While the Grandees were complacent in their power, however, Burke knew its vulnerability and, replying to Fox in the Commons on 9 February 1790, he mounted his first public attack on the Revolution, and the principles which motivated it:

They made and recorded a sort of institute and digest of anarchy, called the Rights of Man, in such a pedantic abuse of elementary principles as would have disgraced boys at school; but this declaration of rights was worse than trifling and pedantic in them; as by their name and authority they systematically destroyed every hold of authority by opinion, religious or civil, on the minds of the people. By this mad declaration they subverted the state.

Four days later, he had identified the danger in England: 'I was much surprised to find religious assemblies turned into a sort of place and exercise and discipline for politicks, and for the nourishment of a party which seems to have contention and power much more than Piety for its object.' Then, on 20 February, he was writing to Sir Philip Francis* of how he had wept to hear of 'the abominable offences of 1789' (not least, the humiliation of Marie Antoinette), adding:

I mean to set in full view their [the revolutionists] wicked principles and black hearts. I intend to state the true principles of our constitution in church and state, upon grounds opposite to theirs. I mean to do my best to expose them to the hatred, ridicule, and contempt of the whole world; as I shall always expose such calumniators, hypocrites, sowers of sedition, and approvers of murder and all its triumphs.

Paine returned to London in March, and the morning after his arrival called at Debretts, the bookseller in Piccadilly, to learn how Burke's pamphlet was progressing. The news was sparse and contradictory. The pamphlet was already at the press, but Burke was at a loss as to how to proceed, and had already revised some of the sheets six, seven, and one nine times. Dinner Bell Burke at a loss for words — impossible; and later, at Fox's house, they laughed at the notion, and Paine promised that, when Burke published, he would reply.

Until then, there was the bridge; always the bridge. Once the project had absorbed him. Now he was tiring of its continual problems. More than five years had passed since he had built the first model at Bordentown — five years of delay and frustration — and now there was the need to find a site to exhibit the prodigy if there was to be any hope of obtaining a contract of sale. In May, the bridge (110 feet long, 24 feet wide and 'portable as common bars of iron') arrived in London by sea and in August was being erected at Paddington Green.

The site was open so that 'no advantage could be taken of butments without the expense of building them', but after five days' work under Paine's supervision the bridge was half complete, and by 7 August was already attracting sightseers.

I have had a visit from Sir Joseph Banks and some members of the Royal Society who appear as much pleased as if they had an interest in it — the first person who found his way in (why we keep it enclosed and the gates shut) was old Lord Bessborough.

I was not there as it was before any of the iron was put up, but he and Mr Bull had a good deal of talk about Rotherham — and the old man went away highly pleased, gave the workmen half a crown and desired leave to come again. Similar cases are happening every day, and the only way to render admission convenient will be by tickets and then people will not be consulting with themselves what they are to give.

At last it seemed as if Paine's perseverance was to be rewarded — then one of his backers, the American merchant Peter Whiteside, was declared a bankrupt and, on 29 August, Whiteside's creditors served a judgment against Paine at the White Bear Hotel, Piccadilly. While the trial model at Paddington was to remain open to visitors at a shilling a head until the summer of 1791, and while Paine was convinced that his design would 'produce a pretty general revolution in Bridge Building', the whole venture appeared to be damned by ill fortune. Better, perhaps, to concentrate on politics. In that, leastways, there were no debtors, and fewer delays, for affairs across the Channel were on the move again.

All France had celebrated Bastille Day, and in Paris the Marquis Lafayette had staged a grand *Fête de la Féderation*, attended by more than 300,000 people — including Louis, Maris Antoinette and the Dauphin. Three hundred priests had celebrated mass at an altar in the amphitheatre on the Champs de Mars and in the silence which followed the King had declared: 'I, King of the French, swear to employ the power delegated to me in maintaining the constitution decreed by the National Assembly, and accepted by me.'

Cannon thundered, mass bands played, and the Queen held the Dauphin aloft, proclaiming: 'Here is my son. He and I both join in those sentiments.' The crowd frenzied with delight: 'Vive le Roi. Vive la Reine. Vive M. le Dauphin.'

What better evidence existed of the new mood, the new liberty of France? Yet Burke still worked on his pamphlet to expose such 'wicked principles', such 'black hearts'.

Burke's reflections had one, overriding goal — to alert Europe to the dangers of revolution and, thus, mobilise the forces of counter-revolution. They made little pretence at either objectivity or formal structure ('I beg leave to throw out my thoughts, and express my feelings, just as they arise in my mind'), relying on prescription to extirpate innovation:

> The very idea of the fabrication of a new government, is enough to fill us with disgust and horror. We wished at the period of the Revolution [of 1688], and do now wish, to derive all we possess as *an inheritance from our forefathers*. Upon that body and stock of inheritance we have taken care not to inoculate any cyon alien to the nature of the original plant. All the reformations we have hitherto made have proceeded upon the principle of reference to antiquity; and I hope, nay I am persuaded, that all which may be possibly made hereafter, will be carefully formed upon analogical precedent, authority and example.

It was the pivot on which all the rest turned; Burke's defence of inviolate property ('Nothing is a due and adequate representation of a state, that does not represent its ability as well as its property . . . The characteristic essence of property, formed out of the combined principle of its acquisition and its conservation, is to be *unequal*'); of an established church ('The consecration of the state, by a religious establishment, is necessary also to operate with a wholesome awe upon free citizens . . .'); of a fixed order ('We have an inheritable crown; an inheritable peerage; and an house of commons and a people inheriting privileges, franchises, and liberties, from a long line of ancestors').

For Burke, these were the rights of man.

> This idea of a liberal descent inspires us with a sense of habitual, native dignity, which prevents that upstart insolence almost inevitably adhering to and disgracing those who are the first acquirers of any distinction. By this means our liberty becomes a noble freedom. It carries a noble and imposing aspect. It has a pedigree and illustrating ancestors. It has its bearings and ensigns armorial. It has its gallery of portraits; its monumental inscriptions; its records, evidences, titles. We procure reverence to our civil institutions on the principle on which nature teaches us to revere individual men; on account of their age, and on account of those from whom they are descended.

Against which Burke ranged anarchy:

> Amidst assassination, massacre, and confiscation, perpetrated or contemplated, they [the National Assembly] are forming plans for the good

of future society . . . This Assembly, which overthrows Kings and kingdoms, has not even the physiognomy and aspect of a grave legislative assembly — *nec color imperii, nec frons ulla senatus*. They have a power given to them, like that of the evil principle, to subvert and destroy, but none to construct, except such machines as may be fitted for further subversion and further destruction.

Point and counterpoint, Burke's critique ranged from the profound — 'A perfect democracy is therefore the most shameless thing in the world . . . No man apprehends in his person he can be subject to punishment' — through the romantic — 'little did I dream that I should have lived to see such disasters fallen upon her [Marie Antoinette] in a nation of gallant men, in a nation of men of honour and of cavaliers. I thought that ten thousand swords must have leaped from their scabbards to avenge even a look that threatened her with insult. But the age of chivalry is gone' — to the hysteric — 'we are taught to look with horror on those children of their country who are prompt rashly to hack that aged parent in pieces, and put him into the kettle of the magicians, in hopes that by their poisonous weeds and wild incantations, they may regenerate the paternal constitution'.

The whole, whilst accepting that the *ancien régime* may have been flawed ('Your government in France, though usually, and I think justly, reputed the best of the unqualified or ill-qualified monarchies, was still full of abuses'), and admitting that no constitution is immutable ('A state without the means of some change is without the means of its conservation'), became the handbook of reaction, taking the Glorious Revolution of 1688 as its text:

> The lords spiritual and temporal and commons do, in the name of all the people aforesaid, most humbly and faithfully submit *themselves, their heirs and posterities for ever*; and do faithfully promise that they will stand to maintain, and defend their said majesties, and also the *limitation of the crown*, herein specified and contained, to the utmost of their powers.

This was Burke's godhead, a constitution armed by prescription. The reverse was the blasphemy at which he raged, a chimera of reason inspired by metaphysicians, for, while he might recognise change, he feared it; while he might applaud liberty, he denied its share to the 'swinish multitude'. On 1 November 1790, *Reflections on the Revolution in France* was published — contradicting all that Paine represented. Four days later,

at The Angel, Islington, Paine sat down to write his reply — the first
part of *Rights of Man*.

By design or accident, Burke had it wrong, and the latter was inconceivable. He was too well versed in politics to confuse his own intentions. The pamphlet, all 360 pages of it, was a calculated insult to France,
and gratuitous too, for the French showed little inclination to dabble in
English affairs. Not that this was mere incivility, its purpose was more
malign — to hold out the examples of English liberties as a lesson to
the French.

Burke presumed, not least in his stress on precedent. Almost a hundred pages were devoted to the topic, and all on what foundation: that
at some distant point in time a contract had been agreed that bound men
to the end of time? This was no more than a new guise for the old tyranny that George had attempted to practise on the Colonies, and Burke had
been quick enough to protest their independence of such prescription then.
And now? Now was no better than then. The notion was arrant nonsense,
and Paine wrote:

> There never did, there never will, and there never can, exist a Parlia-
> ment, or any generation of men, in any country, possessed of the power
> of binding and controlling posterity to 'the end of time', or of com-
> manding for ever how the world shall be governed, or who shall govern
> it . . . The vanity and presumption of governing beyond the grave is
> the most insolent and ridiculous of all tyrannies. Man has no proper-
> ty in man; neither has any generation a property in the generations
> which are to follow.

But that was not all. It was not so much that Burke attempted to regulate
the future by the past, more that he made an arbitrary thing of time itself.
Why 1688? For no other reason than, like some clockmaker, he needed
a point of reference by which to adjust all the cogs and wheels of his
sophistry. So again, why 1688 and no other time, since time began?

> The error of those who reason by precedents drawn from antiquity,
> respecting the rights of man, is that they do not go far enough into
> antiquity. They do not go the whole way. They stop in some of the
> intermediate stages of an hunded or a thousand years, and produce
> what was then done, as a rule for the present day . . . but if we pro-
> ceed on, we shall at last come out right; we shall come to the time
> when man came from the hand of his Maker. What was he then? Man.

Man was his high and only title, and a higher cannot be given him . . .

If the mere name of antiquity is to govern the affairs of life, the people who are to live an hundred or a thousand years hence may well take us as a precedent, as we make a precedent of those who lived an hundred or a thousand years ago. The fact is, that portions of anti-quity, by proving everything, establish nothing. It is authority against authority all the way, till we come to the divine origin of the rights of man at the creation.

The point was well made. Burke was fond enough of invoking the spiritual to justify the temporal, of maintaining that 'religion is the basis of civil society . . . that man is by his constitution a religious animal'. Yet the contradiction still escaped him; that he made a religion of man's constitution, calling up God to hallow 1688 and dismiss all that had gone before — save for the rights of kings. Here, at least, Burke was quick enough to discriminate, finding a new chronology to sanction monarchy:

Everything must have had a beginning, and the fog of time and anti-quity should be penetrated to discover it. Let then, Mr Burke, bring forward his William of Normandy, for it is to this origin that his argu-ment goes. It also unfortunately happens, in running this line of suc-cession, that another line parallel thereto presents itself, which is, that if the succession runs in the line of conquest, the Nation runs in the line of being conquered, and it ought to rescue itself from this reproach.

Once one shuffled time to set the pack straight, there was no end to the arrangement, and knaves came as high as kings, all sanctioned by fortune. It must be ten years and more since Franklin had told him of how, when in Paris as American Minister, he had been approached by a noble who offered himself up as the King of America on the grounds that he was a Norman, of more ancient family and more honourable des-cent (having never been bastardised) than the Dukes of Normandy, and that there was already a precedent in the Kings of England having come out of Normandy. The good Doctor, it seemed, had ignored the first let-ter, but the second was more specific — his correspondent did not threaten to conquer America, simply proposed that, if his offer was not accepted, an acknowledgement of £30,000 might be made for his generosity.

It may, therefore, be of service to his [Burke's] doctrine to make this story known and inform him, that in the case of that natural extinction to which all mortality is subject, Kings may again be had from

Normandy, on more reasonable terms than William the Conqueror; and consequently that the good people of England at the Revolution of 1688, *might have done much better*, had such a generous Norman as *this* known *their* wants, and they had known his!

And there it was again, the Revolution of 1688. Burke made light of the treason of the affair ('a small and temporary deviation from the strictest order of hereditary succession'), yet it was as treasonable as any other. True, no blood had been spilt (that was to come in 1715 and 1745), but for all that his goodly Whigs had sent their King and his popish retinue packing. And now he talked up the majesty of the constitution, to talk down the French.

The man was jesuitical; little wonder that some still suspected his Catholic grounding. Only recently, in *Lessons to a Prince*, an anonymous Elder Statesman had suggested that, if Burke's religion could have its proper effect, dissent would be silenced by the 'holy severities of the inquisition'. The jibe was unworthy of the author, though in his *Reflections* Burke had, indeed, tolled 'Church and State, State and Church' like a rosary to sanctify his establishment.

By engendering the Church with the State, a sort of mule animal, capable only of destroying, and not breeding up, is produced called The Church established by Law . . . Let Mr Burke continue to preach his antipolitical doctrine of Church and State. It will do some good. The National Assembly will not follow his advice, but benefit by his folly. It was by observing the ill effects of it in England that America has been warned against it; and it is only by experiencing them in France, that the National Assembly have abolished it and, like America, have established UNIVERSAL RIGHT OF CONSCIENCE AND UNIVERSAL RIGHT OF CITIZENSHIP . . .

With every respect to what are called denominations of religion, if everyone is left to judge his own religion, there is no such thing as a religion that is wrong. But with respect to religion itself, without regard to names, and as directing itself from the universal family of mankind to the Divine object of all adoration, it is man bringing to his Maker the fruits of his heart; and though those fruits may differ from each other like the fruits of the earth, the grateful tributes of everyone is accepted.

Yet Burke dismissed them. Whilst confessing the ignorance of French affairs, he damned the composition of the National Assembly, the source of its inspiration, and the constitution it had set about devising — always crying up prerogative, prerogative for a constitution he could not produce.

I readily perceive why Mr Burke declined going into the comparison between the English and French constitutions, because he could not perceive, when he sat down to the task, that no such thing as a Constitution existed on his side of the question. His book is certainly bulky enough to have contained all he could say on the subject, and it would have been the best manner in which people could have judged on their separate merits. Why then has he declined the only thing that was worthwhile to write upon?

There was no escaping the answer. Burke had abandoned the ground of constitutional argument, to rest his case on the outworn formula that the people should 'humbly submit themselves, their heirs, and posterities for ever' to kingship. Had the man learned nothing from events in America? Seemingly not. For all the reams of protestation, it appeared that he still needed a lesson in the truth that a constitution was not a thing in name only, but a fact; was not an ideal, but had real existence, and that where one could not be produced in visible form, then it did not exist.

A Constitution is a thing *antecedent* to a Government and a Government is only the creature of a Constitution. The Constitution of a country is not the act of its Government, but of the people constituting a Government. It is the body of elements, to which you can refer, and quote article by article; and contains the principles on which the Government shall be established, the manner in which it shall be organised, the powers it shall have, the mode of elections, the duration of Parliaments . . . the powers which the executive part of the Government shall have; and in fine, everything that relates to the complete organisation of a civil Government, and the principles on which it shall act, and by which it shall be bound.

Paine drank, and remembered. Fourteen years had passed since he had worked through the subject in *Common Sense*. In the meantime, he had gained much in self-confidence, and more in public esteem. Now Tom Paine was a name of consequence, his reflections needed no introduction; and rereading what he had written, he knew that this was a constitution defined. No government arising out of such principles had the right to alter itself. If it did, it would be arbitrary, it could do as it pleased.

On such grounds then, how did France and England compare? The French proposed that every man paying an annual tax of 60 sous (2s 6d) should be an elector, in England the franchise was a matter of caprice; the French proposed that representation should be based on the number of the electorate, in England, Yorkshire had a million inhabitants, Old Sarum three houses, yet each returned two MPs; the French proposed that the right of peace or war should be vested in the nation, in England it lay with the crown; in France it was proposed that all placemen should be abolished, and there should no longer be titles, in England . . . in England, Burke had introduced a programme for economical reform to eliminate the practice of places — to become a secret pensioner of the government himself. The story was confused, though it had been in circulation for two months and more. To air the charge publicly would provide the opportunity for a denial, whilst, if it held, it exposed the man for a hypocrite, and a pandering one at that. As he wrote, Paine's anger mounted that Burke, so long his mentor, should now play the Judas to betray mankind to elevate his new paymasters.

Paine watched the clamour in the yard below. The Norwich coach was due to depart. It was the same at noon each day: the same clamour of ostlers, and potboys, passengers and their friends, and, over all, the coachman in his private majesty. The warning bell tolled. The last passenger eased aboard. Tom Bates's lurcher bayed. The post horn sounded. The crowd in the galleries laughed or wept according to their mood and Paine wondered that these were the people that Burke had sold, the mob he now reviled.

> How is it then that such vast classes of mankind as are distinguished by the appellation of the vulgar, or the ignorant mob, are so numerous in all old countries? The instant we ask ourselves this question, reflection feels an answer. They arise, as an unavoidable consequence, out of the ill constructions of all the old Governments of Europe, England included with the rest. It is by distortedly exalting some men, that others are distortedly debased till the whole is out of nature. A vast mass of mankind are degradedly thrown into the background of the human picture, to bring forward with greater glare, the puppet-show of State and Aristocracy.

And who were they, this body of men who held themselves accountable to nobody? Burke made much of nobility. Let him show what it was, for one thing was sure. Titles were but nicknames, and every nickname was a title:

> The thing is perfectly harmless in itself but it marks a sort of foppery

in the human character, which degrades it. It reduces man into the diminutive of man in things which are great, and the counterfeit of woman in things which are little. It talks about its fine *blue ribbon* like a girl, its new *garter* like a child . . . It is, properly, from the elevated mind of France that the folly of titles has fallen. It has outgrown the baby cloathes of Count and Duke, and breeched itself in manhood. France has not levelled, it has exalted. It has put down the dwarf, to set up the man.

The yard below was empty now, save for the dog that had returned to its hutch, and Paine drank and considered what he had written. It was a digression, important perhaps, but a digression none the less; distracting the mind like a bauble from the essence of the case — that France now regarded the nation as the fountain of all sovereignty, whilst in England, Burke would retain such privilege for the king. Here was the difference which differentiated all the rest; which provoked Burke to call on the sovereigns of Europe to mount a Holy War against the sovereignty of the people, to pit their absolute Rights against the Rights of Man.

Not one glance of compassion, not one commiserating reflection that I can find throughout his book, has he bestowed on those who lingered out the most wretched lives, a life without hope in the most miserable of prisons . . . Nature has been kinder to Mr Burke than he is to her. He is not affected by the reality of distress touching his heart, but by the showy resemblance of it striking his imagination. He pities the plumage, but forgets the dying bird. Accustomed to kiss the aristocratical hand that hath purloined him from himself, he degenerates into a composition of art.

For inheritance was the property he now revered, yet sovereignty could never be the property of any man or family. The reverse. It belonged to the nation, not to any individual, and

a Nation has at all times an inherent, indefeasible right to abolish any form of Government it finds inconvenient, and to establish such as accords with its interest, disposition, happiness . . . Monarchical government, the enemy of mankind, and the source of misery, is abolished; and sovereignty itself is restored to its natural and original place, the Nation. Were this the case throughout Europe, the cause of wars would be taken away.

Almost two centuries had passed since Henry IV of France had proposed establishing a European Congress (or, as the French styled it, a Pacific Republic), in an attempt to abolish war in Europe. The plan failed. The dream remained prompting memories of childhood Sundays at the small Meeting House on Cage Lane. Now, perhaps, it would be realised. Now that France had adopted enlightened principles, perhaps there would be peace — if the rest of Europe allowed.

That was the rub, for, while man was no enemy of man, kings and their placemen saw a profit in blood-letting, and already Burke was calling for a war on peace. And again Paine felt that bitterness of the betrayal. Couldn't Burke understand that only the Rights of Man were descendable; that, if one generation was disposed to slavery, it did nothing to lessen the rights of succeeding generations to be free. Wrongs had no legal descent.

Ironic, he had learned the line from Burke himself, and now? Now the man was too far gone in his prejudices, and, with the book complete, Paine began the Preface:

> From the part Mr Burke took in the American Revolution, it was natural that I should consider him a friend to mankind; and as our acquaintance commenced on that ground, it would have been more agreeable to me to have had cause to continue in that opinion than to change it . . .
>
> When the French Revolution broke out, it certainly afforded to Mr Burke an opportunity of doing some good, had he been disposed to it; instead of which, no sooner did he see the old prejudices wearing away, than he began sowing the seeds of a new inveteracy, as if he were afraid that England and France would cease to be enemies. That there are men in all Nations who make their living by war, and keeping up the quarrels of Nations, is as shocking as it is true; but when those who are concerned in the government of a country make it their study to sow discord, and cultivate prejudices between Nations, it becomes the more unpardonable.

It was done. Since November the days and weeks had fused into one — but now the first part of *Rights of Man* was complete, yet the world outside his window looked the same as when he had begun. The same bustle and confusion, the same noise; and, while the faces might be different, these were still the people he loved, the people Burke feared and despised. That was the difference between them.

Part One of *Rights of Man* was published on 13 March 1791, with a dedication to George Washington:

> I present you a small Treatise in defence of those Principles of Freedom which your exemplary Virtue hath so eminently contributed to establish. That the Rights of Man may become as universal as your Benevolence can wish, and that you may enjoy the Happiness of seeing the New World regenerate the Old, is the prayer of Sir of
> Your much obliged and
> Obedient Humble Servant,
> THOMAS PAINE.

The reaction was immediate, the Constitutional Society ordering 25,000 copies for distribution throughout Britain; and Pitt remarking to Lady Hester Stanhope: 'Paine is quite right, but what am I to do? As things are, if I were to encourage Tom Paine's opinions I should have a bloody revolution.' Burke was more decisive. In the five months since its release, the sales of *Reflections* had been laggardly, and, while there had been a score of parodies on his contemplation of 'the swinish multitude' ('Hog's Wash, Pig's Meat, Mast and Acorns'; 'A Salamagundy for Swine, with contributions by Brother Grunter'), the jurist Samuel Romilly had taken to remarking publicly that former admirers of the work 'had begun to be ashamed of their admiration' since reading Paine.

It was all very well for the purist Horace Walpole to deride Paine's style; it required more than that to answer *Rights* and assuage Burke's pride. The law, he asserted, would satisfy both, but, sensing the public mood, the government refused to act. For all Burke's fulmination, and the fears of those he represented, there was still widespread sympathy for the French, and in April Charles James Fox went so far as to tell the Commons that the new constitution of France was 'the most stupendous and glorious edifice of liberty which had been erected on the foundations of human intregrity in any time or country'.

This was too much for Burke. A few days later he used a debate on the Quebec Bill to mount a diatribe against *Rights of Man*, the incendiary principles of the revolutionaries, and the infamous treatment of the King. Fox intervened, baiting Burke: 'From his Rt. Honourable Friend he had learned that the revolt of a whole people could never be countenanced or encouraged, it must have been provoked . . .' Tempers rose. Burke complained that Fox had 'ripped open the whole course and tenor of his public life'. Charles Grey* interrupted. Burke flared, he:

had frequently differed from Mr Fox in the past . . . never for a single moment interrupted their friendship . . . indiscreet at his time of life to give his friends occasion to desert him . . . now risk all and as public duty and private prudence taught him, exclaim: 'Fly from the French Constitution.'

Amiably Fox interposed that there was no loss of friendship. Then, to the astonishment of the House, Burke declared that he knew the price of his conduct, had 'done his duty at the price of his friend . . . their friendship was over'. Fox wept openly, and reminded Burke of their 25 years of 'most familiar intimacy'. Burke was unyielding. That intimacy was now at an end.

On the government front bench, Pitt savoured the scene. The patchwork of interests that had been the Whig party since 1688 was finally and ir-revocably dividing against itself, leaving Fox to lead the radical wing, and Burke to become increasingly isolated from the mainstream of the party as his fears infected, and his ideology was adopted by reaction. And if the first part of *Rights* helped divide Britain, much the same oc-curred in America.

Early in the 1780s John Adams had asserted that 'History is to ascribe the revolution to Tom Paine'. With the publication of *Rights* in the United States, he was to modify his views. As Vice-President, and leader of the conservative wing which favoured a constitution on the English model, opposing proposals for universal suffrage and pressing to make the Presidential office hereditary, he had recently published his own, vehe-ment attack on the progress of affairs in France — *Discourse on Davila*.

Adams's work reflected a broad swathe of American opinion, but the publication of *Rights* in the summer of 1791 did much to reverse the trend, and in the process triggered a bitter dispute between the republicans under Jefferson, James Madison and Edmund Randolph*, and the con-servatives. An edition of *Rights* published by S.H. Smith carried a brief recommendation from Jefferson:

> I am extremely pleased to find that it will be re-printed, and something is at length to be publicly said against the political heresies which have sprung up amongst us. I have no doubt our citizens will rally *a second time* round to the *standard* of Common Sense.

Jefferson, as Secretary of State, had not intended his private comments to the printer for publication, for there was no mistaking his target — Adams and the friends of reaction. Smith, however, was well aware of the capital to be gained from such an encomium, and the work literally exploded in the public's consciousness. It was bad enough that *Rights* was dedicated to the President; worse that a Secretary of State should deploy Paine against the Vice-President. Jefferson was gravely embarrassed, writing apologetically to Adams: 'I was thunderstruck with seeing it come out at the head of the pamphlet'; but others felt he had not gone far enough ('There is no use in fighting eight years for liberty, if she must lick the spittle of a Vice President') whilst Randolph was promoting Paine's name as the new Postmaster-General in Washington's Cabinet.

The controversy continued, but the move came to nothing, possibly due to Adams's hostility; he had recently been reported as saying that 'I detest that book and its tendency from the bottom of my heart'. Even if it had been offered, it is doubtful if Paine would have accepted the post — he was too embroiled in French affairs. As soon as *Rights* was with the printer, he was *en route* for Paris where events were moving towards a new crisis.

For almost two years the National Assembly and its committees had been piecing together a new civil constitution for France, their task becoming more difficult by the day. Each article widened the rift between the mounting antipathy of the *monarchistes* and the growing ambitions of the radicals, but until the spring of 1791 the centrist, Patriot party in the Assembly had managed to maintain the balance of power, and provide France with comparative stability. They lived within the shadow of their own legislation, however, not least, the Civil Constitution of the Clergy.

The decree had been issued in July 1790, in an attempt to make Catholic worship a part of the general structure of public life. The reform, including a provision for a reduction in the number of dioceses, and for the payment of the clergy by the state, was generally accepted by the church with one, crucial proviso — that such a programme demanded the approval of the Pope as well as the state. Eight months passed before Pius IV pronounced, anathematising the constitution and condemning its contents as being contrary to 'the most sacred dogmas' of Holy Church.

The Assembly anticipated just such a reply, and, in November 1790, had given all priests holding public office two months to swear an oath of loyalty to the new constitution. The diktat opened a bitter schism in the church. A number of bishops refused to take the oath, the Bishop of Narbonne commenting wryly: 'My God, if I had only been a Bishop I might have given way like the others, but I am a gentleman', and only half of the priesthood assenting. The move divided France as much as its church, and provided a new focus for reaction.

Then came the Papal pronouncement, encouraging dissent, infuriating the Protestants and free-thinkers in the Assembly, and convincing Louis in his opinion that: 'This Law is contrary to my religious opinion; I see it as the signal for the endless persecution of my kingdom.' For two years he had compromised with the Revolution, accepting its terms publicly, whilst writing to his cousin, the King of Spain, as early as October 1789:

> I have chosen Your Majesty, the head of the second branch of my family, as the person to whom I entrust my solemn protests against all the decrees contrary to royal authority to which I have been compelled by force to assent. I beg Your Majesty keep my protest secret until its publication becomes necessary.

The time was near. In the countryside, the White Terror was making its first appearance — anarchical, murderous and often inspired as much by brigandage as anti-republican sentiment. In the towns, crowds appeared on the streets wearing monarchist cockades in support of recalcitrant priests. Beyond the frontiers, the army of royalist *emigrés* grew restless with inactivity, whilst in the Tuileries Marie Antoinette read Burke ('No compromise with rebels! . . . appeal to soveriegn neighbours . . . trust to the support of foreign armies'), as Louis dispatched missions to friendly countries seeking their intervention in French affairs to re-establish the old order.

The Revolution had lost momentum, its bondage had become too great; better to move now before the Assembly, the National Guard or the Paris mob placed further restrictions on his movements. At Easter, his family had planned to take communion at Saint Cloud, but the gates of the Tuileries were shut by the crowd. For two hours there was uproar, then the King abandoned the journey. Effectively, Louis was a prisoner of the palace, and Paine was amused by the irony. At least he was free in what Gouverneur Morris was pleased to call his 'wretched apartment'.

Since returning to Paris in March, Paine had divided his time between trying to find a French publisher for *Rights*, and following the growing confusion of public affairs. In the Assembly, the rift between left and right widened daily; at the Tuileries, the King played each against the other, and all with the sanction of the church, always the church.

The creed made no difference; whether Quaker in Pennsylvania or Papist in France, they invoked their Gods to dabble in temporal affairs. Voltaire may have written that if God did not exist it would be necessary to invent him but for this . . . this mummery; for Pius to anathematise the constitution, for Louis to receive absolution for subverting the state. No wonder Burke's best sales were among the *emigrés*. His was their sort of God; a God who bound all in their place to posterity, then called it a constitution.

The Revolution might have its faults, but the alternative was a monster, and in May, Paine was in the Assembly when Robespierre proposed the abolition of the death penalty: 'Capital punishment is but base assassination, punishing one crime by another, murder by murder.' The ghosts returned — of Amy Hutchinson at the stake in Ely; of the macabre pilgrimage to Tyburn Tree — as the motion was seconded by the jurist Duport: 'Let us at least make revolutionary scenes as little tragic as possible. Let us render man honourable to man.'

The resolution was defeated but this, in essence, was what the Revolution represented, to make man honourable to man, so that, as Condorcet would have it:

A moment will come when the sun will shine only on free men on this earth, on men who will recognise no master but their reason; when tyrants and slaves, priests and their stupid hypocritical instruments will exist only in history or on the stage; when men will study the efforts and sufferings that characterised the past only to guard vigilantly against any recurrence of superstition and tyranny.

The dissenting aristrocrat admired Paine and his writings, going so far as to say that all friends of liberty should revere 'Common Sense', and through the early summer of 1791 Condorcet and Paine spent much time together discussing the problems of France — and the future of the King. The rumours of Louis's duplicity abounded; only recently he had dismissed his confessor for taking the constitutional oath, and if he continued to pursue such a course there could be only one, logical outcome — to declare France a republic.

Fifteen years had passed since Paine had written 'Men who look upon themselves as born to reign, and others to obey, soon grow insolent'; since he had considered that 'The palaces of kings are built on the ruins of the bowers of paradise', since he had proposed that 'the Crown be demolished . . . and scattered among the people whose right it is'. That had been in 1776, but the same still applied. France should demolish sovereignty for, while feigning humility, Louis remained insolent — though until he betrayed his designs he would remain at the Tuileries as 'King of the French'.

Condorcet and Paine did not have long to wait. On the morning of

21 June, Lafayette (Commander of the National Guard) burst into Paine's room before he was up. 'The birds are flown,' he raged. At 10 o'clock the previous evening, the King, Marie Antoinette and the royal children had slipped out of the palace in disguise (Louis calling himself the valet Durand, and dressed in a grey coat and wig), and been driven out of Paris in an inconspicuous travelling coach.

By early morning on the twenty-first they were close to Meaux, while in Paris Paine shook the sleep from his eyes and replied to Lafayette: 'It's well. I hope that no attempt will be made to recall them.' But there was. As soon as the King's flight was discovered, riders were dispatched eastwards towards the frontier. All through the day (the longest of the year), the royal family jolted and rattled their way across the hot, dusty high roads of northern France, haunted by fears of being recognised.

At Étoges an hour was lost through an accident to the horses, and a broken trace. At Chalons, they changed horses and were identified — but the Mayor delayed for six hours before posting the news back to Paris where Paine was confiding to a friend: 'You see the absurdity of mon-archical governments; here will be a whole nation disturbed by the folly of one man.'

By early evening the royal family were at the small town of Sainte-Menehould, to be met by a royalist escort. However, the posting master of the town had recognised Louis, and, when the coach moved out, the escort was prevented from following. At Clermont it was the same; a royal escort waited, but the coach was compelled by the townspeople to go on alone. Shortly before midnight, the carriage entered Varennes where the royal family were escorted to a room above a grocer's shop and Louis admitted to a local judge that he was, indeed, the King. The flight was at an end, and early on the morning of the twenty-second, the royal family took the road back to Paris — under heavy guard.

The journey ended on Saturday, 25 June. From six in the morning until seven in the evening the coach had driven with its blinds drawn against the dust and heat. On entering Paris, the National Guard carried their muskets under their arms, as if at a funeral, whilst instructions had been posted that the crowd should remain silent ('Whoever applauds the King shall be flogged. Whoever insults him shall be hanged') and that all bystanders should be covered and wearing the tricolour. The crowds were dense, among them Paine — bareheaded. The mob were quick to notice the imagined insult: 'Aristo! Aristo! à la lanterne! à la lanterne!' For a moment it seemed as if Tom Paine, author of *Rights of Man*, would be strung from a lamp-post to decorate Louis's passage, but in broken French he apologised for his mistake and the crowd fell silent again to watch the King pass.

On his flight, the King's secret papers condemning the Revolution and all it represented had been discovered at the Tuileries. On his return, the debate on his future opened. Since the twenty-first there had been a growing clamour demanding that Louis forfeit the crown, or at least that there should be consultations with the constituencies as to whether he should be returned to the throne. By the month's end, Paine, Condorcet and three others had founded the Republican Society which on 1 July posted a manifesto on the door of the National Assembly:

> Louis has abdicated the throne . . . the nation can never give back its confidence to a man who is false in his trust, perjured in his oath . . . the reciprocal obligation which subsisted between us is dissolved. He no longer holds any authority. We owe him no longer obedience . . .
>
> The history of France presents little else than a long series of public calamity, which takes its source from the vices of the Kings . . . The catalogue of their oppressions was complete, but to complete the sum of their crimes, treason was yet wanting. Now the only vacancy is filled up, the dreadful list is full; the system is exhausted; there are no remaining errors for them to commit, their reign is consequently at an end.

As the law required, the manifesto was above the signature of a French citizen, Du Chatelet, a member of the Club, but the words were Paine's — the first time that there had been an open call for France to declare itself a republic. The following morning the manifesto was published in full in *Patriote française*, and caused an uproar.

The talk in the cafés around the Palais-Royal was all of the manifesto; two members of the Assembly accused Paine of criminal imbecility; and, while the Assembly itself might reject the plan, Paine's opinion of himself blossomed. It was all very well for Morris to dismiss him as 'inflated to the Eyes, and big with a Litter of Revolutions' — the man was no friend of liberty, never had been, whereas the young Palmerston* openly admitted that 'republican principles are now avowed on every street', and Condorcet was in discussion with Sieyes to open a journalistic exchange in which the Abbé would lend his reputation to the principles of the Declaration of Rights.

The Sieyes letter was carried in the *Moniteur* on 6 July; on 11 July, Voltaire's remains were transferred to the Pantheon on a triumphal car drawn by twelve horses, four abreast; and on 16 July, Paine's reply appeared in the *Republicain*:

> Whenever the French constitution shall be rendered conformable to
> its declaration of rights, we shall then be able to give France, and with
> justice, the appellation of a Civic Empire; for its government will be
> the empire of laws, founded on the great republican principles of elec-
> tive representation and the rights of man. But monarchy and hereditary
> succession are incompatible with the basis of its Constitution.

Lafayette accepted the principle, though doubting whether it could be
realised within 20 years. He underestimated the pace of events. Within
18 months Paine's words, and what they represented, were to transform
the course of French history; in the meantime, however, he had business
in London.

10 'THE SPRING HAS BEGUN'

The political mood in England was shifting, gradually. While the majority of the upper and middle classes still sympathised with French aspirations, reaction not only read Burke but outstripped him and, on 14 July 1791, a 'King and Country' mob began a three-day rampage through Birmingham, sacking chapels and the homes of wealthy dissenters, and burning the laboratory of the radical scientist Joseph Priestley.* Though isolated, the incident was a foretaste of what was to come, county gentry and Tory magistrates (and the two were often synonymous) not only encouraging the rioters, but also selecting targets for their violence.

In London, however, counter-revolution still remained discreet. In late June, Paine had received an invitation from Horne Tooke and the Revolution Society to address 'A Select Meeting of the Friends of UNIVERSAL PEACE AND LIBERTY' at the Crown and Anchor on Bastille Day. With his letter to Sieyes complete by 8 July, Paine left Paris for London with the radical Lord Daer, and Étienne Dumont. The latter, a moderate, had little time for either Paine's principles or his self-esteem.

> He believed that his book on the 'Rights of Man' could take the place of all the books in the world, and he said to us quite sincerely that if it were in his power to demolish all the libraries in existence he would do it, so as to destroy all the errors of which they are the depository — and with the 'Rights of Man' begin a new chain of ideas and principles. He knew by heart all his own writings, and nothing else.

It was always the same. Whenever Paine became the focus of public attention or controversy (and the Manifesto that he had left behind in Paris had caused furore enough) his self-esteem burgeoned, to become unbearable when reinforced by his rectitude. For almost 20 years (first in England, following the publication of *The Case of the Officers of the Excise*; then in America with the public response to *Common Sense*), success had primed his vanity — yet without it, there would have been nothing. That's what Morris and Dumont and their like could not understand; that, without a belief in himself and all he represented, he would still have been Tom Paine, the staymaker of Thetford, or at best an outrider in the Excise at Lewes.

And it was not just that he was taking on the 'repository of errors' that was history; there was all the vested privilege that that entailed. Burke had had his opportunities, and talked often enough of his days at Trinity, Dublin, his time as secretary to the second Marquis of Rockingham; but even he was poor in comparison to those whose cause he pleaded with their classical education, their well-stocked libraries, and the wealth and the time to study at leisure. As for himself? Paine shrugged off the self-pity. As for himself, he had learned enough to teach others, though, once he lost the confidence in what the critics were pleased to call his conceit, once he doubted himself, then M. Dumont's criticisms would indeed be justified.

As it was, the Revolution Society still thought enough of 'Common Sense' to invite him as guest of honour to their meeting, and it was said that more than a thousand guests had already accepted the invitation. Paine arrived in London on 13 July, to learn the following morning that the meeting had been cancelled. Though nothing was clear, the word was that the landlord of the Crown and Anchor had been 'persuaded' as to the inadvisability of hosting a gathering to celebrate Bastille Day — but was pleased enough to entertain members of the Royal Society, among them Mr Burke, who was doubtless considering his latest work.

In the three months since his confrontation with Fox, Burke had become increasingly isolated, the *Morning Chronicle* reporting:

> The great and firm body of the Whigs of England, true to their principles, have decided on the dispute between Mr Fox and Mr Burke, and the former is declared to have maintained the pure doctrines by which they are bound together, and upon which they invariably acted. The consequence is that Mr Burke retires from Parliament.

The journal anticipated events. Burke retained his seat, and worked up his reply: 'An Appeal from the New to the Old Whigs' which appeared in August 1791, within days of the rearranged meeting of the Revolution Society at the Thatched House Tavern. Paine drafted the main resolution for the function — 'The Address and Declaration of the Friends of Universal Peace and Liberty' — which rejected a republican government for England, but professed:

> If we are asked what government is, we hold it be nothing more than a national association; and we hold that to be the best which secures to every man his rights and promotes the greatest quantity of happiness with the least expense. We live to improve, or we live in vain; and

therefore we admit of no maxims of government or policy on the mere score of antiquity or other men's authority, the old Whigs or the new.

The Address, which was carried unanimously, provided the first, clear indication of the content of Paine's reply to Burke; it contrasted the extravagances of government ('affording more pretences for places, offices, pensions, revenue and taxation') with the plight of the poor ('we hold that the moral obligation of providing for old age, helpless infancy, and poverty, is far superior to that of supplying the invented wants of courtly extravagance, ambition and intrigue').

It was a conflict that Burke could not, or would not, understand. The 'Appeal' was much the same miscellany as before, defending the principles of the old Whigs on the grounds of precedent and the Revolution of 1688, to castigate the new Whigs who had adopted more advanced views. Only nine months had passed since the publication of *Reflections*, yet Burke plagiarised himself:

the nameless thing that has been lately set up in France . . . a foul, impious, monstrous thing wholly out of the course of moral Nature . . . a constitution which, as it now stands, is a tyranny beyond any that can be found in the civilised European world of our age.

All this and more, whilst extolling a constitution which he still could not produce, save in some mystic 'original contract between crown and people'; whilst proclaiming the incontestability of property, forgetful of the contestability of some two million acres of common land that had been appropriated by enclosures in the past half century; and whilst huzzaing-up his own right to publication to drown out his critics 'if, that is, such writings should be thought to deserve any other than the refutation of criminal justice'.

So much for Burke's notions of liberty. The man made a play of his principles, then cast it with mutes, though, with the latest news out of France, he would have to take care that like the strolling player he was not left to strut and fret his hour upon the stage — to be heard no more. After the alarms of the summer, affairs were again taking a steady course in Paris, and it was widely reported that Louis would soon put his name to the new constitution. The prospect contradicted all Burke's worst fears, and gave the lie to his contempt for *Rights of Man*.

None the less, the 'Appeal' demanded a reply, for two could say with Burke: 'An orator, above all men, ought to be allowed a full and free use of the praise of liberty.' It was now six months since the first parts of *Rights* had been published to outsell *Reflections* twice over, and in the autumn of 1791, Paine began work on the second part at 7, Upper Marylebone Road, the home of his friend from the days in Lewes, Clio Rickmann.

It was a quiet and pleasant time for Paine. Fifty-four years of age, and widely respected, it seemed that he had seen two revolutions through to their successful completion: on 17 October 1781, Cornwallis had surrendered to Washington at Yorktown; and on 13 September 1791, Louis XVI, King of the French, gave his approval to the revised constitution. If he had not lived through such times, it would have been hard to credit them; hard to credit that little more than 16 years had passed since he had first taken ship to the New World with Franklin's note in his pocket ('The bearer, Mr Thomas Paine, is very well recommended to me as an ingenious, worthy young man . . .') to learn the lessons of a new world and then see them applied in the old.

Through the autumn and winter of 1791, Paine spent his days writing or visiting friends and acquaintances — Mary Wollstonecraft,* William Blake,* Joseph Priestley, Horne Tooke, the French and American Ambassadors — and sitting for a portrait by George Romney.* In the evenings, after dinner, he played chess and draughts with the Rickmann family, or took part in discussions which carried through until the early hours of the morning. It was a good life, which he had rarely known, but always there was *Rights of Man* to complete.

For all the entertaining, for all the choruses: 'He comes — The Great Reformer Comes', Burke and reaction still needed answering. While affairs in France appeared settled enough, the emigrés' call for war against the Revolution became more insistent, and only recently Leopold of Austria and Frederick of Prussia had issued the declaration of Pilnitz asserting their willingness to restore the French monarchy — given the support of Europe's other crowned heads.

The move came to nothing (only Sweden offering unconditional support), but it was a dangerous game they played attempting to dictate to the French in their present mood. With the constitution just signed, Leopold and Frederick gambled with the future of Louis and his family, while Marie Antoinette planned counter-revolution at the heart of the Revolution itself to write in an echo of Burke: 'Everything has been overturned by force and force alone can repair the damage.' If Burke pursued his present course, and the *emigrés* now took *Reflections* as their handbook, his text would see Louis to the scaffold.

Paine wrote:

The Revolutions which formerly took place in the world had nothing in them that interested the bulk of mankind. They extended only to a change of persons and measures, but not of principles, and rose and fell among the common transactions of the moment. What we now behold may not improperly be called a '*counter-revolution*'. Conquest and tyranny, at some early period, dispossessed man of his rights, and he is now recovering them. And as the tide of all human affairs has its ebb and its flow in directions contrary to each other, so also is it in this. Government founded *on a moral theory, on a universal system of peace, on a indefeasible hereditary Rights of Man* is now resolving from west to east by a stronger impulse than the Governments of the sword resolve from east to west.

Even Burke could not deny that much. He had devoted time enough to applauding American liberties and here, at least, he was right. The achievement of independence would have been of little consequence, if it had not been accompanied by a revolution in the principles and practice of government, a revolution inspired by reason rather than prejudice. This, surely, was the American lesson: that if man was wholly a creature of society then government was no more than a national association acting on the principles of society, and that once this common interest was unbalanced, both society and government became disturbed.

And here again, Burke was right. While he might have shifted his ground in the 'Appeal', he had protested often enough the public's right to oppose bad government whether in England at the Glorious Revolution, or the American colonies under George, and heaven alone knew:

> If we look back to the riots and tumults which at various times have happened in England, we shall find that they did not proceed from the want of a Government, but that Government was itself generating the cause; instead of consolidating society it divided it; it deprived it of its natural cohesion, and engendered discontents and disorders which otherwise would not have existed . . . Whatever the apparent cause of any riots maybe, the real one is always the want of happiness. It shows that something is wrong in the system of Government that injures the felicity by which society is to be preserved.

He would go this far with Burke, no further, for while Burke accepted the right to resist bad government, he rejected the inevitable conclusion that the history of resistance clearly indicated that monarchical government had been in total violation of any principle. There was little advantage in labouring the point that government by precedent, indifferent to principle, was one of the vilest systems. He had treated it often enough before. But what of the option? What of representative government? While Burke might confound such a system, it was no simple democracy that was for sure.

Athens had known democracy, but not representation; for them government was but a citizens' meeting and while the principle might be admirable, it was incapable of extension; of embracing greater populations, greater territories without the application of representation.

> By ingrafting representation upon Democracy, we arrive at a system of Government capable of embracing and confederating all the various interests and every extent of territory and population . . . It is the easiest of all forms of Government to be understood and the most eligible in practice . . . not more than a common centre, in which all the parts of society unite.

Unlike monarchy, there was no mystery to the thing, no cant, no sophistry; no separating out between knowledge and power; no secrets behind the curtain, for:

> In the representative system, the reason for everything must publicly appear. Every man is a proprietor in Government, and considers it a necessary part of his business to understand . . . The Government of a free country, properly speaking, is not in the persons, but in the laws. The enacting of those require no great expense; and when they are administered the whole of civil Government is performed — all the rest is court contrivance.

Surely that was straightforward enough for even the most obtuse to understand. Yet Burke and his kind still wrapped government in mystery, and invoked the Bill of Rights to disguise the rest. But what was it, this Bill of theirs? No more than a bargain between power-brokers to divide up the profits and privileges of the nation — one saying 'I will have so much', the other 'And I the rest' — and then call it a Glorious Revolution.

In fact, such pretension was no more than a new despotism, the Whigs had made sure of that.

> It is not because part of the Government is elective that makes it less of a despotism, if the persons possess afterwards, as a Parliament, unlimited powers. Election in this case becomes separated from representation, and the candidates are candidates for despotism.

Yet Burke ennobled the travesty with the title of a 'constitution'. The effrontery mocked man and his Creator, denying that a true constitution was the property of a nation, not simply those who exercised government. The summary pleased Paine. It was taut, elegant: a constitution based upon representation to serve the interests of society as a whole for

> Whatever manner the separate parts of a Constitution may be arranged there is *one* general principle that distinguishes freedom from slavery, which is *that all hereditary Government over a people is to them a species of slavery, and representative Government is freedom.*

He reread the words, drank, and preened himself. Small wonder that he had helped build a new empire and established himself as a political author of eminence; *Common Sense* had met with a success beyond anything since the invention of printing and given him the ear and confidence of America itself. Considering his beginnings, it was no mean achievement. The Reverend Knowler might have had his adventures, but they were as nothing compared to this, and all thanks to a perseverance that broached no difficulties, to a disinterestedness that compelled respect. What was it they had sung recently at the Revolution Society in the London Tavern: Paine's Welcome to Great Britain:

> He comes — the great Reformer Comes!
> The joyful tidings spread around,
> Monarchs tremble at the sound!
> Freedom, freedom, freedom, freedom —
> Rights of man, and Paine resound!

Incredible, though little more than his due, and for a moment he called up his new friendships — Fox and Priestley, Condorcet and Lafayette, Washington and Jefferson — and forgot the old. The corruption was deep-rooted, feeding his vanity whilst sapping his conscience and, angry at this betrayal, Paine emptied the glass and wrote:

> When in countries that are called civilised, we see age going to the workhouse and youth to the gallows, something must be wrong in the system of Government . . . Civil Government does not consist in executions; but in making that provision for the instruction of youth and support for age, as to exclude, as much as possible, profligacy from the one and despair from the other . . .
>
> Why is it that scarcely any are executed but the poor? The fact is a proof, among other things, of a wretchedness in their condition. Bred up without morals, and cast upon the world without a prospect, they are the exposed sacrifice of vice and legal barbarity. The millions that

are superfluously wasted upon Governments are more than sufficient to reform these evils, and to benefit the condition of every man in a Nation, not included within the purlieus of a Court.

As the old marching song had it, this was the world turned upside-down, where those most in need got least from a system that taxed the poor to afford the rich. While the court, its placemen, and Mr Burke on his £1,500 a year, were pleased to stand equity on its head, the bitterness of want and misery increased in proportion to the levying of new taxation — and even the physicians' bills out of St James's were now sent to the public to be paid. The system was as monstrous as it was corrupt, yet given reform the world could be righted, and 'spring would be summer, not the other way round'.

In the quiet of Clio Rickmann's house, Tom Paine toyed with the fantasy, and, remembering all he had learned of the world of little causes that led to ruin, wrote up his welfare programme: of maternity grants ('were twenty shillings given immediately on the birth of a child, to every woman who should make the demand . . . it might relieve a great deal of instant distress'), and married couple benefits ('and twenty shillings to every new married couple who should claim it in like manner'); of child allowances ('To pay as a remission of taxes to every poor family . . . four pounds a year for every child under fourteen years of age'); and education grants ('to allow for each of those children ten shillings a year for the expense of schooling for six years'); of old age pensions ('This support is not of the nature of a charity, but of a right . . . To pay every such person of the age of fifty years, and until he shall arrive at the age of sixty, the sum of six pounds per annum out of surplus taxes, and ten pounds per annum during life after the age of sixty'); and death grants ('Also twenty thousand pounds to be appropriated to defray the funeral expenses of persons who, travelling to work, may die at a distance from their friends').

By the operation of this plan, the poor laws, those instruments of civil torture, will be superseded, and the wasteful experience of litigation prevented. The hearts of the humane will not be shocked by ragged and hungry children, and persons of seventy or eighty years of age, begging for bread. The dying poor will not be dragged from place to place to breathe their last, as a reprisal of parish upon parish. Widows will have a maintenance for their children, and not be carted away, on the deaths of their husbands, like culprits and criminals; and children will be no longer considered as increasing the distresses of their parents . . . The poor as well as the rich will then be interested in the support of Government, and the cause and apprehension of riots and tumults will cease.

Ye who sit in ease, and solace yourselves in plenty — and such there are in Turkey and Russia, as well as in England — and who say to yourselves, 'Are we not well off?' have ye thought of these things? When ye do, ye will cease to speak and feel for yourselves alone.

This would be a true revolution, a revolution of humanity — and it was affordable. Given some small sacrifice from those who would least miss it (and a progressive tax on income would raise almost £4 million a year for the Treasury), the curse of poverty would be banished from England, but when — and ill-clothed, hungry and desperate, the ghosts of his past moved into the future until he could see them no more.

The old year turned into the new, and fifteen years had passed since the publication of *Common Sense*. Then he had been in more of a hurry, and the times were well fitted to his mood. The years between had taught him cynicism. It was hard enough to persuade men to share their votes, let alone their wealth; but the thing needed saying for these were the rights of men and he recalled an afternoon in Philadelphia those many years ago when he and Jefferson had first talked of 'life, liberty, and the pursuit of happiness'. The ideal remained:

Some gentlemen have affected to call the principles upon which this work and the former part of the 'Rights of Man' are founded 'a new fangled doctrine'. The question is not whether the principles are new or old, but whether they are right or wrong . . .

It is now towards the middle of February. Were I to take a turn into the country the trees would present a leafless wintery appearance. As people are apt to pluck twigs as they walk along, I perhaps might do the same, and by chance might observe that a *single bud* on that twig had begun to swell. I should reason very unnaturally, or rather not reason at all, to suppose *this* was the *only* bud in England which had this appearance.

Instead of deciding thus, I should conclude that the same appearance was beginning, or about to begin, everywhere; and though the vegetable sleep will continue longer on some trees and plants than others, and though some of them may not *blossom* for two or three years, all will be in leaf in the summer, except those which are *rotten*.

What pace the political summer will keep with the natural, no human foresight can determine. It is, however, not difficult to determine that the spring has begun.

Save for the dedication to Lafayette, the work was complete. Burke was answered. The work might not persuade him, he was too far gone for that. With others, however, it would be different, for mankind was always ready to understand its true interests, as long as they were presented clearly enough, and he signed the work 'Tom Paine, London, February 9th, 1792'.

Since late 1791, Paine had been passing sections of his manuscript to the publisher, Chapman, and by mid-January more than a hundred pages had been set, with the plan for completion before the opening of Parliament. The government, however, was increasingly alarmed by the growth of radicalism and, while Paine was writing: 'By what I can find, the Government Gentry begin to threaten. They have already tried all the underplots of abuse and scurillity without effect', Pitt's agents were pressuring Chapman to refuse publication.

The story is confused: Paine charged that, with funds provided by the government, Chapman had offered him £1,000 to buy out the copyright so that he lost control of the work; Chapman counter-charged that, when drunk, Paine had offended his wife. Whatever the truth, a notice appeared in the *Gazeteer* on 25 January that:

MR PAINE, it is known, is to produce another book this season. The composition of this is now past, and it was given a few weeks since to two printers, whose presses it was to go through as soon as possible. They printed about half of it and then, being alarmed by *some intimations*, refused to go further.

A fortnight later, Paine ordered Chapman to hand over all the printed sheets to his new publisher, J.S. Jordan. On 13 February the first copies were complete, and, while Paine was writing a note in an attempt to cover Jordan against any prosecution ('Sir: Should any person . . . enquire of you respecting the author and publisher of the Rights of Man, you will please to mention me as the author and publisher of what work, and show to such a person this letter'), Gouverneur Morris was writing to Washington:

I have read Paine's new publication today, and tell him that I am really afraid that he will be punished. He seems to laugh at this, and relies on the force he has in the nation. He seems to become every hour more drunk with self-conceit. It seems, however, that his work excites but little emotion, and rather raises indignation.

Morris was wrong on the first count, right on the second. If Part One of *Rights* was successful, and 50,000 copies had already been sold, then, Part Two was destined to become one of the best-sellers of all times. More than 200,000 copies were sold in England (with a population of little more than ten million people) in the first year alone, to fuse dissent and introduce a generation of unprecedented repression. In the three years since Dr Richard Price had delivered his 'Discourse of the Love of our Country' at the Old Jewry, and provoked Burke's *Reflections*, the radical movement had gained both in strength and purpose, and, in January 1792, the Society for Constitutional Information (of which Paine was a member) and the Revolution Societies were joined by the London Corresponding Society.

Although varying in their programmes from the comparatively moderate radicalism of the Revolution Societies, largely committed to the Settlement of 1688, to the more extreme demands of the LCS, they found common cause in Paine's programme for social reform. In the spring of 1792, the moderates in the Society for Constitutional Information were ousted by the Painites, while reports were coming in from throughout the country of the impact of the second part of *Rights*.

From Sheffield, the Deputy Adjutant General, on a tour of Britain to check on the reliability of the troops, was writing: 'that the most seditious doctrines of Paine and the factious doctrines of the people who were endeavouring to disturb the peace of the country had extended to a degree much beyond my conception'; from Leeds a businessman was reporting of 'Paine's mischievous work compressed into a sixpenny pamphlet, and sold and given away in profusion'; from Durham a correspondent was noting that: 'During the late disturbances of Shields and Sunderland, General Lambton was thus addressed: "Have you read this little work of Tom Paine's?" "No." "Then read it — we much like it" '; whilst North Wales was said to be 'infested by itinerant Methodist preachers who descant on the Rights of Man and attack Kingly Government'.

By late spring, Pitt's government was haunted by the spectre of revolution at home, and war abroad. Only six months previously, Pitt himself had been talking of 15 years of peace, but on 20 April, France had declared war on Austria. It was an ill omen, and largely the product of the growing confusion in French internal affairs. Louis and Marie Antoinette wanted war in the vain hope that a French defeat would lead to the restoration of the *ancien régime*. Lafayette and the moderates wanted war, believing that a short campaign would help consolidate the Revolution. The radicals wanted war to promote Fraternity in the interests of Liberty and Equality. On the left, only Robespierre stood out against the militants. To France's cost, he was ignored. Within the month, the French were in retreat, and on 10 May the commanders in the field decided to cease hostilities — leading to acrimonious charges that the Republic had been betrayed.

Inexorably, the Revolution was moving towards a new crisis, and, while the right in England followed events with a horrid fascination, the left still took their examples from France, and quoted Paine on rights that free-born Englishmen may well have considered in private, but had rarely broached in public. The political mood was polarising, rapidly, and by April, the new Whigs in the House had begun to distance themselves from the radical movement out of doors; Charles Grey, a close friend of Fox and Sheridan, announced the formation of the Friends of the People, aimed primarily at reforming parliamentary representation.

It was a retreat from Fox's republican eulogies of only twelve months before, but, if the new Whigs chose moderation, the government preferred reaction. Replying to Grey, Pitt shifted his ground on the need for reform. Once he had supported such a measure but

> This is not the time to make hazardous experiments . . . to follow a madness which has been called liberty in another country; a condition at war with true freedom and good order; — a state to which despotism itself is preferable; — a state in which liberty would not exist for a day; — if it appeared in the morning, it must perish before sun set.

Pitt's defence of liberty was to take on a bizarre character. By 21 May, the King had issued a Proclamation for Preventing Seditious Meetings and Writings:

> Whereas divers wicked and seditious writings have been printed, published, and industriously dispersed . . . We do strictly command our magistrates in and throughout our Kingdom of Great Britain, that they do make diligent enquiry, in order to discover the authors and printers of such wicked and seditious writings.

By the late summer, the government had funded and unloosed 'King and Country' mobs throughout the country, whose prime targets were Paine, and *Rights of Man*. In Lincoln, among other places, he was hung in effigy 'amidst a vast multitude of spectators'; in Yorkshire, he replaced Guy Fawkes on Bonfire Night; whilst one small village reported that the executioner's hands ran with blood from pounding the image of Paine into pieces — and all to the tune of 'Old Satan had a darling boy;/Full equal he to Cain;/Born peace and order to destroy;/His name was — THOMAS PAINE'.

Within the next two years, government spies and *agents provocateurs* had penetrated virtually every radical group in Britain, and in 1794, Habeas Corpus was suspended and the first of the Combination Acts passed. This was liberty in chains, and the hulks on the mud-flats of the Thames filled with dissenters, awaiting passage to Botany Bay. For 30 years following the publication of *Rights* and Pitt's volte-face in the Commons, coercion mocked the liberty of free-born Englishmen. In May 1792, however, it was the prohibition on 'seditious meetings and writings' that concerned Paine most.

He could shrug off the abuse of hacks such as Peter Pindar ('And vomit forth their grisly bands;/Surrounded by this squalid host,/Paine shall their leader be, and boast;/PAINE, GORDON, and REBELLION, shall shake hands'); could dismiss the savage cartoons of Gilray; could laugh at the new medals cast showing him hanging in chains ('We dance, Paine Swings'); but he could not ignore the far-reaching implications of the Royal Proclamation.

On 14 May, while staying in Bromley, Kent, he learned that the government had issued a summons against his printer, Jordan. Seven days later, the Proclamation was published in the Commons, for Fox to argue that its ambiguity disguised the government's sole intention of prosecuting the author of *Rights of Man* — and that evening a summons against Paine to appear before the Court of the King's Bench on 8 June was served at Clio Rickmann's house.

Two days before the hearing was due, Paine opened his counter-attack. In an open letter to the Home Secretary, Dundas,* he denied charges that he had tried to hide from prosecution ('the apartments that he occupied at the time of writing the work last winter, he has continued to occupy to the present time'); he alleged that he was being prosecuted for advocating exactly what the government was claiming to defend, but was unable to produce (a constitution); and he closed with a bitter aside against Burke:

I believe that Mr Burke, finding himself defeated, has been one of the promoters of this prosecution; and I shall return the compliment by showing, in a future publication, that he has been a masked pensioner at £1,500 per annum for about ten years. Thus it is that public money is wasted, and the dread of public investigation produced.

On 8 June, the hearing was postponed until December, but the full charge published. Running to 40 pages, it accused Paine of 'being a wicked, malicious, seditious, and ill-disposed person, and being greatly disaffected to our said Sovereign, the now King, and the happy constitution and government of this kingdom'. With minor variations, the phrase was repeated 15 times through the document, punctuating the Attorney-General's prosecution of *Rights of Man*. Having failed by other means, the law was closing in about Paine, while his opponents circulated rumours that he was on the point of flight to Paris where the climate was more conducive to his radical talents.

Since the disastrous beginnings of the war with Austria, conditions in France had degenerated sharply. There were growing disturbances in the Provinces; in the Assembly, the Jacobins* charged the Girondins* of being in the pay of the Court, whilst the Girondins charged that the Jacobins, who had opposed the war, were plotting a counter-revolution; and with the economy deteriorating and food prices rising, the sansculottes took to the streets of the capital again.

On 20 June, a march of 8,000 shopkeepers, working women, artisans and National Guardsmen armed with pikes, pitchforks and muskets invaded the Assembly, and then moved on to the Tuileries. Louis was in an ante-room when the mob burst in roaring: 'Tremblez tyrans! Voici les sansculottes!' A spokesman quietened the crowd to read a petition, and above the uproar that followed — 'Vive la Nation' — Louis replied: 'Yes, Vive la Nation. The nation has no better friend than me,' then toasted France from a bottle of wine.

It was a triumph for the monarchy, if short-lived. Almost exactly three years before, the aristocracy had joined with the Third Estate to challenge the King. Almost exactly twelve months before, Louis had agreed to a constitution that encapsulated the ambitions of the bourgeoisie. Now it was the turn of the proletariat (or that section of it represented by the districts of Paris), and on 13 July, as alarmed by the activities of the sansculottes as by the threat of the Austrians, the Assembly declared 'La patrie en danger'. It was a dangerous step towards populist absolutism, ominously symbolised the following day — 14 July — when the crowds ordered Louis to burn down the Tree of Feudalism on the Champs de Mars. Protesting at the indignity, his guard escorted him to the comparative safety of the École Militaire.

Momentarily the crisis was averted, and, dismissing news of the troubles in Paris as the temporary, if inevitable, product of change, Paine continued work on his 'Letter Addressed to the Addressers of the Late Proclamation'. Since the publication of the Proclamation in May, a steady flow of loyal addresses had been reaching St James's Palace, one from the Clergy of the Diocese of Worcester setting the general tone, begging:

> to return our warmest thanks to your Majesty for your Majesty's latest wise and provident proclamation. In our present circumstances, Sir, nothing but experience could make it conceivable that any of your Majesty's subjects, in the full enjoyment of every blessing which the best government can bestow, should be so weak or wicked as to endeavour to raise groundless jealousies and discontents in the minds of the people, and to disseminate such principles and writings among them as tend to destroy . . . our excellent constitution.

The Addresses published in the following months bore down, monotonously, on the same theme, whilst repeating almost word for word the charge that Paine was a 'wicked, malicious, seditious, and ill-disposed person'. Little more than twelve months before, Pitt had confessed that Paine might, indeed, be right. Now he was orchestrating an unprecedented campaign to discredit both the man and his works. It was a challenge that Paine himself could not ignore. If he was worried for his safety, he was equally concerned publicly to renounce the charges brought against him.

> Could I have commanded circumstances with a wish, I know not of any that would have more generally promoted the progress of knowledge, than the late Proclamation, and the numerous rotten Boroughs and Corporation Addresses thereon. They have not only served as advertisements, but they have excited the spirit of enquiry into principles of government, and a desire to read the RIGHTS OF MAN, in places, where that spirit and that work were before unknown.
>
> The people of England, wearied and stunned by parties, and alternatively deceived by each, had almost resigned the prerogative of thinking. Even curiosity had expired, and a universal languor had spread itself over the land. The opposition was visibly no more than a contest for power, whilst the mass of the nation stood torpidly by as the prize.

His books had changed all that, and, if he were now to take a turn in the country, he would see the buds of political summer blossoming — save at Westminster. There was nothing to be hoped from there, for it had neither the right ('no government has a right to alter itself, either in part or in whole. The right, and the exercise of that right, appertains to the nation only . . .'), nor the will to reform itself, and its abuses, out of existence. All that had happened since the publication of the second part of *Rights* had made that clear, the Cabinet behaving as if a conspiracy of the elements was forming around it. In such a situation, at such a time, there was nothing to be gained from government; but what of the alternative?

> Instead, then, of referring to rotten Boroughs and absurd Corporations . . . the real and effectual mode would be to come at once to the point, and to ascertain the sense of the nation by electing a National Convention. By this method, the general WILL, whether to reform or not, or what the reform shall be, or how far it shall extend, will be known . . . It will then be seen whether seventeen millions of taxes are necessary . . . concealed pensioners will then be obliged to unmask . . . the source of influence or corruption, if such there be, will be laid open to the nation . . . THE NATION WILL DECREE ITS OWN REFORMS.

While the organisation of such a convention would not be difficult (election being based on male suffrage for all over 21 years of age), the principle of the thing would put government to the test. Pitt, Dundas, Burke and the rest all made high claims for the current system (only recently Pitt had again been talking up 'the beauty of the constitution . . . a monument to human wisdom, which had hitherto been the exclusive blessing of the English nation'); a convention would quickly reveal that it did not stand as high in the public's estimation as they fondly supposed. The trick was neatly played. If the government refused a convention, their case would be exposed. If not, the same applied.

The notion pleased Paine; he would riddle them at their own game, though the risks increased daily. Since early July there had been rumours that the government might anticipate its own prosecution by issuing a new warrant for his arrest, and he held off publication of 'An Address' through August and into September. It was not as if it was needed; anyone but a fool could see that liberty was a puppet which danced to the government's strings, while there was other business to hand.

On 23 August, Paine had been awarded French citizenship by the National Convention, and ten days later the electors of the Pas de Calais were the first of four *départements* to invite him to represent them at the Convention itself. On 6 September, their messenger, Achille Audibert, arrived in London to extend the invitation, and bring news that Lafayette had defected to the enemy. The report was unconfirmed and Paine rejected it as inconceivable, whilst accepting the offer from the citizens of Calais. This was all the more reason for Pitt and his friends to take care, and he tried out the new title — Deputy Paine — before catching himself in the conceit. It was easily done, yet unnecessary. 'Common Sense' required no prefix.

Vanity eroded what remained of Paine's caution, and, on 12 September, he delivered an address with 'inflammatory eloquence' at a meeting of the Friends of Liberty. Government agents were in the audience and the following evening, after dining with friends off Ludgate Hill, the poet William Blake* took him aside to warn that the Home Office had given orders to search Rickmann's house, and seize Paine's papers — 'You must not go home, or you are a dead man.'

Paine protested his determination to remain (with the present mood in the country, the government would hardly dare risk a hearing in open court), but Audibert reinforced Blake's advice: 'You have a great career yet to come in France. Let us go.' The argument prevailed, and late in the evening Paine, Audibert and the lawyer John Frost left for the Channel coast by fast chaise.

For the last time, Paine followed the familiar route through Chatham, Rochester and south of Sandwich with its now faded memories of Mary Lambert ('What are the iron chains that hands have wrought?/The hardest chains to break, are those of thought'); and wondered an instant whether this was how Louis Capet felt on the road to Varennes? The comparison entertained him. They were both in flight, though in different directions — Louis from freedom to repression; he from repression to freedom. The tragedy was that, for all his public protestations, the King would not accept that his private interests would best be served under the new constitution, and Paine tried out his new title again — Deputy Thomas Paine. The distinction was fitting, and sounded well.

The Customs House at Dover was alert for trouble, though Paine's party was still ahead of the warrant for his arrest. It made little difference. It was only four months since the publication of the Royal Proclamation against seditious literature — and Paine's reputation had preceeded him. Outside, a small crowd chanted his name, and for more than an hour Audibert, Frost and Paine were held incognito as their baggage was searched, their papers examined. Audibert protested his French citizenship. He was ignored. Frost asked to use the toilet. He was refused. It was Paine, however, who was their quarry — and his luck held.

When the Customs' men finally came to open his trunk, the first thing they came across was two sealed letters he was carrying for the American Minister in London, and two private letters addressed to himself — one from President Washington, the other from Thomas Jefferson, US Secretary of State. As an officer opened Washington's note, Frost took it from him and read the concluding paragraph aloud:

> As no one can feel a greater interest in the happiness of mankind than I do, it is the first wish of my heart that the enlightened policy of the present age may diffuse to all men those blessings to which they are entitled and lay the foundations of happiness for future generations.

The Presidential signature was there, together with the seal of office. For all the Royal Proclamation, this was dangerous business in which to tamper, and the small party was allowed to board the Channel packet. Twenty minutes later the warrant for Paine's arrest reached Dover, but the small ship already stood off the pier. Paine was safely *en route* to France to discover the irony that the repression from which he fled under monarchy was to find a new guise in the republic of 'the Terror'.

11 'TO JUDGE A KING'

Calais was *en fête*. A band played at the quayside. The National Guard lined the route to the *Hôtel de Ville*. The Mayor made a speech of welcome. Paine replied, and, though his French was limited, no one cared. Citizen Paine, author of *Les Droits des hommes*, symbolised the Revolution itself, its hopes and its universality. It was as if the small town had inherited a legend, this man who had marched with Washington; who had been the first to propose a republic for France; and who was now a fugitive from the reaction across the Channel.

For two days Paine remained in Calais before taking the road to Paris, to find the city in chaos. Three months before he had shrugged off news of the sansculottes, though he had long feared the malign influence of the *émigrés*. Now the two elements interacted, and the Revolution degenerated into anarchy. In late July, the Duke of Brunswick, commanding the Prussian forces, issued a Manifesto threatening 'an exemplary and unforgettable vengeance, by delivering up Paris to military execution and complete destruction' if the Royal family was not respected, or the Tuileries was invaded again. Recognising its dangers, Louis repudiated the Manifesto, but it was too late; one Deputy proclaimed: 'The moment the danger exists, every Citizen is a soldier' — the theory of revolutionary nationalism, when the defence of revolution by a 'nation in arms' was born.

On 3 August, all but one of the Paris sections petitioned for the deposition of the King. Seven days later, as Louis and his family found shelter with the Assembly, the Tuileries was stormed, and the Jacobins of Paris established a revolutionary Commune. The broad front of bourgeois interests which had dominated the Revolution from its early days was collapsing, with both the Jacobin and Girondin factions appealing to the Paris mob, if on different grounds — the one on republican principles, the other, in the belief that a victory in the field would ensure their continuing power.

It was a contest which was destroy the ideals of the Revolution, piecemeal. On 17 August, Louis was deposed and imprisoned with his family at the Temple; two days later, Lafayette defected; and on 26 August, first reports reached Paris of the fall of the frontier fortress of Longwy. Again the talk was of teachery, and with Verdun endangered the new Minister of Justice, Georges Danton,* insisted that the time had come to 'tell the people that they must throw themselves on their enemies *en masse . . .* The tocsin that will ring will be no mere signal for alarm; it will

215

sound the charge against the enemies of the nation.'

While Danton's challenge nerved the nation to fight (within the week, 1,800 volunteers a day were leaving for the frontier), it had a darker side. For the sansculottes the 'enemies of the nation' were already amongst them and on Sunday, 2 September, the Massacre of the Prisons began. In the next 72 hours, 1,300 prisoners were butchered, and the gutters of Paris ran with blood. At the Conciergerie, the mob hacked 378 prisoners to pieces, then piled them in heaps in the Cour de Mai. At the Abbaye bonfires were lit to illuminate the mass killings. At the Châtelet, the executioners sat within a circle of corpses drinking brandy mixed with gunpowder to 'aggravate their fury'.

Paris was developing a taste for blood, and the authorities did little to check it. With the last of the killings on 7 September, Danton was dismissive of complaints: 'I don't give a damn for the prisoners. Let them look after themselves as they can', later adding: 'It often happens, in times of revolution, that one has to applaud actions that one would not have wanted or dared to perform one's self.' It set the tone for much that was to follow and when Paine arrived in Paris on 19 September the city was quiet, sullen, haunted by recollections of all that had passed.

The Paris Commune might write to all the *départements* of France 'that some of the fierce conspirators detained in its prisons, have been put to death by the people . . . in order to restrain by intimidation the thousands of traitors hidden within its walls', but there could be no justifying this horror. It seemed as if the Revolution was devouring itself. Paine had hoped for peace, and there was war. He had hoped for justice, and there was anarchy. He had hoped for the rights of man, yet it seemed that the wrongs still multiplied.

What was it that Lafayette had once said: 'For a nation to love liberty, it is sufficient that she knows it; and to be free, it is sufficient that she wills it' — and now he, too, was gone, and this meant more than all the rest. How many years was it since he had first heard of the man and his exploits? Almost too long to recall, and the memories crowded in. Lafayette replying to the Comte d'Artois's challenge: 'You demand an Estates General?' 'Yes, Monseigneur, and even better than that.' Lafayette bursting into his room on a June morning little more than a year ago, to roar: 'The birds have flown.' Lafayette and Jefferson; Lafayette and Condorcet; Lafayette and the dedication to the second part of the *Rights*:

> After an acquaintance of nearly fifteen years in difficult situations in America, and various consultations in Europe, I feel a pleasure in presenting to you this small treatise in gratitude to your services to

my beloved America, and as a testimony of my esteem for the virtues, public and private, which I know you to possess.

The betrayal defied logic, and yet logic itself was betrayed. It was all very well for Danton to argue that the means justified the ends, but could any ends be served by the obscenity of what had occurred? Three years before, at the fall of the Bastille, Paine had noted: 'These outrages were not the effect of the principles of the Revolution, but of the degraded mind that existed before the Revolution, and which the Revolution is calculated to reform.' Then he had written with hope. Now he began to doubt, and on 20 September 1792, Paine 'entered his name in the role of the National Convention' as the Deputy for the Pas de Calais, and took his seat with the Girondins, to the right of the President's chair.

The new Convention, replacing the Assembly, still consisted largely of the bourgeoisie (250 of the 749 Deputies were lawyers), though with radically different views. Whilst the moderate Girondins initially held the majority in the Chamber, they were under continual pressure from the more radical Jacobins led by Robespierre and Marat* who had their power base amongst the Paris Commune and the sansculottes. As Carlyle was to write half a century later: 'The weapons of the Girondins were Political Philosophy, Respectability, and Eloquence. The weapons of the Mountain (the Jacobins) . . . those of mere Nature; Audacity and Impetuosity which may become Ferocity, as of men complete in their determination, in their conviction.'

At the best of times, it would have proved an unstable combination. In France in the fourth year of the Revolution it was to prove disastrous, though initially it seemed that a common programme might be achieved. On 21 September, there was unanimity in favour of abolishing the monarchy (the Girondist Gregoire declaring: 'The history of kings is the martyrology of nations'); on the twenty-second, the new Republican calendar was adopted; and on the twenty-fifth, Paine wrote his 'Address to the People of France': 'In entering this great scene, greater than any nation has yet been called upon to act in, let us say to the agitated mind, be calm. Let us punish by instructing, rather than by revenge.'

It was a sentiment that was to find little sympathy amongst the Jacobins. Less than three weeks before, the mob had indicated where future power lay, and while the left continued to maintain the appearance of consultation, it was always with an eye to the gallery where the sansculottes watched, and waited.

On 29 September, an all-party Committee was elected to redraft the constitution. Nine members were named: two Jacobins, four Girondins, and three Girondin sympathisers — Sieyes, Condorcet (now Vice-President of the Convention), and Paine. Robespierre had looked for a place, was excluded, and turned his talents to nullifying its work, proposing to the Convention that any discussion of the constitution should be deferred until after a debate on the future of Louis Capet.

For the next two months, the Committee worked under the shadow of the issue, Condorcet drafting the paper, Paine preparing the preamble, and writing to Danton that in the new constitution France:

> must speak for other nations who cannot yet speak for themselves. She must put thoughts into their minds, and arguments into their mouths, by showing the reasons that have induced her to abolish the old system of Monarchical Governments, and to establish the representative . . . there is more to be hoped for from enlightening foreign nations than there is to be feared from foreign courts.

After the horrors of September, and charges in the Convention that Robespierre and Marat had plotted the massacre, Paine's optimism was reasserting itself. Whilst Danton might dismiss moderation contemptuously ('Revolutions are not made with rose water') Condorcet commanded the Committee, and he was not a man to pander to the mob — and Paine cursed his own treachery. He was beginning to sound like Burke with his 'swinish multitude', yet in England they hung him in effigy, the Jacobin incarnate.

The situation was ironic: that in one place he was branded a moderate, in another, a firebrand; the more so when in France they talked of trying a king, whilst in England they were preparing his prosecution as a 'wicked, malicious, seditious, and ill-disposed person'. In his room at White's Hotel, off the Passage des Petits Pères, Paine drafted a note to the Attorney-General, Sir Archibald MacDonald:

> My necessary absence from your country affords the opportunity of knowing whether the prosecution was intended against Thomas Paine, or against the Rights of People of England to investigate principles and systems of government; for as I cannot now be the object of prosecution, the going on with the prosecution will show that something else was the object, and that something else can be no other than the People of England . . .
>
> The terrible examples that have taken place here upon men who, less than a year ago, thought themselves as secure as any prosecuting Judge, Jury, or Attorney-General can do now in England, ought to

have some weight with men in your situation. That the Government of England is as great, if not the greatest perfection of fraud and corruption that ever took place since governments began, is what you cannot be a stranger to; unless the constant habit of seeing it has blinded your sense. But though you may not choose to see it, the people are seeing it very fast, and the progress is beyond what you may choose to believe.

If no more, that was true. The pace of events accelerated daily, until there was no place to stand in safety; not in England, nor in France, nor in all Europe. All were threatened by the despotism of the extremes. For an instant the notion haunted him, the negation of all his ideals, then he completed the note ('As I have no time to copy letters, you will excuse the corrections'), and returned to the Convention. The devil take abstractions, there was not only a constitution to draft for France, but a debate on the future of Louis Capet to attend.

Since early October, a Commission of Twenty-Four had been examining 'the crimes of the ex-King', and on 6 November their report was presented to the Convention. The evidence was exhaustive — of counter-revolutionary papers, of subsidies to the *émigré* army, of expenses for the flight to Varennes — but still the Deputies were cautious. They remembered the trial of another king. The Long Parliament had been blamed not for executing Charles, but for creating an *ad hoc* tribunal to do so. It was a mistake the Convention would not repeat, and for seven hours a day for the next two months they debated what should become of Louis.

Paine was ambivalent. He remembered Louis from that first visit to Paris 12 years before, and his support for the American cause — but was that enough to excuse his perfidy? He accepted Louis as a man, but not as a monarch — but which predominated, the monarch or the man? He recognised that, if Louis were tried, the world would condemn France — but who could forgive his intriguing with a counter-revolution that threatened France itself? For eight days after the debate began, Paine remained silent, then on 21 November his case was read to the Convention.

Louis should stand trial. As an individual, he was beneath the contempt of the Republic; weak, narrow-minded, badly reared, as all like him. No, prosecution should not be of the individual, but of a king as one of a band of crowned robbers — then nations would come to know, and detest monarchy. But compassion for the individual was still required, a compassion reflecting national magnanimity, not the result of a burlesque notion of pretended inviolability.

The issue was to become central to Paine's case: that charity towards

Louis would reflect well on the Republic, and thus mollify its critics. Still the debate continued. For a further two weeks the Deputies discussed their right to try a king: some argued that, as Louis was now deposed, no more should be done; some that capital punishment was a crime against nature, and Louis should be allowed to live as a warning to others; and one, the young Secretary to the Convention, Saint-Just,* that Louis was never a commoner, always a king, and that kingship itself was a crime.

It was Robespierre, the Arras lawyer who little more than 18 months before had been pleading for an end to capital punishment, who was to make the decisive speech. On 4 December, he damned the moralistic prejudices of the Girondins; scorned the notion of invoking a constitution which every act of the Convention denied. Louis had declared war on the Revolution. His life was forfeit. The Convention's only duty was to judge him: 'il faut le condamner sur-le-champ à mort, en vertu d'une insurrection.'

Since mid-November, attempts had been made to intercede on Louis's behalf — Danton offering to secure his freedom if Pitt would raise £40,000; the army promising him safety if the Prussians would recognise the Republic — but now the matter was decided. Louis should be tried, and two days later Saint-Just read Paine's views on the conduct of the trial:

> It is not only against Louis XVI that we are going to judge, it is the monarchy . . . it is a general conspiracy of kings against people, and the more Louis will appear innocent, the more it will be evident that kings have the art of deceiving. It is on the basis of these proofs of conspiracy that it is necessary to judge Louis XVI.

Paine listed the charges: that Louis was guilty of pledging his oath to the nation, then violating it; guilty of having conspired with other kings against the sovereignty of the people of France; guilty of furnishing those despots with money for the purpose of subjugating the French nation; guilty of having favoured the *émigrés* and the conspirators; guilty of having sent to the frontiers armies too weak so that they were cut to pieces by the enemy.

Others could be added, but that was sufficient; the indictment carried more weight than the charges now levelled against him in England. And here, again, the irony. The date for Paine's trial had been set for 19 December at Guildhall, and he expected little justice from a packed jury (what was the government's axiom: two guineas a day and dinner for a verdict; a guinea and no dinner for acquittal?); yet here he was, 'a wicked, seditious and ill-disposed person', trying to ease the verdict against Louis of France. Once there had been nothing but contradictions. Then, for a while in America, it seemed as if they had been resolved. Now they were back again.

In one place he had condemned a mob; in another, condoned it. In England, he was prosecuted by a king; in France, he shielded one, and on Christmas Eve by the old calendar Paine heard the result of the Guildhall trial. As expected, the verdict was guilty, in part, at least, as a result of the Attorney-General's release of his letter of a month before. His counsel, Erskine, had suggested the note was a forgery. The explanation carried little weight, and, after Erskine's closing address, the Foreman of the Jury needed no instructions: 'My Lord, I am authorised by the jury here to inform the Attorney-General that a reply is not necessary for them, unless the Attorney-General wishes to make it, or your Lordship.'

As MacDonald demanded, the sentence against Paine was outlawry, and the government proceeded to tighten its measures against both publishers and their publications. Britain was entering a dark age, the King issuing proclamations for the mobilisation of the militia; for the fortification of the Tower; for the deployment of a 'formidable array of weapons' not against France, but *Rights of Man*. As a report to the Convention of January, 1793, stated:

> The Minister [Pitt] stated that this work had perverted all men's minds; that it had formed a revolutionary sect which proposed to overthrow the English government and replace it by a National Convention; that this sect had its secret committees, its clubs, its correspondences; that it had intimate ties with the Jacobins in Paris; that it sent out apostles to excite revolt throughout England; that a conspiracy to overturn the throne was in readiness . . .

In his place in the Chamber, Paine remembered the meeting in the Thatched House Tavern little more than 18 months before and how they had set the National Anthem to his name — though he had done no more than articulate their hopes. In England as in America that had been his role: to express the thoughts of those who could not express themselves. In the early days in Philadelphia, and with a recollection of Wilkes, he had written: 'There is nothing which has so general influence . . . as the press' — and for 20 years he had been perfecting and improving his techniques as a publicist.

It was not a talent to be lightly dismissed, though it needed placing in perspective. While Paine was arguably the most powerful, radical publicist writing in English in the late eighteenth century, his works were primarily a synthesis of much that had gone before — an echo of the pamphleteers of the Commonwealth period, refined by the theories of Locke and Voltaire, Rousseau and the *encyclopédistes*. Ultimately his achievement was in applying such theories to everyday life; in making them accessible to the 'mere people' and by articulating their thoughts, crystallising their dissent.

But where would it lead? At the tribune in the Chamber, a Deputy still read the report from England: 'In this climate of opinion, it was sufficient for the Minister to sound the tocsin against anarchy, to cry that the constitution was in danger . . . so that the conspiracy against all revolution became by necessity universal.' The words masked the coercive nature of Pitt's policies but while he, Paine, was free, what of the people he had left behind? He had given them a voice, then abandoned them: Godwin, and Horne Tooke, and the publisher Jordan, and the advocate Thomas Muir who had been sentenced to 14 years' transportation by the Scottish bench for calling a National Convention. It had been easy enough to drum up the proposal in an 'Address to the Addressers', but it was men like Muir who bore the cost.

Again Paine pondered the irony that in England it was the rights of man that endangered the constitution, in France, the rights of kings, and, two days after hearing the Guildhall verdict, the defence opened its case at the trial of Louis XVI. Simply dressed in an olive silk coat, and seated in a straight-backed wooden chair, Louis heard the young advocate de Sèze represent that, under the Constitution of 1791, the King was inviolable, and that if he were to be tried it should be as an ordinary citizen with the normal guarantee of two juries (an indictment jury, and a trial jury) — 'I look for judges amongst you, and see only prosecutors.'

The Convention suspected that the political intent of the trial was being disguised by judicial procedure, Saint-Just denouncing: 'Justice cannot prevent great crimes from being concealed. A crime may not be seen to be committed, but its effects are no less real.' He was right. The Girondins were playing for time in the hope that the latent royalism of the countryside would make it impossible for the Convention to carry the trial to its logical end. The Jacobins, however, were intractable. They would settle for nothing less than a sentence of death, Robespierre remarking: 'Louis must die, because France must live' — and in the gallery the sansculottes became more restive by the day.

The alternatives were irreconcilable. As Paine told Gouverneur Morris in the last week of 1792, the King's last hope lay in finding a compromise which would satisfy the pride of the Jacobins, whilst allaying the fears of the Girondins, and the only solution that offered itself was to hold Louis hostage for the good behaviour of the European monarchy, to be followed at the war's end by banishment, ideally to America. Morris was quick the grasp the idea, writing to Washington that the Convention:

> have it in contemplation not only to refer the judgment to the electors of France, that is, to her people, but also to send him and his family to America, which Paine is to move for. He mentioned this to me in confidence, but I have since heard it from another quarter.

The Girondins' attempt to refer the whole issue back to the country was rejected by the Convention, and on 14 January 1793, there were only three questions left for the Deputies to decide. First: Is Louis guilty? Second: Do you wish your verdict to be referred to the people? Third: What punishment does Louis deserve? The voting began on the same day. On the question of the King's guilt, Paine voted 'Yes' with the majority; a Jacobin victory. On the question of referring the verdict to the country, Paine voted 'No' with the majority; again, a Jacobin victory.

Only the nature of the sentence remained to be decided, though the Girondins, now fearing total defeat, again attempted to obscure the issue by proposing that a two-thirds majority should be required to pass sentence. Danton was dismissive: if France had gone to war by a bare majority, why should not the fate of the King be decided in the same way? The motion was defeated, and voting on the sentence began at 8 o'clock on the evening of 17 January, to continue for the next 36 hours.

It was a bizarre scene, an eyewitness describing how the end of the chamber had been converted into a temporary lounge where 'ladies in charming negligées were eating ices and oranges, drinking liqueurs' . . . how sleeping Deputies were shaken awake to cast their votes . . . how bets were laid and taken in the nearby coffee houses . . . how women pricked cards to follow the vote . . . how the public gallery was filled with spectators drinking wine and brandy . . . and how the sansculottes menaced the Deputies.

The streets of Paris were filled with armed men who now openly intimidated Girondin supporters: one Deputy commented that they voted under poignards; the wife of another reflected cynically 'What charming freedom we now enjoy in Paris'; the Abbé Sieyes explained: 'What was the tribute of my glass of wine in that torrent of brandy' — after reversing his position and voting for the death of the King. In those January days of 1793, moderation lived in fear in Paris whilst in the pale light of the chamber a succession of Deputies went to the tribune to enter their verdict. For once Paine spoke, word perfect, in French: 'I vote for the detention of Louis until the end of the war, and after that his perpetual banishment.'

When the last of the votes had been counted the President, Vergniaud, declared the result: a majority of five for the sentence of death. There was uproar. Both sides suspected fraud. A scrutiny was held and again Vergniaud announced the result: 361 for capital punishment, 360 against. Majority, 1.

On the nineteenth, the Girondins made their last play. The majority was so close, the idea of a reprieve so attractive, that they pressed for a vote on a stay of execution. Again the roll was called. Again the Deputies mounted the tribune, and again Paine rose, this time to stand silent whilst a Deputy, Bancal, read his opinion: 'Very sincerely do I regret the Convention's vote of yesterday for death . . . '

The gallery bayed. Marat was on his feet. The Jacobins wanted nothing of Paine's pleading: 'I deny the right of Thomas Paine to vote on the subject. As a Quaker, his religious views repudiate the infliction of capital punishment.' There was chaos, the sansculottes roaring down from the gallery, the Deputies on the floor crying 'Free speech'. Eventually, above Vergniaud's call for order, Bancal continued reading with Paine, mute, beside him:

> My language has always been that of liberty and humanity, and I know by experience that nothing so exalts a nation as the union of these two principles, under all circumstances. I know that the public mind of France, and particularly that of Paris, has been heated and irritated by the dangers to which they have been exposed; but could we carry our thoughts into the future, when the dangers are ended, and the irritations forgotten, what today seems an act of justice may then appear an act of vengeance.
>
> My anxiety for the cause of France has become for the moment, concern for its honour. If, on my return to America, I should employ myself on a history of the French Revolution, I had rather record a thousand errors dictated by humanity, than one inspired by a justice too severe . . .
>
> France has but one ally, the United States of America . . . It happens unfortunately that the person now under discussion is regarded in America as the deliverer of their country. I can assure you that his execution will there spread universal sorrow, and it is in your power not thus to wound the feelings of your ally. Could I speak the French language I would descend to your bar, and in their name become your petitioner to respite the execution of the sentence on Louis.

Again, Marat was on his feet. This was not what the gallery wished to hear; such pleading must be discredited. 'I assert that this is not Thomas Paine's opinion. It is a faithless translation.' Above the din, a Deputy asserted: 'I've read the original and the translation is correct', while Paine acknowledged the opinion as his own. Bancal read on:

> Your Executive Committee will nominate an Ambassador to Philadelphia; my sincere wish is that he may announce to America that the National Convention of France, out of pure friendship to America, has consented to respite Louis. That people, your only ally, have asked you by my vote to delay the execution.
>
> Ah, Citizens, give not the tyrant of England the triumph of seeing the man perish on a scaffold who helped my dear brothers of America to break his chains!

For a third time, Marat rose to his feet, incensed. Above the uproar, he roared that Paine had 'voted against death because he was a preacher', to which Paine replied: 'I vote against it both morally and politically.' When the uproar subsided, the count continued and the following morning, with the mob howling 'Justice' at its doors, the Convention voted by a majority of 70 that Louis XVI should die within 24 hours.

Paine rose early on Tuesday, 21 January. He had an appointment to keep in the Place de la Révolution. The day was grey, overcast; a light rain was falling, though the crowds seemed not to notice it. They massed the streets on the two-mile route to the scaffold, but were silent; and for a moment Paine listened to the silence before hearing the distant sound of drums. The crowd shifted, and somewhere above him on the terrace of the Tuileries gardens a child cried, then was quiet again.

So this was the prelude to the death of a king, and the practice and the principle became confused. Almost 20 years had passed since he had written of the evil of kings, 'the popery of government', yet only yesterday he had pleaded for this man's life. The head of the column was in the Place now, the drums louder, a metronome counting out not only a king's time but that of the Revolution itself. Robespierre and Marat might not see it, but the two were inextricably linked; this ritual of death degraded the Revolution, negated all that it stood for.

Only Louis and his confessor, Henry Edgeworth, left the carriage, to stand in the shadow of the guillotine. Three guards moved forward to remove the King's coat. He shrugged them off, stripped to the waist, then climbed the scaffold alone. The crowd saw that he was a man just like any other. For a moment, the drums ceased — 'People, I die innocent.

I forgive those who are guilty of my death, and I pray God that the blood which you are about to shed may never be required of France' — then resumed. The King's last words were drowned by the sound.

The executioner, Sanson, moved forward, and guided Louis to the plank of the guillotine, where he lay, hands bound and face down. For Paine, all time was compressed in the instant, a *mélange*: of 'the poorest he . . . that hath a life to lead as the greatest he', and the death of another King; of 'a Citty upon a Hill, the eies of all people . . . uppon us', and a Declaration of Independence; of a July day of 1789, and the affirmation of the rights of man. Then the blade fell. The King of the French was dead.

The crowd erupted: 'Vive la Nation!' 'Vive la Republique!' The cavalry guard raised their helmets on the points of their sabres. Those nearest the scaffold dipped their handkerchiefs in the King's blood, and, as the body and severed head were escorted away to the Madeleine, the sans-culottes danced a farandole around the guillotine, singing the Marseillaise. Could Burke have been right after all? The rain had stopped, a breeze had blown up from the south-east, and Paine wondered a moment that the wind always seemed to blow from the left.

Possibly the ultimate irony of Paine's life was that, while he was amongst the first to condemn the institution of monarchy, he was amongst the last to defend the life of a king; the royalist Bertrand de Moleville wrote that it was 'to the eternal shame of the Convention that Thomas Paine, misguided by the fanatacism of the most ardent demagogery, was the most wise, the most humane, the most courageous, in a word, the least culpable of all his colleagues'.

The compliment did little to recommend Paine to the political mood of Paris in 1793. Although the Girondin moderates continued to command a majority in the Convention after the execution of Louis, their authority was being sapped, inexorably, by the Jacobins and their allies from the Paris sections. Initially the shift was disguised by the success of French arms against the Austro-Prussians: Savoy and Nice had been occupied; General Custine was across the Rhine and moving on Frankfurt; General Dumouriez was sweeping through Belgium to defeat the Austrians at Jemappes. It seemed that the Revolution was on the march, but the mood of the Paris mob remained volatile, and they had tasted blood.

Exactly a week after Louis's death, the Republic declared war on England and Holland, a Girondin initiative to forestall the Jacobins. For Pitt the declaration was to unite England against her traditional enemy, and provide him with the excuse necessary to intensify the campaign of repression that was to exorcise the name of Paine for more than a quarter of a century. For France it meant that, while Danton boasted: 'We hurl at their feet, as a gage of battle, the French king's head', the Republic was ringed by powers determined to revenge the 'heinous crime' of regicide and destroy the Revolution — if it did not destroy itself. By early spring the French forces were again on the defensive, and in France itself there was growing unrest. The Vendée in the south-west was in open revolt against the government, and Lyons (the second city of France) was soon to fall to the royalists.

The Revolution was again in crisis, and the Girondins under growing pressure from the left. As early as 15 February the Convention had talked out Condorcet's constitution in part, as Robespierre explained, because it made only a passing reference to the Supreme Being. Paine was cynical. For three years the Assembly had wrestled to contain the clergy, and less than two years had passed since the Pope had laid what amounted to an interdict upon France. Yet here was Robespierre calling up religion, and he was by no means alone. The Jacobins were learning a new faith, a faith in the mass.

As conditions in France deteriorated, the Paris mob became more demanding, more menacing. In the four years since Louis had called the Estates General, they had watched the locus of power move steadily away from the right. Their time was close, and, reacting to the situation in mid-March, the Convention established a Revolutionary Tribunal, as much to curb the excesses of the sansculottes as to prosecute treason. It was a dangerous move towards despotism (Vergniaud declaring that they were 'laying the foundations of an Inquisition a thousand times more terrible than that of Spain') which was soon to be turned against the moderates themselves.

On 5 April, the Jacobin Club, under Marat's Presidency, issued an inflammatory address:

> Friends, we are betrayed. To arms! There is counter-revolution in the government and in the National Convention. There, in the citadel of our hopes, our criminal representatives pull the strings of the plot they have contrived with a horde of despots coming to cut our throats.

The attack could not be ignored. The Convention voted for Marat's indictment, and on 24 April he appeared before the Revolutionary Tribunal. The major charge turned on the address, but the six-hour hearing was dominated by the subsidiary issue of Deputy Thomas Paine.

Earlier in the year, Paine had moved out of White's Hotel into 63,

Rue du Faubourg Saint-Denis. A comfortable house, with a high-walled garden, it had once belonged to Madame de Pompadour, mistress of Louis XV. Now Paine shared it with two other Englishmen: William Johnson and William Chopin. A neurotic, Johnson read the Jacobin address of 5 April, and decided on suicide: 'I came to France in order to enjoy Liberty, but it has been assassinated by Marat. Anarchy is even more cruel than despotism.' After writing a will dividing his property between Paine and Chopin, Johnson stabbed himself twice — superficially.

Reading Johnson's suicide note, Paine's Girondin sympathies overrode his better judgement. He decided to use the letter, and it was published in full a week before the trial. Called to give evidence, Paine suggested that Johnson had attempted suicide because Marat intended to denounce him; Marat counter-charged that it was Paine he intended to denounce, not Johnson. The 'Friend of the People' was acquitted, in triumph, to be crowned with a laurel leaf and carried shoulder-high from the Palais de Justice to the Convention.

Marat's enmity for Paine was reinforced, and, only two days after his acquittal, the Paris sections drew up a list of 22 Girondin Deputies 'guilty of the crime of felony against sovereign people', and demanded their expulsion from the Convention. Paine's name was not included, but he read the signs well enough and, by early May, was writing to Danton:

> I am exceedingly disturbed at the distractions, jealousies, discontents and uneasiness that reign among us and which, if they continue, will bring ruin and disgrace on the Republic. When I left America in the year 1787, it was my intention to return the following year, but the French Revolution, and the prospect which it afforded of extending the principles of liberty and fraternity through the greater part of Europe, have induced me to prolong my stay upwards of six years. I now despair of seeing the great object of European liberty accomplished, and my despair arises not from the combined foreign powers and priestcraft, but from the tumultuous misconduct with which the internal affairs of the present revolution is conducted . . .
>
> There ought to be some regulation with respect to the spirit of denunciation that now prevails. If every individual is to indulge his private malignancy or his private ambition, to denounce at random and without any kind of proof, all confidence will be undermined and all authority be destroyed. Calumny is a species of Treachery that ought to be punished as well as any other kind of Treachery. It is a private vice productive of public evils, because it is possible to irritate men into disaffection by continual calumny who never intended to be

disaffected. It is equally as necessary to protect the character of public officers from calumny as it is to punish them for teachery or miscon-duct . . .

Calumny becomes harmless and defeats itself when it attempts to act upon too large a scale. Thus the denunciation of the sections of Paris against the twenty two deputies falls to the ground. The depart-ments that elected them are better judges of their moral and political characters than those who have denounced them. This denunciation will injure Paris in the opinion of the departments because it has the appearance of dictating to them what sort of deputies they shall elect. Most of the acquaintances that I have in the Convention are among those who are on the list, and I know there are not better men nor better patriots than what they are.

His fears were soon realised. On 18 May, the Convention denounced the Paris authorities as 'anarchic, greedy for money and power'; a week later, two leaders of the Commune were arrested; and on 31 May, with the city in turmoil, Danton turned Paine away from the doors of the Con-vention with the advice that if he entered his name might well be added to the list of proscribed Deputies drawn up by the Jacobins against the Girondists.

Bitterly, Paine turned for home. There was no longer a place for moderation in Paris in the summer of 1793. Four years before, at the fall of the Bastille, he had written: 'I think there is now no possibility of anything hindering their [the French] final establishment of a good con-stitution.' And now? Now the Revolution was in ruins and on the after-noon of Sunday, 2 June, a crowd of 80,000, supported by cannon, beseig-ed the Convention. Their demand was straightforward: 'Purgez la Con-vention; tirez le mauvais sang!' The Deputies attempted to leave, but were forced to return and accede to the mob's demand for the internment of 29 Girondin Deputies, and two Ministers. The bourgeois Revolution had finally lost its bearing. The Terror was about to begin.

On 7 June, Robespierre pressed for tighter laws against foreigners and whilst, as a Deputy, Paine was excluded, the legislation had special significance for him — in the past four months he had intervened on behalf of a number of Britons (including at least one of Pitt's agents) to prevent their arrest, or obtain their release from gaol. Ten days later, the electors of the Pas de Calais voted an Address to the Convention declaring their lack of confidence in Paine, and, on 23 June, the Convention approved the new, and hastily drafted constitution. The Jacobin document differed significantly from that of Condorcet and the Girondins, but Paine had expected no less. The same could not be said for the preamble with its new Declaration of the Rights of Man acknowledged 'in the presence of the Supreme Being'.

The opportunism of the thing sickened him. Only recently Robespierre had been heard to remark that, if God did not exist, it would be necessary to invent him. The man was Voltaire's parrot, yet while the one had excoriated religion ('Ecrasez l'infame!') the other now exploited it for political ends. It was always the way: in England, the established Church had made its godhead of the Glorious Revolution; in Philadelphia, they had raised 147 spires to the name of God; and now here, in France, the Jacobins invoked a Supreme Being to sanctify their power.

Paine felt the cynicism flower within him, and drank. The house and the garden were quiet, and there was no call to go to the Convention. They had no need of him there, and a tired man and lonely he tolled his 56 years and wondered where they had gone? Once there was so much, now so little was left, and he finished the bottle. It was coming on 20 years since he had first been called a drunkard and now, an outcast from England and on sufferance in France, he might well live up to his reputation. Hard drinking was no stigma after all; Pitt and Sheridan were both six-bottles-a-day men, while Burke's affection for claret could well account for the extravagance of his outbursts in the Commons. The man was mad, quite mad. A little time before, it seems, he had sprung to his feet in the midst of a debate on the Aliens Bill and, after much fumbling in his bosom, produced a dagger which he had hurled on the floor of the House, all the while storming against 'murderous atheists'. Perhaps Burke and Robespierre did have something in common after all.

July was a lost month for Paine. Occasionally he would sit around the garden. Occasionally he would play marbles or hopscotch or chess with Johnson or Chaplin or Clio Rickmann, who had recently fled from England. Occasionally he would talk of his childhood, but for the rest of the time, 'borne down by public and private affliction', he drank hard and long. It did something to ease the bitterness; or was he simply revenging the world of his disenchantment, by taking revenge on himself? Was that how it was: that, like a summer soldier, he shrank from the crisis to reach for a bottle, when so much still remained to be done?

And, in the garden where a king's mistress had once held court, he remembered an army of ragged men in line of march across a winter countryside and sensed their disbelief that Tom Paine should have turned sunshine patriot. Small wonder they despised him; he despised himself. Paine emptied the glass. He had had more than enough. There was work to be done. Robespierre and his kind demanded a reply, though it would be little more than he had promised himself since that childhood afternoon when he first learned that God Almighty could act like a passionate man who killed his Son. Then he knew too little to answer. Now he began to write:

> The circumstance that has now taken place in France of the total abolition of the whole national order of priesthood, and everything appertaining to compulsive systems of religion, and compulsive articles of faith, has not only precipitated my intention, but rendered a work of this kind exceedingly necessary, lest, in the general wreck of superstition, of false governments, and false theology, we lose sight of morality, of humanity, and of the theology that is true.

With the present mood in Paris, and more Girondins imprisoned by the day, they were dangerous words, but they had to be said:

> As several of my colleagues, and others of my fellow citizens of France, have given me the example of making their voluntary and individual profession of faith, I also will make mine; and I do this with all the sincerity and frankness with which the mind of man can communicate itself.
>
> I believe in one God, and no more, and I hope for happiness beyond this life.
>
> I believe in the equality of man; and I believe that religious duties consist in doing justice, loving mercy, and endeavouring to make our fellow creatures happy.

Robespierre was damned. He was as bad as the others:

> I do not believe in the creed professed by the Jewish church, by the Roman church, by the Greek church, by the Turkish church, by the protestant church, nor any church that I know of. My own mind is my own church.
>
> All national institutions of churches, whether Jewish, Christian, or Turkish, appear to me no other than human inventions, set up to terrify and enslave mankind, and monopolize power and profit.
>
> I do not believe by this declaration to condemn those who believe otherwise; they have the same right to their belief as I have to mine. But it is necessary to the happiness of man, that he be mentally faithful to himself. Infidelity does not consist in believing, or in disbelieving; it consists in professing to believe what he does not believe.

It was the Jacobin position, exactly. For all their protestations, the acolytes of this Supreme Being had so far corrupted themselves as to subscribe to a professional belief, in which they did not believe. Could anything be more destructive to morality than that, to trade belief for gain and all the while pretending to have some special mission from God? Jews, Christians, Turks, they all called up their revelations, to charge others with unbelief — Moses with his commandments received from God; Mohammed with a gospel written in heaven and handed down by an angel; Christ and the Virgin Birth.

Nothing that is here said can apply even with the most distant disrespect, to the *real* character of Jesus Christ. He was a virtuous and an amiable man. The morality that he preached and practised was of the most benevolent kind, and though similar systems of morality had been preached by Confucius, and by some of the Greek philosophers, many years before; and by the Quakers since; and by many good men in all ages, it has not been exceeded by any.

Yet the mythologists multiplied, as did their myths: of Genesis and the Garden of Eden, of Satan and the pit, of Christ's birth and resurrection; of a motley of fables which, collected together, men called the 'Word of God'. It only served to mock God himself, for he required no myth-makers. He revealed enough of himself in Creation and needed no commentators on his power:

Do we want to contemplate his power? We see it in the immensity of Creation. Do we want to contemplate his wisdom? We see it in the unchangeable order by which the incomprehensible whole is governed. Do we want to contemplate his munificence? We see it in the abundance with which he fills the earth. Do we want to contemplate his mercy? We see it in his not withholding that abundance even from the unthankful. In fine, do we want to know what God is? Search not the book called the Scripture, which any human hand might make, but the Scripture called the Creation.

The only idea that man can affix to the name of God, is that of a *first cause*, the cause of all things. And incomprehensible and difficult as it is for a man to conceive what a first cause is, he arrives at the belief of it, from the tenfold greater difficulty of disbelieving it. It is difficult beyond description to conceive that space can have no end; but it is more difficult to conceive an end. It is difficult beyond the power of man to conceive an eternal duration of what we call time;

but it is more impossible to conceive a time when there shall be no time. In like manner of reasoning, everything we behold carries in itself the internal evidence that it did not make itself . . .

It is only by the exercise of reason, that man can discover God. Take away that reason, and he would be incapable of understanding anything.

From the window of his room, Paine looked out across the Faubourg Saint-Denis, across Paris, and saw reason in ruins. On 16 October, Marie Antoinette went to the guillotine, to be followed by Brissot, and Sillery, and Duchatel, and Cussy, and Gorsas and Vergniaud — not only Girondins but his friends. The pattern was unvarying: the tribunal; the verdict; the tumbril; the blade. The city made a ritual of its sacrifice to the Supreme Being, and all the while he wrote of reason, aware of the sacrilege.

Vigilius had gone to his death asserting the world was round; Galileo had been compelled to renounce as heresy the structure of the universe he had seen through his telescope; and Bruno gone to the stake for envisaging more than one world. The inconsistency was incredible: that men damned the study of the universe that God had made as profane, preferring myths and fables.

How different is this to the pure and simple profession of Deism. The true Deist has only one Deity, and his religion consists in contemplating the power, wisdom, and benignity of the Deity in his works, and in endeavouring to imitate him in everything moral, scientific and mechanical . . .

It has been by rejecting the evidence, that the word or the works of God in the creation affords to our senses, and the action of our reason upon that evidence, that so many wild and whimsical systems of faith, and of religion, have been fabricated and set up.

And if myths were not enough, there were always the mysteries, the miracles, the prophecies — the former taking care of the past, the latter taking care of the future, as if it was not sufficient to know what had been done, but also what would be done. Burke was metaphysical enough, but this was the matter of fantasy. Yet even now they raised a new God with all its attendant mysteries — and still the grim ritual of the Place de la Révolution continued.

As Paine was later to write to Samuel Adams: 'My friends were falling as fast as the guillotine could cut their heads off, and I expected every day the same fate . . . I appeared to myself to be on my own death bed, for death was on every side of me.' There were good grounds for his fears. The Jacobins, and their newly established Revolutionary Tribunal, extended their list of proscriptions by the day (more than 2,500 were to go to the guillotine by July 1794), while Gouverneur Morris conspired in the wings.

A vain man and tetchy, he had first rounded on Paine 14 years before ('a mere adventurer from England . . . ignorant even of grammar') during the Silas Deane affair. The years between had done little to change his views, the more so because he had long been overshadowed by Paine's standing in French affairs, and his friendship with Condorcet and Sieyes and Lafayette — whilst the business of the keys of the Bastille still rankled.

And even now, in voluntary exile, Paine still appeared to exert an influence disproportionate to his position. Since the summer, almost a hundred US merchantmen had been held in Bordeaux by the French authorities, in reply to the British seizure of vessels bound for France flying the American flag. Morris, as Minister to France, had done little to help and late in August a deputation of officers visited the Faubourg Saint-Denis. They planned a public protest against Morris, but Paine persuaded them otherwise. A petition to the Convention would prove more effective — and it did.

By the end of the month, the American captains had received a favourable reply, to the chagrin of Morris. It was not so much that the petition was succcessful, more that he had again been humiliated by Paine. In the next two months, Morris was to play a shadowy, but devious role in Paine's affairs. Early in September, Paine, longtime a passionate advocate of the American–French alliance, welcomed a suggestion by the Chairman of the Committee of Public Safety, Barrère, that the Convention should send Commissioners to Congress to report, directly, on the state of conditions in France.

Morris, always the patrician, had shown little sympathy for the Revolution, and the French government had twice requested his recall. By the autumn of 1793, however, he was shifting his views, writing to Washington of a meeting he had held with the new French Foreign Minister, Desforgues:

I have insinuated the advantage which might result from an early declaration on the part of the new Minister that, as France has announced the determination not to meddle with the interior affairs of other nations, he can know only the *government* of America. In union with this idea, I told the Minister that I had observed an over-ruling influence in their affairs which seemed to come from the other side of the channel, and at the same time had traced the intention to excite a seditious spirit in America; and that it was impossible to be on a friendly footing with such persons . . . This declaration produced the effect I intended.

It is impossible to establish the grounds for Morris's confidence, or the effect of his insinuations about Paine (virtually the only Englishman of any repute then living in Paris). One thing, however, is certain. In early October, the charge against the Girondins specifically mentioned Paine, maintaining that his defence of Louis had been based on the premiss that the King's death would alienate American sympathies. Immediately, the charge was invalidated by Paine's membership of the Convention — though it placed his name high on the list of the Revolutionary Tribunal.

The net was closing inexorably, and, alone in the Faubourg Saint-Denis, Paine wrote to complete the first part of *The Age of Reason*. Johnson and Chopin had fled, the housekeeper, Georgeit, had gone. He had the old house to himself, a lonely place, and a dangerous one. Robespierre, since late summer the guiding force behind the Revolution, and the man who had recently described Paine as 'one of the most eloquent defenders of the rights of humanity', now held him in contempt; while, in November, a former schoolmaster who had voted with Paine at Louis's trial was condemned by the Tribunal and executed.

There was so little time yet so much to be done, and, recalling Robespierre, he wrote: 'The success of one imposter gave encouragement to another, and the quieting salvo of doing *some good* by keeping up a *pious fraud*, protected them from remorse.' Some good, dear God. Some good; Robespierre protested loudly enough for his principles, whilst consecrating them in blood. Winter was coming on fast, and each evening Paine was thankful for the freedom of the day just passed. The work was almost done, only the summary remained:

First — That the idea or belief of a word of God existing in print, or in writing, or in speech is inconsistent in itself . . .

Secondly — That the Creation that we behold is the real and ever existing word of God, in which we cannot be deceived . . .

Thirdly — That the moral duty of man consists in imitating the moral goodness and beneficence of God manifested in the Creation towards all his creatures . . . and consequently that everything of persecution and revenge between man and man, and everything of cruelty to animals, is a violation of moral duty.

On Christmas Day, Robespierre delivered a report 'On the Principles of Revolutionary Government' to the Convention, denouncing the presence of foreigners. Forty-eight hours later, almost exactly a year to the day since Paine first heard of his outlawry from England, and Louis had first stood trial, the Committee of Public Safety ordered Paine's arrest.

That evening he spent with American friends at White's. Between three and four in the morning there was a knock at the door of his room. A guard waited outside with orders to examine his papers, then escort him to the Luxembourg prison. Paine made only one request, that he should be allowed to hand over the final pages of his latest work to the American, Joel Barlow. Then he was led away.

12 THE GREATEST EXILE

Paine was fortunate. In the winter of 1793, the Luxembourg was the best of the twelve prisons in Paris. Since the autumn there had been more than ten thousand arrests and at the Force, the Conciergerie, the Marie all privileges had been withdrawn, overcrowding and disease were endemic, and many prisoners died before taking the tumbrils to the scaffold. At the Luxembourg it was different. It was a former royal palace; moreover the gaoler, Benoît, was a humane man, and conditions were so easy-going that the Police Administrator was to dub it the principle brothel in Paris — albeit, in the shadow of the guillotine.

As Paine was led to his basement cell ('level with the earth in the garden and floored with brick') he must have wondered at his chances of survival. Nominally the Convention and the Committee of Public Safety, with Robespierre at its head, still ruled, but the Terror was gaining a momentum of its own and it was rumoured that four men were now employed solely to empty the blood from the scaffold into a reservoir dug near the Seine.

It was at the end of the ideal that he had extolled, of the new era 'that shall blot despotism from the earth, and fix, on the lasting principles of peace and citizenship, the great Republic of Man'. So much for Monsieur Rousseau's 'general will'. So much for finding that form of association which, while uniting one with all, still allowed individuals to obey themselves alone. So much for the rights of man.

Only twelve months had passed since he had been condemned in England for asserting that 'The instant formal Government is abolished, society begins to act: a general association takes place and common interests produce common security'; and now here, in France, in the Republic that he had been among the first to propose, all that remained was violence — and the cell door shut behind him.

The disillusion was deep-rooted, and soon to be compounded by Gouverneur Morris's handling of his case, and the Convention's reception of a petition for his release presented by 18 Americans living in Paris:

> As a countryman of ours, as a man who above all is so dear to Americans who like yourselves are earnest friends of Liberty; we ask you in the name of that goddess cherished by only Two Republics in the world, to give Thomas Paine back to his brethren . . .

The Convention's reply, delivered by its new President, Vadier, was uncompromising: 'Thomas Paine is a native of England; this is undoubtedly enough to apply to him the measures of security prescribed by the revolutionary laws.' The confusions piled in. What the devil was he: American, English, French? Franklin had once remarked: 'Where liberty is, there is my country', to which Paine had replied: 'Where liberty is not, there is mine.'

Then it was in jest, but now . . . Now the French, who had granted him citizenship, called him English; the English outlawed him for drumming up the liberties of France, while the American Minister to Paris, Morris, would not decide where he belonged. Since the Silas Deane affair 15 years before, the two men had dissembled friendship, but there was no disguising the differences in their views — Paine, the one-time staymaker, as a foremost republican; Morris, the patrician, with strong, underlying sympathies for the royalist cause.

Five weeks after his admission to the Luxembourg, Paine wrote asking Morris to intercede on his behalf with the Convention. On 14 February, Morris approached the French Minister for Foreign Affairs:

> Sir — Thomas Paine has just applied to me to claim him as a Citizen of the United States. These (I believe) are the facts which relate to him. He was born in England. Having become a citizen of the United States he acquired a great celebrity through his revolutionary writings. In consequence he was adopted as French Citizen, and then elected Member of the Convention. His behaviour since that epoch has been out of my jurisdiction . . .

The tone of the note belies the strength of Morris's negotiating position. With France hard-pressed by a hostile European alliance (between February and September 1793, Pitt had taken Holland, Russia, Sardinia, Spain, Naples, Prussia, Austria and Portugal on to the English payroll), it was essential to ensure America's continuing neutrality and renew the existing treaties between the two countries. The Convention recognised the point well enough, and was sensitive to any move which would jeopardise France's relationship with the United States.

In Paine's case, however, it was a bargaining counter that Morris preferred to ignore. The implication of his note to the French government was clear. The man might be English, or French, or American; it was for France to decide, though, to disguise his duplicity, Morris was writing to Jefferson on 6 March: 'Mr Paine wrote to me a note desiring I would claim him as an American, which I accordingly did, though contrary to my judgement, for reasons mentioned in my last.'

At best, Morris's assertion was a half-truth, but it succeeded in allaying the American government's fears for Paine's future — while he remained in the Luxembourg, and the Terror gathered pace. On Sunday, 30 March, the Dantonist faction was arrested. Less than a year had passed since Danton had taunted Paine with attempting to make revolutions from rose water. Now he greeted Paine in English:

> What you have done for the happiness and liberty of your country, I have in vain tried to do for mine. I have been less fortunate but not more guilty. They are taking me to the scaffold. Well, my friends, I shall go gaily.

Six days later Danton rode a tumbril to the Place de la Révolution.

By early summer, 50 people a week were going to the guillotine, sacrificed to reasons of state and the Supreme Being. Since November 1791, when the National Assembly and passed its first decrees against refractory priests, there had been mounting pressures to renounce Catholicism, and de-Christianise the state. By the winter of 1793, the movement was approaching its climax.

In Paris, altar linen was made into shirts for soldiers, Bibles were sold to grocers for packing paper. At Blois, the republican society closed all churches, advising their congregations to stay at home and obey the law: 'for that is the long and short of gospel morality, and of the teaching of its author, the *sansculotte*, Jesus.' In Nancy, the priesthood renounced their orders and burned their licences in the nave of the Cathedral; while at the church of Vitry-sur-Seine 'a big girl in a white dress decked with ribbons and carrying a bonnet rouge on the end of a pike' stood on the altar supported by busts of Voltaire and Rousseau, as hymns to the Supreme Being were sung.

For Paine, the delirium negated all that it claimed to represent. When man lost faith in mankind and his institutionalised Gods, then all he had left to rely on was himself. It was a lonely, a daunting concept, yet it may do something to account for Paine's egotism and arrogance; for his sense of exile and difference and, ultimately, for his passionate testament to deism. He had begun the work in the Faubourg Saint-Denis. He continued it in the Luxembourg, reading extracts daily to his fellow prisoners, the surgeon Mr Bond, with the request each evening before they were locked in their separate cells that 'Bond should tell the world that such were his dying sentiments'. It was a necessary precaution. Six months before it was already clear that the principles of the Revolution had been betrayed: that 'the Tribunal, styled revolutionary, supplied the place of an Inquisition, and the guillotine and stake out-did the fire and faggot of the Church'.

Now the evidence of the betrayal passed Paine's cell door on the way to the scaffold every night.

No man could count upon his life for twenty four hours. To such a pitch of rage and suspicion were Robespierre and his Committee arrived, that it seemed that they feared to leave a man to live. Scarcely a night passed in which ten, twenty, thirty, forty, fifty or more were taken out of the prison, carried before a pretended tribunal in the morning, and guillotined before night.

Paine felt the fear, all-pervasive, and each night waited for the cell door to open; each day read more of his new work to Bond as if his private faith in reason was all that now remained. The myth of Christianity held nothing for him, and again he recalled a garden in childhood and the cruelties that men attributed to God: of Moses ordering the slaughter of women and children ('Kill any male among the little ones, and every woman that hath known a man by lying with him'); of Joshua's sacking of the City of Ai ('And Joshua burned Ai, and made it a heap for ever, a desolation unto this day'); of Elisha's curse on the children in the name of the Lord ('and then came forth two she bears out of the wood, and tore forty and two children of them'); and again, and above all the rest, of God's sacrifice of his Son.

The whole was a blasphemy, yet men worshipped it still for:

The most detestable wickedness, the most horrid cruelties, and the greatest miseries, that have afflicted the human race, have had their origin in this thing called . . . revealed religion. It has been the most dishonourable belief against the character of the Divinity, the most destructive of morality, and the peace and happiness of man, that ever was propagated since man began to exist.

And what men once practised in the name of God, they now practised in the name of reason. On one night alone 168 prisoners had been taken out of the Luxembourg. Paine's name had been on the list 'and the manner I escaped that fate is curious'. The routine of the guard detail was unchanging. Each evening they marked the doors of those due for trial and execution the following day. Paine's cell, which he now shared with three others, was in a long range of rooms under a gallery, and its door opened outwards to lie flat against the wall.

We, as I have stated, were four, and the door of our room was marked, unobserved by us, with that number in chalk; but it happened, if happening is a proper word, that the mark was put on when the door was open . . . and thereby came on the inside when we shut it at night, and the destroying angel passed by it.

Of the prisoners taken out that night, only eight escaped the guillotine. The horror of the thing mocked all Paine's beliefs. Reason itself was turned upside-down. Yet without a belief in reason there was nothing, and condemned by England, denied by America, imprisoned by France, he worked to refine all that now remained to him: deism.

What is it we want to know? Does not the creation, the universe we behold, preach to us the existence of an Almighty power that governs and regulates the whole? Here we are, the evidence of an Almighty power is sufficiently demonstrated to us, though we cannot conceive, as it is impossible that we should, the nature and manner of its existence . . . Deism then teaches us, without the possibility of being deceived, all that is necessary or proper to be known. The creation is the Bible of the Deist. He there reads, in the handwriting of the Creator himself, the certainty of his existence, the immutability of his power.

Through the late spring and early summer of 1794, Paine worked on the outline of the second part of *The Age of Reason*. At first, the logic was cutting, precise. As the Terror moved towards a crescendo, the work became more wild, fevered:

Of all the systems of religion that were ever invented, there is none . . . more repugnant to reason . . . than this thing called Christianity. Too absurd for belief . . . too inconsistent for practice. Only religion that has not been invented . . . is pure and simple Deism. The scheme of the Christian Church . . . to hold man in ignorance of the Creator. The study of theology . . . is the study of nothing. Not anything can be studied as a science, without our being in possession of the principles on which it is founded . . . We can know God only through his works. The principles of science lead to this knowledge, for the Creator of man is the creator of science Every part of science . . . is a text as well for devotion as for philosophy.

The dilemma multiplied, to rationalise the Trinity of Creator—Reason—Man, to contain the conflict in his mind. Less than two years before it had seemed simple enough, but now he wrote and talked, talked and wrote, while the cortège to the scaffold continued, denying all that he knew, and in June Paine collapsed. For six weeks he was fevered, semi-conscious, to be attended by the prison doctor and two inmates, Dr Graham and Mr Bond, and nursed by his three Belgian cell mates — Joseph Vanhuele, Charles Bastinit and Michael Rubyns.

Three days before Paine recovered full consciousness, Robespierre went to the scaffold. Since the previous autumn, the Jacobin leadership had consciously distanced itself from the grass-roots support on which its power had been founded, treating its membership with growing contempt. Buttressed by coercion, France was moving towards dictatorship and, with the elimination of the Dantonists in the *coup d'état* of April 1794, the *jacquerie* finally established itself in what amounted to absolute power.

It was to be short-lived. By the summer the victims of the Revolutionary Tribunal and Committee of Public Safety were no longer solely enemies of the Republic, but ordinary citizens trapped in a web of fear and hatred. In July, nine shopkeepers, six innkeepers, four weavers, four clockmakers, three grocers, three domestic servants, seven day-labourers, a boy of sixteen, an octogenarian, and three sisters of between 22 and 25 years of age were among those who went to the guillotine.

The Terror had turned on itself. As Danton passed Robespierre's house on his way to the scaffold, he had called out: 'You will be following me soon!' The cry was soon to be echoed through Paris: 'Citizens, beware. It will be your turn next, perhaps tomorrow.' Even Robespierre himself sickened of the bloodshed, resigning from the Committee of Public Safety in mid-May. By then, however, it was too late. For almost a year, the man's name had been irrevocably linked with the Terror, and, on 26 July 1794, he appeared before the Convention for the last time.

Dismissing the charge of dictatorship, and proclaiming the gospel of 'virtue', Robespierre denounced yet another conspiracy against the Revolution, this time from within the government itself. The Deputies sat silent as he tolled off the names of the guilty men — Carnot and Barrère, Cambot and Mallarmé. What was it that this austere moralist sought: dictatorship or martyrdom? To his enemies, the former; to his friends, the latter; and that evening he talked of the Convention speech as his 'last will and testament', and spoke of 'drinking the hemlock' of self-immolation.

The following day, among an uproar of 'A bas le tyran!' the Convention ordered Robespierre's arrest. On 27 July, 45 anti-Robespierrists had

gone to the guillotine. In the following forty-eight hours, 83 Robespier-
rists were to die. The Terror was ending. No precise figures are available
of those who died during its reign, estimates putting the numbers at between twelve and fourteen thousand, but a search of Robespierre's records
revealed a brief memorandum: 'Demand that Thomas Paine be decreed
of accusation for the interests of America as well as of France.'

The note confirmed Paine's suspicions of Robespierre, and within three
weeks he was writing to the Convention requesting his release:

> the strange power that Robespierre, by the most consummate hypocrisy
> and the most hardened cruelties, had obtained rendered any attempt
> on my part to obtain justice not only useless but even dangerous . . .
> This being my situation I submitted with patience to the hardness of
> my fate and waited for the event of brighter days.

Seven months had passed since he had entered the Luxembourg, and
while friends such as Achille Audibert supported his appeal ('A friend
of mankind is groaning in chains — Thomas Paine who was not so politic
in regard to a man unlike himself, but dared to say that Robespierre was
a monster to be erased from the list of men'), there was still no sign of
American intervention on his behalf.

The last he had heard of Gouverneur Morris was in the spring, and
Congress still believed that he was negotiating on Paine's behalf. When
the new US Minister to France, James Monroe,* was received in late
August he was surprised to find Paine still in gaol, the question of his
nationality unresolved. Six months had passed since Morris told Jefferson that he had claimed Paine as an American citizen. It seemed that
the man had lied. With Morris writing for the royalist cause, Monroe
began to explore the Paine case, while Paine himself wrote to Peter
Whiteside (his backer in the bridge project) in an attempt to discover
his exact status.

> In about ten days I received an answer to my letter, in which the writer
> says: 'Mr Monroe told me he had no order (meaning from the Presi-
> dent, Mr Washington) respecting you, but that he (Mr Monroe) will
> do everything in his power to liberate you, but, from what I learn from
> Americans lately arrived in Paris, you are not considered, either by
> the American government or by individuals, as an American citizen.

Paine was stunned. When they had need of him, America had been
glad enough of his service, yet now they disowned him. Effectively, he

was stateless — save in England, where they hung him in effigy. Impassioned, Paine wrote a 43-page memorandum to Monroe, and on 18 September received an unequivocal reply:

> By being with us through the Revolution you are of our country, as absolutely as if you had been born there; and you are no more of England, than every native of America is . . . The crime of ingratitude has not yet stained, and I trust never will stain, our national character. You are considered by them, as not only having rendered important services in our own Revolution, but as being on a more extensive scale, the friend of human rights.

The reassurance was some consolation, but the days dragged by from September and into October, and there was still no sign of his release. With Robespierre gone, and the new government promoting moderation, Paine was restless for freedom and, remembering his own words 'Wrongs cannot have a legal descent', laughed bitterly at the irony. It was almost 20 years since he had first encouraged America to claim its liberty, while now they forfeited his own.

Held in the Luxembourg, Paine failed to understand the complexity of Monroe's position. Gouverneur Morris had left behind a cat's cradle of intrigue, and it was not until 2 November that the new Minister felt confident to write to the President of the Committee of General Surety on Paine's behalf:

> The citizens of the United States cannot look back upon the time of their own Revolution without recollecting among the names of their most distinguished patriots that of Thomas Paine; the services he rendered to his country in its struggle for freedom have implanted in the hearts of his countrymen a sense of gratitude never to be effaced as long as they shall deserve the title of a just and honourable people.
>
> The above named citizen is at this moment languishing in prison, affected with a disease growing more intense with his confinement. I beg, therefore, to call your attention to his condition and to request you to hasten the moment when the law shall decide his fate, in the case of any accusation against him, and if none, to restore him to liberty.

Two days later, Paine was released. In ten months and nine days almost a thousand prisoners had left the Luxembourg for the scaffold; but he was free. An ageing man, and sick, he pondered the rights of man, and the contradictions they entailed. Then Monroe drove him home.

13 'MASTER OF AN EMPTY HOUSE'

Effectively the French Revolution came to a close with the fall of Robespierre. In five years, France had shifted from the absolutism of Louis XVI through the comparatively moderate demands of the Estates General and the carefully circumscribed programme of the bourgeoisie, to the dictatorship of the Jacobins, sanctified by the Supreme Being. Now it was the turn of counter-revolution, though during the early months reaction moved with caution.

The sansculottes still commanded large sections of Paris, while a rump of Jacobins composed a powerful minority in the Convention. By the autumn, however, the new centre−right grouping felt confident enough to begin closing the Jacobin Clubs, and on 8 December, the date of the political amnesty granting freedom to those Girondins who had escaped the guillotine, the moderate Deputy A.C. Thibaudeau was proposing Paine's return to the Convention:

> I reclaim one of the most zealous defenders of liberty — Thomas Paine (applause); a man who has honoured his century by the energy with which he has defended the rights of man, who has gloriously distinguished himself by the role he has played in the American Revolution. I have never heard a single reproach uttered against Thomas Paine. Naturalised as a French citizen by the Legislative Assembly, he was named representative of the people. His expulsion from the Convention was merely the fruit of intrigue . . . He lives in distress. I urge that he be recalled to the Convention (applause).

The motion was adopted unanimously, and a month later, when the Committee of Public Instruction proposed awarding pensions for literary services to French citizens, Paine's name headed the list:

> the man of genius, without fortune, dear to all friends of humanity . . . a cosmopolitan persecuted equally by Pitt and Robespierre . . . a notable epoch in the life of this philosopher who opposed the arms of Common Sense to the sword of tyranny, the Rights of Man to the Machiavellianism of English politicians.

Paine was sceptical. The French pushed too hard to make reparation: 'First they voted me out of the Convention for being a foreigner, then they imprisoned me on the ground of being a foreigner, then they voted me in again by annulling the vote that declared me a foreigner.' The old arrogance was reasserting itself, though now tinged with bitterness. Ten months in the Luxembourg were not to be dismissed with a few well-chosen words. Once he had placed his trust in men, but that was before Congress had dismissed him for exposing Silas Deane; before Burke had betrayed himself; before Washington had forgotten the meaning of friend-ship — and already the Convention talked of expunging the word '*revolu-tionaire*' from the language and of drafting a new constitution.

This would be the third in as many years, and the preamble set the mood for what followed:

> Hitherto the efforts of France have been directed solely to destroy . . . Absolute equality is a chimera; virtue, talents, physical and in-tellectual power are not equally distributed by nature . . . Property alone attaches the Citizen to his country . . . The people should never be allowed to deliberate indiscriminately on public affairs; a populace constantly deliberating rapidly perishes by misery and disorder.

The words could have been Locke's, or the authors of the Revolutionary Settlement: that property was the measure of the man. Had nothing chang-ed in the past century, nothing been learnt since 1789? Was this to be the monument to the Revolution, to erect a constitution on the premiss that 'all who are to have any share in the legislature should be possessed of some independent income'? The scheme deserved a reply, if only to commemorate those who had died believing that man had rights other than property.

Again Paine wrote to expose the absurdities of hereditary government, to extol the merits of representation, and now the words were sharpened by experience: 'the rights which any man, or any family had to set itself up to govern a nation, was no other than the right which Robespierre had to do the same thing in France.' For a year the man had nullified all he claimed to represent for: 'The true and only basis of representative government is equality of rights.'

By the summer of 1795, the Convention, having contained the Jacobins and with a growing right-wing bias, was moving fast to approve the new constitution, and Paine hammered out his reply:

> Personal rights, of which the rights of voting a representative is one, are a species of property of the most sacred kind . . . In any view of the case it is dangerous and impolitic, sometimes ridiculous and always unjust, to make property the right of voting . . . The offensive

part of the case is that this exclusion implies a stigma on the moral character of the person excluded . . . To take away the right, is to reduce a man to a state of slavery, for slavery consents to being subject to the will of another.

The *Dissertation on the First Principles of Government*, a summary of much that Paine had written in the previous 20 years, was published in late June 1795, and on 7 July he went before the Convention to argue that certain of the articles of the proposed constitution were 'repugnant to reason and incompatible with the principles of liberty'. The Deputies listened indifferently as Citizen Lanthera read Paine's text, and no one rose to support the case. It was Paine's last appearance before the Convention. Three months later the body abolished itself by voting in the new constitution with a bicameral legislature based on property qualifications and headed by a Directory of five members — who took up their residence in the Luxembourg, and ordered that Condorcet's remains be transferred to the Pantheon.

The irony was inescapable: not so much that the new men of power now lodged in what had so recently been his prison; more that they should elevate Condorcet whilst burying his ideals. Only two years had passed since Paine had worked with Condorcet framing a new constitution for France, and he remembered its opening words:

The object of all union of men in society being the maintenance of their natural rights, civil and political, these rights are the basis of the social pact: their recognition and their declaration ought to precede the Constitution which assures their guarantee. The natural rights of men, civil and political, are liberty, equality, security, property, social protection and resistance to oppression.

First, Robespierre and the Jacobins had plagiarised the document, then been party to Condorcet's death. Now reaction disguised their betrayal of his beliefs by making a talisman of Condorcet himself. It was always the way, expedience mocking reason until there was no reason left. At 58 years of age, Paine had once considered himself an authority on the subject; now it seemed that he had spent half a lifetime building a credo on sand to watch its foundations being sapped, inexorably, by the tide of unreason.

The response that had greeted the publication of the first part of *The Age of Reason* early in 1794 was a case in point. The work had provoked an uproar among churchmen and laymen alike who, if they could not find fault with his logic, reverted to criticism of his private life, not least of his drinking habits. It was not that he was the first man to profess deism (Voltaire himself had been inspired by English deists such as Lord Herbert of Cherbury* and Matthew Tindal*); more that he had taken the gospel out of doors. And why not? If the church could preach that, even if those in authority were evil, the authority and its power were good and from God; then why not tear down the whole shibboleth? A year had passed since he had talked through his ideas with Mr Bond in the Luxembourg. Now Paine wrote to refine the second part of *The Age of Reason, An Investigation of True and Fabulous Theology*.

By the late summer of 1795 Paine was tired, disillusioned, sick. The first he understood: 20 years at the centre of affairs was fatiguing enough for any man. The second he fought to contain: a poisonous growth in the mind. The third was pitiless: an abscess on his side, a memento of prison, pulsed with a life of its own until it seemed that the pain and the disenchantment fused, to live off each other, and he wrote and drank and remembered the Luxembourg and concentrated all the bitterness he knew on Washington.

There had been a time when the two men had called each other friends; when Paine had written in defence of Washington, when Washington had befriended Paine. So much for friendship. For ten months and nine days he had remained in prison, without a word from Washington, without any sign of intervention by the President of the United States. Paine was unaware of Morris's duplicity, and this personal betrayal was worse than all the rest. They might outlaw his principles in England; they might acclaim him, gaol him, release him, dismiss him in France; but without the surety of friendship there was nothing. In September 1795, Paine wrote a curt note to Washington accusing him of being party to his imprisonment, but within days was writing a partial retraction to Madison: 'I ought not to have suspected Mr Washington of treachery but he has acted towards me the part of a cold blooded traitor.'

Confused and paranoid, the gaol sickness returned, and Paine collapsed for a second time. He was virtually helpless with a form of paralysis.

> Mrs Monroe showed him all possible kindness and attention. She provided him with an excellent nurse, who had for him all the anxiety and assiduity of a sister. She neglected nothing to offer him care and comfort when he was totally unable to help himself.

For all the attention, Monroe was writing in the late summer of 1795: 'The prospect is that he will not be able to hold out more than a month or two at the furthest.'

By the year's end, however, Paine was making a slow recovery, to read the early replies to the publication of the second part of *The Age of Reason*. The criticisms were much the same mixture of theological outrage and personal abuse as before, except for that of Richard Watson, Bishop of Llandaff. In defending his creed in *An Apology for the Bible*, Watson accepted much of what Paine had written — the doubtful authenticity of much of the Old Testament; the discrepancies in the genealogy of Christ — and went so far as to write: 'There is a philosophical sublimity in some of your ideas when speaking of the Creation of the Universe.'

Watson's grounds for criticism were largely moral: that objections to a Christian God for permitting the existence of evil applied equally well to the God of the deists. While stinging Paine into a later reply, the argument at least commanded his respect. As for the rest, he was contemptuous, writing to Samuel Adams:

> I endangered my life in the first place, by opposing in the Convention the execution of the King . . . and I endangered it a second time by opposing atheism, yet *some* of your priests cry out in the war whoop of priestcraft, what an Infidel, what a wicked man is Thomas Paine! They might as well add, for he believes in God, and is against shedding blood.

In the spring of 1797, Thomas Williams was the first printer brought before an English court charged with publishing a blasphemy, *The Age of Reason*. Erskine, who had lost his patronage for defending Paine five years before, represented the prosecution, and, while Paine wrote to Erskine condemning his inconsistency ('he admits the right of controversy, he reserves the right of calling that controversy, abuse'), and repudiating the charge ('of all the tyrannies that effect mankind, tyranny in religion is the worst'), he had other and more pressing concerns.

Five months before Paine was released from the Luxembourg, Congress had dispatched John Jay to London to negotiate a new agreement between Great Britain and the United States. Paine viewed the move with suspicion, and with the signing of the treaty vehemently protested that to declare that: 'the *United States has no other resource than in the justice and magnanimity of his Majesty*, is a satire upon the Declaration of Independence, and exhibits a spirit of meanness on the part of America, that were it true, I should be ashamed of her.'

To Paine, the betrayal was twofold — on the one hand, of America's

republican principles; on the other, of America's oldest ally, France —
and the ultimate responsibility lay with the man whom he suspected of
his own betrayal: Washington. In Paris, Monroe attempted to dissuade
Paine from dabbling in affairs of state. It was a hopeless task: 'He [Paine]
thinks that the President winks at his imprisonment, and wished he might
die in gaol.' The suspicion might be ill-founded but by early in 1796, with
the Directory deciding that the Jay Treaty nullified the alliance between
France and the United States, Paine determined that the time had finally
come to expose the full extent of Washington's perfidy. The man had
counterfeited friendship for too long.

To avoid embarrassing Monroe, who was on the point of being recalled from his post as Minister to France, Paine moved to Versailles and
there, in the summer of 1796, he wrote his open letter to the President:
'As censure is but awkwardly softened by apology, I shall offer you no
apology for this letter. The eventful crisis to which your double policies
have conducted the affairs of your country, requires an investigation un-
cramped by ceremony.'

The issues were varied, complex, but all turned on Washington. As
President he sat at the centre of the web, and had done so since the States
had met at Philadelphia ten years before to draft the Constitution. No
one could doubt the need for the measure — Paine himself had discussed the importance of consolidating the separate states into a Federal
government with Gouverneur Morris and others as early as 1782 — but
the outcome was as corrupt as the intentions had been virtuous.

At his desk in Versailles, Paine remembered his first sight of the new
constitution, and the letter he had written to a friend in New York:

> A thousand years hence, for I must indulge in a few thoughts, perhaps
> in less, America may be what Britain now is. The innocence of her
> character, that won her the hearts of all Nations in her favour, may
> sound like a romance, and her inimitable virtue as if it had never been.
> The ruins of liberty, which thousands bled to obtain, may just furnish
> materials for a village tale, or extort a sigh from rustic sensibility;
> while the fashionable of that day, enveloped in dissipation, shall deride
> the principle, and deny the fact.

Then his fears had been shadowy. In the meantime, they had lengthen-
ed. Echoing John Adams, the Federalist party had placed its confidence
in 'the wise and good and rich' to draw representation so tight that it
choked the meaning of the word; had indulged in aristocratic posturings
and recoiled from the Revolution in France; and had gone so far to ape

English manners that Adams had suggested that the Presidency should become an hereditary office, and Jay proposed that the Senate be appointed for life.

> the right to set up and establish hereditary Government, never did, and never can, exist in any generation at any time whatever . . . it is of the nature of treason, because it is an attempt to take away the rights of all minors living at that time, and of all succeeding generations. It is a degree beyond treason; it is a sin against nature.

This was the corruption that Washington presided over: the corruption of the Republic itself. With such a man, nothing was safe, and it did something to account for his own confinement in the Luxembourg. Washington could have intervened but 'it has sometime been known by those who know him, that he has no friendships, that he is incapable of forming any; [that] he can serve or desert a man, or a cause, with constitutional indifference'.

For what applied to Paine was doubly true of France. Before the Treaty was released, the whole of Jay's mission to London was cloaked in secrecy, yet Washington could still write to the Committee of Public Safety on Monroe's appointment:

> He [Monroe] is instructed to bear to you *our sincere solicitude for your welfare, and to cultivate with zeal the cordiality so happily subsisting between us* . . . I beseech you, therefore, to give full credence to whatever he shall say to you on the part of the United States, and most of all, when he shall assure you that your prosperity is an object of our affection.

This was the treachery of Washington, who could protest friendship while scheming to abandon America's closest ally in preference for her most recent enemy. And all the while the man preened himself as if he had won American independence single-handed, as if American liberty had been in his gift. The facts contradicted the pretensions. Washington came late to the political movement — and Paine recalled his remark little more than a month before Bunker Hill: 'Independence, sir? If you ever hear of my joining in any such measures you have my leave to set me down for everything wicked' — whilst as for his military achievements: 'it would have been prudent in Mr Washington not to have awakened enquiry on that subject. Fame then was cheap; he enjoyed it cheaply; and nobody was ever disposed to take away the laurels that, whether they were *acquired* or not, had been given.'

As a commander, Washington's sole merit lay in constancy, but constancy was the common virtue of the Revolution. As for the rest? Paine checked, remembering his own defence of Washington 20 years before. Then 'Crisis Five' had been a necessity — the need to maintain unity subordinated all else against the machinations of the Philadelphia cabal — but in hindsight a different interpretation could be placed upon events. True, Washington had foiled Howe in the early campaigns, but more as a result of masterful inactivity than military éclat. True, Washington did command the Continental Army; but it was Gates who drubbed Burgoyne at Saratoga; Greene who recovered the southern States when they had been overrun; and without the French it was questionable whether Cornwallis would have been taken at Yorktown.

> I have had, and still have, as much pride in the American revolution as any man, or as Mr Washington has a right to have, but that pride has never made me forgetful whence the great aid came that completed the business . . . It is as well the ingratitude as the pusillanimity of Mr Washington, and the Washington faction, that has brought upon America that loss of character she now suffers in the world, and the numerous evils her commerce had undergone, and to which she is still exposed.

The case was well argued. After this, Washington would have less reason to cry himself up. All that was needed was the close:

> If there is any sense left in the heart, to call a blush into the cheek, the Washington administration must be ashamed to appear. And as to you, Sir, treacherous in private friendship (for so you have been to me, and that in the day of danger) and a hypocrite in public life, the world will be puzzled to decide whether you are an APOSTATE, or an IMPOSTER? — Whether you have abandoned good principles, or whether you ever had any?

Paine dated the letter 3 August 1796, and dispatched it for publication to Benjamin Franklin Bache, editor of the *Aurora*. Franklin used excerpts from the letter in support of Jefferson and the Republicans in October and November, and published the full text in a pamphlet in February 1797. It sparked off a controversy which was to haunt Paine for the rest of his life. Critics considered it little less than a blasphemy. Twice in as many years Paine had offended the conscience of America, first with *The Age of*

Reason, then with the Washington letter. Although Washington's reputation was waning, he remained the godhead of the Federalists and wryly Paine remembered the savage comment that 'the people of America had been guilty of idolatry in making a man their God' by those who now numbered themselves amongst Washington's closest confidants, and composed a private epitaph to friendship:

> Take from the mine the coldest, hardest stone,
> It needs no fashion: it is Washington.
> But if you chisel, let the stroke be rude,
> And on his heart engrave — Ingratitude.

As incapable of compromise as he was careless of self-interest, the bitterness of Paine's own experiences were to poison his last years, and by the late 1790s he was already despairing of the young Republic. Since 1795 the Directory had tightened its control on government and, while stability was returning to France, it was at the expense of the utopian hopes of the revolutionary years. As a young Burgundian noblewoman, imprisoned during the Terror, was to write of 1797:

> All over France the pleasures of life were cultivated quite uninhibitedly. The revolutionary regime was over once and for all. No-one now spoke of informers or gendarmes. I have never seen people enjoying themselves as much as this . . . life was just one great carnival.

The aristocracy may have passed on, but the bourgeoisie took their place — a new 'republic of friends' based on common social interests. And while life in France itself was a 'carnival' for the middle class if not for the peasantry, French arms triumphed throughout Europe and the exploits of Bonaparte became the talk of the salons. At 27 years of age, he had commanded the French army brilliantly in the recent Italian campaign, and on 5 September 1797 (the 18th Fructidor on the revolutionary calendar) his troops had supported the Directory in a *coup d'état* that overthrew the Councils and brought parliamentary government to an end in France.

Paine was ambivalent. On the one hand, the *coup* was dangerous for its concentration of executive powers in the hands of the Directory; on the other, it had checked a widely suspected Anglo-royalist conspiracy with all that that implied. In early October, Paine explained his support for the new regime in 'A Letter of Thomas Paine to the People of France':

Considering the events of the 18th Fructidor in a political light, it is one of those that is justifiable only on the supreme law of absolute necessity, and it is the necessity abstracted from the event that is to be deplored. The event itself is a matter of joy,

coupling it with his continued suspicion of the intentions of the Pitt administration.

Peace talks between the two countries had recently broken down and, by January 1798, Paine was not only contributing to a government fund for an assault on England ('though it is not convenient for me in the present situation of my affairs, to subscribe to the loan . . . my economy makes it possible for me to make a small patriotic donation'), but also elaborating his own invasion plan which was adopted by the Directory. And they were not alone. Bonaparte, who claimed to sleep with a copy of *Rights of Man* beneath his pillow, was intrigued by Paine's proposal, though two years were to pass before the two men were to meet.

For Paine it was a comparatively quiet time, living in the Paris apartment of Nicholas de Bonneville, and writing the occasional article for his journal *Le Bien Informé*. For Bonaparte, they were crucial years in his progress to power. In mid-1799, he returned from the disastrous Egyptian campaign to find the government divided against itself, and on 11 November (the 19th Brumaire) led a *coup* against the constitution ('The Constitution has been thrice violated already — all parties invoked it — each in turn trampled on it. Since that can be preserved no longer, let us save its foundations — Liberty and Equality'), to establish the Consulate, with himself as the first amongst equals.

At the Bonnevilles' apartment on the rue du Théâtre Français, Paine considered the comparisons between Washington and Bonaparte. Both were military men. Both were ambitious and, while Washington had already held high office, Bonaparte now waited his chance. It was soon to come. On 14 December 1799, he appointed himself Chief Consul. Little more than ten years after the fall of the Bastille, France again had a ruler as absolute as any Bourbon, and among Bonaparte's first acts was to move the seat of government from the Luxembourg to the Tuileries explaining that it was 'a good military position'.

Within the month, Paris heard news of the death of Washington; Bonaparte issued a general order commanding the French army to wrap their colours in crêpe for ten days in honour: 'of a great man who fought against tyranny and consolidated the liberties of his country'; and Paine considered the snare of words. Almost 25 years had passed since he had talked through the Declaration of Independence with Jefferson, for

Washington to turn its ideals topsy-turvy; almost a decade had passed since he and Condorcet had talked over the Rights of Man, and now Bonaparte mouthed the principles to mask his intentions.

It seemed that the First Consul's ambitions were limitless, but first England had to be broken. In the spring of 1800, Bonaparte visited Paine at the Bonnevilles' apartment to declare that a statue in gold should be erected to Paine in every town, and invite him to attend a Military Council to act as an adviser for the proposed invasion of England. Paine agreed, with one proviso — that the sole object of the sortie would be to bring liberty to his fellow countrymen.

Bonaparte was reassuring; none the less, Paine only made a single appearance at the Council. Asked his opinion of the prospects for invasion, he replied:

> It is now several years since I have been in England and therefore I can only judge of it by what I knew when I was there. I think the people are very disaffected, but I am sorry to add that if the expedition should escape the fleet I think the army would be cut to pieces. The only way to kill England is to annihilate her commerce.

The Council agreed. Bonaparte was incensed. The two men never spoke together again. Years later, the artist Walter Savage Landor, an admirer of Paine, recalled a meeting with him in Paris and Paine's prophecy that Bonaparte would make himself Emperor, but that his intemperate use of power would cause the French 'to wish for their old Kings, forgetting what beasts they were', adding:

> You will shortly see the real strength and figure of Bonaparte. He is wilful, headstrong, proud, morose, presumptuous; he will be guided no longer; he has pulled the pad from his forehead, and will break his nose or bruise his cranium against every table, chair, and brick in the room, until at last he must be sent to hospital.

The prediction gave Paine little comfort. He was 62 years of age, and it seemed that all he had so long represented was in ruins. In England, Pitt's government hung liberty from the gibbet. In France, the Republic was subordinate to Bonaparte. In America . . . in America there was news that, with Washington's death, Jefferson and the Republicans could well be returned to power. How many years was it now since he had sailed for Europe? Twelve, no thirteen. Then it had been for a short visit, but a revolution had intervened, and he recalled Lafayette in exile, and

Condorcet, and Danton dead. The Revolution in France was lost and on 1 October 1800, Paine wrote to Jefferson:

> If any American frigate should come to France, and the direction of it should fall to you, I will be glad if you will give me the opportunity of returning. The abscess under which I suffered almost two years is entirely healed of itself, and I enjoy exceeding good health.

By the spring of 1801, following his election to the Presidency, Jefferson was replying:

> You expressed a wish to get a passage to this country in a public vessel. Mr Dawson is charged with orders to the Captain of the 'Maryland' to receive and accommodate you back if you can be ready to depart at such short warning . . . I am in hopes that you will find us returned generally to the sentiments worthy of former times. In these it will be your glory to have steadily laboured, and with as much effect as any man living. That you may long live to continue your useful labours and to reap the reward in the thankfulness of the nation, is my sincere prayer.

There was only one difficulty to be overcome. While Britain and France were already in the process of negotiating a peace settlement, Paine risked capture by a British ship of the line until the terms were finalised, and it was not until September 1802 (little more than a year after the signing of the Peace of Amiens), that he sailed for America from Le Havre.

Clio Rickmann was on the quayside to see him off. More than 30 years had passed since the two men first met in Lewes, before so many events that had changed the world. Now Rickmann stood alone until he could see the ship no longer, then wrote a farewell to his friend:

> Thus smooth be thy waves, and thus gentle the breeze,
>   As thou bearest my Paine far away;
> O waft him to comfort and regions of ease,
> Each blessing of freedom and friendship to seize,
>   And bright be his setting sun's rays.

Paine's reception in America was to mock both Jefferson's sentiments and Rickmann's hopes.

Even before he landed in Baltimore on 20 October 1802, Paine's critics were alerted: 'If during the present season of abasement . . . any portent could surprise, sober men would be wholly confounded by the article current in all the newspapers that the loathsome Thomas Paine is invited to return in a national ship by the first Magistrate of the People.' The accusation that Jefferson had used his high office to obtain Paine a passage in a US frigate was one of the lesser charges, however.

The Church militant and the Federalist right, one incensed by *The Age of Reason*, the other by the letter to Washington, combined to villify Paine: 'What! Invite to the United States that lying, drunken, brutal infidel who rejoiced in the opportunity of basking and wallowing in the confusion, devastation, bloodshed, rapine and murder in which his soul delights.'

It was hardly the welcome that Jefferson had led Paine to expect. If this was the 'thankfulness of the nation', the reception contradicted the words; whilst, as for 'a return to the sentiments of former times', it seemed that America was as divided as ever before. In 1787, when he had sailed for Europe, Paine had hoped that the wounds inflicted by the Revolution would heal, that Patriot and Tory would make common cause in the interests of the young Republic.

Superficially they had, though on different terms. While the Federalists pursued their exclusivity, took England as their model, and were deeply suspicious of the French; the Republicans represented a wider franchise, and remembered their debt to France. The conflict was bitter, one Federalist journal writing to warn the electorate in 1800:

> If Mr Jefferson is elected the taxes will fall on the landed interest, all the churches will be over-turned, none but Frenchmen employed by government, and the monstrous system of liberty and equality, with all its horrid consequences, will inevitably be introduced.

Paine was the incarnation of such fears, and the Federalists mercilessly exploited his deism to discredit Jefferson and his Republicans. Not that the President was unduly concerned. The two men's friendship was too resilient for that. When Paine reached Washington in mid-November, Jefferson welcomed him warmly, ignoring the concern of advisers that the man was as much an embarrassment to the President as to his party. Paine was to remain in Washington for three months, discussing policies with Jefferson (among them a plan for purchasing Louisiana from the French government), bringing news to his family of acquaintances in Paris, dining with Republican friends, and writing.

The calumnies of the Federalist press demanded repudiation and his seven 'Letters to the Citizens of the United States of America', written between December 1802 and February 1803, were a summation of Paine's hopes and fears for the Republic:

> I now know from the information I obtain on the spot, that the impressions that distressed me when abroad, for I was proud of America, were all too well founded — She was turning her back on her own glory, and making hasty steps in the retrograde path of oblivion. But a spark from the altar of *Seventy Six*, unextinguished and unextinguishable through the long night of error, is again lighting up in every part of the union, the genuine flame of national liberty.

In the letters that followed, Paine excoriated Federalist ambitions: 'A faction, acting in disguise, was rising in America . . . They were beginning to contemplate government as a profitable monopoly, and the people as hereditary property.' The words crystallised the disillusion, and from somewhere in his past — Joseph's workroom, Dr Bevis's chambers? — he recalled the lines of a Commonwealth pamphleteer of 150 years before:

> Oh England, stand amazed. Many of your trustees have conceived wickedness. They promised liberty but behold slavery, they pretended justice but behold oppression; they pretended reformation but behold deformation . . . Our condition is much worse than at the beginning, for then we knew our sickness and remedy but now such are our distempers that we may more easily know them than cure them. 'Tis their privilege is our bondage, their power our pestilence, their rights our poverty, their wills our law, their smiles our safety, their frowns our ruin.

The process was unchanged, unchanging; in England, in France, and now here, in America, the ideal for which men had fought and died was threatened again. The betrayal of Burke and Lafayette and Washington had been bitter enough. It was nothing compared to this, the betrayal of the Republic itself, and Paine wrote reiterating the case for a Federal state, secured by representative government:

> To ELECT and REJECT is the prerogative of a free people . . . if ever America loses sight of this principle, she will no longer be *the land of liberty* . . . an abuse of power, and trust, however disguised by appearances, or rendered plausible by pretence, is one time or another to be accounted for.

The seventh letter was written from Paine's old home at Bordentown and within days of its completion he was to witness how bitter the feuding had become, how much animosity his name aroused. The New York stage left from Trenton but, when his long-time friend, Colonel Kirkbride, tried to book him a seat, the owner swore that he'd 'be damned if he'd take Paine as a passenger' for the man was an infidel, or a deist, or both. Kirkbride received the same reply from the proprietor of the rival stage, and eventually Paine and Kirkbride rode north out of Trenton in a hired chaise — mobbed by a menacing crowd.

The road was familiar, Paine had marched it more than quarter of a century before, one of a tired column that straggled across a winter land-scape on the long retreat to the Delaware. Now the countryside was fresh with spring, but he still remembered the ghosts of that army, and the picket guard reading the first of his Crisis papers: 'These are the times that try men's souls', and the retaking of Trenton on Christmas Day 1776. Even hostile commentators had been compelled to admit that it was a 'brilliant little affair', yet now he fled the place, and as the din of the crowd fell behind Paine recalled a single line that he had written those many years ago: 'Tyranny, like hell, is not easily conquered.'

Was this where it began and ended, with the tyranny of the crowd? For an instant the memories fused — of the night mobs on the London streets: 'Wilkes and Liberty'; of the menace of the sansculottes: 'Aristo, à la lanterne'; of the angry faces on the road out of Trenton: 'Infidel, Anti-Christ' — and Paine wondered that they could rail at the temporal and the spiritual with equal celerity. He had written of the Rights of Man, and they were persecuted. He had written of the Age of Reason, and that was persecuted, too. They were Paine's inheritance, the twin Gods of his pantheon, but now he wondered whether reason and man were compatible, and remembered Burke. He had been dead for five years, and yet . . . Paine shrugged off the apostasy, and drove for New York.

At 67 years of age, he still had work to do. Within days of his arrival in the city he was the guest of honour at a dinner at Lovett's Hotel and, at White Plains on Independence Day 1804, a 10,000 strong crowd toasted 'Thomas Paine — the bold advocate of National Liberty — the People's Friend'. But the hostility remained, and in September the *Evening Post* was carrying an epitaph to his name:

> And having spent a lengthy life in evil,
> Return again unto thy parent Devil.

The editor, Federalist William Coleman, was premature, though after almost three decades at the centre of American and European affairs, the horizon of Paine's interests was narrowing. Dividing his time between New York and his small farm at New Rochelle, his last years degenerated into a round of domestic wrangling and petty political feuds.

In the summer of 1804, Madame Bonneville, who had fled France with her three children, moved into Paine's farm, but tiring of the countryside soon moved into New York, leaving Paine to write to a friend:

> I am master of an empty house. I have six chairs and a table, a straw bed . . . a tin kettle, an iron pot, an iron baking tin, a gridiron, cups, saucers, plates and dishes, two candlesticks and a pair of snuffers . . . When you come you must take such fare as you meet with, for I live upon tea, milk, fruit pies, plain dumplings, and a piece of meat when I can get it.

It was here, in May 1807, that the local Tories engineered Paine's final political indignity. Led by Elisha Ward, the election supervisors refused him the right to vote. When Paine remonstrated, Ward called the Constable — 'I commit you to prison' — but did not press the case. Paine's bitterness was complete. He had been outlawed in England, imprisoned in France, denied by America, but old now, and sick, this was the cruellest cut — that he, Thomas Paine, should be refused the vote by those for whose representation he had fought for so long.

It was his last visit to New Rochelle, though his life was little easier in New York. During his first two years in the city, Paine continued to comment on political issues, but in the spring of 1805 he wrote his last major political pamphlet (*Thomas Paine to the Citizens of Pennsylvania, on the Proposal for Calling a Convention*), and in May 1807 published his last important article (the 'Essay on Dreams'). The old skills remained — 'The God of eternity and all that is real, is not the God of passing dreams, and shadows of man's imagination' — but, under mounting personal attack, he was driven to defend his private reputation.

At the close of 1805, Paine was taken seriously ill, and for several weeks was confined to bed. On recovering, he moved his New York lodgings and his former landlord, William Carver, demanded $150 for six months' back rent. Paine replied tetchily. Carver counter-charged with a letter of savage abuse, accusing Paine of debauchery, ingratitude and drunkenness.

Before Paine's death, Carver retracted, but not before handing over a copy of his original letter to James Cheetham, a one-time radical and by 1805 the publisher of the *American Citizen*, a paper for which Paine himself had written. In the late summer of 1807, Cheetham wrote an article in the *Citizen* accusing Paine of taking his ideas, wholesale, from Locke, and casting doubts on his military record during the Revolution. The charges infuriated Paine. As to the former: 'I suppose Locke has spoken of hereditary and *Elective Monarchy*, but the representative as laid down in *Common Sense* and *Rights of Man*, is an entire different thing to elective monarchy.' As to the latter: 'It is . . . not true that I stuck to my pen in a safe retreat with Congress in the times that tried men's souls.' As for Cheetham himself: 'he is an ugly tempered man, and he carries the evidence of it in the vulgarity and forbidingness of his countenance — God has set his mark upon Cain.'

The controversy smouldered on, but Paine was sickening again. Through the winter and into the spring of 1808 his health deteriorated, and during the summer an acquaintance recalled seeing him alone at the window of his lodgings in Greenwich Village.

The sash was raised, a small table or stand was placed before him, with an open book upon it, which he appeared to be reading. He had his spectacles on, his left elbow rested on the table or stand, and his chin rested between the thumb and finger of his hand; his right hand lay upon the book, and a decanter containing liquor of the colour of rum or brandy was standing next to his book and beyond it.

In Thetford 60 years before Paine had known an exile like this, this sense of loneliness — but then he had had a future before him. And now? Now he watched the world passing by the window, and wondered where the years and the friendships had gone, and what purpose they had served? Once, and Paine smiled at the conceit, he thought that he could change the world when America went to war for Common Sense, and England and France declaimed the Rights of Man — but that was before Hamilton, and Pitt, and Bonaparte. It seemed that, while everything changed, all remained the same, and he recalled how Joseph had talked of an English Commonwealth in which 'the Spirit of the Father is Pure Reason; which as he made knits the whole creation together in a oneness of life and moderation' — yet the dispossessed still crossed Thetford bridge.

For three decades Paine was as much as propagandist of optimism as of reason, careless that the evidence defied his ideals. Ultimately, in fact, the practice and principles of his radical inheritance — more especially the levelling tradition of the Commonwealth period with the emphasis on individualism ('reason being the foundation of all honest laws gives to everyman propriety of interest, freedom of enjoyment, and improvement of his own advantage') coupled to a social conscience ('Was the earth made to preserve a few covetous, proud men to live at ease . . . or was it made to preserve all her children?') — were incompatible.

While this duality of interests was to provide liberal democracy with its ethos for three centuries, Paine refused to accept the innate contradiction that it entailed, even as it took concrete form in the latter stages of the American and French Revolutions. On both occasions he was central to developments which reflected much of his inheritance and which, as an inspired publicist, he played a major role in promoting, while dismissing the leveller caution that 'everyone that gets an authority in his hands tyrannises over others'. For more than half a lifetime, Paine's faith in reason and man's beneficence fuelled his optimism, and disguised from him the realities of power.

Indeed, if Paine had accepted the conflict between private interests and the public good as irreconcilable, it would have negated all that he represented — as much the Rights of Man as the Age of Reason. The idea was intolerable — that his credo was fundamentally flawed — but, as he sat by the window of his lodgings in the summer of 1808, it was possible that he pondered why his springtime hopes had never been realised, for government still remained 'the badge of lost innocence'.

At the close of the year, Paine wrote his last brief letter for publication: 'To the Federal Faction'; completed his will ('reposing confidence in my Creator God'); and asked the Quaker Willet Hicks to try and arrange for his interment in the Friends' cemetary. But even there he was rejected. The Society declared that, while they bore no animosity to Paine, they suspected that his friends might wish to erect a monument to his memory which was against Quaker practice. At 72 years of age the hurts continued to multiply, but Paine was too sick to care, and when Margaret Bonneville promised to bury him on his own farm he could only reply: 'I have no objection to that, but the farm will be sold and they will dig up my bones before they are half rotten.'

On 25 February 1809, Paine became feverish, and by March the first symptoms of dropsy appeared. Paine knew he was dying. The thought did not trouble him. All that he feared was the loneliness that went before death, and he begged Margaret Bonneville to take him into her home. The house was only 80 yards from his lodgings and on 4 May he was carried to 59, Grove Street in an armchair.

In New York the rumours abounded. Paine was dying. Paine was dead. Paine had recanted. Paine was recusant still. On 5 June, Dr Manley put the question to his patient directly: 'Do you wish to believe that Jesus Christ is the Son of God?' Paine considered a moment before replying:

'I have no wish to believe on that subject.' It was the same early on the morning of 8 June when two clergymen, bent on Paine's salvation, burst into his room, to be dismissed abruptly: 'Let me alone. Good morning.'

At 8 a.m. on 8 June 1809, Thomas Paine died, to be buried two days later at his farm in New Rochelle. Only five people followed the coffin to the grave — two negroes who had travelled 25 miles on foot to honour the man who had fought so long for the rights of everyman; Margaret Bonneville and her son, Benjamin; and the Quaker Willet Hicks. As the first earth rattled on the coffin, Margaret Bonneville spoke: 'Oh! Mr Paine. My son stands here as testimony for the gratitude of America, and I, for France.'

It was the epitaph for a man the world sought to forget.

In 1817 the radical journalist William Cobbett, fearing imprisonment in England following the suspension of Habeas Corpus, settled in America for two years. At the close of his stay, Cobbett determined to exhume Paine's body and return with it to England to 'effect the reformation of England in Church and State'.

In October 1819, Cobbett drove by night to New Rochelle, but some locals noticed lights around the graveside as he disinterred the body. The alarm was raised, and a sheriff's posse formed, but it was too late. Cobbett was already on the road for New York where he loaded Paine's remains aboard a packet bound for Liverpool.

After this the accounts differ: one suggests that government agents, alarmed at the possible effects of Paine's return, dumped his body into the Mersey at Liverpool; another that Cobbett left the body to his son, John, on his death in 1835. The second version, which is better authenticated, suggests that, when John was later declared a bankrupt, the Lord Chancellor refused to accept Paine's skeleton as an asset, and that for several years the remains were kept by a day-labourer before passing into the hands of a Surrey furniture dealer.

However, a century later a third, partial account emerged. In the 1930s a letter, based on material supplied by a Brighton housewife, appeared in the *Daily Telegraph*:

My grandmother's first husband, Mr Wilkinson, was a Custom House Officer in Liverpool at the time that William Cobbett brought over Thomas Paine's bones for burial in England. Mr Cobbett gave Mr Wilkinson Thomas Paine's 'jawbone'. My grandmother thought so much of it that she took it with her to her new home when she became the wife of Richard Beverley, a schoolmaster of Eglwysbach, North Wales. My mother used to play with it when a child, but after her marriage and when on a visit to her old home she thought that it should have a decent burial. Her father gave his consent, and she placed it in an open grave in the village churchyard. It must therefore have had a Christian burial.

Paine, the deist, would have been entertained by the posthumous irony.

NOTES

Chapter 1 Early Years

1. To obtain a current approximation of mid-eighteenth-century currency values, multiply by 80.

2. 'Every chartered town is an aristocratical monopoly in itself, and the qualification of electors proceeds out of these chartered monopolies . . . In these chartered monopolies, a man coming from another part of the country is hunted from them as if he were a foreign enemy. An Englishman is not free in his own country, every one of these places presents a barrier in his way, and tells him he is not a freeman — that he has no rights' (*Rights of Man*).

3. Written by the Quaker Nicholson, 'A Blast from the Lord', in 1653.

4. Following common eighteenth-century practice, America is used throughout the book to denote the 13 Colonies which, following independence, became the United States.

5. From a sermon delivered by John Winthrop, leader of the Massachusetts Bay Colony, at sea abroad the *Arabella* (350 tons) during the ten-week voyage from Cowes, Isle of Wight, to New England in the spring of 1630.

Chapter 2 London: The Two Cities

1. This vignette is based on an essay in Goldsmith's *Letters From a Citizen of the World To His Friends In The East*.

2. In *Rights of Man*, Paine writes of 'the youth that comes up to London full of expectations' to find that 'unless he gets immediate employment is already half undone; and boys bred up in London without any means of livelihood and, as it often happens, of dissolute parents, are in still worse off condition, and servants long out of place are not much better off. In short, a world of little causes is continually arising, which busy or affluent life knows not of, to open the first door to distress. Hunger is not among the postponable wants, and a day, even a few hours in such conditions is often the crisis of a life of ruin. These circumstances which are the general cause of little thefts and pilferings that lead to greater . . .'

3. Written by Paine thirty years after Mary Lambert's death, and sent to Sir Robert Smith the morning after he had asked Paine: 'What Is Love?'

4. 'Affronted in one country by polygamy, which gives them their rivals as inseparable companions, enslaved in another by indissoluble ties, which often joins the gentle sex to the rude, and sensibility to brutality. Even in countries where they may be esteemed most happy, contrained in their desires in the disposal of their goods, robbed of freedom of will by the laws, and slaves of opinion which rules them with absolute sway, and construes the slightest appearance of guilt; surrounded on all sides by judges who are at once their tyrants and seducers, and who having prepared their fault, punish every lapse with dishonour — Nay, usurp the right of degrading them on suspicion — Who does not feel sorry for the tender sex? Yet such I am sorry to say is the lot of women over the whole world' ('An Occasional Letter on the Female Sex', *Pennsylvania Magazine*, August 1776).

5. The remark, together with a wealth of other waspish detail about life at the court of George II, comes from Lord Hervey's *Memoirs*, originally published (in expurgated form) in 1848. In 1932, a limited edition of the uncensored manuscript (held in the Royal Archives, Windsor Castle) was published.

6. 'One turns candleholder, or a lord in waiting, another a lord of the bedchamber, a groom of the stole, or any insignificant office to which a salary is annexed, paid out of public taxes, and which avoids the direct appearance of corruption' (*Rights of Man*).

Chapter 3 'An Ingenious, Worthy Young Man'

1. Paine's poem 'To a Farmer's Dog', written in Lewes and first published in the *Pennsylvania Magazine* in 1775, carried the introduction: 'The following story, ridiculous as it is, is a fact. A farmer at New Shoreham, near Brighthelmsea (now Brighton) having voted at an election for a member of Parliament, contrary to the pleasure of three neighbouring justices, they took revenge on his dog, which they caused to be hanged for starting a hare upon the road.'

Chapter 4 Common Sense

1. 'On Conciliation with the American Colonies', 1775.
2. As early as 1768, a French agent in New York was reporting to Paris: 'If things could only go on as they were doing, it was all that France could desire . . . the colonies would learn to do without the aid of the mother country and England would be ruined.'

APPENDIX

Adams, John (1735–1826): cousin of Samuel Adams, educated at Harvard, and admitted to the Bar in 1758. In 1765, John Adams became a leader of the Massachusetts Whigs opposing the Stamp Act. Due to illness, he withdrew from political activities in 1771, but in 1774 was appointed a Massachusetts delegate to the first Continental Congress. In 1776 he was one of the Committee that drafted the Declaration of Independence, and seven years later was a signatory to the Treaty of Paris which ended the Revolution. Between 1785 and 1788, Adams was the United States' first envoy to Britain and, after serving for eight years as Vice-President (1789–97), was elected the second President of the US in 1797 — an office that he held for three years. Always vain, and often cantankerous, Adams's combination of legal and political interests played an important role in steering the Colonists to independence — though his radicalism was limited by a legalistic mind that tended to place the law above the public it served, and by a background which, in 1797, led him to propose that the governing representatives of the people should be only 'the rich, the well born and the able'.

Adams, Samuel (1722–1803): a graduate of Harvard, Adams went into business in Boston, failed miserably, and by 1764 was devoting himself almost exclusively to politics. A member of the Massachusetts House of Representatives from 1765 to 1774 (and its Clerk for eight of those years), Adams was at the forefront of the Colonists' opposition to the Stamp and Townshend Acts, and in 1774 managed the Boston Tea Party. One of the first Colonial leaders to advocate separation from Britain, and a vehement opponent of making any concessions to George III, Adams was a delegate to the Continental Congress from 1774 to 1781, and Governor of Massachusetts from 1794 to 1797. A brilliant agitator and polemicist, Samuel Adams was a central figure in the eleven-year campaign (1765–75) that led to American independence.

Bacon, Francis (1561—1626): Baron Verulam of Verulam, Viscount St Albans. London-born, and educated at Trinity College, Cambridge, Bacon was called to the Bar in 1582, and elected MP in 1584. An extraordinary contradictory character, Bacon was on the one hand a ruthless political opportunist; on the other, a philosopher of seminal power. As to the former, he was to spend more than half his lifetime selling his talents to any master who could improve his position: in 1606 he became Solicitor-General; in 1616 Lord Keeper, and in 1618 Lord Chancellor (the year in which he played a major part in the trial and execution of Sir Walter Raleigh). Bacon's naked political ambitions, however, won him many enemies and in 1621 he was charged before the House of Lords with receiving bribes to influence his judicial decisions. Offering no defence, he was heavily fined, banished from Parliament and the Court, and briefly imprisoned in the Tower. As to his philosophical genius, Bacon abandoned the deductive logic of Aristotle and the Schoolmen, and, in emphasising the importance of experiment in interpreting nature, and rejecting the convention that truth is derived from authority, he became the practical creator of scientific induction. In 1605 he published *The Advancement of Learning*, a study of the state of knowledge in his own times; in 1620, his master work *Novum Organum*; and, in 1623, *De Augmentis Scientiorum*. Bacon died, heavily in debt, in 1626 having caught a cold while stuffing a fowl with snow to observe the effects of low temperatures on the preservation of flesh.

Beaumarchais, Pierre Augustin Caron de (1732–99): French playwright and man of affairs. The son of a Paris watchmaker, Beaumarchais was brought up in his father's trade, but when in his mid-twenties he was noticed by the court. At 24 years of age, Beaumarchais married the widow of a wealthy court official, and twelve years later made a second advantageous marriage. His first two plays were only moderately successful, but in 1775 he completed *The Barber of Seville*, and nine years later *The Marriage of Figaro*, each of which was widely acclaimed, and both of which were later to provide the basis for two of Mozart's most successful operas.

Blake, William (1757–1827): English poet, painter, engraver and mystic.

Brunswick, Duke of (1735–1806): fought in the Seven Years' War; commanded the combined Prussian–Austrian forces in France in 1792, when he issued the so-called Brunswick manifestos threatening to deliver up Paris to 'military execution' if any violence was offered to Louis XVI or Marie Antoinette. Died of wounds after his defeat by Napoleon at Auerstadt.

Bunker Hill (June 1775): an assault by 24,000 British troops under the command of General William Howe to dislodge 1,600 Colonists from a redoubt built on the heights overlooking Boston. The position fell on the third attack, when the Colonists' supply of powder gave out — leaving 1,000 British and 400 American dead on the field.

Burgoyne, John (1723–92): entered the British army at 17, and later eloped with the daughter of the Earl of Derby. Lived in France for seven years, then returned under the patronage of his father-in-law to take a Captaincy in the Dragoons, then a Lieutenant-Colonelcy in the Coldstream Guards. Entered Parliament as a Tory in 1761, and in 1762 served with distinction in the British campaign against the Spanish. 'Gentleman Johnny' was commissioned Major-General in 1772, and two years later began his playwriting career with 'Maid of the Oaks', staged by Garrick at the Drury Lane Theatre. Ordered to Boston in 1775, he used his influence in London to create serious problems for his C-in-C, General Gage. Late in the year, he returned to London, to be posted to Canada in 1776 and lead the offfensive that ended with the surrender at Saratoga in October 1777. When Burgoyne returned to London on parole he was almost unanimously condemned for the failure of his Saratoga campaign, and George III deprived him of command of his Regiment. With the Whigs return to power, he was briefly reinstated, and later managed the impeachment of Warren Hastings. In his later years Burgoyne devoted much of his time to the theatre, writing a highly successful play, *The Heiress* (dedicated to his father-in-law), in 1786.

Burke, Edmund (1729–97): educated at Trinity College, Dublin, Burke came to London in 1750 to practise law, a career which he soon abandoned for writing and then politics. For two years (1761–3) he was private secretary to the Secretary for Ireland, and in 1765 was returned as MP for the pocket borough of Wendover. A Rockingham Whig, Burke did not hold office until the fall of North's Ministry in 1782 (and then only a non-Cabinet post), though he was possibly the most powerful, consistent and able spokesman amongst the varying Whig interests. During his long period in opposition, Burke was at the forefront of criticism of George's North American policies (*American Taxation*, 1774; *Conciliation with America*, 1775), and of the movement demanding political reform (*The Present State of the Nation*, 1769; *Thoughts on the Causes of Present Discontents*, 1770; *Economical Reform*, 1780), though as far as the latter was concerned, his proposals went no further than his innate conversation would allow. The *Reflections on the Revolution in France* (1790) revealed the full power and extent of Burke's conservative nature — and became the handbook of reaction throughout Europe. A man continually haunted by the 'horrid spectre' of the mob, Burke appreciated the need for moderate reforms — though always within the boundaries drawn by the Declaration of Rights of 1689. One of Britain's foremost political thinkers, his philosophy powerfully influenced the development of the Conservative Party. In his last years, largely as a result of his speeches and writings on the French Revolution, Burke split with the Whigs and became a man without a party. He died at his home in Beaconsfield in July 1797, leaving George Canning to write: 'Here is but one event, but that is an event for the world — Burke is dead.'

Bute, Earl of (1713–92): succeeded to the title at ten years of age; appointed a Lord of the Bedchamber to Frederick, Prince of Wales, in the late 1730s. On the death of Frederick in 1751, Bute became Groom of the Stole to his son, George, and played a major role in the future King's upbringing. At the accession of George III, Bute was appointed one of the principal Secretaries of State, and in 1762 became George's first Minister — to lead one of the most unpopular governments ever to hold office. In 1763, Bute retired but remained close to George until the late 1760s when he retreated to the country to study botany and science.

Clinton, Sir Henry (1738–95): son of the Governor of New York, Clinton entered the Guards in 1751 and served with gallantry throughout the Seven Years' War. A Major-General by the age of 34, he was posted to North America in 1775, and succeeded Howe as Commander-in-Chief in 1778. After the capitulation at Yorktown, Clinton resigned his command and returned to England, to be appointed Governor of Gibraltar in 1794.

Clive, Lord (1725–74): soldier and administrator; served only twelve years of his life in India, latterly as Governor of Bengal, but widely held to be the founder of the British empire in India.

Common Sense: the second, Bradford edition carried an appendix addressed to the North American Quakers who had affirmed their loyalty to George in a formal address. Four months after its publication, and with the Friends still opposing independence and calling on conscience to avoid taking up arms, Paine was writing in the *Pennsylvania Journal*:

O ye partial ministers of your own acknowledged principles! If the bearing arms be sinful, the first going to war must be more so, by all the difference between wilful attack and unavoidable defence. Wherefore, if ye really preach from conscience, and mean not to make a political hobby horse of your religion, convince the world thereof by proclaiming your doctrine to our enemies, for they likewise bear arms.

By the summer of 1776, *Common Sense* had been published in England and in translation, had appeared in France (where, according to Silas Deane, it had a greater run than in North America), Germany and Holland.

Condorcet, Marquis de (1743−94): the son of a cavalry officer, Condorcet was educated by Jesuits at Rheims before entering the College of Navarre in Paris to begin his mathematical studies. A brilliant scholar, he soon won the recognition of D'Alembert (a leading French philosophe and editor of the mathematical section of the *Encyclopédie*), whilst for his 'Essai su le calcul integral' he was admitted to the Academy of Science when he was only 22. In 1781, having contributed a number of articles to the *Encyclopédie*, he gained membership of the French Academy. A liberal humanist, Condorcet was a powerful advocate of the Revolution and was elected by Paris to the National Assembly, and later was a Deputy for the Aisne in the National Convention — where he voted against the death of Louis XVI. During the Terror, Condorcet was condemned by Jacobin extremists, fled to the country, remained in hiding for eight months, but was finally arrested to die in gaol. His last work, *Progrès de l'esprit humaine*, written when he was in hiding, is Condorcet's testament to his faith in the perfectability of humanity.

Continental Congress: The first Congress met at Philadelphia (September/October 1774) to co-ordinate a Colonial response to the Coercive Acts. Six months later, in the aftermath of Lexington−Concord, the second Congress met and created the Continental Army. For six years this second Congress (effectively a gathering of ambassadors from all the Colonies whose authority was derived solely from public approval), directed the American war effort and created a framework for the future government of the United States — the Articles of Confederation, 1777. It took Congress a further four years to have the Articles approved, by which time the weakness of their central premiss was clear — that in agreeing that 'these united Colonies are, and of right ought to be, free and independent States', they failed to recognise the need to provide a central core to manage the future affairs of the United States. For eight years, however, the Articles of Confederation were the law of the land to be replaced, after an intense constitutional debate, by the Constitution of 1789.

Cornwallis, Charles, Second Earl (1738–1805): educated at Eton, gazetted an Ensign in the Grenadier Guards at 17 years of age. Served in Europe during the Seven Years' War; elected to Parliament in 1760, and appointed Lieutenant-Colonel of his Regiment in the same year. Five years later appointed a Lord of the Bedchamber to George III, and ADC to the King the following month. Sailed for America with 2,500 troops in 1776, and landed at Staten Island. Fought up the Hudson under Howe's command, but was out-generalled by Washington in the Delaware/Trenton campaign. In 1777, Cornwallis's command occupied Philadelphia, reinforced Howe at Germantown, and captured Fort Mercer. In 1778, Cornwallis was promoted Lieutenant-General, and second-in-command to Henry Clinton who had succeeded Howe as C-in-C. Late in the year, Cornwallis returned to England and did not rejoin Clinton until the late autumn of 1779, to take command of British operations in the Carolinas and Georgia. The surrender of Cornwallis at Yorktown in October 1781 effectively ended the American Revolution.

Corporation and Test Acts: two amongst a series of punitive acts passed against dissenters in the seventeenth century. The Corporation Act (1661) restricted office-holding in municipal government to members of the Church of England; the Test Act (1673) required all holders of office under the crown to take the sacrament according to Church of England usage.

Cumberland, Duke of (1721–65): second son of George II; commanded the British force which brutally crushed the Young Pretender's rebellion at Culloden in 1745, earning him the lasting title 'Butcher Cumberland'.

Danton, Georges (1759–94): of peasant stock, Danton was practising law in Paris at the outbreak of the Revolution. A founder with Desmoulins and Marat of the radical Cordeliers Club, he was soon to establish himself as a major political force and, in August 1792, was appointed Minister of Justice. Six months later, after voting for the death of the King, he became one of the nine original members of the Committee of Public Safety. Throughout 1793, Danton worked with Robespierre to crush the moderate Girondins though, with the object achieved, he then worked with Desmoulins to curb the savagery of the Terror. The break with Robespierre and the Jacobins was inevitable and in April 1794 Danton was condemned to death by the Revolutionary Tribunal which he had set up.

Declaration of Independence: Although John Adams, a member of the committee appointed by Congress to draft the Declaration, stated that: 'it was not Franklin but Timothy Matlack, James Cannon, Thomas Young and Thomas Paine who were the authors of it,' there is no corroborative evidence to suggest that Paine had any part in drawing up the Declaration. On the contrary, in a letter to the *Pennsylvania Packet* in March 1777, he was writing: 'I had no hand in forming any part of it, nor knew anything of its contents until it was published.'

Desmoulins, Camille (1760–94): studied law in Paris, but turned to writing. By 1789, in the van of the republican movement and following the fall of the Bastille, became known by the ominous title of 'Procureur Général de la Lanterne'. Four months later he launched his brilliant weekly journal *Revolutions de France* which appeared until July 1792. A close friend of Danton, he was elected to the National Convention and voted for the death of Louis. Until late in 1793 both he and Danton gave their support to Robespierre but then, as the Terror gathered pace, Desmoulins began publishing the *Vieux Cordeliers* urging the government to adopt more clement policies. It was to cost him the friendship of Robespierre and the Jacobins, and in April 1794 he went to the guillotine.

Dundas, Henry Viscount Melville (1742–1811): Scottish lawyer, elected to Parliament in 1774. An advocate of Lord North's American policy, Dundas became Secretary of State for the Home Department in 1791 and was responsible for implementing much of the repressive legislation introduced by the Pitt ministry.

Fielding, Henry (1707–54): born in Somerset, and educated at Eton and Leyden, Fielding became the author–manager of the Little Theatre in the Haymarket, London in the 1730s before turning novelist. His works include *The Adventures of Joseph Andrews* (1742) and *Tom Jones* (1749). In 1747, thanks to the influence of his patron, Lord Lyttleton, Fielding was made a Justice of the Peace in Westminster.

Fox, Charles James (1749–1806): the third son of Lord Holland, Fox was educated at Eton and Oxford and entered the Commons at 19 years of age. In the early 1770s he served in a number of offices in Lord North's administration, but was dismissed in 1775. An outspoken, and formidable critic of the government's North American policy, Fox remained out of office for seven years and then, in 1782, was appointed a Secretary of State in the Whig administration that came in with North's retirement — to abandon the Whigs and form a coalition ministry with North in 1783. It was an ill-fated, and short-lived arrangement and, when Pitt the Younger formed his first government later the same year, Fox was condemned to the opposition benches for more than two decades. A longtime friend of Edmund Burke, the two men led the Whig opposition until their Commons quarrel over the French Revolution. For the next thirteen years, Fox and a small band of radical Whigs fought unremittingly against the repressive legislation of the Pitt administration. At Pitt's death in 1806, Fox was recalled to office, opened negotiations for a peace with France, and died when on the point of introducing a bill to abolish slavery.

Fox, George (1624–91): founder of the Society of Friends, Fox was the son of a Leicestershire weaver whose parents hoped that he would enter the Anglican Church. At 19 years of age, however, he felt a 'divine call' to forswear all previous associations and, with England in the midst of a civil war that turned as much on spiritual as temporal issues, he wandered the countryside searching for knowledge of God. In 1647, Fox began his open air ministry (he regarded churches as unimportant, calling them 'steeple houses'), preaching that all who followed the 'Inner Light' of the Living Christ were assured of salvation. By the 1660s, the Society of Friends commanded an extensive following throughout England and Wales and in 1666, the year after Fox and his followers refused to take the oath of adjuration, more than a thousand Quakers were in gaol. Fox visited the West Indies and America in 1671–2 and Holland and Germany in 1677 and died in London in 1691. Virtually self-educated, yet with a profound knowledge of the Bible, Fox established an order whose humane views on a wide range of educational and welfare issues were to prove as powerful in the social as the spiritual field.

Francis, Sir Philip (1740–1818): born in Dublin, educated in London, Francis became a member of the Council of Bengal during Warren Hastings's governorship and supplied Burke with much of the background material on which Hastings's impeachment was based. He is believed by many to be author of the 'Junius' letters which appeared between 1769 and 1772.

Franklin, Benjamin (1706−90): a Bostonian, Franklin left school at ten years of age and, after working for his father as a tallow chandler for two years, was apprenticed to a printer. At 16 he began submitting articles to the *Dogood Papers* and in 1723 moved to Philadelphia where, under the patronage of the Governor, he was commissioned to go to London to buy printing equipment to estabish a print shop of his own. Back in Philadelphia in 1726, the 20-year-old Franklin took over the management of the *Pennsylvania Gazette* and turned it into the most successful Colonial periodical of the day. Between 1732 and 1737, Franklin published *Poor Richard's Almanac* and became increasingly involved in civic affairs, his plans leading to the establishment of the American Philosophical Society (1743), the University of Pennsylvania (1751), and the Pennsylvania Hospital (1752). A man of insatiable curiosity and boundless energy, Franklin started to learn French, German and Italian when in his twenties, and began his investigations into electrical phenomena when in his forties — research, culminating in his invention of the lighting rod and the publication of *Experiments and Observations on Electricity* (1751−4). In 1753, Franklin was appointed Deputy-Postmaster-General for the Colonies, and in 1757 was posted as agent for the Pennsylvania Assembly to London where he was already well known for his scientific work. Eight years later, Franklin was the London agent for four colonies, and with the passage of the Stamp Act began his long attempt to conciliate between the government and the Colonists, petitioning the King on the Boston Port Bill and being pressed by Lord Howe and his brother to act as a diplomatic intermediary between the two countries as late as the Christmas of 1774 — ten months after the incident of the Wedderburn letters. In 1775, however, Franklin returned home to help with the drafting of the Declaration of Independence before being posted to Paris by Congress where, by 1778, he had won the French government's recognition for the new republic. In his mid-seventies, and by now a revered figure, Franklin signed the Treaty of Paris (1783), whilst at 82 years of age he was a signatory of the US Constitution. A generous, warm-hearted and compassionate man, Benjamin Franklin was a diplomat of international standing, whilst as a humanist he represented all that was best of the Age of Enlightenment.

Gage, Thomas (1719?−87): British C.-in-C. in America, 1763−75. Educated at Westminster School, Gage entered the army and was promoted Captain in 1743. After serving in the Low Countries and under Cumberland at Culloden, he purchased his Majority in 1748 and was promoted Lieutenant-Colonel in 1751. Two years later he sailed with his regiment for America, accompanied Braddock's ill-fated expedition in 1755 (when he came to know Washington), and in 1760 was appointed military governor of Montreal, being made up to Major-General the following year. Over the next 14 years, Gage (known as 'Honest Tom' to his men) was at the centre of the growing crisis in North American affairs, and in 1773 he was appointed Governor of Massachusetts, in addition to his post as C.-in-C. Even before Bunker Hill and the siege of Boston, a clique in London, aided by Burgoyne in Boston, were plotting Gage's removal and, in October 1775, he surrendered his command to William Howe and returned to England.

Gates, Horatio (1728–1806): general in the Continental Army. The son of the Duke of Leeds's housekeeper, he joined the British army in his teens, served in North America and Martinique, and retired with the rank of Major in 1765. With Washington's help, Gates settled in Virginia and when war broke out was appointed Washington's ADC. Transferred to the Northern Department, he commanded the American army at Saratoga, which led to the suggestion by the Conway cabal that he should replace Washington as Commander of the Continental Army. Gates was again involved in an abortive move to replace Washington in 1779, but after his apparent cowardice at the Battle of Camden he retired to his farm in Virginia and played little further part in the war.

Girondins: the loosely affiliated centre party that originally took its name from a group of deputies from the Gironde region. Until late in 1792, the Girondins and their allies commanded a convincing majority in the Convention, holding the Presidency up until the middle of November, but their power waned rapidly after the trial of Louis XVI.

Godwin, William (1756–1836): educated at dissenting schools, Godwin served in the ministry for five years before turning republican and a 'complete unbeliever' in 1787. Six years later, and inspired by the Revolution in France, he published an *Enquiry Concerning Political Justice* which established his reputation and won him the admiration of Coleridge, Wordsworth and Shelley who was later to become his son-in-law. A year later, 1794, Godwin published his masterpiece, *The Adventures of Caleb Williams*, with the aim of giving 'a general review of the modes of domestic and unrelated despotism'. In 1797, Godwin married Mary Wollstonecraft.

Goldsmith, Oliver (1728–74): born in Kilkenny, where his father was curate, Goldsmith took his BA at Trinity College, Dublin, in 1749. Travelled in Europe for next seven years, returning to London penniless. For three years Goldsmith lived in virtual poverty before winning recognition as a writer. By 1764 he was one of the nine founder members of Dr Johnson's famous Literary Club; in 1766 *The Vicar of Wakefield* secured his reputation as novelist; and in 1773 his comedy *She Stoops to Conquer* was given its first performance.

Gordon, Lord (1751–93): a violent anti-Papist, Gordon entered Parliament at 23 years of age. In 1778 an Act was passed providing Roman Catholics with relief from certain disabilities, and two years later Gordon (as President of a Protestant association) headed a march of 50,000 to the House of Commons demanding the repeal of the legislation. The crowd got out of control and for four days there was serious rioting throughout London, causing an estimated £180,000 worth of damage. On 7 November 1780, the troops were called in, the riots put down (with the death of 289 rioters), and Gordon arrested. Charged with High Treason, he was acquitted, and later adopted the Jewish faith. Gordon died of gaol fever in Newgate, where he was held for a libel of Marie Antoinette.

Grey, Charles (1764–1845): a lifelong Whig, and close friend of Fox, with whom he helped to found the Society of the Friends of the People in 1792. But 40 years were to pass before Grey was to head the government which passed the Reform Bill of 1832.

Hamilton, Alexander (1757–1804): born in the West Indies, Hamilton wrote a series of papers in defence of the Colonies whilst still a student in New York. In the early days of the Revolution he served as a Captain in the artillery and was appointed an ADC to Washington in 1777. At the war's end, Hamilton studied law, established his practice in New York, and entered Congress in 1782. For the next five years he played a major role in preparing for the constitutional convention of 1787. Already a prominent figure in the Federal party, Hamilton wrote 51 of the 85 papers later collected in *The Federalist*. In 1789 he was appointed Secretary of the Treasury and did much to establish US finances on a sound basis. Six years later he resigned from office, but remained the leader of the Federalists until his death in 1804.

Hancock, John (1737–93): born in Massachusetts, and a graduate of

Harvard, Hancock inherited one of Boston's leading mercantile firms from an uncle and, by the time of the passing of the Stamp Act in 1765, had become a prominent opponent of the British government's North American policy. In 1768, British customs officials seized and burned his sloop *Liberty* claiming that it was trading illegally and the court action that followed enhanced his radical reputation. In 1774–5 Hancock served as President of the Massachusetts Provincial Congress; and in 1775–7 was President of the Second Continental Congress. As such, he was the first man to sign the Declaration of Independence. In 1780, Hancock became the first Governor of Massachusetts, a post he held until his death.

Hastings, Warren (1732–1818): appointed Governor-General of India in 1773, a post from which he resigned in 1784. On his return to England, a parliamentary enquiry was opened into his conduct of Indian affairs and after impeachment at the bar of the House of Lords, Hastings's trial began in February 1788, the trial managers including Burke, Fox and Sheridan. After 145 sittings, lasting more than seven years, Hastings was finally acquitted.

Heath, William (1737–1814): general in the Continental Army. A farmer and militiaman, Heath sat on the Massachusetts General Council in 1761, and from 1771 to 1774, and then became a member of the Provisional Congress of Massachusetts. A keen soldier, he served with the militia during the French war and joined Boston's Ancient and Honourable Artillery Company in 1765. Heath's active service during the Revolution began at the siege of Boston, but Washington quickly recognised Heath's limitations as a commander and, although Commander of the Eastern Department for one tour in 1777, he played no major role in the campaigns of the Continental Army.

Herbert of Cherbury, Lord (1583–1648): statesman and philosopher, Herbert published his *De religione gentilium* in 1645. The work, which argues that all religions recognise five, principal articles (that there is a Supreme God, that he deserves to be worshipped, that virtue is a major element of that worship, that there should be penitence for sin, and that there are rewards and punishments in after-life), established Herbert as the first of the deistical writers.

Hobbes, Thomas (1588–1679): graduated at Magdalen Hall, Oxford, 1608, and made first European tour as tutor to William Cavendish, afterwards second Duke of Devonshire, in 1610. Returning home, he acted occasionally as amanuensis to Francis Bacon and then, in the 1630s, made two further trips abroad — meeting Galileo in 1636. Hobbes's interest in science and philosophy was stimulated by contacts with leaders of European thought and he planned a philosophical trilogy to establish that physical phenomena are explicable in terms of motion; that specific bodily motions are involved in human cognition; and from this, to explain the proper organisation of man in society. In 1640, with England in political ferment, Hobbes went into voluntary exile in Paris, and in 1646 became tutor in mathematics to the Young Prince of Wales, later Charles II. Six years later, Hobbes published his masterpiece: *Leviathan, or the Matter, Form, and Power of a Commonwealth, Ecclesiastical and Civil*. In moral theory he argued for rules solely on a pragmatic basis (as a means to 'peaceable, social, and comfortable living') whilst, as a political theorist, he first analysed the conditions needed for peace and security and then, by constructing a model of the social contract, defined the conditions in which an ideal state can be satisfied. Natural right rather than natural law was central to Hobbes's theory: a right to self-preservation. No one is obliged to act according to the law of nature if injurious to his own security — yet stability is not achieved unless the law of nature is generally observed. Hobbes resolved this fundamental quandary by supposing that all citizens give a guarantee of good behaviour to their fellow citizens by establishing a power that will keep all in awe — and that all will obey the authority of this selected individual or assembly. Such an authority is responsible only to God; its rights are as absolute as its power; and, once established, its power is permanent — even though its subjects may wish to depose it. At the close of *Leviathan*, however, Hobbes attempted to define the conditions under which submission to a new sovereign authority might be legitimate, reiterating his traditional view that, when a ruler can no longer protect the citizen, the citizen has the right to abandon him and transfer his allegiance to a new authority. With Charles I only recently executed, the idea gave serious offence to Charles II's court-in-exile, and in 1651 Hobbes returned to England to make his peace with the Commonwealth. With the Restoration, Charles II granted Hobbes a pension, but in 1666, in preparing a Bill against atheism, a House of Commons' Committee was ordered to investigate the *Leviathan*. Hobbes burned all of what he regarded as incriminating papers and, though the Bill was dropped, he was never again given permission to publish anything on subjects relating to political conduct. In the eighteenth century, Hobbes's reputation was overshadowed by that of Locke, but he was reinstated in the nineteenth century and has since become recognised as one of Britain's greatest political thinkers.

Hume, David (1711–76): born in Edinburgh, Hume studied at Edinburgh University before taking up law. After a short spell in commerce, he settled for a period in Anjou, France (the countryside of Descartes's youth) where between the ages of 23 and 25 he wrote his masterpiece: *Treatise on Human Nature*. Hume denied the claims of metaphysicians such as Descartes that there are innate ideas, and of theologians that we can know the ultimate reason for anything, maintaining that ideas depend upon empirical experiences. At the same time, his views on the artificiality of justice and political obligations challenged the social contract theories of Locke and, later, Rousseau. The work was first published in London in 1739 and 'fell still born from the press'. Two years later, Hume published his *Essays Moral and Political* with greater success, but his atheism prevented his appointment to the chair of Moral and Pneumatic Philosophy at Edinburgh, and of Logic at Glasgow. In 1750, Hume wrote (but did not publish) his 'Dialogues Concerning Natural Religion' which examined the various 'proofs' for the existence of a God. Two years later, by which time he had become Keeper of the Advocates' Library in Edinburgh, his *Political Discourses* were published — to provide him with a pre-eminent reputation as an economist. By the 1760s, Hume was in Paris as secretary to the British Ambassador and was fêted by the city's intellectuals — among them Rousseau who, in 1766–7, he tried to help by settling in England. Hume, Britain's greatest empiricist, died of cancer in 1776.

Jacobins: members of the Jacobin Club who, in the three years from 1791 to the Club's disbandment in 1794, moved progressively to the left as the Revolution developed. Originally known as the Club Breton, and later as the 'Friends of the Constitution', the Club inherited its popular nickname from the Dominican monks whose Paris premises it hired in the Rue Saint-Honoré. Membership cost £1 5s 0d a year, and from October 1791 onwards public meetings were held nightly to debate major political, social and economic issues and formulate policies for the guidance of Jacobin supporters in the Assembly, and later the Convention.

Jay, John (1745–1829): the son of a prominent New York merchant, Jay was of patrician stock with conservative sympathies. After reading for the Bar and practising as a lawyer, he served on the Continental Congress, succeeding Laurens as President in 1778. Nine months later Jay was appointed US Minister to Spain, and in 1782 was party to the peace negotiations between the United States and Britain. Returning to America he served first as Secretary of Foreign Affairs, then as the first Chief Justice of the US. In 1794, while still holding the latter office, Jay was dispatched to London to negotiate a settlement of the differences between Britain and the United States — a move which led Republicans to accuse the Federalist party, of which Jay was a prominent member, of selling out their French allies. In 1795, Jay was elected Governor of New York and served for two terms, but with the election of the Republicans in 1800 retired to his country estate.

Jefferson, Thomas (1743−1826): born in the frontier wilderness of Virginia, where his father worked as a civil engineer, Jefferson graduated from William and Mary College and then read for the Bar. In 1769, Jefferson was elected to the Virginian House of Burgesses where he joined the radical party. In 1774 his authorship of *A Summary View of the Rights of Americans* placed him high among the leadership of the revolutionary cause, and gave him a place as a Virginian delegate to the first Continental Congress. Two years later, Jefferson was largely responsible for drafting the Declaration of Independence. The next eight years he devoted mainly to Virginian affairs. As a member of the State legislature, Jefferson pressed to replace aristocratic authority by republican ordinance, and introduced a range of measures to abolish primogeniture, entail and an established church. In the two years 1779−81, when Virginia was under constant attack from the British, Jefferson was Governor of the State, but at the war's end in 1783 he returned to Congress and in 1784 was posted to Paris to help with the drafting of a treaty of commerce between France and the United States. A year later, he succeeded Franklin as the US Minister in Paris, a post he held until his appointment as Secretary of State by Washington in 1789. The next four years were to be crucial to the future structure of American politics. Washington had appointed Alexander Hamilton as his Secretary of the Treasury, a man who contrasted vividly with Jefferson in both personality and outlook: the former a thrusting, energetic figure representing the business ethos; the latter more concerned with law and individual liberties, whose interests were agrarian rather than mercantile. By 1793, when Jefferson negotiated the Neutrality Proclamation shortly before the onset of war between England and France, the party lines were clearly drawn — Jefferson heading the Democratic Republican Party; Hamilton the Federalist Party. In late 1793, Jefferson resigned his office but in 1796 became the Vice-President under John Adams and five years later, 1801, the third President of the United States, when he set about the task of republicanising the government. Jefferson was elected for a second term, but refused a third nomination in 1808. A humanist, inspired by the ideals of an open and tolerant society, Jefferson was among the leading architects not only of American independence, but also of the form of government adopted by the young United States.

Johnson, Dr Samuel (1709−84): the son of a bookseller, Johnson was educated at Litchfield Grammar School and Pembroke College, Oxford, before moving to London. From 1747 to 1755 he worked on his famous *Dictionary*, and lived in virtual penury. In 1762, Johnson was provided with a government pension of £300 a year which eased the drudgery of the hack work which he had had to undertake to make a living. In 1764, he was a founder member of the Literary Club whose membership came to include Boswell, David Garrick, Edmund Burke, Oliver Goldsmith, Adam Smith, Sir Joshua Reynolds and Richard Brinsley Sheridan. In 1773, Johnson toured Scotland with Boswell (*Journey to the Western Isles*) and six years later published his *Lives of the Poets* (1779−81). A full-blooded Tory, Johnson's political writings spanned more than 30 years, from his work in the *Gentleman's Magazine* in the 1740s to his pamphlet *Taxation and Tyranny* published in 1775.

Kalb, Johann (1721−80): a general in the Continental Army. The son of a Bavarian peasant, Kalb served as a mercenary in Europe, then travelled to America for the French government to report on Colonial attitudes to Britain. Returning to Europe, Kalb took to soldiering again and reached the rank of Brigadier in the French army before sailing to America with Lafayette in 1777. Appointed a Major-General, he served as Lafayette's second-in-command in 1778. Two years later, he commanded the Maryland and Delaware contingents on their march to the relief of Charleston, and died of wounds received at the Battle of Camden in August 1780.

Lafayette, Marquis de (1757−1834): orphaned at the age of twelve, Lafayette joined the French army at fourteen, was married at sixteen (to a daughter of one of the most powerful families in France), was a Captain at eighteen, and sailed for America before he was twenty. Congress commissioned him as a Major-General, and he was immediately befriended by Washington. Although embarrassed by his youth and inexperience, the Continental Army soon came to appreciate Lafayette's éclat — he helped check the British advance at Brandywine, and bettered the Hessians in a skirmish in November 1777. In the next eighteen months, Lafayette proved himself as one of Washington's keenest commanders, and in 1779 he returned to France to promote the American cause. By April 1780, Lafayette was back in America, and commanded a light division at Yorktown. Lafayette returned to France in 1781, and in 1789 represented the Auvergne at the Estates General, to table a Declaration of Rights based on the US Declaration of Independence. Twelve days after the fall of the Bastille, he was appointed commander of the National Guard and by 1790 was one of the most popular men in France — though hated by the Jacobins for his moderation. When war broke out with Austria, he commanded the French army in a series of successful engagements, but mounting Jacobin pressure led to his replacement and flight to Belgium. Lafayette was imprisoned by the Prussians for five years before being released by Napoleon and offered the post of Minister to the United States, which he declined. Until the Bourbons returned, he played little further part in public affairs, but in 1817 entered the Chamber of Deputies to sit on the extreme left. From 1825 to 1830 Lafayette was leader of the Opposition, and during the Revolution of 1830 again commanded the National Guard.

Lamartine, Alphonse (1790−1869): French poet, statesman and historian; author of *Histoire des Girondins* (1848).

Laurens, Henry (1724−92): began life as a clerk in a counting house, Laurens became one of the wealthiest merchants in Charleston. Attended the Provincial Congress in 1775, and was Vice-President of South Carolina in 1776. In November 1777, Laurens was elected President of the Continental Congress. The following year he played a significant role in exposing the Conway cabal, but resigned in December 1778, over the Silas Deane affair. In August 1780, Laurens sailed for Holland to negotiate a treaty of friendship, was captured at sea by the British, and imprisoned in the Tower of London. In the spring of 1782, Laurens was exchanged for Lord Cornwallis, and in the autumn of the same year served as a US Commissioner during the peace negotiations in Paris. After a further 18 months as an unofficial emissary to England, Laurens returned to America to die on his plantation.

Lee, Arthur (1740−92): the youngest of four famous Virginian brothers, Arthur Lee was educated at Eton and Edinburgh University, where he took a medical degree. After a brief home visit, Lee returned to London to read for the bar. A keen supporter of Wilkes, he met Beaumarchais at Wilkes's house in 1775, where the embryonic plan to establish

Hortalez & Cie was first discussed — though he was subsequently cut out of the business by Beaumarchais and Deane. Incensed, Lee worked to expose Deane, but was recalled from Europe in 1779. Between 1782 and 1784 Lee represented Virginia in Congress.

Lee, Charles (1731–82): general in the Continental Army. Educated in England and Switzerland, Lee entered his father's regiment at 16 years of age. After service in North America and Portugal, Lee was retired on half-pay, to serve as a mercenary with the Polish army. In 1774, Lee returned to the American Colonies, aligned himself with the Patriots, and in 1775 Congress appointed him Major-General, subordinate only to Washington. In October 1776, Lee was with Washington at the Battle of White Plains, but when the US force divided Lee remained behind at Peekskill with some of the best American troops. His later refusal to rejoin Washington's force led to the suspicion that he had hoped for Washington's defeat so that he could be appointed to the command. Captured by the British in December 1776, Lee proposed a plan which would 'unhinge the organisation of the American resistance'. General Howe ignored Lee's advice, and in 1778 he was exchanged with other American prisoners, to be re-appointed to field command. After the Monmouth campaign, Lee was court martialled, and he was dismissed from the service in 1780.

Locke, John (1632–1704): born in Somerset and educated at Westminster School and Christ Church, Oxford, Locke entered the household of his long-time patron, the first Earl of Shaftesbury, as a physician in 1667. Under Shaftesbury's encouragement, developed his philosophical interests. For the next 22, troubled years the two men were either in Court favour (in 1672 Shaftesbury was appointed Lord Chancellor, Locke a secretary of the Board of Trade) — or in exile, living variously in France and Holland. In 1687, Locke joined the supporters of William of Orange in Rotterdam, where he wrote his *Treatises on Government* — a reply to the patriarchal, divine-right theories of Sir Robert Filmer. Locke, refuting Hobbes who suggested that primitive society was simply a war of everyman with everyman, insisted on the natural morality of primitive man, arguing that men contract into society by surrendering personal power to a ruler or magistrate. However, if this contract is broken by the ruling authority, then the authority itself can be deposed. Together with his theory on property, this sanctioning of rebellion provided the ideological framework for the Glorious Revolution of 1688, and was fundamental to the 'thinking' both of the American Colonists and the French revolutionaries. In 1690, Locke published his *Essay Concerning Human Understanding* which, while accepting the possibility of the rational demonstration of moral principles and the existence of God, denied the notion of innate ideas. Effectively, Locke was the founder of philosophical liberalism and, with Bacon, of English empiricism.

Madison, James (1751−1836): Fourth President of the United States. A Virginian who took his degree at Princeton, Madison was elected to the Continental Congress in 1779. After working with Jay and Hamilton, and writing 29 of the Federalist papers, Madison began to have doubts about the extent of the powers invested in central government and joined the Jeffersonian Republicans. In 1801, Madison was appointed a Secretary of State and in 1809 was elected President. At the close of his second term of office he retired to his estate and took no further active part in politics.

Marat, Jean-Paul (1743−93): studied medicine and practised in London and Paris. With the approach of the Revolution, Marat joined Danton and Desmoulins in the Cordeliers Club and established his virulent journal *L'Ami du peuple*. By 1792, Marat was a Deputy in the National Convention, where he was idolised by the sansculottes and dreaded by his fellow Deputies, not least for the central role he had played in inspiring the September massacres in the prisons. After the trial and execution of Louis, Marat joined Robespierre and Danton in attacking the Girondins. By the summer of 1793, however, he was a sick man who could only write sitting in his bath — where he was stabbed to death by Charlotte Corday on 13 July 1793.

Mifflin, Thomas (1744−1800): general in the Continental Army. The son of Quakers, Mifflin graduated from the College of Philadelphia before entering business and then politics. He was one of the most radical members of the Continental Congress of 1774, and after a period recruiting and training troops was appointed Washington's ADC in 1775. Eighteen months later, Mifflin held the rank of Major-General and, though he proved hopelessly negligent during the Philadelphia campaign, he still held Washington's favour — whilst being deeply involved in the Conway cabal which sought Washington's removal as C-in-C. In 1779, Mifflin resigned from the army, but was a delegate to Congress from 1782 to 1784.

Mirabeau, Comte de (1749−91): during a wild and extravagant early life, Mirabeau was imprisoned twice by his father for his debts and high living, sentence to death by the parlement of Besançon, and spent more than three years in prison on the orders of the French government. Released in 1780, Mirabeau spent the next five years making a precarious living out of writing. Entering the Estates General as a candidate for both Marseilles and Aix in the *tiers état*, Mirabeau soon established himself as a major political force. By the autumn of 1789, however, he had already begun to have doubts about the course of the Revolution, and early in 1790 was in close contact with the court. Whilst distrusted by the *monarchistes*, and loathed by the Queen, they needed his skill to contain the more extreme demands of the revolutionaries — but the popular movement had already progressed beyond his hope of placing Louis at the head of a reformed government. In January 1791, Mirabeau served as President of the National Assembly for two weeks, but his health was already deteriorating and he died in April of the same year.

Monroe, James (1758–1831): Fifth President of the United States. A Virginian, Monroe was elected to the State Assembly at the close of the War of Independence, and to Congress in 1783. Entering the US Senate in 1790, he opposed Washington and the Federalists, and after an eighteen-month spell as Minister to France was recalled to America. From 1799 to 1802, Monroe was Governor of Virginia and in 1803 he helped to negotiate the purchase of Louisiana from France. After a further spell abroad, Monroe returned to the US to take a second term of office as Governor of Virginia and then, in 1811, to be appointed a Secretary of State. Five years later he was elected to the Presidency, and re-elected almost unanimously in 1820.

More, Hannah (1745–1833): born at Stapleton, near Bristol, Hannah More published her first work in 1762. By the mid-1770s she was established in London's literary society, but driven by her religious convictions, she retired to Cowslip Green, near Bristol, where she worked to improve the conditions of the poor — albeit on her own, authoritarian lines. A powerful social influence in the late eighteenth and early nineteenth centuries, her most successful later works included *The Manners of the Great* and *The Religion of the Fashionable World*.

Morris, Gouverneur (1752–1816): educated at Kings College (now Columbia), Morris was admitted to the Bar at 19 and established a successful law practice in New York. A landed aristocrat, he had initial doubts about the Independence movement but supported the Patriots when it became clear that war was inevitable. Elected to Congress in 1778, Robert

Morris (no relation) later invited him to become his assistant as Superintendent of Finances, and the two men worked closely together for the next four years. In 1789, Morris sailed for France to become one of the most prominent figures in the American community in Paris, where mob violence reinforced his innate conservatism ('Give votes to the people who have no property and they will sell them to the rich'). Washington appointed Morris Minister to France in 1792, but two years later he was replaced by Monroe at the request of the French government. After a further four years in Europe, Morris returned to America to spend his last years on his estate, a bitter man who had 'lost all loyalty to the nation'.

Morris, Robert (1734–1806): Liverpool-born, Morris arrived in America at 13 years of age to work in a Philadelphia counting-house, becoming a partner in the company when he was 20. Morris attended the first Continental Congress in 1774 and in 1775 was appointed to the Council of Safety. The following year he drew up the commercial instructions for Deane and was responsible for much of Congress's military procurement programme — whilst still managing his own business. The confusion between Morris's public and private affairs led to growing suspicions about his integrity — the more so when Deane was recalled from Paris. Henry Laurens charged Morris's company with fraud, but a detailed investigation cleared his name and he was appointed Superintendent of Finances during the US financial crisis of the early 1780s, an office in which he was notably successful, and which was to win him the accolade 'Financier of the Revolution'. An advocate of strong central government, Morris supported the Federalist party and served in the Senate from 1789 to 1795. In the mid-1790s Morris's commercial empire collapsed and in 1797 he was arrested for debt, to spend more than three years in prison. He died, a comparatively poor man, in Philadelphia.

Necker, Jacques (1732–1894): Geneva-born, Necker moved to Paris to become a banker's clerk in 1747, and at 30 years of age had established his own banking house. In 1777, he was made Director General of Finance, but his reforms alienated the Queen and her circle and he was dismissed. Eleven years later he was recalled to office, and won popularity by recommending the summoning of the Estates General. Three days before the fall of the Bastille he was again dismissed by the King, was again recalled, to serve in government for a further 14 months before resigning in September 1790.

Newcastle, Duke of (1693–1768): succeeded to title on death of uncle; supporter of Walpole, holding office of Secretary of State for 30 years. In 1754, he succeeded his brother, Henry Pelham, as Prime Minister, but retired two years later. In 1757, however, Newcastle became Premier again and held the post until the accession of George III when he was replaced by the Marquis of Bute.

Newton, Isaac (1642–1727): born in Lincolnshire, and educated at Trinity College, Cambridge, Newton began a study of the laws of gravitation in 1666 but abandoned them, temporarily, to conduct experiments into the nature of light which led to the development of the reflecting telescope. By the 1680s, and already a Fellow of Trinity and a member of the Royal Society, he returned to his research into gravitation and in 1684 demonstrated his theory. In 1696, Newton solved two celebrated problems proposed by Bernouili to the mathematicians of Europe, and in 1716 solved a problem posed by his great rival Leibniz — a rivalry that turned on the priority of the discovery of the differential calculus. A direct descendant of the methods pioneered by Bacon, Newton was knighted in 1705, and was President of the Royal Society from 1703 until his death.

North, Lord (1732–92): entered Parliament at the age of 22, Chancellor of the Exchequer, 1767; Prime Minister, 1770. A genial and easy-going man, North admirably suited George III's purpose. Although he threatened resignation on a number of occasions, North held the Premiership until 1782, his mastery of the Parliamentary machine complementing the King's policy-making — a combination which was to lose Britain its North American colonies.

Orléans, Duc d' (1747–93): a profligate who inherited his title in 1785, he became prominent as a liberal critic of the King in 1787 and before the calling of the Estates General spent much of his fortune publishing and disseminating the works of radical authors throughout France. In June 1789, Orléans led the nobles who seceded from their own order in the Estates General. Three years later, with the abolition of titles, he took the name Philippe Égalité, and represented Paris in the National Convention — to vote for the death of Louis. In 1794, Orléans was arrested, tried and guillotined.

Palmerston, Lord (1784–1865): three times Prime Minister of Great Britain in the 1850s.

Penn, William (1644–1718): the son of Admiral Sir William Penn, he was sent down from Oxford for having become a Quaker and in 1667 was gaoled for attending a Friends' meeting. Two years later, imprisoned in the Tower, the 25-year-old Penn wrote *No Cross, No Crown*, a tract attacking religious orthodoxy, and in 1671 he spent six months in Newgate for his Quaker principles. In 1681, Charles II granted Penn a settlement on the Delaware and Susquehame Rivers as a refuge for persecuted sectarians. Within a year of his arrival in North America in 1682, he had attracted more than three thousand settlers to join him and until 1684 he worked at establishing the new colony, laying out the ground plan of Philadelphia (based on the grid principle devised by Wren for the rebuilding of London after the Great Fire), and assisting with the constitutional organisation of New Jersey and Delaware on the grounds of religious toleration and political democracy. In the mid-1680s Penn returned to England to intercede, successfully, on behalf of his co-religionists with James II; an act which led to accusations of his treasonable adherence to the deposed King after the Glorious Revolution in 1688. Finally acquitted of the charges in 1695, he spent a further two years in Pennsylvania (1699–1701), before returning to England where he died in 1718.

The Philosophes: a highly cosmospolitan, yet loosely organised coalition of religious sceptics, cultural critics and political reformers who dominated European thinking during the Age of Enlightenment of the eighteenth century. If Bacon was their mentor then it was Kant who, at the close of the period, gave them their watchword: *Sapere aude* — 'Dare to know.'

Price, Dr Richard (1723–91): born in Wales, Price was educated at a dissenting academy in London. A well-known nonconformist preacher (he received his DD from Glasgow), Price also won a reputation as a commentator on political and economic affairs, and was invited by the US Congress to assist in planning the finances of the young Republic.

Priestley, Joseph (1733–1804): educated at a dissenting academy, Priestley became a Presbyterian minister in 1775 — but his reputation depends on his work as a scientist. Elected a Fellow of the Royal Society in 1766, and a member of the French Academy of Sciences in 1772, Priestley was a pioneer in the chemistry of gases, and one of the discoverers of oxygen. Three years after the Birmingham mob burned out his laboratory (partly because Priestley had written to refute Burke's *Reflections*), Priestley moved to America where he lived until his death.

Rainborough, Colonel Thomas (d. 1648): son of Captain Wm. Rainborough; served in the New Model Army where he commanded a regiment. Leader of the republican section amongst the officers and elected MP for Droitwich, 1646. Died at siege of Pontefract Castle, 1648. His brother-in-law, John Winthrop, Governor of Massachusetts, 1630–49, was one of the most influential figures in forming the political institutions of the northern American colonies.

Randolph, Edmund (1753–1813): a Virginian, Randolph became governor of his home state in 1786 and the following year was a member of the Convention which framed the US Constitution. In 1794 he was made a Secretary of State, but was falsely accused of bribery, and virtually ruined.

Robespierre, Maximilien (1758–94): known to his contemporaries as 'The Incorruptible', Robespierre was born in Arras, studied law and established his practice in his home town. A distinguished advocate, he was soon appointed a Judge at the Salle Épiscopale, and at 25 years of age was admitted to the Arras Academy for the Advancement of Science, of which he was later to become President. A humanitarian (he won the first prize at the Metz Academy for his 'Report on Degrading Punishments'), and a radical, he regularly represented the interests of the poor whilst alarming the privileged classes with his attacks on royal absolutism and arbitrary justice. Elected to the Estates General in 1789, he quickly established himself as a leader of the left and, in April 1790, presided over the Jacobins. A passionate supporter of the Declaration of the Rights of Man (September 1791), Robespierre fought for universal suffrage, religious and racial toleration, and defended the minority interests of Jews and black slaves. As the Revolution progressed, Robespierre's principles were to bring him into growing conflict first with the moderate Lafayette, then with the Girondins. After he was elected leader of the Paris Deputies in the National Convention in September 1792, the Girondins mounted a concerted attack on Robespierre's intentions, accusing him of having dictatorial ambitions in the very first session of the Convention. Three months later he was to speak eleven times during the trial of Louis XVI. With the King's execution in January 1793, the confrontation between Jacobins and Girondins entered its final phase, ending with the triumph of the Jacobins in June, and Robespierre's appointment to the Committee of Public Safety in July. From this moment on, Robespierre's role became increasingly ambivalent. While he supported the intensification of the Terror ('It is our leniency to traitors that is ruining us'), he protested at the arrest of the Girondins, and was sickened by the massacres condoned by the representatives of the Convention in the French provinces declaring them 'dishonourable to the Revolution'. By April of 1794, and with the elimination of Danton and Camille Desmoulins (the so called Indulgents of the National Convention), Robespierre was established in virtually absolute power. For the next three months he nominated all members to government committees, took complete control of the Revolutionary Tribunal, and on 4 June was elected President of the National Convention by an overwhelming vote. None the less, as financial and government affairs drifted towards ruin, and the Committee of Public Safety (from which Robespierre himself has resigned) unleashed the Great Terror, opposition to Robespierre grew — to be synthesised when Saint-Just demanded the creation of a dictatorship in Robespierre's name. Six weeks after the National Convention had voted him to its Presidency, the Deputies finally turned on Robespierre and his allies. On 27 July, he was arrested, and guillotined the following day. Possibly the most enigmatic and controversial figure to emerge from the Revolution, Robespierre was vilified by his counter-revolutionary critics for his social and egalitarian ideals, though the growth of the popular movements in the nineteenth century led to a reappraisal of his importance in the radical movement.

Romney, George (1734—1802): one of the foremost English portrait painters of the eighteenth century.

Rousseau, Jean-Jacques (1712—78): born in Geneva, the son of a watchmaker, Rousseau was boarded out with a Calvinist pastor when he was ten years of age. Six years later Rousseau was locked out of Geneva having forgotten the curfew hour, quit the city and was befriended by the Catholic convert, the Baroness de Warens, at Annecy. She sent him to Turin to be baptised and on his return he became her factotum and, later, her lover. For six years with occasional breaks, Rousseau remained at Annecy and then, after short spells in Paris and Venice (where he was secretary to the French Ambassador), he returned to Paris where his opera *Les Muses Galantes* won him the acquaintanceship of Voltaire and Diderot (editor of the *Encyclopédie*). In 1749, on the road to Vincennes where Diderot was imprisoned for his anti-clerical materialism, Rousseau read in the *Mercure de France* of the Dijon prize essay: 'Has the revival of the arts and sciences done more to corrupt or purify morals?' Diderot encouraged Rousseau to enter for the competition, suggesting that, if he adopted the controversial stance that such a revival had indeed corrupted morals, it would distinguish him from the other competitors. Although contrary to all his own beliefs, Diderot was right. Rousseau's essay, which maintained that the Baconian belief in empiricism and progress had seduced man away from his natural and noble estate, won the Dijon prize in 1750 — and he was lionised by Paris society. Five years later, Rousseau published *Discours sur l'origine de l'inégalité parmi les hommes* which again emphasised the natural goodness of man, and the corrupting influences of civilisation. Rousseau's views had already set him apart from the philosophes of the Baconian school when, in 1762, he published his masterpiece, *Contrat Social*. The tone of the work is established at the outset: 'My purpose is to consider *if*, in political society, there can be any legitimate and sure principle of government, taking men as they are, and laws as they might be'. The qualification is crucial for the *Contrat* is not a plan for reform, rather a philosophical reflection on the nature of man and the structure of law and government. While depicting man in the state of nature as brutish, and recognising that civil society can provide man with freedom, Rousseau none the less rejects the idea that man must choose between being ruled and liberty to conclude that: 'Men can be both ruled and free if they rule themselves. For what is a free man but a man who rules himself?' The problem posed by this conclusion is to achieve a stable, civil order if each man does, indeed, rule himself — a problem which Rousseau only solved by postulating a contract in which citizens surrender their individual rights to the 'general will' which, thus freed from sectarian and private interests, must serve the collective, and impartial good. In the same year as the publication of the *Contrat Social*, Rousseau also completed work on *Emile* which, whilst primarily concerned with education, continued his assault on both monarchy and government. In combination, the two works enraged the establishment and Rousseau fled first to Moitiers in Neuchatel and then, at the invitation of Hume, to England (1766—7) where he wrote *Confessions*. For the last ten years of his life, Rousseau lived in virtual permanent flight from persecution and he died, insane, in a cottage at Ermenonville in July 1778, his remains being transferred to lie beside those of Voltaire in the Pantheon, Paris, in 1794. Together, the two men provided the rationale for the Revolution of 1789, while in the years that followed Rousseau's slogan: 'Liberty, Equality, Fraternity' was to be carried at swordpoint throughout Europe.

Rush, Benjamin (1745—1813): a member of the Continental Congress (1776—7), Rush signed the Declaration of Independence and later joined Washington's Continental Army as Surgeon-General. In 1792 he was appointed Professor of Medicine at University of Pennsylvania.

Rutledge, John (1739−1800): studied law at Middle Temple, London; delegate for South Carolina to Continental Congress, 1774−5; President of South Carolina Assembly, 1776−8; elected Governor of South Carolina, 1779. Returned to Congress in 1782, and in 1784 he began his judicial career on being appointed to the state chancery court. In 1791, Rutledge was elected Chief Justice of South Carolina, and in 1795 was nominated Chief Justice of the US by Washington, Congress rejecting the nomination because of Rutledge's bitter attack on the Jay Treaty.

Saint-Just, Louis-Antoine (1767−94): studied law at Rheims, and arrived in Paris at 19 years of age. In 1791, Saint-Just published *L'Esprit de la Révolution* and the following year was returned as a Deputy to the Convention where he became a devoted follower of Robespierre — to die with Robespierre on the guillotine of 28 July 1794.

Sandwich, Lord (1718−92): gambler, debauchee, and with Wilkes a member of the notorious Hellfire Club of the late 1750s. In 1770 Sandwich was appointed a Secretary of State under Lord North and in 1771 he became First Lord of the Admiralty — a post he held for the next eleven years, a time in which he won as notorious a public reputation for his corruption and jobbery as he had a private one for his profligacy. Now best remembered for having given his name to the sandwich — a filling between two slices of bread which he had served at his club so that meals would not interfere with his gambling sessions.

Shelburne, Lord (1737−1805): a Whig, Shelburne entered Parliament in 1761 and was appointed President of the Board of Trade in 1763. With the fall of Lord North's government in 1782, Shelburne served as Secretary of State in the short-lived Rockingham administration, and on Rockingham's death became Prime Minister, to hold office for less than two years.

Sheridan, Richard Brinsley (1751−1806): Dublin-born dramatist and politician. Between 1775 and 1779, Sheridan produced a series of dazzling comedies including *The Rivals*, *The School for Scandal*, and *The Critic* before turning his attention to politics. He served as an under-secretary in the Whig ministry of 1782, but his parliamentary reputation dates from his speeches during the impeachment of Warren Hastings. A devoted friend of Fox, the two men led the opposition to Pitt's administration until 1806. Sheridan died in poverty in 1816.

Sieyes, Abbé (1748–1836): studied theology, to become Vicar General of Chartres. A leading radical, he published a number of important pamphlets before the meeting of the Estates General, which he attended. A Deputy for Paris in the National Assembly, he took part in the Declaration of the Rights of Man (August 1789), and later sat in the National Convention, voting for the death of Louis XVI. For four years after the fall of the Jacobins, Sieyes played only a secondary role in French affairs but in 1799 was elected to the Directory and later the same year plotted the *coup* of the 18th Brumaire with Bonaparte. As a member of the Consulate, he drafted a constitution for France, but on disagreeing with Bonaparte he resigned his post and played little further part in affairs.

St Vincent, Earl (1735–1823): entered Royal Navy in 1749; Lieutenant, 1755; Commander, 1759; made a KB in 1782. Given command of Mediterranean Fleet in 1795 and, though heavily outnumbered, defeated a Spanish fleet off Cape St Vincent in February 1797, for which he received his Earldom and pension of £3,000. In early 1800s as First Lord of the Admiralty he reformed a range of abuses common at that time.

Tindal, Matthew (1655–1733): a Fellow of All Souls, Oxford, Tindal published *Christianity as old as the Creation* in 1730. The work, which was to become the deists' handbook, aimed at eliminating the supernatural element from religion and proving that morality is religion's only claim to the reverence of mankind.

Tooke, Horne (1736–1812): educated at Eton and St John's, Cambridge, Tooke read law before taking the living of Brentford, Middlesex. Tooke met Wilkes while the latter was in exile in Paris and became one of his most powerful protagonists during the earlier Middlesex election campaigns. In 1770 the two men fell out, though Tooke continued to pursue radical policies — demanding political reform, opposing the enclosure movement, and when imprisoned writing the *Diversions on Purley* to promote a subscription for the Colonists 'barbarously murdered at Lexington in 1775'. Tooke stood, unsucccessfully, for Parliament twice in the 1790s; was tried for, and acquitted of, high treason in 1794; stood for, and won, the rotten borough of Old Sarum in 1801 — but was prevented from taking his seat by a special Act of Parliament.

Townshend, Charles (1725−67): entered the Commons at 22 years of age, was appointed First Lord of Trade and the Plantations in Grenville's Ministry (1763−5), and became Chancellor of the Exchequer in 1766 to draft the ill-starred Acts that bear his name.

Turgot, Robert Jacques (1717−81): destined for the church, but read for the law and joined the philosophes. Appointed intendant at Limoges, 1761, and Comptroller General of Finance in 1774 with the accession of Louis XVI. Attempted to introduce a series of radical reforms to establish a more efficient and economical administration, but in doing so alarmed and antagonised the nobility who pressurised Louis to remove him after only 20 months in office — a decision that contributed, significantly, to the events of 1789.

Vernon, Admiral (1684−1757): an RN Captain at the age of 21, and Rear-Admiral at 24, Vernon sat as MP from 1727 to 1741. He was nicknamed 'Old Grog' from his grogram coat, and in 1740 ordered the dilution of rum with water which, ever since, has been known as 'grog'.

Voltaire (1694−1778): the son of a French official, and educated at a Jesuit seminary, Voltaire was destined for the bar but before he was 20 he was already winning notoriety as a satirist. In 1716, he was banished from Paris for lampooning the regent, the Duc d'Orléans, and on his return was thrown into the Bastille for repeating the offence. By the 1720s the authorities were refusing to allow the publication of his work for its championship of Protestantism and religious toleration. For all this, he had established himself as a favourite of the Court — until the Chevalier de Rohan-Chabot denounced him as a parvenu. Voltaire replied with a series of acid epigrams; the Chevalier's hirelings revenged him by assaulting Voltaire, who then challenged Rohan-Chabot to a duel — a gesture that was to cost him a second spell in the Bastille. In 1726, he was freed on the understanding that he would move to England where he made the acquaintance of, amongst others, the Duchess of Marlborough, Pope and Gay. Voltaire was deeply influenced by his English experience, developing an admiration for the scientific principles of Bacon and Newton, and the constitutional works of John Locke. On his return to France in 1729, he published his *Letters on England* — including three short chapters on the Society of Friends. For the next 20 years, Voltaire's output of plays, histories and philosophical works was prodigious, and in 1749 he accepted an invitation to become Chamberlain to Frederick the Great with a pension of 10,000 francs. He remained in Germany for five years, then moved to the outskirts of Geneva where he wrote the satirical master-piece *Candide*. In France, there was growing reaction to the radical implications of the works of the philosophes and Voltaire's home at Ferney became a retreat for the exiles of reaction, Voltaire himself declaring war on the bigotry of *L'Infâme*. In 1778, Voltaire returned to Paris for the premier of his latest tragedy, but died within days of his arrival. A commanding figure among the small group of philosophes who provided the intellectual groundwork for the revolutions that were to come, Voltaire was interred at the Pantheon in Paris.

Walpole, Robert (1676−1745): son of a Norfolk landowner, Walpole was educated Eton and King's College, Cambridge. Elected MP, 1701; appointed Secretary at War, 1708; and then highly lucrative Treasurer of the Navy, 1710. Expelled from the Commons and held in the Tower for alleged corruption, 1712, but reinstated as First Lord of the Treasury and Chancellor of the Exchequer with Whigs' return to power at accession of George I in 1715. Resigned in 1717 but, with collapse of South Sea Bubble in 1721, Walpole was again recalled as First Lord of the Treasury and Chancellor. Held both offices, and effectively became Britain's first Prime Minister, until February 1742. The corruption of Walpole's regime earned it the title 'Robinocracy' from his critics; none the less, his politics provided Britain with 18 years of peace and powerful mercantile expansion.

Washington, Colonel George (1732−99): First President of the United States. In 1754, the 22-year-old Washington was posted with a detachment to protect workmen building a fort at the forks of the Ohio River from the French — but the fort had been captured before he arrived. At Great Meadows, near the present-day Pittsburg, Washington built Fort Necessity where he stood off a French attack and won himself his full Colonelcy, and a laudatory tribute in a Colonial journal:

> Since the perfidious French in hostile Ranks
> The English drove from smooth Ohio's Banks.
> Since Washington entered the List of Fame,
> And by a journey to Lake Erie came.
> Since he defeats a French detached Band,
> Under the brave Junonville's command.

In triggering off the French and Indian War that followed, the incident proved to be a major cause of the Seven Years' War.

Watt, James (1736—1819): Scottish inventor, who refined the Newcomen engine, thus pioneering the effective development of steam power.

Wesley, John (1703—91): the founder of Methodism, Wesley was educated at Charterhouse and Oxford. Ordained in 1725, he became leader of a small group of devout Christians derisively called The Holy Club or Methodists. After three years in North America, Wesley returned to England in 1738 and the following year he founded his first Methodist chapel in Bristol. For the next 50 years Wesley travelled through Britain and Ireland preaching some 40,000 sermons on the gospel of Methodism, mostly to the working class. An Anglican, Wesley was determined his movement should remain within the established Church, as it did throughout his lifetime.

Wilkes, John (1727—97): the London-born son of a distiller, Wilkes studied at Leyden before becoming one of the most notorious rakes of mid-eighteenth-century London. A Whig, Wilkes entered politics in 1757 as a supporter of Pitt the Elder. Following the accession of George III in 1760, he became a vehement critic of government; was imprisoned in the Tower for his editorship of the *North Briton*; was outlawed from England; returned to fight the Middlesex elections; was re-elected to the seat four times, and each time declared ineligible; and finally admitted to the House in 1774, the year of his Lord Mayoralty of the City of London. A born publicist, Wilkes played a central role in taking the political debate 'out-of-doors' and laying the foundations for later constitutional reformists.

Wollstonecraft, Mary (1759—97): born in London, Wollstonecraft earned a living as a teacher and governess before turning to writing. In 1790, she published *Vindication of the Rights of Man*, and the following year *Vindication of the Rights of Woman*. Following a visit to Paris during the Terror, she wrote *View of the French Revolution*. Returning to London in 1795, Wollstonecraft went to live with William Godwin. The couple married in April 1797, after Mary became pregnant, and she died shortly after giving birth to a daughter — Mary Wollstonecraft Shelley.

SELECT BIBLIOGRAPHY

General

Arendt, Hannah *On Revolution* (Viking, New York, 1963)
Forster, Robert and Elborg (eds) *European Society in the Eighteenth Century* (Macmillan, London, 1969)
Gay, Peter *The Enlightenment, An Interpretation* (Weidenfeld and Nicolson, London, 1970)
Goodwin, A. (ed.) *The American and French Revolutions* (Cambridge University Press, Cambridge, 1965)
Hampson, Norman *The Enlightenment* (Penguin, Harmondsworth, 1968)
Hobsbawn, E.J. *The Age of Revolution* (Weidenfeld and Nicolson, London, 1962)
Laski, Harold J. *Political Thought from Locke to Bentham* (Greenwood Press, New York, 1920)
—— *The Rise and Fall of European Liberalism* (George Allen and Unwin, London, 1936)
Nicolson, Sir Harold *The Age of Reason* (Constable, London, 1960)
Rude, George *Revolutionary Europe* (Collins, London, 1960)
The Annual Register, 1775-1794

France

Acton, Lord *Lectures on the French Revolution* (Macmillan, London, 1910)
Carlyle, Thomas *The French Revolution* (1837)
Elton, Lord *The Revolutionary Idea in France* (Edward Arnold, London, 1923)
Furet, Francoise and Richet, Denis *The French Revolution* (Weidenfeld and Nicolson, London, 1970)
Godechot, Jacques *France and the Atlantic Revolution in the Eighteenth Century* (The Free Press, New York, 1965)
Lefebvre, George *The French Revolution* (Routledge and Kegan Paul, London, 1962)
Thompson, J.M. *The French Revolution* (Blackwell, Oxford, 1943)
de Stael, Baroness *Considerations on the Principal Events in the French Revolution* (1818)
An Impartial History of the Late Revolution in France (New Annual Register, 1794)

Great Britain

Dickinson, H.T. *Liberty and Property* (Weidenfeld and Nicolson, London, 1977)
Inglis, Brian *Poverty and the Industrial Revolution* (Hodder and Stoughton, London, 1971)
Jarrett, Derek *Britain, 1688-1815* (Longmans, London, 1965)
—— *England in the Age of Hogarth* (Rupert Hart Davies, London, 1974)
Marshall, Dorothy *Eighteenth Century England* (Longmans, London, 1962)
Namier, Sir Lewis *The Structure of Politics at the Accession of George III*, 2nd edn (Macmillan, London, 1957)
Pares, Richard *George III and the Politicians* (Clarendon, Oxford, 1952)
Plumb, J.H. *England in the Eighteenth Century* (Penguin, London, 1950)
Porter, Roy *English Society in the Eigtheenth Century* (Pelican, London, 1982)
Veitch, G.S. *The Genesis of Parliamentary Reform* (Constable, London, 1913)
Watson, Steven *The Reign of George III* (Oxford University Press, 1960)
Williams, Basil *The Whig Supremacy* (Oxford University Press, 1939)

United States

Bailyn, Bernard *The Ideological Origins of the American Revolution* (Harvard University Press, Cambridge, Mass., 1967)

Boorstin, Daniel J. *The Americans, The Colonial Experience* (Random House, New York, 1958)

Ierley, Merritt *The Year That Tried Men's Souls* (A.S. Barnes, New York, 1976)

Ketchum, Richard *The Winter Soldiers* (History Book Club, London, 1973)

Lucas, Stephen E. *Portents of Rebellion* (Temple University Press, Philadelphia, 1976)

McWhiney, Grady and Wiebe, Robert (eds) *Historical Vistas*, Readings in US History, Vol 1 (Allyn and Bacon, Boston, 1963)

Pearson, Michael *Those Damned Rebels* (Heinemann, London, 1972)

Steeg, Clarence Ver and Hofstadter, Richard (eds) *Great Issues in American History from Settlement to Revolution* (Random House, New York, 1969)

Trevelyan, Otto *The American Revolution* (1899)

INDEX